The Princes of Naranja

The Princes of Naranja

AN ESSAY IN ANTHROHISTORICAL METHOD

By Paul Friedrich

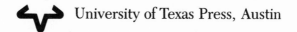 University of Texas Press, Austin

First edition, 1986

Requests for permission to reproduce material from
this work should be sent to:
   Permissions
   University of Texas Press
   Box 7819
   Austin, Texas 78713-7819

Library of Congress Cataloging-in-Publication Data
Friedrich, Paul, 1927–
   The princes of Naranja.
   Bibliography: p.
   1. Local government—Mexico.   2. Villages—Mexico.
3. Political anthropology—Mexico.   I. Title.
JS2108.F75   1986   306'.2'0972   86-16075
ISBN 0-292-76432-4
ISBN 0-292-76502-9 (pbk.)

οὐκ ἀγαθὸν πολυκοιρανίη· εἷς κοίρανος ἔστω,
εἷς βασιλεύς . . .

(No good thing is a multitude of lords; let there be one lord,
One king . . .)   —*Iliad* II.204–205

The blood of your brother is crying out to me from the earth.
                                                   —Genesis 4:10

Contents

FOREWORD by Dennis Tedlock   *xi*

PREFACE   Outline and Problems   *xiii*

PART ONE. SEVEN PRINCES

1. Seven Political Life Studies   3

FIELDNOTES INTERLUDE

2. Political Pragmatics and Practicalities: Notes on Three
   Ejidal Meetings   77

PART TWO. STRUCTURE AND HISTORY

3. Political Ethnography: "Confidential Friend" and Related
   Categories   89
4. Political Organization   *115*
5. Political History: *Libido Dominandi* and the Rise of
   Elías (Scarface) Caso (1926–1956)   *132*

PART THREE. "POLITICAL ECONOMY"

6. Political Economy, Oligarchy, and the Leaders   *179*

PART FOUR. EXPERIENCE AND METHODS

7. Fieldwork Categories: Sources of Shattered Bits   *203*
8. "Writing It Up"   *220*
9. Background: Personal and Intellectual   *246*

APPENDICES

Economic Appendix A. The Ejidal Bank and Naranja Ejido
Economics   *263*

Economic Appendix B. The History of Anita Rías
(Fieldwork Datum No. 11)   268

Homicide Appendix   271

Psychological Appendix A. Camilo's Rorschach   276

Psychological Appendix B. Boni's Rorschach   281

Psychological Appendix C. Aquiles' Rorschach   285

NOTES   291

SOURCES   299

Maps, Charts, Tables, and Illustrations

The Zacapu Region and Environs	xv
Tarascan Territory	xvii
Skeletal Chronology of Key Political Events	xviii
Brandenburg's Ladder of Political Prestige	32
Camilo's Position in Scott's Table of Organization	33
Ejidal Assembly	81
Sociogram of Friendship	94
Residence Map	102
Naranja Street Map	103
Sociogram of Ceremonial Kinship	109
Table of Ceremonial Kinship	112
Two Fundamental Cacical Processes	135
The Expropriated Groups	158
A History of Anthrohistorical Writing	226

Foreword BY DENNIS TEDLOCK

When anthropologists write books, it is their custom to put the results of their fieldwork in one volume and give an account of what actually happened in the field in a separate volume. The first kind of book stands at a great distance from its subject, casting the anthropologist in the role of an omniscient narrator. The second has a confessional character, revealing the previously hidden subjectivity of the narrator. There has long been a need to overcome the opposition between these two genres, uniting the full range of anthropological thought and sensibility between the same two covers. It is easier to theorize about this need than to take the risk of doing something about it. In writing the present book, Paul Friedrich has taken a risk that will make it easier for the rest of us to do what we should have started doing already.

This book is remarkable not only in bridging genres, but in its substance as well. Very seldom does field experience in a single community bridge as many years as does Friedrich's in Naranja, and very seldom are accounts of such an experience given still further depth by a fine-grained knowledge of ethnohistorical sources. It is also remarkable to learn so much about practical politics. Or to learn what sorts of things literate natives might read—including, in this case, a classic work on politics.

Anthropological writing is customarily short on dialogue, whether between the researcher and the natives or among the natives, and here again Friedrich opens the way to new possibilities. Along with quoted dialogues come discussions of the general characteristics of the speech of the main actors, including subtle dimensions of the voice that lie behind mere words as printed on the page. This and other kinds of detail—about diet and dress, for example—give the book an extraordinary richness. Seldom do fieldworkers put sights and sounds so clearly in the eyes and ears of their readers. And seldom do they build the kind of emotional depth that provokes readers to responses ranging from laughter to horror.

Almost never do we find natives depicted in the act of reflection, or of self-objectification or self-explanation, but in this book we have, for example, a native explaining with crystal clarity that political comrades do not make good compadres. Friedrich had come close to reaching this conclusion just by looking at his collected "facts," but instead of simply crediting himself with an insight into a "hidden" dimension of social structure, he chose to tell us of his discovery that the natives also think about such things.

Intellectual autobiography gets little play even in full-length confessional works, but the present book suggests that even general discussions of field methods ought to include this dimension. And the chapter on "writing it up" is unique in the literature on anthropological methods, so far as I know. Doubly unique, in fact: not only do anthropologists not describe the "writing-up" process, but Friedrich describes it according to topics that are unusual in their own right. That is to say, he has given us an interesting statement on writing, not just anthropological writing.

Perhaps the strongest single thing about this book lies in characterization. In other writings, native character is either not present at all, or only in the "national" sense, or it is represented only by a single person (in life histories), or is weakly developed in the supporting cast that surrounds the anthropological autobiographer. But here we have native characters in the plural. I've never read anything quite like it.

Once I had started in on this book I found it hard to put down. And by the time I reached the end, I had learned enough about the way things go in Naranja to worry about what might happen to some of the characters in the future. In the case of Daniel, the musician who puts the beauty of his art ahead of his politics, I was left feeling afraid for him. I hope he avoids side streets, and that he is careful when he goes walking alone in the mountains.

Preface: Outline and Problems

This book is about peasant leaders and some ways of getting to understand them. Concretely, it describes agrarian leadership and factional politics in a small village of peasants that was still Tarascan Indian at the time of fieldwork, and it tells "how to" by setting forth demystified field methods and writing crafts and strategies. More generally, it explores the meaning of fieldwork by explicitly conjoining two enterprises that are inextricably interconnected. The first is a full exposition of the results of fieldwork, historical research, and write-up, that is, a substantial text of anthropological history. The second is a retrospective, introspective discussion of the personal background, fieldwork practices, and what is called the composition of a text. Of course, the section on ideas and methods contains rich, illustrative description, just as the empirical treatment of a history and a structure says or implies much about method. Incidentally, the more methodologically and theoretically oriented reader is invited to read Part IV first, and then go back to the history, life history, and ethnography of Parts I–III. The book can be read either way, although the order adopted below is somewhat more integrated and cumulative.

Let me outline the main parts of the book. The first third or so goes directly into the biographical character studies or political life histories of seven of the local leaders as they were seen and envisaged in the field in 1955–1956 (indeed, four of these texts are pretty much what was written during the year following that fieldwork). Each of the leaders stands out for his particular synthesis of traits and life styles that are partly idiosyncratic, partly stereotypical, and partly archetypical. Let's look at the *dramatis personae* as a sort of preface: "Bones," with his *sangfroid* as a former fighter-gunman now serving as town judge; Ezequiel, whose poignant marital history seems inseparable from his role as a wealthy patriarch and old-fashioned radical; Camilo, the volatile "second cacique" (town boss) and husband of the leading usuress; Toni, scion of a rival political family, accomplished assassin, and the fastest agricultural worker in town; Boni, roguish, ultra-courteous philanderer, loyal fighter in the vendetta, and an explicit pantheist; Melesio, furtive, vengeful, and culturally the most conservative (e.g., in clothes and language); and finally, the complex, "sentimental," and most ardently ambitious Aquiles. In this third of the book "the symbols and meanings" are synthesized into an organic whole.

To galvanize and interrelate the unique individuality of the seven strong men, there follows a "fieldnotes interlude" of raw data—"raw" in the sense of being what I recalled (with the help of notes) and typed out minutes (or, in one case, a day) after three intrinsically exciting and also irritating meetings of the agricultural commune (*ejido*).

The second third or so of the book (Parts II–III) deals with the recent history and structure of politics in the village of Naranja (pronounced "nahráng-hah"—it's the Spanish word for "orange," substituted for the Tarascan name, Naranshani). More specifically, this book is about the political structure and dynamics over one generation, and the one-generational history of a politics, with emphasis on leaders, factions, and primary bonds such as friendship. The leaders and their cohorts and their foes, along with their differences, also have much in common in their feelings, for example, about ceremonial kinship and how it binds them to one another (analyzed in the first chapter in Part II). The leaders also share other, more or less political values: attachment to the land and the peasant lust for land; political ambition to control others; and habituation to small-arms violence. The next chapter (4 below) is devoted to the formal and informal aspects of political organization in a narrow sense (e.g., the patterns for assemblies). The last chapter in Part II is a detailed political history contextualized in several interpretations of the "cacical process." Many strands in the book as a whole are brought together in Part III, "Political Economy," which also points ahead to the more philosophical concerns in Part IV and the final chapter in the companion volume, *Agrarian Revolt in a Mexican Village* (Friedrich 1977).

My focus on complex persons and shifting informal politics is part of a strategy for leading the reader to greater insight and identification with the issues by ignoring some of the conventional boundaries between the individual and the cultural/economic systems, and more generally by circumventing or bridging many familiar categories and classes of description in anthropology and history. This also applies to the historical and temporal complexity of the book's orchestration; the reader who wants a simple temporal structure is invited at this time to look elsewhere.

The final third of the book, Part IV, "Experience and Methods," consists of retrospective chapters written in the 1980s. Following on the foregoing analysis, I now sketch twelve (about half) of the main methods and kinds of evidence that were used when studying Tarascan peasant leaders: for example, locally kept chronicles, the collection of gossip, the psycho-

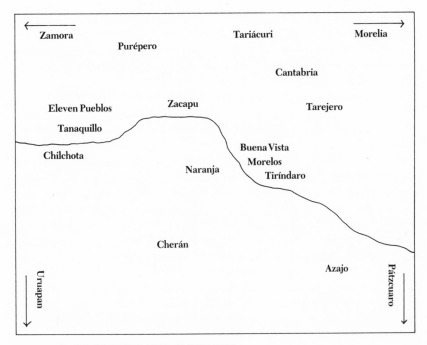

THE ZACAPU REGION AND ENVIRONS

logical interview, and the usual sort of "participant observation" by the anthrohistorian in fiestas, town meetings, and the like. Then comes a chapter on the personal experience of writing up the results of fieldwork, and a spelling out of seven "principles of composition" (for instance, what is called "partial holography"); I am told that this chapter is without precedent in the literature. The next section in this same chapter discusses the more substantive or "content" categories of an anthropological history such as the individual life history and the microsociology of primary groups (e.g., "confidential friend"). I conclude this chapter with a general model for the study of local-level politics and anthropological political history that should be of value for comparable problems, especially in the Third World. Finally, as an autobiographical postscript, there comes a chapter on the minimal, relevant facts in the anthropologist's life prior to fieldwork: what experiences and education bore most directly on my "precept and practice"? What sort of interpretive apparatus was interacting with a partly Indian culture? This is, in short, a sort of intellectual portrait of the fieldworker to match up with the leaders being studied. In a somewhat novel manner, then, the observer has been seen as part of the field or universe of observation.

I am concerned, then, with the fieldworker, the experience and the techniques of fieldwork, the individuals, groups, and cultures being studied in the field, the stylistic, tactical, and theoretical problems of writing a fieldwork-based book, and implicitly with the potential audiences for such a book—all of which leads into questions that are unanswered and surely to some extent unanswerable. As for the "natives" in these equations, I would emphasize that I early on discarded the idea of a "paid informant," and indeed of "informant" itself at a time when these terms were standard fare, and relied instead on friends, acquaintances, or helpers—or just folks who felt like being helpful for a few minutes or even hours. There are more boring ways of spending one's spare time than chatting about local politics with a curious and likable gringo. I made this tactical change partly for financial reasons: at about $90.00 a month with a wife and two infants I simply could not afford to pay "informants." But necessity soon became a virtue as I realized the intellectual, emotional, and practical advantages of not alienating the villagers by applying the usual methods. After all, didn't Juan Belmonte revolutionize bullfighting because he had to, because he was lame?

The Princes of Naranja is a sequel or companion volume to *Agrarian Revolt in a Mexican Village*, which has become a classic case study in political anthropology and the anthropology and local history of Central America. The earlier book, dealing with the village and its region through fifty years of agrarian history, raised issues about local politics and agrarian reform that are basic to our understanding of peasants and farmers all over the world (including the United States, where large numbers of family farmers continue to be forced off their land every year by agribusiness and its associates). *Agrarian Revolt* was theoretically relevant in terms of the problematic interface between a changing economic and political system, on the one hand, and, on the other, the character of leaders, notably the colorful, violent, and psychologically complex Primo Tapia. The earlier study is now carried forward and, as it were, capped by considering leadership, ideology, factionalism, and agrarian economics in the "ethnographic present" of 1955–1956, with particular condensation in the life histories. At another level, both of these works are structured in terms of the trilogy of biography, ethnography, and historiography and exemplify the possibilities of interaction between the individual/personal, the social/cultural, and the historical. It is intriguing that an anthropological history mainly researched thirty years ago should be "flush with some of the basic theoretical concerns today (1985)," as one reader put it. Moreover, the patterns of caciquismo analyzed below have if anything expanded and intensified in Mexico, thereby felicitously enhancing the relevance of this book.

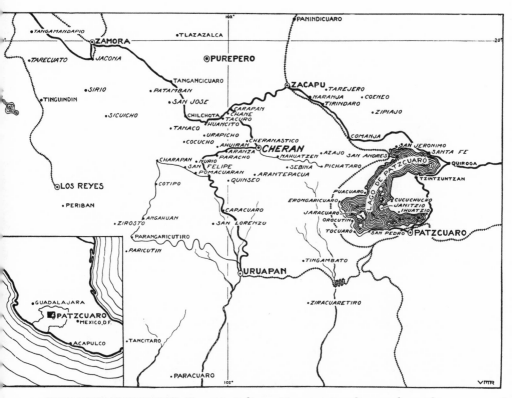

TARASCAN TERRITORY. Towns in italic are Tarascan in culture and speech. Towns in roman are either of mestizo origin or are primarily mestizo in population and culture and Spanish in speech. The inadequacies of existing maps make it difficult to show all the Tarascan towns with accuracy. Reproduced with permission from Beals 1946:6.

The first two-thirds of the book, describing local-level politics in anthrohistorical terms, has been drawn from the second volume of my 1957 doctoral thesis, *Cacique: The Recent History and Present Structure of Politics in a Mexican Village*, plus diverse subsequent workings, notably in 1965–1966 and 1985–1986, some of which appeared in published and anthologized articles, plus a swatch of fieldnotes added in the 1980s (for a full chart of the times of input, see Chapter 8). Personal names have been altered except for those of a few historically salient persons, notably Joaquín de la Cruz and Primo Tapia, who figure in *Agrarian Revolt* and largely as a consequence of that seem to have entered the larger stream of Mexican history and (political) anthropology and, indeed, have become the subject of a not inconsiderable amount of additional academic study.

Skeletal Chronology of Key Political Events

1900–1920	Mestizo cacicazgo; agrarian movement initiated under Joaquín de la Cruz
1919	Joaquín de la Cruz assassinated
1926	Primo Tapia assassinated; breakup of regional unity
1928	Tomás Cruz assassinated; first partition of Naranja ejido
1931	Second partition of Naranja ejido
1935	Expropriation of the first group of ejidatarios
1937	Caso faction divides against itself
1941	Expropriation of the second group
1945	Attempt to overthrow Scarface, led by Martín
1952–1955	Major fission led by Juan Nahua
1955–1956	Maximum centralization under Scarface

My theoretical-ideological statement in *Agrarian Revolt* (pp. xii–xiii) merits paraphrase here because it is, if anything, more relevant to *The Princes*. No one can study agrarian politics without becoming emotionally and morally involved. This is partly because the peasants themselves are deeply preoccupied with factionalism, political violence, land disputes, and some subset of the diverse historical details that bear on today's situation. Any one peasant spends far more time, energy, and thought on agrarian questions than one would guess from the anthropologies and histories, which typically dispatch the subject in a few pages or a chapter (granted recent exceptions such as Frans J. Schryer's *The Rancheros of Pisaflores*). Since I have bucked a number of scholarly traditions and tried to write completely, trenchantly, *and* sensitively on subjects about which most peasants feel strongly, it is fitting to state two relevant values of my own.

First, peasants have a right to the land around their villages, especially if there is a tradition or history of such ownership or usufruct. I approve of land reform in such cases, that is, of expropriation and redistribution. The need is real and the reform just, whether or not connected with anarchism, socialism, or any other ideology that may be held to be objectionable in some societies. But peasants also have a right to some sort of equity in the distribution of that land among themselves. The attempts of leaders to arrogate large amounts of land to themselves contradict the same laudable principles of agrarian reform.

Perhaps as important as the moral and humanistic problems is the scientific (here anthropological) historical one. A basic assumption of mine (elaborated more fully in Chapters 8 and 9) is that history and structure are determined by a complex of causes and contexts that include the natural environment; the economic relations of production and consumption; the organization of symbols we anthropologists call "culture"; the psychological factors of emotion, cognition, and character; and, finally, the more or less explicit ideologies by which people order their political lives. These and other things interact in a vast universe of (mainly mutual) implications and determination, although we may, for scientific reasons, zero in on a limited problem. Thucydides, "the first scientific historian," probed the causes of the Peloponnesian Wars. I, to some extent following him, have been deeply and indeed passionately concerned to anatomize and demonstrate the workings of one remarkable case of local-level politics, particularly its factionalism and leadership.

My debts are diverse. The research was supported financially by a starter grant of $1,500.00 from the Wenner-Gren Foundation, a Buenos Aires Convention Fellowship from the Mexican Government ($90.00 per month), a small loan from my father, and, during some of the write-up, allotments from the Lichstern Fund. My former wife Lore Friedrich twice typed most of the 1957 doctoral manuscript that underlies the later drafts in the first two-thirds of the book, and discussed parts of it with me. Lois Bisek retyped the entire text in 1984. Part IV was read in various sections to University of Chicago audiences, and I am grateful for the helpful comments made on those occasions. For their critical readings and suggestions on this part—made on the much different 1982 version— I wish to thank David Brent, John Comaroff, Ray Fogelson, my wife Deborah Friedrich, David Koester, David Price, James Redfield, Milton Singer, and George Stocking. Deborah gave valuable advice on three of the life studies, as did Ray Fogelson, Margaret Hardin, David Schneider, Marc Swartz, and Melford Spiro on "Bones" and "Camilo." Deborah and Fred Strodbeck commented astutely on the chapter which analyzes small group relations, as did Paul Liffman on this and Chapter 5, and John Attinasi, Deborah, Tim Buckley, and Lloyd Rudolf on Chapter 9. Dale Arntson read and critiqued Parts II and III. Gail Mummert-Zendejas, through her thesis, her questions, and her detailed answers to my questions, provided an invaluable factual backstop to the enterprise, as well as some fascinating information and insight into Naranja in the early eighties. The entire text of the book was reviewed, that is, read aloud and intermittently discussed, in a special seminar on anthrohistory at the University of Chicago, and I am grateful to the students for their questions: Pat Allen, Bruce Applebaum, Dale Arntson, Coby Jones, Valerie Hector, Laura Lewis, Paul Liffman, and Robert Moore. Economist Kenneth Miranda helpfully checked out the economics at the eleventh hour. All parts of the book profited from the earlier comments of Sidney Mintz, and Friedrich Katz made some strategic suggestions. My more generic intellectual debts for the point of view in the work as a whole are to the anthropologists Clyde Kluckhohn and Ralph Linton, and to my father, Carl Friedrich.

PAUL FRIEDRICH
Chicago, 1986

Part One. Seven Princes

Since the arrangement of a biography is given by time
or by the free associations of the narrator rather than
by externally imposed categories such as "economics"
or "religion," careful scrutiny should afford many clues
as to the actual interconnections of many pattern
systems. . . . The interdependence of one set of
patterns with another with which the connection is
hardly obvious from our point of view may sometimes
be detected as "felt" by the participant.

—CLYDE KLUCKHOHN,
The Personal Document in Anthropological Science

Note: The historical present in Parts I–III below means 1955–1956 unless clearly qualified
as 1986.

CHAPTER 1

Seven Political Life Studies

1. "BONES," THE FIGHTER[1]

Gonzalo Gómez: An Introduction

The comparatively tall figure, of medium weight, is still physically lithe and well-coordinated despite the action-packed years suggested by his white hair. His facial structure is heavy, his cheekbones prominent, and his forehead slopes back sharply to the white hair of his circular cranium, a perfect fit for the broad-brimmed, Michoacán-style sombrero with its pointed peak. His face is so often covered with stubble that one makes a mental note on seeing him cleanly shaven. During the eighteen months that I occasionally observed him, "Bones" invariably sported the cheap, ankle-length boots that are replacing *huarache* sandals, blue jeans or khakis, a white shirt and white cotton jacket, neither of them either very clean or very dirty, seeming at all times to contain a reasonable amount of dry soil. At times of cold he dons a khaki aviator-style jacket with a fur collar.

He often seems to effuse a personal brand of grimness, his eyes clouded and hostile, or betraying some distant purpose or suppressed intent. In his most characteristic pose he is sitting or standing before the town hall—the focus of political activity—with his athletic back erect, staring off into the distance with his grey eyes, the jaws clenched, not wiggling or moving any part of his body. In this state of apparently complete repose he can think or daydream for half an hour or more. Almost in caricature, his elegant gestures of hand and the precise articulation of his fingers ex-emplify the style with which Tarascan Indians punctuate any emphatic personal opinion. His gentle, almost pressureless handshake symbolizes the Tarascan desire to avoid bodily contact in most public domains. In for-mal contexts the man is called Gonzalo or even Don Gonzalo, but his friends usually refer to him and address him as Gonza, and his intimates address him and his enemies sometimes refer to him as Bones.

Life History and Political Role: The Formative Years (1898–1920)

When Gonzalo was born fifty-eight years ago (that is, in 1898), most of the folk in his village spoke only the Indian language, and they felt a strong identity with Indian customs. His own mother was Tarascan, and Gonzalo and his five siblings grew up surrounded by Tarascan customs, with Tarascan as their first language. But Gonzalo's father was one of those landless, wage-earning peons who, because of marriage or economic necessity, had migrated into another village. He was one of the few on record to have moved into the then "very Indian" and violently ethnocentric Naranja. As Gonzalo himself recalls, "Before 1925 they didn't use to let people 'of reason' [i.e., non-Indians] settle here. We used to get drunk and then someone would want to kill a *mestizo* [i.e., non-Indian]. That's why there are still so few of them here" (even today the village contains only 5 percent mestizos, and its inhabitants are known in the region "for their race" [*por la raza*]). Gonzalo's father, then, had to learn Tarascan to survive, and his specific, habitual errors of speech are still remembered by the son. The linguistic split between this father and the community—especially Gonzalo's young friends within the community—must have engendered conflicts and dichotomies within his own mind that were subsequently paralleled by or at least connected with conflicts in agrarian politics. Today Gonzalo still speaks Tarascan and seems more at home in it than in Spanish. He feels that his language sets him off from the people "of reason" (*de razón*). After the first six months of my fieldwork he always used to greet me in Tarascan, and enjoyed swapping a few phrases—usually terminated by a double entendre that I could not understand.

His infancy and childhood were marked by extreme physical deprivation. About ten years before his birth most of the best land in the valley, a great marshy swamp lying north of the village, had been seized by a Spanish company collaborating with wealthy local mestizos and backed by the national government—an instance of "the rape of the pueblos" by mestizos and foreigners then taking part in many parts of Mexico and accompanied by national inflation and other ruinous developments. In this case, the swampy lands were drained and fabulously productive plantations created, but, by the same token, the Indian population was no longer able to get fish, fowl, and the superb rushes from the marsh (from which they produced mats for market). The great majority of villagers, including Gonza's parents, were forced to eke out a subsistence as hired peons for the new landlords, or on the great sugar plantations to the south. Gonza's father usually made the trek to the "hot country" several times a year, his mother carrying and dragging along the children to the disturbing and poverty-ridden environment of the migrant laborers' camps. One of his brothers died in childhood. His father died when the boy was ten, and his mother perished two years later. After these deaths he lived with an older sister and two older brothers, both of whom soon died of fever. The Gómez family may be said to have typified the new proletariat, the children, in particular, suffering from malnutrition, sickness, and tropical diseases (malaria is often mentioned) in a general ambience of economic and social disintegration.

Until agrarian reform, the children of poorer villagers received little if any formal education, and Gonza never attended the tiny elementary school that functioned in the village until shortly before the Mexican Revolution (1910–1920); this deprivation may have made him initially responsive to the ideals of education in agrarian reform, but also may have motivated his later hostility to schoolteachers. His years of adolescence, in any case, were mostly spent riding herd for the new landlords of the valley and for one of the wealthy mestizo families in league with them. Gonza usually slept in the stables of the latter; old women still think of him as a former stable boy. He became the expert horseman he remains to this day, and during the same years formed the friendships and animosities that were to govern his later conduct. I suspect that he began to hate or at least resent his mestizo employers.

Gonza seems to have been highly susceptible to agrarianism from early on. Since Naranja lay on one of the main east-west roads and rail lines, army detachments and guerilla bands repeatedly passed by during the Revolution, threatening or shooting men and raping women. From his twelfth to his twenty-second year, Gonzalo, the orphaned stable boy, heard or saw many acts of violence and challenges to the foundations of his culture. He clearly recalls how agrarian unrest germinated in the village during the long years of the Revolution as the seminal notions of Emiliano Zapata and Francisco Villa—or, more precisely, of the Zapatistas and Villistas—reached the town. In 1912, when he was fourteen, a mob of enraged Indians attacked a party of drunken mestizos, killing six. He enjoys describing how the local priest was driven out in 1918. Yet he was not known for violence until the onset of the agrarian revolt itself (1920).

Gonzalo's First Conversion (1920)

Perhaps the most significant experience in Gonza's early life was his early and unwavering identification with the agrarian hero Primo Tapia. Tapia differed fundamentally from Gonzalo Gómez, and yet their social roles were complementary. After a good education, because of a generous uncle, Tapia spent fourteen years in the United States as a migrant worker in the mines and farms of the West, but also as an acolyte of anarcho-syndicalist revolutionaries in Los Angeles, and then as an organizer for the "Wobblies" (Industrial Workers of the World). Returning to Naranja in 1919 or 1920, he organized shock brigades of partisans and, more generally, pulled together the agrarian movement in the entire Zacapu Valley. Gonzalo, as a boy, had known Tapia and was one of the first to join his movement as a disciple and fighter; he often slept in Tapia's house, that is, the house of one of Tapia's aunts, and frequently accompanied him on trips as a bodyguard; his place in local history as one of the "original fighters" has been attested by persons of otherwise extremely divergent political orientations.

Gonzalo is still profoundly grateful to Tapia for his ideological orientation, the adaptation to Tarascans of a blend of anarcho-syndicalism and communism. As he says, "Primo used to explain everything to us, that such-and-such ideas were false, that such-and-such ideas were good, and that it was a pure lie that we would be sent to Hell for taking part in agrarianism. He understood everything, and he used to explain it well." "In Tarascan?" I ask. "Yes, he always used to talk to us in Tarascan. He could speak Tarascan, and Spanish, and . . . and . . . English! Ever since I joined him I have never gone to church. I never go in *there*. Primo still holds me out *here* (*Y me tiene aquí todavía*). Primo organized us. He was one of us." As some villagers put it, "Gonza was the first who sided with Primo Tapia." From my point of view, Tapia brought to Naranja a comprehensive and effectively communicated world view, a panorama of drastic change, and Gonzalo Gómez was perhaps the most susceptible of the new "corevolutionaries."

An "Original Agrarian" (1920–1926)

Gonza's poverty-stricken childhood and presumable penchant for aggression must have helped validate the ideology of land reform, that is, expropriation—even made it attractive. During the revolt, he figured as one of Tapia's young myrmidons. His enemies, now, accuse him of executing planned assassinations and even armed robberies and assaults, but his part in the often nocturnal violence cannot be exactly determined. He vaguely admits that "there was a lot of killing, but I don't like to think of that anymore." Certain it is that he spent much of his time in the sierra south of Naranja to avoid retaliation from the federals, the landlords' militia, and the pro-landlord faction in the village. In 1924, the men of Primo Tapia, to quote Gonza, "ran the opposition out of town, and they couldn't return without signing the agrarian census. They were foolish (*tonto*), reactionary. We were getting the ejido lands for the good of the town, and they opposed us." His position is rational: agrarian reform was an adaptive change. Later the same year, the agrarian factions won the struggle against the Spanish landlords. The Indians of Naranja obtained rights over almost fifteen hundred acres of extremely fertile black soil. Until the death of Tapia, all phases of production and distribution were communalistic.

During these stressful years Gonza emerged as one of "Tapia's well-

known killers," as enemies put it. In August 1924, at the age of twenty-
six, he shot and killed a member of one of the land-owning families that
had been solidly supporting the landlords; the face-to-face political homicide was catalyzed by sugarcane brandy during a drunken brawl at a
fiesta. In 1925, a group of agrarians, including Gonza or "Bones," ran the
leading witch (a woman) out of town. Later that year he participated in a
gun-battle on the streets of the county seat in which three from the village lost their lives. Agrarian reform thus required and fostered a social
status, that of "fighter" (*luchador*), for which personalities such as Bones
were fitted.

But on April 26, 1926, Primo Tapia was captured by federal troops
under direct orders from the national president, and lynched in the evening. Gonzalo and three agrarian comrades dashed off by horse to the
state capital, made inquiries, and tried to secure a federal safe-conduct or
injunction (*amparo*). Two days later they bore home the mutilated body.
The sadistic lynching of Primo Tapia outraged Gonzalo Gómez.

A Fighter in Village Factionalism (1926–1947)

With the death of Tapia, regional control disintegrated as the local chieftains in the agrarian communities turned against each other and their
neighbors. During the ensuing decades of factionalism—often resem-
bling a Hatfields-and-McCoys feud—Bones sided with the Casos under
Scarface. His motives for opposing the other faction, the Ocampos, were
complex, as is usually the case: they wanted to partition the land into family plots (the ostensible reason for the feud); then they had "offended
him" and "refused to recognize his worth," that is, they had wounded his
amour propre and thwarted his "egoism"; and he was related to some of
the Casos at that time through friendship and through shared illegalities;
finally, members of the opposing faction had twice tried to ambush him,
Bones proving "too fast and alert" (*listo*). He already was a heavy drinker
at this time and is said to have been ugly in his cups, especially when in
the company of Juan Nahua Caso, his partner and *compadre* or ritual co-
parent (i.e., the parent of one's godchild or the godparent of one's child).
In 1929 Bones killed a man in the Ocampo faction during a drunken
brawl. Three years later he and several other Naranja agrarians killed a
man in revenge for one of their number. The group was led by the cacique
in an adjoining mestizo hamlet which was vigorously reinforcing the Casos
in their struggle; by 1932, political ambitions and ideological or class interests had come to outweigh factors of cultural solidarity in the formerly
so ethnocentric community of Naranja.

Two years later, as the Casos were emerging victorious, Bones again
notched the record with a killing that, though accidental, is described
with lowered voice and undertones of horror. A certain member of the

Ocampo faction had stolen and eaten Bones' brown cow—a sufficient cause for rage (*coraje*), which can trigger a homicide that is congruous with the larger frame of politics. Shortly after the theft, Bones, somewhat drunk, asked the thief and gourmand to come and "discuss a little matter on the edge of town." The man consented and walked out with Bones, followed by a friend. On reaching the railroad tracks on the outskirts both men drew their pistols from their holsters or pants, but, being at close quarters, almost side by side, grappled instead of shooting and went down, wrestling. The thief's wife had been told and came running up behind the men, screaming and panting. She hurled herself into the combat to interpose her body before Bones—who was probably in a rage—and so save her husband. This is absolutely standard: a woman breaks into the fray because it means comprehensive disaster to become a widow, or worse, a widowed mother of orphans. As she was twisting in between the men, Bones got his pistol free and fired, accidentally hitting her in the mouth. A few seconds later he put a bullet through the stomach of his adversary just as the latter's friend shot Bones in the back, the ball passing under his kidneys. Not infrequently do killings in Mexican villages transpire like this: a small group of fired-up, disheveled peasants in the twilight on the edge of town or in the weak lighting of a fiesta grapple, and shoot impulsively, as the powdery *tupuri* dust rises and settles on their white cottons and red and black blankets. Both of Bones' antagonists left town shortly thereafter for security reasons and have not been seen since.

Gonza had spent his youth as a cowhand and horse trainer, and, with the new affluence of the *ejido* collective, he was not long in purchasing a fine bay mare: "In those days one wanted to own a fine horse," and fine horses are remembered for decades in Naranja. It was only natural for him to join the town's mounted militia during the thirties, and he soon became outstanding in the popular exercises of, for example, riding erect while straddling two horses, springing from one horse to another while in full gallop, jumping from a horse to the ground and back again, and other Cossack feats. The equestrian orientation remains strong to this day in the village: to have been the best rider is no mean accomplishment. The Naranja militia to which Bones and Scarface and others belonged was often instructed by cavalrymen from the county seat, and frequently distinguished itself at large parades, once winning a statewide contest. Local mounted militias were a key factor in the struggle for power in the village, the region, and even the state and national arenas, particularly during the conservative counterrevolutions of the twenties and the bitter factionalism of the thirties: candidates who could bring a few thousand such men into the state capital stood a better chance of getting elected. The eventual dissolution of the local militias by the government symbolized the end of a sort of era in Mexican politics, and greater control by "the Center" in Mexico City.

With the election of national president Lázaro Cárdenas in late 1934, as will be elucidated below, the Ocampos began to lose decisively. Gonza, a fairly loyal friend of Scarface Caso, was rewarded and charged with the office of town judge during the critical years of 1935 and 1936, that is, during the time of the First Expropriation (see Chapter 5). A judge, obviously, can render invaluable service by ignoring the offenses of one faction while calling in the county police or even federal troops in cases that stand to incriminate the opposition, in this instance the disintegrating Ocampos. Shortly after Gonza relinquished his legal responsibilities, however, the struggle began between the followers of Scarface, and, on the other hand, his Cousin Pedro González. Bones, reverting to a more familiar role in June 1937, killed an Ocampo (who was probably siding with Pedro) "by treason" (*de traición*), that is, in this case, by drilling him from behind a stone wall with his rifle as the victim walked down the street. Just one year later he took part in a similar bushwhacking of three mestizos from a neighboring hamlet; by this time the Naranja agrarians were lending a helping hand to various mestizo allies in killing or expelling the surviving individuals who remained loyal to the landlords. A few months after this Bones bushwhacked a member of the always large group of "fanatical Catholics" in the county seat; the man had threatened Bones while the latter was drunk and Bones shot him "in order to anticipate." Here, as so often, we see a combination of political and personal motives that are difficult to unravel. Violence in such a fighter often derives from political ambition, and aggressiveness in the streets may well outweigh forensic shortcomings at town meetings. As for bushwhacking, this style made one villager say, "Bones never shone until they gave a free rein to criminality. He has killed many, but always from behind. A turkey in a flock never does anything alone."

The main reason for Bones' renewed violence was the new schism within the village between the two first cousins, who were similar in personality and ideology. Internecine violence mounted, as did the alcoholism of many leaders and fighters. During the last years of the 1930s Bones drank more and more heavily, testifying, perhaps, to the strains of what is always called "the struggle," or, perhaps, to deeper-lying personal problems. He now cemented his reputation as a "bad man" (*un hombre malo*) when in his cups. He and his friends Juan and Boni constituted the formidable triumvirate of alcoholic gunmen who, as much as anything, won the battle for Scarface Caso. The more somber, if not sober, aspect of Bones' drinking was that it began to get out of control, to become a chronic need, with the consequence that he, like Boni, was frequently troubled by mild attacks of delirium tremens and began to shake so badly that he had to resign from the mounted militia. "My fingers shook like leaves in the wind." Like all the people of his culture, Gonza conceives of alcoholism as an external force usually beyond a man's conscious control, a fate that befalls you. "I was seized by the vice."

In 1939, as if in punishment for his "vice," Bones, as he was crossing the plaza, wandering, completely drunk by one account, was shot and gravely wounded in the arm, shoulder, and abdomen. The aggressors were two important *pistoleros* who had been engaged by the opposing factional leader, Pedro González Caso. I should perhaps reiterate at this point that almost all the persons in the Naranja drama are peasants like Gonza who are fighting over land, and that only in a few cases is one justified in using the opprobrious epithet of "pistolero," with its meaning of professional, hired gun. For a variety of reasons, in any case, mainly those of friendship, the attempt on Gonza's life unleashed a whirlwind of reaction among his many friends and compadres in the Caso faction: within two hours one of the assailants had been hunted down and riddled where he was hiding in the tall maize of the ejido, and one hour later the second miscreant was dispatched by Juan Nahua Caso in a head-on encounter in the Naranja side alley known as "The Street of the Dead."

Gonza has been very lucky. He emerged from this narrow brush with death in 1940 augmented in prestige and enjoying the even greater attachment of his Caso comrades; people just hadn't fully appreciated his sterling qualities until they nearly lost him. But these were troubled times for the Naranja commune, partly because great national unrest had marked the 1939 presidential elections, the bloodiest in Mexican history. Locally, fourteen members of the opposing González faction had allegedly "risen up in arms" as supporters of the losing candidate, that is, they had supposedly deserted the community during the seeding season in order to maneuver in the mountains. Much questioning and admittedly limited documentary evidence has left it uncertain whether this "rebellion" ever took place at all. Many now claim that nobody ever "retired into the sierra." Nevertheless, the Casos invoked the Agrarian Code, according to which anyone who leaves the ejido lands for even one year is subject to expropriation proceedings and anyone who fails to cultivate it for two years can automatically be deprived of his plot; by the same code, anyone who *does* cultivate a plot for two years acquires rights to its use. In late 1940, therefore, about harvest time, the Casos alleged that the land had been allowed to lie fallow and the fourteen opposition peasants in question, many of them "original agrarians" like Gonza, with as much agrarian right to the land as anybody, were expropriated; early the next year, their plots were redistributed by fiat to men who backed or would back the Casos. Gonza was "elected" president of the ejidal organization together with the former militiaman Ezequiel Peñasco as treasurer (see the next life study), and Bones' close friend Melesio Caso as secretary. On these men devolved the job of enforcing the drastic Caso action, which was no longer part of a reform but only of an acquisitive struggle. Bones was the right man for this place and time. In 1942 he shot and killed a man, allegedly because he had stolen a liter of Bones' brandy, actually because he was one of the expropriated and a member of the opposing faction. This also was an act of "rage," but, as in the case of some of Bones' previous homicides, it coincided felicitously with the exigencies of the factional struggle. By the time he retired as president of the ejido in 1943, Bones and his men had succeeded in preventing the reclamation of the contested plots by the expropriated peasants, and the benefited Caso peasants had acquired rights by virtue of having tilled the soil in question for the minimum of two years.

During 1945, concomitant with the election of a new governor, political unrest again broke out all over the state of Michoacán; in neighboring Tiríndaro the ejidal president was shot to death. Bones, with Boni and another friend, was arrested for the first and only time in his life and briefly detained—on false charges, as it turned out. A few weeks after his release the opposition faction, staring defeat in the face, made two desperate, final efforts. First, three of Scarface's peons were butchered in the sierra—with mutilation, the Casos claim. In the swift retaliation that characterized them through the whole period, Bones, Boni, and Juan Nahua Caso ambushed and killed two of the lesser supporters of the opposition that same afternoon as they were walking up the highway to the county seat. Comparatively few of the outstanding leaders and fighters, incidentally, have died with their boots on, the brunt being borne by lesser men: "The soldiers die, and the generals live," as Scarface puts it. The second desperate attempt was to try to assassinate Scarface using pistoleros, but this, too, was met with force involving a coincidental convergence of nepotic power that will be described in due course below (Chapter 5).

By 1947, the Casos had won the factional war, although many homicides were yet to come. In that year Bones was an accomplice in a murder that was felt to be infamous because the victim, a nephew of Pedro González, was shot through the back while trotting home from work on his donkey with his three-year-old son riding in front. The son, of course, was also wounded, and injury to children is not accepted as a part of factionalism, although it occasionally occurs and is consonant with an extension of blood vengeance. Taken together with his accidental shooting of a woman, Bones' record here reinforced the tendency for opponents to call him a criminal or an assassin.

Gonzalo's Second Conversion (1947)

Power may have begun to corrupt Gonzalo Gómez. One evening later in that same year of 1947, while wandering along the main street of town, allegedly besotted again and brandishing his pistol, threatening to kill so-and-so, he chanced to encounter one Bruno González, a respectable, determined, short peasant who had been peacefully tilling his acres during the entire period of internecine strife I have been describing. Bruno, a middle-of-the-roader, had recently been elected mayor of Naranja through the influence of Scarface, who wanted to bring him into the political process. But now Bones, the drunkard and político, swayed up to him and exclaimed, "You think, because you're mayor, that you're a big shot you son of the fucked one . . ." These are fighting words although, like all so-called "fighting words," they require other conditions to cause a fight. But here and now Bruno said, "And what are you?" (y tú, qué), yanked his pistol, and sent several bullets into Bones' midriff and intestines.

During the long convalescence that followed, Bones' friends and doctors remonstrated and he pondered his heavy drinking and abdominal wounds. Too drunk for his own defense, he had nearly been killed by a man, as they say, "without valor." He came to what may have been the second basic decision or spontaneous conversion in his life. He resolved never to drink again, and has never touched a drop since. Today he is careful to avoid drinking groups, and if he must take part in some conviviality, a friend always sedulously orders him a Pepsi-Cola or other soft drink. By the same token, since 1947 he has shot nobody, with two probable exceptions. The affirmation of law and order by the industrious and pacific Bruno over the bully Bones was a turning point in Naranja's recent political history. Since 1947, violence has declined somewhat; by 1955, the little ex-mayor who shot Bones was still prospering as the head of a patriarchal household with an ideal defense: three grown sons. But enemies claim that Bones was the one who bushwhacked Augustín Galván in 1955 (a critical homicide to which I return in Chapters 5 and 9), and even that he was in collusion in the killing of Toni Serrano in 1959. In a more facetious tone, in his absence, one knowledgeable leader in the opposition, for example, affirmed heatedly that Bones has killed "at least fifteen," which is probably true, since I am only citing cross-checked homicides (see Homicide Appendix). This same witness added, "Yes, he kills them, he goes to the wake, and he drinks coffee with the bereaved."

Gonzalo's Role in Local Intrigue (1952–1957)

No strictly political killings took place during Gonza's tenure as town mayor in 1952, perhaps testifying to the "new look" of "peace and solidarity" toward which the Casos have been straining ever since their victory; having gained control, the ruling princes want to be able to calumniate any opposition as a threat to the commonweal. But there lurks a constant danger to any such faction of unity, and that is a schism within its own core—such as began during Bones' mayoralty. With the formerly unifying hostility against Pedro's faction now weakened, many of the princes felt an increasing resentment against the control by the kinship nucleus of the Casos. Juan Nahua Caso was a member of that nucleus and a friend of some of its leaders, so that his rising influence and his eventual election as mayor in 1954 looked to insure the status quo. But beneath the surface smoldered Juan's feeling that he had never been rewarded adequately with political office despite (and perhaps because of) his status as a fighter, and he was galled by the spectacle of Camilo Caso and others operating in higher state politics. Juan and some of his colleagues, including Bones, were in collusion with Pedro González and some of his faction. All persons in the nascent Nahua faction (which included several other able Nahuas) are said to have been motivated by their hatred for the obese wife of the "interminable cacique," Scarface. Intellectually, they were guided by Juan's elder son, a left-wing law student in Mexico City at that time, and an excellent orator. By the height of the "Juan Nahua case" there were actually three separate factions, all led by splinters of the former Caso faction and sharing the same ideology. Personal animosity was perhaps most intense between Gonzalo Gómez and the oldest of the Caso nephews, Camilo, who was serving as alternate to the national senator from the state of Michoacán. Locally, this nephew once shouted out, "All right, Bones, let's go to the edge of town or before the ejidal assembly and see who comes out dirtiest!" The attempt by Juan to overthrow his Caso kinsmen eventually was broken by the intervention of higher authorities in the informal politics of the state, by the astute intriguing of Aquiles Caso, to which I return below, and, finally, by the inevitable method of violence: Juan and his intellectual son were ambushed and narrowly escaped with their lives, after which they fled to Mexico City. (I visited Juan in his shack in a horrible slum and was rewarded by an invaluable one-hour interview.)

But we are here interested in the defection of Gonzalo Gómez. Why did he betray his leader, Scarface Caso, whom he had been supporting at considerable risk for over twenty-five years? First, he shared the widespread envy and jealousy toward the primary leaders, and had never forgiven the Casos for declaring that the little mayor who shot him had acted in conformity with his office, even, some say, that Bones deserved what he got. Thus there was an element of blood revenge. Second, Gonza liked the ambitious "plan for material improvements" that had been drawn up by Juan's son. Third, the supporters of Juan, including Bones, saw him as a sort of point man who would take the small-arms fire upon himself when the Casos went into action—which is just what happened.

How did the Casos go about winning back Gonzalo Gómez? At first nothing was done, but gradually after Gonza's re-election as mayor in 1953, his faith in the new, would-be cacique was undermined by Aquiles Caso, the town secretary, who argued that Juan would have Bones assassinated as soon as he held the balance of power in the town. Aquiles also pointed out faults in the "plan for material improvements": although Juan's son had been born and bred in the village, he was interpreted to Bones as a man of the city who "could not understand Naranja's problems," Aquiles thus exploiting the contrast between the well-read law student and the illiterate Bones. But perhaps most persuasive were the small and indirect bribes: whenever the civil authorities had "done justice," Aquiles, as town secretary, would refuse a part of the fine on the grounds that his private income was sufficient, insisting that Bones take "now ten, now twenty pesos" as his due (the truth of this claim is problematical, incidentally, in light of what we know about Bones otherwise). Within a space of several months Gonza, for whatever reason, allegedly became "very fond" of the young secretary (*me tenía mucho cariño*), let him run the court, and then reneged against the rebellious faction of Juan Nahua. Some time after Juan's precipitous retirement to Mexico City, Bones was elected town judge, supposedly as a reward for betraying his decades-long comrade in arms and cups. Bones' presence in this office and his ability to disarm others have both been contributing to the order of sorts or "communal unity" in Naranja—despite the justifiable denunciations by the Pedro González faction against the "murderer in the judgeship." In Naranja, as in many Mexico pueblos, the most redoubtable gunmen are often at or near the center of the political rulership.

Gonzalo as a Senior Prince in 1955–1956

Bones is today one of the inner princes and one of the eight or nine leaders in the dominant faction who, at secret nocturnal meetings, make policy decisions affecting the entire village. Because of disputes over ejidal plots and attempts by expropriated families to regain their plots, meetings of the town and, even more, the ejido are often called by delegates from the Department of Agrarian Affairs. During these convocations the delegate is careful to turn, now to Bones, now to Toni or Ezequiel, for an opinion. But Bones is more laconic than most of these leaders, when it comes to public speaking, nor does he hold forth in conversation, unless the subject is sex or politics. When the politics "gets hot," as it did in 1956, he enters into arguments with short but relevant sentences on the need for Naranja to gain and maintain control in the region. And once he "took the word" at length à propos of an occasion with unusual moral portent. One of two brothers had seduced a young wife and was carrying on a liaison. One Sunday afternoon (during a basketball game, which I was watching too) the mother-in-law of the young woman started a public scene with the adulterous brother and slapped him several times. In the ensuing melee one of the two brothers nearly knifed her other son, the minor leader called Carlos. Gonzalo, while arbitrating the case, made many statements highly revelatory of values, and adduced numerous proverbs— all in support of the position that no man is guilty of an act of rage (*coraje*) and that the blame accrues to those who stimulate or precipitate such rage. Most of the villagers would agree to some extent with this legal concept. By the same token the two enraged brothers were let off with a mild admonition, whereas heavy blame and imprecation were heaped on the mother of the man who had nearly been knifed. (For a close analogy, see the judgment of The Mestizo, p. 183 below.) During the same hearings Gonza expatiated more generically that the defendants and the whole town should outgrow their reputation of being "only killers" (*puros matones*) and that deep grievances such as lay beneath this near-knifing ought to be settled "in the town hall and not in the fields."

Character and Culture: Sexual/Marital History[2]

In 1919, at the comparatively advanced age of twenty-one, Gonzalo eloped with a young sister of one of the two most important fighter-leaders in the agrarian movement under Tapia. He and his have-not parents-in-law lacked the minimum for a wedding in the traditional style, and so the couple just joined up (*así no más*). Moreover, the disturbed times were not conducive to marital fidelity. After three years, at the height of the revolt, he deserted his wife to join in another common-law marriage with a woman by whom he had three children who died in infancy and one son, Benito, who is now a minor leader.

Abandoning his second wife after six years, Gonza drifted during the thirties, associating simultaneously or successively with numbers of women in the village or the county seat. A friend, when asked about his affairs, grinned and responded, "*Mil amores*"; most of the "thousand loves," especially the longer relationships, seem to have been with Tarascan-speaking women. Documents and interviews for the 1930s contain occasional references to "a woman" in Gonza's house; certainly the available widows and faithless wives are often quicker to surrender to such a leader. Several enemies accuse him of having seduced or assaulted the wife of a political enemy. While it would be absurd to interpret Naranja politics as primarily a struggle over the connubium, there is no question but what both factions are steeled by real or fancied threats to their women-folk, and that the women themselves reinforce these threats.

When sex is the subject, Gonza is articulate. Once, in a group discussion of premarital relations, he casually remarked, "We begin to fuck (*chingar*) at fourteen." With whom? I asked. "With whomever we can lay our hands on, with a widow or a girl." When do sex relations with the bride begin? After the bride-capture or elopement? "Yes, and before it too." And he is given to double entendres when the conversation is running in Tarascan (where word play is common among these leaders just as it is rare in their Spanish). One day, for example, a friend in the Caso faction commented on a woman peddler across the street. What had been her wares, vegetables? Gonza answered in the affirmative and touched off a guffaw by playing on the word for a kind of wild green which also means vulva or vagina, that is, "pussy," in several dialects of the Eleven Pueblos. And he can be scurrilously funny. One evening after a day in the Tarascan sierra on a trip, we were sitting on the curb in the plaza of the great tourist attraction, Pátzcuaro. One of us saw a local girl walk by on heels and noted, "She is pretty," in Tarascan, at which the old goat or, better, burro, Gonza, chuckled and said, "Bite my cheek." Seeing that his interlocutors were amused, he continued, laughing harder all the time, "Bite me on the cheek, give me a kiss, embrace me, darling (*malecita*), with your legs pointing upward." He finished bent over, shaking with mirth. (Such conversations, which should give some idea of Gonza's style, had to be recorded mentally where—even if I'd had one—a tape-recorder would have been out of place.) Incidentally, Gonza's humor always referred to ventro-ventral heterosexual intercourse.

Gonza's naturalism about sex, which he sees as an often humorous form of pleasure, is probably related to his lack of anxiety about death and his resignation to homicidal rage. I did not detect signs of what might be called "moral anxiety"; *chercher la femme* was a part of life, and death was part of factionalism. His amatory and homicidal histories have generated, if not affection, then at least sporadic amusement, even comic relief, in a culture where "Indian humor" laughs at broken crockery and physical pain. During my fieldwork in neighboring Tiríndaro a girl was abducted, carried to the sierra, and raped by three adolescents. Such sexual violations, occurring every year or two, invoke value conflicts: the women, the priest, and some of the more moral men are upset or outraged, whereas the majority of the men either resign themselves or joke about it. In this case, it was judged in Tiríndaro that one of the boys would have to marry the girl, which he was then forced to do. Bones and five of his companions talked at length about the episode while seated before the Naranja town hall; while recognizing the gravity of the act, they also jested a few times about the youths taking such good advantage of their opportunities.

One realistic index of Gonza's sexual past is his present relations with women in their fifties, or even older, with whom he often seems to be on the verge of joking. I could sometimes watch him at a distance, conversing with such a Naranja matron, breaking into a chuckle, or buckling over and shaking his head in a gesture that contrasted sharply with his habitual iron reserve. The contempt and vilifications of his enemies must be weighed in balance against his jesting and friendship with so many of the women who have grown up along with him, and for whom he still seems to feel affection even though their sometimes shabby dress and unkempt hair suggest the demoralizing effects of the past forty years. I have discussed Bones at some length with women in their sixties and seventies; several hated him as "bad," but the consensus was that he *used* to be "wild" and "one of the hot-tempered ones" (*uno de los bravos*),[3] but that he unquestionably belonged "with the community."

A few years ago Gonza finally joined in common-law marriage with a much younger Tarascan woman who struck me as cheerful and fairly attractive. At fifty-eight, he appeared to have settled down. But he threw back his head and laughed when someone remarked casually that men copulate until their death. He absents himself from the town hall for a week or ten days, sometimes simply to relax in his cozy, one-room house near the plaza, enjoying the company of his wife and two elderly female in-laws. Or he may be working.

My focus above on many aspects of politics and the essentials of sexual and marital life necessarily obscures the role of work in Gonzalo's life. At least a third of the year, that is, for over one hundred days, he, like the other ejidatarios and hired men, is in the fields of the sierra or of the valley, plowing with a team, seeding, harrowing, cross-harrowing, weeding, harvesting, looking after his livestock, and, in general, keeping up his callouses.

Relations with Children and Men

As noted, Bones was involved in the wounding of a small child as a part of politics. In light of this and other "grim antecedents," one might be struck by the tenderness and concern that he shows toward tots. I have often seen him cuddling and kissing his baby granddaughter in public, something not too usual for a Naranja man. Once he walked the length of the plaza to pick up a little boy, move him back from the street, and warn him to be careful. Gonza's affection for children is probably linked to his friendly dealings with mature women and his jocular attitude toward old (and implicitly senile) men (*muy viejitos*). No one of these three categories threatens him; some of the old women and all the young folk address him as "Don Gonzalo." By way of contrast, his occasionally expressed hostility or suspicion toward adolescent and adult males may well symbolize an anticipation of strife or envy from this quarter of the population. In the same spirit, the most extraordinary reserve obtains between Gonza and his son, Benito, and his stepson by the same wife, Mateo; both men are in their middle twenties, married, living together in a joint fraternal household, and already minor leaders who have held office in the civil or ejidal administration. Yet in hundreds of times where they were in the same company I hardly ever heard a word pass between father and son or stepson. No other men that I knew kept their distance this way. I think that all this was expressive of unusual ambivalence: precisely because of Bones' past, they evinced respect to a marked degree. Bones is fond of both these sons, and their presence in the town hall probably influenced his volte-face from liquor in 1947 and his recent more commendable comportment.

Gonza is more reticent about himself than any other leader, so that the life study had to be pieced together like a mosaic from other people's statements or from such brief disclosures as emerged naturally from him or could be cultivated for five or ten minutes during a talk about some other subject. His closeness and reserve stem in part from his illiteracy; he is the only illiterate leader. And unlike others for whom Tarascan was or remains the first language, he has had little contact with Spanish-speaking cities; I believe he has never left Michoacán, and I know he has never been to the United States. This "lack of education," as he terms it, has caused him anxiety. He was the only leader I approached on the subject whom I could not persuade to take a Rorschach test; all others whom I asked agreed readily (although I admit I did not feel like asking the leading caciques of the two factions, Scarface and Pedro). Several persons have accused Bones of persecuting schoolteachers. Once in the early 1950s he and two other relatively uneducated stalwarts threatened with drawn pistols a recently arrived *and politically ambitious* young pedagogue. During the first months of my field trip Gonza was cold and even uncivil. But one thing that warmed him was a peculiar scene where I, on request, was fighting with a young man who was training as a boxer in Zacapu; hurriedly recalling my study of the manly art (at Harvard!), I knocked this man down repeatedly. More decisive were my sorties into the arena of Tarascan. He began asking questions in Tarascan and laughing at my answers; his effortless superiority increased his confidence. Our mutual relations improved greatly after a lengthy interview about house-building which involved the names of all the house parts (which are handled in the language by the same suffixes used for body parts). Once I was telling a small group before the town hall about the translations of the Bible into Tarascan by nearby missionaries. I wound up by handing over a copy of *The Gospel According to Saint John*. Gonza took it like the tail of a rat suspected of carrying the bubonic plague and swung it around in a semicircle, keeping it away from his body, before handing it on to one of the Caso cousins.

Gonzalo's Primary Groups

Central to both the political culture and the individual psychology of the village are the several kinds of primary or immediate bonds that surround every normal person. Thus, fathers, sons, and brothers are obligated to political loyalty and blood vengeance. As is detailed in Chapter 3 below, these primary bonds have somewhat specialized meanings and functions for leaders and fighters: thus, ceremonial coparenthood (the *compadrazgo*) binds them outward to nonleaders. Friendship, and kinship in the broadest sense, constitute one's most immediate and significant integration with the community, and one's optimal form of security; every time a man acts politically in accordance with such bonds he is recommitting himself to the principles implicit in the system. Our evaluation of Gonza's behavior and moral status should therefore realistically reflect his primary picture.

After seeing his political record, one feels enlightened to learn that Gonza is well liked by many people and, in his own opinion, has "many good friends." Many of the major princes in the dominant faction named him as a "best friend" or a "friend of confidence" (*amigo de confianza*), and Gonza, when questioned by me on the subject (in private, of course), stretched out his arms inclusively and said, "Many," in a rather mestizo style, before going on to list eleven of them with the (unusual) implication in his intonation that he could have named a goodly number more. (Most men, on the contrary, carefully itemize about a half-dozen and seem sure that there is a boundary line, and where to draw it; see Chapter 3 below.) Gonza has friends for several reasons, partly because of the same down-to-earth understanding that he shows in conversation, partly because of the texture of humor which he weaves with his persiflage and salacious (if unoriginal) puns. Many exculpate his killings on the ground of (justifiable) rage, the former effects of alcohol, and the exigencies of "the struggle" (in which the revolt period and the subsequent destructive factionalism may not be distinguished sharply). Finally, his homicidal and amatory exploits inspire amusement and respect, if not always admiration. In Mexican terms, he is macho; in Tarascan terms, he is a "virile rooster" who "knows how to defend himself" (*horénasti kwáhpikwarin*).

Gonza's ties of friendship contrast strongly with those of kinship; after fifty-eight years of almost constant residence in the village he turned out to be the godfather of the wedding for a few of the younger leaders, but could name only three men linked to him by the respectful status of *baptismal* compadre. This gap in his personal network reflects his career as an agrarian fighter and an agrarian atheist who scrupulously avoids entering a church. Such compadres as he has were mostly leaders in the abortive

Juan Nahua fission, and neither the dominant cacique, Scarface, nor most of his nephews are compadres or close friends of Gonza—whose sociometric position may thus be said to accurately index the chthonic hostility he has felt to most of the Casos ever since they "betrayed him" in 1947. I was not terribly surprised to learn, after my departure from Naranja, that Bones was thought by some to have been involved in the successful ambush of Toni, the Caso fighter whose life is sketched in the fourth part of this chapter.

Gonza's natural kindred within Naranja has always been very limited. His mestizo father gave him no ties, of course, and most of his siblings died in infancy or childhood, as has been detailed. True, his brother-in-law by his first marriage was a leading fighter, but Gonza was soon divorced, and then this affinal ally was killed. Gonza's son and stepson, of course, support him politically. As against these positive if limited ties, Gonza's only living brother split with him during the schism of the late 1930s and has ever since followed a publicly acknowledged if undistinguished role in the rank and file of the opposition; such a standoff between full blood brothers is almost unique in Naranja's recent history.

Conclusions

Except for his clothing and his role in agrarian history, it can be said that Naranja's drastic culture change has hardly affected Gonza. At many points he has resisted change, as, when mayor in 1952, he blocked the construction of a new state highway that might have brought "progress" by connecting his town with the city of Uruapan on the southwestern edge of the Tarascan area. Although faithfully anticlerical in the tradition of Tapia, Gonza does compromise with what has been called "Tarascan folk religion" to the point of participating in such semi-pagan fiestas as "The Day of the Dead" and "Tiger Day" (when until recently he used to dance in a tiger suit and a deer-head mask on the nearby "Mountain of the Moon"). Such religious adjustments partly clarify his status in the moral order of the town. Gonza, as noted, lives in a small, one-room adobe house (with a dirt floor and neither electricity nor running water). His careful grooming of a fine roan mare symbolizes his adherence to traditional values. His lack of private property, aside from his house, ejido plot, and several private fields (mainly planted to beans), mutely attests to his own fast living and his relative lack of acquisitiveness. But it is curious that Bones Gómez, former alcoholic, killer, and womanizer, has ended up living in monogamous union and nominally enforcing a species of law and order as a community judge, partly with the compelling symbol of his old .45, which he proudly claims he no longer needs to carry (largely a true statement), but perhaps more by the strength of his reputation as "valiant."

My most vivid memory of this valor goes back to a moonlit night when, while passing alone through the Naranja plaza, I was detained by an ine-briated man, unknown to me, who held me with an extended and increas-ingly heated and minatory harangue in Tarascan that I simply could not follow. Suddenly, Gonza appeared, gliding swiftly down the long porch before the town hall and school buildings, staying in the shadow. He took my interlocutor firmly by the elbow and led him away. As he left I saw a .22 pistol in its holster over the small of his back.

[*Postscript:* By 1970, fourteen years after the "historical present" above, "Don Gonzalo," already a "little old man" (*viejito*), was living in a different little house and seldom emerging (*casi no sale*). No one responded to my prolonged knocking. By 1984, I am informed, his wife had left him and gone to live in a far-away city. No longer able to work, he was residing in a one-room shack attached to his son's house.[4]]

Let us now turn from the Gonzalo Gómez text, which synthesizes from several periods of composition, to the political life study of Ezequiel, pretty much as it was written up from the field experience for *Cacique* in 1956.

2. EZEQUIEL

Some men weave together in the fabric of their life history many of the clashing colors and broken threads of an unhappy, if eventful epoch. At about the turn of the century a very swarthy infant called Ezequiel was born into one of the more propertied branches of the landholding Peñasco lineage; he and Gregorio are the only two princes who did not "suffer" in their youth. But the quantity of beans and the condition of one's manta shirt are not the only indices of childhood discontent. At the age of four-teen Ezequiel attached himself to one of the numerous troops of federal soldiers that were passing through the Zacapu area. The soldiers, con-vinced of his alleged age by the tall, large-boned frame, toughened by heavy field work, were not long in provisioning him with a uniform and rifle. During the last four years of the Mexican Revolution he was able to participate in numerous battles and skirmishes as one of those teen-age Indian riflemen who used to swell the armies of Carranza and Zapata and to irrigate with their blood the dry soil for which they were fighting.

Ezequiel was not fond of army life. About 1920 he deserted and went to the United States, where he remained for almost five years, working, like Primo Tapia, in the mines of Arizona and the sheep ranches and sugar-beet fields of the Rocky Mountain states, and, incidentally, drinking heav-ily, mixing with laborers of all nationalities, and getting married to a Mexican girl named Carmela. But the battlefields of the Revolution and the Great Escape of migrant labor in the United States were not sufficient to release Ezequiel from the rigorous dictates and compelling bonds of the indigenous patriarchy. When he returned to Naranja in 1925 "for a short visit, his family did not let him go again. His mother had picked a certain Concha. Ezequiel disliked her. On the day when they were going to get married, he hid himself in the house of a friend. He was weeping and complaining, and said that he would go away to the North again, but his *parents and godparents* made him get married to Concha. He was never able to go back to Carmela." This event in Ezequiel's life exemplified a striking feature in the Naranja culture that was to be so shattered by the agrarian reform and subsequent changes. In the case of Ezequiel, a grown man of twenty-three with a wealth of the experiences that make for maturity and independence was literally compelled, in accord with the old Naranja customs, to marry a girl whom he didn't like but with whom he had been compromised through parental arrangement. In all fairness one should add that the girl also disliked Ezequiel!

Ezequiel did not figure in the heroic period of radical agrarianism, and almost all his relatives were actively opposed to Primo Tapia because they already possessed sufficient private land or because they were sharecropping for the hacienda; Ezequiel himself is for this reason accused by some enemies of having been a "White Guard," although in actuality he, like Ildefonso Serrano, declared himself in favor of Tapia. He joined the militia shortly after his return and forced marriage. He was in Naranja on the day of Primo's martyrdom and clearly remembers the details. Subsequently Ezequiel, like most of his family, affiliated himself with the Ocampo faction, and he was elected town secretary for the two years of 1927–1928, although he has never been to school. He was one of the fifty-odd agrarians from Naranja who, under the Ocampos, formed part of the four-hundred-man army from the Zacapu region that helped the government to eliminate the Cristero (Christian reactionary) rebels in southern Michoacán and Jalisco. Ezequiel is fond of telling about this mopping-up expedition and his activities as town secretary. During these years he was also active in organizing and encouraging the agrarian movement in the mestizo towns of the Zacapu region, as well as communities in the Tarascan area, a job that often caused him to spend entire nights far from home. He seems then to have withdrawn from politics as the Casos and the Ocampos continued their struggle. Ezequiel's political activity was minimal from 1929 to 1934. He actually spent most of the time away from town (and Concha), going to the United States for brief sojourns and working as a migrant laborer in other Mexican states such as San Luis Potosí and Vera Cruz, "looking for adventures," as he puts it. Ezequiel probably owes his life to this partial retirement from the mayhem days of the Ocampo period.

Ezequiel's agrarianism has always been soundly tempered by a keen concern for his personal safety. With the defeat and departure of the

Ocampos in 1934, he boldly switched sides and declared his allegiance to the triumphant Casos. He entered again with great energy into the agrarian struggle that was revived by the new president, Lázaro Cárdenas. During these years of the middle thirties he was secretary and then president of the Radical Agrarian Socialist Federation of Primo Tapia and operated as what might be called a "politically ambitious scribe," traveling to distant regions or drawing up documents for the granting of ejidos in the Naranja town hall, which, as "the soul of agrarianism in the Zacapu region," contained five typewriters and a telephone. Ezequiel frequently made speeches at the ejidal meetings during the thirties.

Ezequiel, because of his intelligence and aggressiveness, began to emerge as one of the leaders of the faction of Scarface. He was a member of the tough-riding militia described in Bones' life history above. In 1944, Ezequiel Peñasco was elected president of the ejidal commissariat, following directly on Bones Gómez. The struggle between Scarface and Pedro González was reaching its climax; the former narrowly escaped from an assassination attempt. By 1945 the governor of Michoacán, supported by minority factions all over the state and by González people in Naranja, was making one of the periodic attempts to overthrow the ruling Cárdenas machine. The González party obtained a presidential order from Cárdenas' successor, Manuel Avila Comacho, restoring their ejido parcels to Agustín Galván and five others after four years of exacerbating litigation.

Would the order of the national president suffice to restore the coveted ejido plots to these five old agrarians? The dramatic report of a federal delegate, dated November 4, 1945, recounts how he went to Naranja to oversee the execution of this presidential order. He describes how he was met by a large group of women and some men, including the president of the ejido, Ezequiel, who were all "visibly aggressive." The delegate read them the order. Ezequiel said that they were going to disobey. Despite the definitely menacing posture of the Naranjeños, the federal delegate convoked a meeting of the ejidatarios. The gathering was hostile and uncommunicative, and Ezequiel continued to flatly affirm that he would refuse to obey. At these meetings the principal ejido officers sit around a rickety table at the front of the room, under a single electric bulb, while in the background there are massed the ejidatarios, the women squatting on the dirt floor, only their black eyes showing above their shawls. The men stand against the wall, muffled in their serapes. Suddenly the meeting was interrupted by the entry of Camilo Caso, then secretary of the regional committee, with an angry frown on his face and a pistol under his belt. The ejidatarios and Ezequiel immediately shouted at him "not to sign anything." The federal delegate beat a hasty and well-advised retreat to Zacapu, because he "lacked guarantees." From the municipal seat he issued a summons to Ezequiel, but Ezequiel refused to present himself, and the case was again pigeonholed. Numerous written accusations testify that the Caso party, represented by Ezequiel, was prepared to use violence against the delegate. "The bells had been tolled, the people aroused," and "grave consequences" barely avoided.

This little page in Naranja history exemplifies several things. It illustrates one of the numerous conflicts of authority that have taken place between the national organizations, sometimes even backed by the president, and the partially autonomous local levels backed, as in this case, by the informal political structure in the state. Specifically, the federal delegate, coming from the national bureaucracy and President Avila Camacho, could not enforce his orders against the ejidal authorities of the Naranja community, bastion of "Cardenismo," and Camilo Caso, the left-wing Indian friend of the preceding president and the ultimate sovereign in Michoacán, "Father" (*Tata*) Lázaro Cárdenas. The spirit in which national orders are thus defied is reminiscent of and derivative from the anarchical strains of the earlier communal ethnocentrism, Primo Tapia's anarchism, and Francisco Múgica's stand for state's rights. But only the spirit is analogous; Ezequiel and the ejidatarios were but acting as cogs in an informal statewide structure of authoritarian power. The present case also sounds the violent, rebellious tones that have characterized the pronunciamentos of Ezequiel and other princes on many other occasions. This tone is heard, for example, in a letter written directly to the Secretary General of the Agrarian Department in 1943, and signed by Ezequiel, Bones, and Melesio, accusing Agustín Galván of being a "bandit," and concluding with the words "we are not disposed that the orders given by you shall be completed . . ." Thus do the princes flout national directives.

Ezequiel has remained loyal to Scarface through all vicissitudes, and Scarface trusts him more than several of his own nephews. In 1953 and 1954, during the dangers of the "Juan Nahua case," Ezequiel was the only major prince who did not desert the Caso nucleus. His faithfulness is based on his conviction in the upper-level political connections of Scarface and on the fact that the latter has covered up some of Ezequiel's illegal activities, especially embezzlement and land-grabbing. Ezequiel was again given office in 1949 and served for five years as president of the important Regional Committee.

Ezequiel is one of the older princes, like Nico and Toni, who still profess a radical agrarian ideology in no equivocal terms. His speeches in council and his general thinking hark from a former period when all means were fairly used in the unconditional fight against the landlords and the clergy. Memories of class warfare showed themselves during the tense ejidal assembly in 1955 when Gregorio Serrano chose to stick with his original decision to abide by a federal directive nullifying his candidacy as ejidal president because he still lacked the final deed to his plot. Ezequiel was genuinely angered. He said, "You talk about the law, about obedience! But during the struggle, in the question of land, we often had to fight the government, and to ignore it, and we didn't worry about honor! *Primo thought first of his people, of the community, and not about things like honor!*" And Ezequiel stalked out of the assembly. There is no Tarascan word for honor.

The most salient feature of Ezequiel's ideology, however, is his still fervent anticlericalism. He partook in the public burning of the holy images in the plaza during the thirties and the conversion of the Naranja church into a political meeting house for the Radical Agrarian Socialist Federation. His is the last laugh, or chuckle, when he recalls the priest who used to weep as he preached in Tarascan about the immediate hell awaiting all who participated in the agrarian movement. "We participated, and we ran him out, and we burned the 'santos' in the plaza, and they still haven't sent us to the inferno!" Needless to say, he views with a jaundiced and envious eye the recrudescent power and influence of the priest in Tiríndaro, and the now open and expensive religiosity of the Naranja women.

Having surveyed Ezequiel's political role, let us return to certain more personal strands of his development. About the time of his activities as secretary and then president of the ejido (1941–1945), his wife, Concha, whom he had married under such pressing circumstances, began to break under the strain of life-long companionship with a man who was either absent from Naranja, or engaged in the all-absorbing agrarian politics. "She went crazy. . . . She used to get on the bus and go off to other parts . . ." and the greatly aroused Ezequiel spent much time searching for her. This turn of events now provokes much contagious mirth in Naranja (in Ezequiel's absence!), but at the time it constituted a major scandal, giving rise to a Tarascan folk song that goes as follows:

I have wandered everywhere, everywhere,
looking for Silvina
She is going to take a little Red Bus,
A Red Line Bus
To go to Uruapan

Looking for Silvina
I have wandered everywhere, everywhere,
I have wandered everywhere, everywhere,
But I haven't found her.

Silvina (a pseudonym to avoid being too "personal"), was eventually found, and the Peñasco family appears now to be fairly well ordered again. Ezequiel is an excellent father and an industrious provider. But present mirth, stability, and the production of seven children should not obscure the clear picture of this object lesson in the sad complications that often arise from forced marriage by parental arrangement. The "inner" Ezequiel is partially visible today when he becomes very "stupid" (*necio*) in his cups, and may wander about all night in other towns or start accusing other princes of being "ignorant or uneducated," until one of his sons half-coaxes, half-drags him home. For this reason the princes treat him coldly when he is drunk, and go to great lengths to avoid him. His ponderous, heavy-tongued description of the torture of Cuautémoc would try the patience of the most dedicated ethnological fieldworker.

Ezequiel's speech habits are more distinctive than those of some princes. He always expressed himself in a comparatively slow and considerate way, constantly interjecting phrases and words which do not contribute directly to making the point but which do permit the speaker and the audience plenty of time to mull over the communication. An example follows: ". . . this, I would like to tell you, this . . . that . . . well, that comrade, here on my left, is not taking into account, completely, that is, how shall I say it, that in the case of the school buildings, out here, in the plaza, we have always tried to . . . to . . . ." and so forth. Ezequiel generally takes twice as long to make a point as any of the other princes. Nevertheless, he is very "verbal," and often holds forth at length during meetings, often carrying his point, and takes pleasure in telling long stories. His Spanish vocabulary is larger than that of the average Naranjeño.

Ezequiel is the hardest worker of all the princes, although closely seconded by Boni and Toni. He toils long hours every day in his various fields and frequently spends the night sleeping in the hills next to a bean patch. That this industry has borne fruit is evidenced by his numerous livestock and his large two-story house with its cement floor. I once encountered him plowing in the black soil of the ejido. He was sweating profusely, barefoot, and talking constantly to his team of oxen to keep them lined up. He was concentrating so intensely on the furrow that he didn't see me until he had finished and began to turn around. His oldest, married son, one of the half-dozen whom he directs with a patriarchal hand, was tilling in the adjacent ejido plot, and displayed the same fixed attention to the furrow.

[*Postscript:* By 1984, his wife dead, Ezequiel was living alone. Too old to work, he was "caring for his horses."]

Let us now turn to the political life study of Camilo, synthesized in 1985–1986 from the chapter in *Cacique*, from a published article (Friedrich 1968), and from a short biographical monograph (unpublished).

3. CAMILO, AGRARIAN CACIQUE [5]

Introduction

Camilo Caso looks and can play his part: wealthy, powerful cacique from an agrarian village. Avoiding mestizo suits and the black felt hat, he dresses more like a peasant on holiday: cheap pointed shoes, pressed khaki trousers, clean white shirt, and a Michoacán sombrero with its small colored tassel dangling down behind. When in the county seat he usually totes a .45 or a .38 pistol over his right hip, but hidden by the bottom of his snugly fitting athlete's warm-up jacket. He has pretty much forgotten how to speak Tarascan, but usually understands the obscene jokes and puns, can get the drift of extended discourse, and makes it almost a point of honor to explain the etymology of Tarascan place names to mestizo politicians. Of medium stature, agile, very swarthy, with slightly puckered lips and flashing dark brown eyes, Camilo was felt by both villagers and outsiders—and understandably so—to look "very Indian, because of the skin, and the face."

Childhood, and Agrarian Revolt

Camilo Caso Mendoza instances radical upward mobility through the interaction of agrarian politics, family traditions, and resolute ambition. His mother's first child, he was born—out of wedlock, his detractors claim—in Naranja in 1911. His father, a young, landless Indian, was strongly affected by Zapata's proclamations, joined one of the agrarista armies after Camilo's birth, and was killed in a battle four years later. His departure from the village left the mother, Ana Caso, to fend for herself as one of the poorest in a town that already was suffering from the severe disturbances created by the desiccation of the marsh and by the ongoing Mexican Revolution (1910–1920). Older villagers remember vividly—or at least tend to emphasize—that Ana used to wear only a dress of the white cotton fabric called "manta" (although the norm was to have such manta under a heavy skirt of black wool and a brightly colored apron). As one crone put it to me, "Doña Ana had very few feathers" (*era de muy poca pluma*). So it was that this proud and vigorous young woman, from 1911 until the birth of her second son in 1917, was forced to tax the limits of her great energy and will in order to support herself and her little boy. This she managed primarily by migrating south into the "hot country" with her younger brother Elías (later Scarface), who was then in his teens and probably gave little evidence of becoming the dominant agrarian cacique in the Zacapu Valley of the 1940s and 1950s. While Elías was cutting sugarcane in the huge "Banks" plantations, Ana helped with earning a living by making tortillas for the other laborers in the camps. Brother and sister made the treks every year, carrying along the infant Camilo, and usually returning just in time for a sumptuous fiesta in Naranja. The frequent movement and the excitements of his seminomadic infancy and childhood must have contributed their fair share to the restless and independent character of Camilo today. They also gave him an early experience of the cultural conflict and clash of values that have been such a salient feature of his development: Naranja and Ana were still Indian in culture, speaking Tarascan, whereas the sugarcane plantations were mestizo.

Camilo's mother stayed back in Naranja after the birth of Boni through a second union, still supporting herself by making tortillas: today she is reputed to be the best tortilla maker in the pueblo, and is much sought after to perform her art at fiestas. For her oldest son, memory seems to have begun during these years, and he now recalls, above all, the bitter physical deprivation—granted that it is impossible to disentangle actual memory from what seem to be culturally approved formulae: "I used to run around half naked, and all we had to eat was tortillas and squash—lots of squash!" Nana Ana and Elías were implicated in the agrarian unrest that was growing largely under the leadership of their uncle, until he was assassinated by agents of the landlords in 1919; he has perdured for Camilo as a vague ideal whom he could invoke but never realistically hope to equal. When Camilo's own uncle, Primo Tapia, came back from the north to lead his Indians in the revolt, Camilo was transformed into a highly conscious if small-fry participant, witnessing the intermittent violence of the times, including the battle, with his mother at the forefront, for the first fruits of the newly won ejido lands. He also saw what the second most valiant agrarian looked like after he had been killed by five "White Guards" using ox goads: "very ugly" (*muy feo*). During Primo's hegemony, 1924–1926, Camilo, by then in his teens, often saddled up his uncle's horse, held the stirrup for him as he mounted, and ran messages for him in the small hours of the morning. Primo Tapia's mélange of radical principles made a deep impact on the youth, susceptible, like many adolescents, to political programs of violent, revolutionary reconstruction. Ever since Camilo has to some extent been a man of ideology, or, as some say of him, "he has good principles."

Student, Schoolteacher, Political Fledgling

Camilo somehow picked up two years of primary-school education during the hectic confusions of the heroic period. In 1925, one year after the winning of the ejido, Camilo, then fourteen, "was sent to Morelia by Primo Tapia" as the first candidate for higher education from the group of former have-nots who made the reform in Naranja. But the pink-stone charms of the provincial capital seem to have had little effect on the rough-edged boy, nor does it appear that studies came first, although he avers that he stood at the head of his class and that for six months he headed up a project for teaching apiculture and aviculture. More significant during the storms and stress of these years were the political embroglios then agitating the capital of the state. Camilo was converted into a "convinced Communist" and became a member of a "Communist cell" that read and discussed Marxist literature. As one of the minority of "Cardenistas with principles," moreover, he refused to participate in a student strike against the then governor-elect, Lázaro Cárdenas. But when the latter took office, Camilo ended his studentship and began to teach in primary schools. There is a missing link in my evidence here, but I assume that at some point Camilo also adjusted or was compelled to adjust to the tough policy against active Communists in the state which was initiated by the Cárdenas people about 1929.

For the next decade, that is, from his seventeenth to his twenty-seventh year, Camilo taught in a series of Michoacán village and city schools, including three years down in the tropical coastal area where he had spent so much of his childhood. Today I see something of this tropical south in him, in his violent gestures and quick smile, or sudden anger. The ten years as an itinerant schoolmaster, moreover, greatly widened his social and political horizons; he made many friends, did much desultory reading, and expanded his network of acquaintances and alliances. He also periodically helped and consorted with his uncle Pedro González, by then already a dangerous and eloquent politician in the capital. To paraphrase Eric Wolf, Camilo picked up some of the etiquette of mestizo communication and became sure of foot along the often shadowy or hidden passageways of state politics.

Regional Leader (1938–)

Camilo left off grade-school teaching in 1938 and went home to Naranja de Tapia to farm his recently awarded ejidal plot and to lend support to his hard-pressed uncle Scarface in the complicated schism with his other uncle and mentor, Pedro González. The very next year, Camilo, sponsored by Scarface, was elected president of the Regional Committee, succeeding yet another uncle, Guillermo de las Casas, who had supposedly betrayed the faction and switched to Pedro's. Camilo thus moved into front center in local and regional politics, particularly when it came to the infighting and litigation for new ejidos in neighboring areas, and to the expropriation of opposition ejidal families in the town. Camilo also in some sense came into his own in what—because of the role of the village as "the soul of the agrarian movement in the region"—is called the Regional Committee of Naranja (one of about fifty such regional committees in the state, it is part of the League of Agrarian Communities originally organized by Tapia; see Chapter 4). During his tenure, Camilo continued to enlarge his contacts and options, notably during "the bad year" of 1945, when he was packed off to Morelia by his uncle Scarface so that he would not be shot by the aroused opposition. Scarface values him because of his "culture," that is, education, and "ability to speak," and Camilo reciprocates with an intense loyalty that stems from the early years when his maternal uncle really functioned as a sort of father during the long sojourns in the sugar plantations. Relations between the two men are marred by violent disagreements, however, in which Camilo, Boni, and Aquiles often side with each other; an unshakable loyalty, in fact, unites these three; some of Boni's homicidal assaults have been "to defend Camilo— he's my brother, after all" (es mi hermano, pues). The arguments and temporary rifts between nephews and uncle are generally blamed on the intriguing of Scarface's wife, the bête noire of local politics.

Camilo, as a member of the inner, policy-making oligarchy, took part in many decisions to kill persons of the opposition during what I call the Libido Dominandi period (see Chapter 5). Despite his "culture," he more than holds his own as one of the pistol-packing nephews who "never fail Scarface." In 1945, for example, he, Boni, and their cousins Juan Nahua Caso and Héctor Caso successfully assaulted five opponents on the outskirts of town, killing two and wounding the others. In fact, his past and present activities have made Camilo somewhat callous about political homicide: ". . . so we go into politics, kill people, and all that" is a typical remark (así es que hacemos la política, matamos, y todo eso). Once, in 1956, it looked as though the regional control of the Naranja princes would be toppled because of the conspiracy of certain men in the county seat who were in cahoots with prominent políticos in the state capital. Camilo's reaction to the recrudescent threat was, "They want to command in everything around here, but, if we lose, three or four of them will go to the graveyard, so what's the difference?" A political refugee from Naranja now working in the Zacapu factory once described Camilo as a "killer" (matón), thus expressing the opinion of someone at the receiving end of Caso politics.

In 1950, Camilo was replaced as head of the Regional Committee by Ezequiel (the subject of the second life study above). Soon thereafter he was nominated by the national Party of Institutional Revolution (PRI) and then duly elected alternate to one of the then national senators (a leading Michoacán politician and son of a liberal lawyer and friend of Primo Tapia who was assassinated in 1921). During most of his incumbency as alternate (suplente) Camilo remained in the Zacapu region, farming his lands and making agrarian politics, although often enough in Mexico City. The distinguished and edifying, albeit not very lucrative, office went to him because he is seen by urban lawyers and politicians as a representative or token of "the indigenous masses"—or at least he can fill that bill on their slates. Also, in terms of concrete power, he is one of the caciques in a tough Cardenista region that continues to prove its worth in "the struggle"; Naranja fighters can be used for homicides and as bodyguards in distant cities. In 1954, shortly after the expiration of his term as alternate, Camilo was appointed the county treasurer in Zacapu with indefinite tenure, a post in which he continues to this day (always wearing a pistol to work). Questioned as to the likelihood of becoming a state or national congressman, he nonchalantly rejoins, "That is for later."

Ideology and Tactics

In the same line as his uncles Tomás Cruz, Pedro González, Scarface Caso, and Primo Tapia (granted that the latter was in a higher bracket), Camilo has emerged as one of those Naranja leaders who have become state politicians—in his case, regional leader, senatorial alternate, and county treasurer. He and Scarface thus contrast more and more with the urban, middle-class lawyers and politicians who, they feel, are coming to dominate the scene. Both can wax furious against these men, "who use us, the peasants, like stepping stones." As Camilo put it once, "Their parents had money. We suffered. They didn't." Both men are Indian in many culturally significant senses, knowing Tarascan, residing in an indigenous community, and taking part in the agricultural cycle and even some fiestas. And both can play the bright Indian, whether describing local customs or illustrating a bit of the native lingo. But their asseverations as native sons also function as a mask, as alibis for political exploitation, as an implicit justification for land-grabbing and graft and for the social fact that both are now categorized as "rich" and "político."

Because of his boyhood participation in the agrarian struggle, his student radicalism, and his leadership of the regional committee in the thirties and forties, Camilo sees himself as an "old fighter" and so sets himself off from both the younger blood and the outside, mestizo politicians. His experiences have also made him articulate about ideology, and when his nerves are frayed by politics he will hold forth, sometimes more with vehemence than coherence, about "the principles of Primo Tapia and Lázaro Cárdenas," which he defines mainly in terms of past leaders and past achievements. To some degree he is saddled with an ideology without any means of carrying it anywhere. Today the cornerstones of agrarianism—expropriation of landlords, anticlericalism, public education, and material improvements—are partly moribund: the land has been won, the priest is gone (mostly), the school is off limits because Scarface's wife, the former teacher, hamstrings any interference, and, finally, material improvements cannot be initiated without the danger of stirring up Scarface's envy and the possible charge of starting a new faction. The old cornerstones have

Brandenburg's Ladder of Political Prestige

1. The head of the Revolutionary Family*
2. The President of Mexico
3. Members of the inner circle and factional leaders of the Revolutionary Family
4. Cabinet members, including the governor of the Federal District; the military chief of staff; the private secretary of the President; managers of major state industries; and directors of large semiautonomous agencies, commissions, banks, and boards
5. Governors of big states and federal territories; ambassadors in prestige posts; regional strong men not in the inner circle; the two presidential legislative spokesmen in the respective houses of Congress; military zone commanders; and the president of PRI
6. Supreme Court justices; senators; undersecretaries of cabinet ministries and assistant directors of large state industries, commissions, boards, and dependencies; the secretary-general and sector heads of PRI; leaders of major opposition parties; and the secretaries-general of the CNC (National Peasant Confederation), and similar organizations
7. Directors and managers of medium-size state industries; directors of secondary federal boards, commissions, and agencies; governors of medium and small states; ambassadors, ministers, and consuls general
8. Municipal presidents in large cities
9. Federal deputies; federal judges; the president and members of regional executive councils of PRI; leaders of minor opposition parties; labor, agrarian, and federal credit bank bosses at the state level; and state cabinet officers
10. State deputies; state judges; district PRI officials; federal officials in the states; and local caciques
11. Municipal presidents; local military commanders; and state and federal officials at the local level
12. Local part officials and municipal councilmen

Source: Adapted from Brandenburg 1964. Camilo was on the tenth rung of this ladder, Scarface on the ninth, or possibly considerably higher.

*The Revolutionary Family is the small network of leaders who run Mexico in general and PRI in particular.

come to function for Camilo as a distant and generally unfeasible ideal, the principles of a turbulent youth that cannot be acted on, and so we find him expropriating fellow villagers, dining with the priest when he comes to say Mass in Naranja, focusing on the elite education of his own children, operating (through and with his wife) as a capitalistic entrepreneur, and making no effort to initiate the numerous material improvements that require his leadership.

The year 1954, however, provided a chance to apply the old principles. One part of Juan Nahua's plan for improvements was to reconstruct the parish house, and for this purpose the parochial priest was invited to

The Organization of the PRI

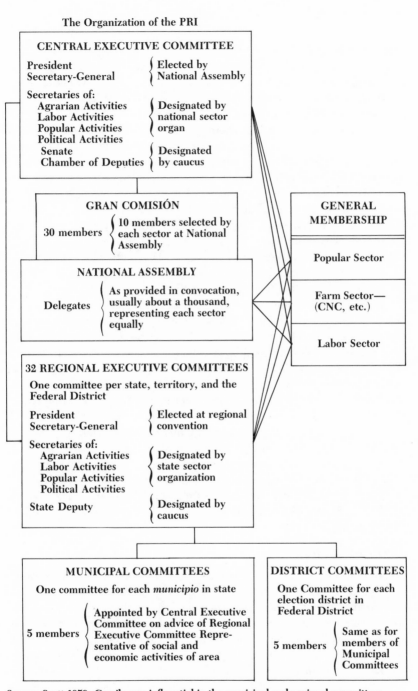

CENTRAL EXECUTIVE COMMITTEE

President
Secretary-General ⟩ Elected by
National Assembly

Secretaries of:
  Agrarian Activities
  Labor Activities ⟩ Designated by
  Popular Activities ⟩ national sector
  Political Activities ⟩ organ
  Senate ⟩ Designated
  Chamber of Deputies ⟩ by caucus

GRAN COMISIÓN

30 members ⟨ 10 members selected by
each sector at National
Assembly

NATIONAL ASSEMBLY

Delegates ⟨ As provided in convocation,
usually about a thousand,
representing each sector
equally

GENERAL MEMBERSHIP

Popular Sector

Farm Sector—
(CNC, etc.)

Labor Sector

32 REGIONAL EXECUTIVE COMMITTEES

One committee per state, territory, and the
Federal District

President
Secretary-General ⟩ Elected at regional
convention

Secretaries of:
  Agrarian Activities
  Labor Activities ⟨ Designated by
  Popular Activities ⟩ state sector
  Political Activities ⟩ organization

State Deputy ⟩ Designated by
caucus

MUNICIPAL COMMITTEES

One committee for each *municipio* in state

5 members ⟨ Appointed by Central Executive
Committee on advice of Regional
Executive Committee Representative of social and
economic activities of area

DISTRICT COMMITTEES

One Committee for each
election district in
Federal District

5 members ⟨ Same as for
members of
Municipal
Committees

Source: Scott 1959. Camilo was influential in the municipal and regional committees.

CAMILO'S POSITION IN SCOTT'S TABLE OF ORGANIZATION

come over from Tiríndaro to speak to a town meeting. This, to Camilo, meant an attempt to revive "fanatical Catholicism." On the afternoon of the town meeting, as the priest was addressing the assembly, Pedro, Boni, and Aquiles Caso appeared on the plaza, with their pistols in their hands, and began asserting loudly that the "Center" in Mexico City was on their side and would give them "guarantees" (that is, a safe-conduct in case of trouble). Their anticlerical act was concluded by firing a salvo over the town hall and then also discharging their pistols over the heads of some women who were staging a religious procession. Camilo and Scarface subsequently brought pressure on the Catholic Church, through the higher echelons of state politics, and the activist priest in Tiríndaro was reassigned (to another trouble spot, actually). Ironically, two leaders and several older persons have told me that the poorest and most ignorant villagers—especially the women—believe that both Camilo and Elías (Scarface) are endowed with supernatural power because two decades of black magic have failed to work against them.

Like his uncles Primo Tapia, Elías Caso, and Pedro González, Camilo combines his pronouncements about agrarian principles with a sophisticated and remarkably self-conscious, if largely homespun, corpus of tactical maxims which must be followed by the princes if they want to retain their present strength—maxims that jibe closely with those of Machiavelli, from which they partly derive, and which make Naranja politics remind one not infrequently of the ideas of the immortal Florentine realist. Once, when asked a question about the intrigues in the region, Camilo responded, "When you have an enemy in your midst, then you bring in someone else from the outside who is weaker than you and throw him against your enemy, keeping your own forces uninvolved. Then, after your enemy is down, you can say farewell to your temporary ally! Haven't you read Machiavelli, Pablo?" Application of this and similar maxims contributed to Scarface's nomination and election as state congressman later that year.

The Economics of Politics

Not only Camilo's appearance but his cognitive world is that of a Tarascan peasant. The urban, mestizo accretions are mainly superficial, and the governing symbols in his mind come mainly from agriculture and from local fauna, flora, and customs (as is clear from his Rorschach, Psychological Appendix A). On his return home in 1938, he began cultivating his own plot, but during the 1940s he continuously expanded his operations so that by the time he was elected alternate to the national senator in 1951 he, with one or sometimes two hired men, was working his own ejido plot and five others as well (with the sanction of the Agrarian Code [63,

159-1] whereby an individual may seed, cultivate, and harvest the plot of a widow, minor, or disabled person, receiving half the crop [*a medias*]). Camilo, a man of considerable strength as well as energy, was thus producing from over thirty acres in the ejido and more than that amount of privately owned land. This is prodigious in face of the crude, almost Neolithic technology, but he managed by rising before dawn, toiling until late afternoon, even sunset, and alternating between two or three teams of oxen. Some ejidatarios used him as a sharecropper simply because they were lazy, or needed money before a harvest, or were otherwise engaged (e.g., in the Zacapu factory), or because they were "dedicated to the vices," as it goes in Spanish. By the early 1950s Camilo had developed back trouble and had to curtail heavy labor. He now sharecrops only three ejido plots, mainly using hired men, and, since these plots belong to widows, he is within the Agrarian Code and so avoids troublesome denunciations by Pedro and other enemies. But it is widely known or at least widely gossiped about that he covertly takes almost all the harvest from one of these plots.

The family income is augmented further by Camilo's wife, who operates as a corn trader, buying before the harvest, sometimes even before the seeding, at twenty pesos per hectoliter, and selling after the harvest at thirty-five, and thus making about fourteen hundred pesos per year per plot. Since she purchases part of the futures from over fifty plots, her annual income substantially exceeds ten thousand pesos, even after we take into account that many debtors refuse to pay up at harvest time or pay only in part (this ten thousand plus converts to well over a million pesos in the values of 1985).[6] The presence of corn traders in Naranja (all of them mestizo women), together with a lack of responsibility among many ejidatarios, has led to over 30 of the 214 ejidatarios getting only a subsistence fraction of their harvest and nearly half of them being in debt, some ruinously so. The activities of Camilo's wife reflect her disdainful and sometimes hate-filled attitudes toward the pueblo, particularly its Indian men, whom she calls, "bad, bad." To collect her debts, incidentally, such a creditor or her representative needs to be at the exit to the ejido as the harvest from the plot in question is being brought out—preferably with a truck, and necessarily with the backing of the ejido authorities. The most inexorable of the collectors, however, the Bank of Ejidal Credit, actually appointed as its man Camilo, "the man of good principles," to extend loans at 7 percent interest, but he, understandably, has frustrated what he calls "these exploiters from the outside" and brokered only a small part of the potential capital. He is sensitive to the contradictions and conflicts between his agrarian principles and, on the other hand, his wife's corn-trading and his own money-lending, and tries to justify himself by claiming that he lends only to friends, relatives, and compadres, "for humanity, out of pity; I am the last man to get paid at harvest." I believe there is something to this.

But let us continue with Camilo's income. He collects some five thousand pesos a year as manager of the Naranja billiard hall, where he also passes many of his evenings keeping in his hand as the town's third-best man with a cue. As county treasurer he earns a nominal salary of nine to thirteen hundred pesos a month (7 percent of the total tax intake), but his actual gains are much higher because, like almost all of Mexico's officials, all of whom are underpaid, he does accept sizable "bites" in the form of bribes and unregistered fines. Summing all this up, the total income of Camilo and his wife is well over fifty thousand pesos a year, making him the third wealthiest man in town (vastly wealthier than I was), and able to support the seven of their eight children studying in Mexico City, keep up a household that is luxurious by local standards, what with its cement floors, gas stove, and a diet for Camilo of "only meat," and finally, make large political investments in the state chapter of the Masonic League and the national Party of Institutional Revolution. He and his uncle Scarface thus combine wealth and power, a combination not unusual in this world, but interesting here when taken in conjunction with the way they rose from poverty and the ambience of agrarian principles.

Orator and Arbiter

Camilo is central not only in politics but also in legal control, and to some extent this is consistent with his abilities. He is the most effective (articulate, persuasive) public speaker of the leaders currently residing in Naranja and seconded only by his half-brother Aquiles and two members of the opposing faction; he is excelled only by the exiled law-student son of Juan Nahua. In his speeches Camilo often displays a volatile, grim passion, pouring out his opinions in correct and sometimes eloquent sentences that contrast with the grammatically atrocious Spanish of his ordinary conversation. At a dramatic session of the Regional Committee I once heard him slashingly attack its "traitorous" president—sitting directly to his left—without spelling out what the man had actually done wrong but making it clear what the Casos thought of him personally. On another such occasion during my fieldwork, a federal inspector convoked a meeting of the ejido to hear out, once again, the much-litigated case of six of the fourteen ejidatarios who had been expropriated back in 1941. As the night was advancing, Camilo suddenly spoke up from among the assembled mass of ejidatarios and allayed the confusion and awkward atmosphere with a twenty-minute address, followed later by a lengthy peroration, all of which apparently convinced the young inspector that, under some of the most basic clauses of the Agrarian Code (153, 165), the six plaintiffs had lost any possible claim simply by virtue of the fact that someone else had been working their plots for fifteen years. In these speeches of Camilo there occur frequent references to "the principles of agrarianism" and "Primo Tapia" and "the struggle" (see Chapter 2, section 3, for the complete fieldnotes on this assembly).

There is always an official judge to try disputes and minor felonies in the town hall, but the real grass-roots judge and lawyer of Naranja is Camilo Caso. In serious cases, the parties concerned immediately call on Camilo, who tries to get the story from many sides and, most of the time, arranges for a settlement of some sort, usually in the form of a payment for damages that entails a rather complicated network of obligations. In cases that go outside Naranja, Camilo advises the parties how to comport themselves, and he or Scarface often make informal judgments of some sort that are transmitted to the forces of federal justice in the county seat. Camilo's impulses toward equal justice for all are clearly going to be adulterated by the size of the bribes and the respective political affiliations of the parties—two factors that remain important at the county level, and only less so at the level of the state in Morelia. In addition to discussing and adjudicating in these instances, Camilo is visited—almost beset, it sometimes seems—by villagers with a wide variety of complaints, particularly people embroiled in personal conflicts: a woman may strike her neighbor's child, the mothers will altercate furiously and then not speak to each other, and so forth—with the end result that one or both of them run off to consult Don Camilo. A more special form of personal conflict arbitrated by Camilo is that which arises from the predominant form of marriage in this Tarascan culture: elopement, with prior agreement by the girl, or bride capture by force. Following such happenings, which means 80 percent of the time, Don Camilo is invited and sometimes implored by the parents of the boy to accompany them on a peace mission to the girl's parents, who are typically disturbed or even angry. It is then up to Camilo to proffer the formal "apology" and make the formal request, because only he and one other man know the semireligious formulae in Tarascan in which petitions of this kind should be couched. Finally, Camilo is visited daily by people who need what amounts to legal aid and advice on matters pertaining to debts, land disputes, inheritance, and marital problems. In his often unremunerated functions as a low-key arbiter-advisor—mainly working in his home—Camilo tries to judge in accordance with local mores, to distribute compensations and punishments over as wide a field as possible, and to protect fellow villagers from state and national law, all of which adds up to a central if controversial role in Naranja social organization. The informality, knowledgeability, and general effectiveness of his arbitration reduce public questioning of his legitimacy, and actually make him more legitimate than Scarface.

Personal Relations

Camilo's personal relations within the pueblo are as clearly defined as they are atypical. He is not popular, but, like his uncle, is respected, more because of his power as a cacique than any specific trait of character. He does not cultivate friendships among "his people," but, on the contrary, has earned the reputation of acting aloof and thinking himself superior to his fellow Naranjeños, including his fellow princes, particularly Bones Gómez (granted that such alienation is expected of a cacique, and hence tends to be exaggerated). His supposed aloofness is not complete, in any case, and he sometimes bursts into a jocular exchange or even a boyish tussle with a bedraggled peasant, suggesting that he used to be a different sort of man when tilling his ejido plots like the rest. His only near friends in Naranja, with whom he does consort on an almost daily basis, are his cousin Héctor and the oldest son of the leading corn trader; strolling down the main street of an afternoon, you might well see these three inside a doorway playing cards. Camilo has some local compadres, but most of them are landless, immigrant mestizos who have sought him out for their own protection and treat him like a patron; he has many compadres in other communities in Michoacán, some of them part of his network of political alliances (see Chapter 3 for some details).

His atypical social relations are the structural and behavioral expression of conflicting and intense feelings about his own background. Such self-consciousness about their own provenience marks the thinking of many of the princes. They feel that they have experienced to the full their community's long transition from a primarily Indian culture to a way of life that borders much more closely on the mestizo one—when it does not actually replicate it. His attitudes are typical or representative: "Yes, I am an Indian" (referring to his swarthiness); "We suffered, we want progress"; and, most of all, "I am Indian, I grew up poor, Pablo, and that I will never forget" (*Yo soy indio, yo crecí pobre, Pablo, y eso nunca se me va a olvidar*).

Let us explore Camilo's cultural ambivalence further. On the one hand, he is actually a bit ashamed of his "race," his "dirty" village, and even of his own vibrant and activist mother, whom he avoids at fiestas. His playing the Indian is, at one level, a means of cultivating the alliance of mestizos. But when the political chips are down and he erupts in one of those cardiac, austral performances, then you find yourself looking into the eyes of a "man of principle" who cannot forget how he rose up from being Indian, which he often equates with being poor.

In 1933, at the comparatively advanced age of 22, Camilo married a girl from Mexico City and, because she was "of reason," and because of his own opposition in those days to religious fiestas, they did without the colorful nuptial *kúpera* dance—perhaps the most diagnostic trait when it comes to categorizing the acculturation of an individual. A year later a son was born to them, closely followed by a second whom they named Elías, that is, after Scarface. But the young mother, transplanted from her urban milieu, became mentally disturbed (*se trastornó*) and ran back to Mexico City with the brother of Camilo's best friend, the other son of the leading corn trader. Perhaps she fled because of the hard realities of life in a Mexican village—seasoned by the specific tensions of the factional struggle; 1938 was one of those "ugly years," the second in the stand-off between Scarface and Pedro, and punctuated by a half-dozen homicides. Shortly after her exodus, in any case, Camilo joined in common-law marriage with a mestiza from another state, one of the ten or so schoolteachers then providing such an extraordinary education for little Naranjeños. He took her in, as the saying goes, and adopted her three children by a previous marriage and has since cared very well for them, as for his two sons from the first marriage and the three daughters that they have had. His concern for these various children and his lavish spending on their private schooling in Mexico City have won him esteem both locally and elsewhere, and testify to his faith in education, if not as a panacea then as the surest means to personal success. You can see his love for these children in the way he talks to them, for example, and he treats them all more or less equally. The one exception is his favored second son, Elías—whom his wife allegedly has always made to "suffer the black sorrow" (the local idiom normally applied to orphans).

In recent years Camilo has been unhappy with his sharp-witted wife, and lives in partial separation from her. There have been two scandalmongered affairs with local wives of otherwise good repute, and he has had several mistresses in Zacapu—currently his young secretary. The mere notion of her existence torments his wife, formerly a handsome woman herself, I would judge, and the liaison may be nothing more than a paranoid fantasy—although, having spent a day researching records in his office, I would say that there were at least some grounds for suspicion. Camilo is away many nights when his children are at their studies in the capital, and he often seems a different man within his own home: once across the threshold, he turns disagreeable, even mandatory, snapping at his wife about trivialities and sometimes giving more attention to her than to playing the cordial host. The deep rifts in Camilo and his ambiguous cultural identity are symbolized by the way this principled man of the Indian people has chosen only mestizas as wives and paramours; there is a bitter, desperate streak in him unmatched by any other prince. One factor in his fate, certainly, is the Mexican double sex standard; another is his own social and geographical mobility; another is his wife's above-mentioned hatred of Naranja and its Indian men; and yet another is her own increasing corpulence (the object of considerable Tarascan-style animadversion); indeed, the corporeal and psychological parallels between the wives of Camilo and Scarface are almost too coincidental to be true—they even wear the same species of black dress and flowing shawl, rather like Greek widow's weeds. But, ultimately, I cannot explain the tragic rift between these two complex, intelligent human beings who loved each other at one time.

Conclusions

One objective of this study has been to communicate some intimations of the complexity of a peasant leader such as Camilo. Salient among his constellation of personal factors would seem to be the following: loyalty to his close kin (uncle, half-brothers, cousins); lack of strong or lasting union with any one woman; an ambivalent attitude toward both Tarascan and mestizo culture, with masking and double-agenting in either case; a tendency toward violence and an aptitude for, even a playfulness about, intrigue; his own "egoistical" economics and political ambition; his ardent espousal of a partly moribund ideology as "the man of good principles"; and, finally, such psychological traits as courage, intelligence, flexibility, resolve, and an engaging devil-may-care and devil-take-the-hindermost outlook on life. These and yet other factors meld to create an intrinsically interesting leader.

The traits of character just sketched also are interwoven with the fascinating issue of Camilo's legitimacy and his perception of it. His intense and justified ambition wells in part from a consciousness of the central role of his lineage in the politics of Naranja and the region, since he inherits from no less than six well-known local leaders, one of them an ancestral representative of the pueblo in the last century, another the originator of agrarian reform, then his uncle Primo Tapia; Camilo was actually responsible for organizing the funding of the first publication of the pioneer biography of Tapia. Another such political forebear and uncle was the able Tomás Cruz, assassinated in 1928 (see Chapter 5), and then there are his uncles Elías and Pedro, whose feud has dominated pueblo politics for two decades. This marked continuity of kinship-political context and the ideological association with the radicalism of Tapia and Cárdenas have reached the point where Camilo and the other Casos and also many non-Casos, including many old women, declare it to be a natural state of affairs that the Casos should rule Naranja—a "natural state" that is of course buttressed by the aptitude to lead, the increasing financial means to do so, and what one political scientist has called "the normative powers of the factual." Camilo's emotions about his family and politics were partly responsible for his switching his patronymic and matronymic names, from Mendoza Caso to Caso Mendoza, "so that my sons would be Casos," although the name change also stemmed from resentment of his runaway father. His young sons, like those of Scarface, fine athletes and law students, will be in a position, even if they do not return to Naranja, to help realize their father's ambition for the perduring domination in this century of the Caso faction and family line.

[*Postscript:* In the late fifties and early sixties, after several notable homicides—including that of Scarface—I infer that a third, neutralist and vaguely conservative, faction emerged, opposed to the traditional cacicazgo. Camilo and his half-brothers left town for varying periods to avoid assassination. But about 1963, the man who had served as national senator, and whose alternate Camilo had been, was elected governor of the state. The rebellious faction was made to disperse and Camilo, now the leader of the Casos, returned "to direct the destinies of his pueblo," as he once worded it to me. Shortly afterward, however, he died of a natural cause. His cousin and intimate friend Héctor also died about the same time of the same cause—a heart attack.]

Let us now turn to a fourth text in our anthropological history, the relatively short life studies of Toni, Boni, and Melesio, pretty much as they were composed for the thesis *Cacique* in 1956–1957.

4. TONI

Three salient traits have characterized the peasant leaders in the Indian community of Naranja over the past sixty years. The first trait is a sheer physical and psychic vitality, a comprehensive toughness that covers the visible behavioral exterior and ultimately derives from the deepest roots of personality. The second trait is generalized cunning, a versatile and highly flexible combination of astute manipulativeness, suspiciousness, lack of guilt about certain norms, psychological perceptivity, and a high degree of adaptivity of one's own personal or political interests to the exigencies and limits of a given situation, all this plus a streak of "Indian humor" (to laugh at bad luck). The third trait is ambition, the lust to power and control over land and men. Such figures as Primo Tapia, Hercules Ocampo, Pedro González and Scarface Caso possess cunning, sheer vitality, and ambition to a striking degree, as do many secondary leaders. One such secondary prince is Antonio Serrano, known to his friends as "Toni."

Toni, aged fifty, was born and raised in Naranja de Tapia. He, like most of the princes, suffered throughout his youth and childhood, as shown most clearly in his first memories. He recalled first that ". . . we were very poor, that we suffered . . . I went almost naked until seven, which caused me great embarrassment (*pena*) . . . afterward I had a shirt that only reached to my knees." His second recollection was that boys used to creep into the hacienda "by the light of the moon" to steal corn, "and this was in the cold months, when it freezes." His third memory was of his father, a muleskinner who used to spend most of his time bringing back sugar, soap, and brandy from the hot country. Subsequently he fished up the recollections of his older brother teaching him how to seed cabbages, and, with noticeable pain, of how his parents had gone to the United States for two years when he was six, and how he, not wanting to stay home with his grandmother, had hidden under the seat of the train, not to be discovered and dragged forth, crying, until the "All Aboard" had actually sounded. His father died of a "fever" one year after his return to Naranja, and Toni, orphaned at nine, after one year of school, had to go to work to help support his mother. He remembers starting with the Cantabria hacendados at twelve, and that the foremen used to beat them. Only a minority of Naranja children lived through a childhood such as Toni's, and many of these remain permanently weakened in body and mind. At nineteen he married his present wife, a short, swarthy woman, whose face is frequently wrinkled by a pleasant but basically unexpressive smile. They had to forego a wedding because of their mutual poverty. None of their ten children have died (possibly a record for Naranja), and three are now married. Toni, a stern but kindly father in the large family, was quick to resume control over his oldest, twenty-six-year-old son, after the latter's return from an eleven-year sojourn in the Great North.

Toni today belongs to the economic upper class, with an ejido plot (5.2 acres) and eight additional acres in the rich bottom lands and the foothills. He also owns the best team of horses in town, a source variously of pride, admiration, and envy. Two years ago he sold his several cattle to finance a combination general store–drinking establishment that is doing well, catering especially to the adolescent set and certain hard drinkers of the sort who, "in order to sup," like to mix a half-bottle of beer with an equal amount of "pure" alcohol. At the comparatively advanced age of forty-six, and then again at forty-nine, Toni crossed over the great divide into the United States and apparently took to the new conditions very well, particularly the high pay and the fast, piece-time working; he wants to sally forth again and is currently organizing a group of Naranjeños. The Serrano family reposes at night on plain rush mats spread over low board beds, or simply raised pallets, under the tile roof of a one-story adobe house that extends back from the frontal store on the main street of town; chickens, dogs, and little pigs frequently scamper or lounge about on the uneven floor (Toni put me up in his house on my first visit to Naranja, and we were always on friendly terms). Unlike many princes, who are greatly augmenting and varying their diet, the Serranos subsist primarily on the typical Indian staples of corn, beans, and chile, consumed in enormous quantities.

Toni has been active in the political struggle since his early manhood. During the heroic period of radical agrarianism he fought with the hacienda militia against Primo Tapia, and subsequently joined the Zacapu militia and continued to operate against the successful agrarians. But in 1927 he blew apart his rifle while discharging it in a state of complete inebriation, got into trouble with the authorities, and subsequently defied and then fled the detachment that had come from Zacapu to arrest him. Having "offended the government," he was readily persuaded by Tomás Cruz that he should change his allegiance "as the Caso party would not injure him in any way"; shortly afterward he participated in the campaign against the Cristero uprising as a member of the large regiment of Zacapu Valley agrarians. During the thirties Toni operated as one of the more talented gunmen surrounding Scarface, participating in several out-of-town skirmishes and assassinations. He has been the subject of at least two assaults, but managed to escape or drive off his attackers because of his physical speed; still a first-class bodyguard, Toni often accompanied Scarface in Morelia during the dangerous period of 1956. The speed with which he brings a pistol into play from under his belt is unforgettable. Toni has also functioned as a leader and office-holder, serving as mayor in 1943, 1953, and 1955, and as ejidal treasurer from 1948 to 1951. His feeling of being neglected and slighted by the Casos makes for a sharp conflict of values, since he is related to some of them by the baptismal form of ritual coparenthood, that is, by the most compelling bond of ceremonial kinship. In intimate conversation, one sometimes hears the revealing phrase, "He is my compadre, but. . . ." This conflict between political attractions and other bonds of the social structure has been experienced by almost everyone during the past forty years. Toni swung to Juan Nahua for a time during the abortive attempt to overthrow the Casos, partly because of thwarted ambitions, partly because of the possibility of collusion in cattle rustling, and partly because of his primary loyalty to the treacherous Serrano lineage. Soon convinced of his errors, he switched again to "backing Scarface" and is today one of the inner circle of Tarascan princes, as measured by his participation, with a half-dozen of the select, in such key events as the Hidalgo fiesta in Zacapu, or the statewide rally in Chupícuaro. Toni has an important voice at the secret meetings where the future steps in ejidal administration are planned.

Toni, like Pedro González and Ezequiel Peñasco, is one of the anticlerical princes of Naranja, and this is especially interesting since his former motivation in fighting for the hacienda was his superstitious belief in the preachings of the priest to the effect that agrarians were doomed to the eternal fire. But he took the risky step of experimenting with this prediction, and found that the dangers of fighting for the Casos were of a purely earthly character. Like many late converts, he soon became an extreme radical, taking a leading part in the burning of the sacred icons before the church in 1939. While accompanying me to the Rosary (i.e., Tiger) fiesta on Calvary Hill, he suddenly exclaimed: "All this is very ugly!". But why? "Here I am, a radical, and going to a religious fiesta!"

Toni's switch to the Caso party, his "conversion" from Catholicism to radical agrarianism, and his maneuvering during the complicated and shifting alignments of the "Juan Nahua affair" all illustrate the deft and cunning way in which he has managed to survive the long series of involved intrigues that have marked and continue to characterize factional politics in Naranja. Toni's astuteness differs from that of Primo Tapia, or Aquiles Caso, in that he is not bothered or distracted by a profoundly felt adherence to higher values, such as material improvements for the pueblo. For him any new intrigue or factional unrest is simply responded to with a wily solution to the following question: "Which side is going to win, and how can I get the most out of it without ruining my relations with the other?" This pragmatic attitude is evidenced by the fact that there is little mutual hostility between him and the leaders of the fallen party of Pedro González.

Toni is comparatively tall (about 5'10" like Nico and Bonifacio), hard and lean, with very dark brown skin and eyes, and straight black hair; he is probably at least 95 percent Indian by race, although his father immigrated from a mestizo rancho. His lips are generally held thin by the tough muscles of his face, while his eyes usually seem hard, steady, and appear to be watching you. He will smile broadly, his gums showing, when first greeting one, and at points in a conversation, but most of the time the facial features are grim and set. Fast, vigorous bodily movements characterize this man. He gestures with sharp cuts of the hand and strides along with rapid, light-footed steps. Everything about him spells a wary purpose and great physical vitality. He, like Ezequiel, is in the fields most of the time, tilling in arrow-straight rows or dexterously cutting wheat, preferring to leave the general store and official duties to someone else. For the fields and hills he dons the Indian dress of huaraches, serape, and so forth, but when going to the town hall or a fiesta he customarily wears blue jeans, a sky-blue nylon or black cotton shirt, an aviator-style leather jacket, and a good, broad-brimmed sombrero. Toni is very like a hard-driving, lean Yankee farmer, except for the additional skills bred by Naranja politics.

He is completely bilingual, speaking Tarascan at home and Spanish on the outside, the latter with a speed, clarity, and organization of ideas that is unusual in Naranja for one of so little schooling: "The reasons are: first . . . second . . ." When he does speak, as at ejidal meetings, it is always in a laconic, condensed, abbreviated way that may be difficult to understand during the first few months of fieldwork. Toni's laconic and precise speech is simply the verbal reflection of a permeating reserve; he is silent for long periods, with an absent-minded, thoughtful look in his eyes, and he often only half listens to what his friends are saying (rejoining "*Sí,*" and echoing the last phrase of his interlocutor).

Toni's mask drops on at least two types of occasion. First, he is an inveterate practical joker (homicides can also be regarded as practical jokes, from a certain point of view). He takes an uninhibited pleasure in delicately extracting an item of material culture from the anthropologist's hip pocket, or filching the change from a girl sitting in front of him on the bus. Such stolen goods are then returned with genuine laughter. On the other hand, this innocuous pickpocketing assumes serious proportions whenever Toni is functioning in civil or ejidal posts; at such times his almost insatiable appetite for public funds leads him, for example, to abscond with all the taxes of a major fiesta, or the fines collected after a notable misdemeanor. These attitudes toward property, related to his generally opportunistic character, have occasionally incurred the wrath or irritation of other princes, especially those who miss out in the graft. Toni's mask also disintegrates under the effects of alcohol. Then Toni, cast in so tough a mold, appears to be trying to physically contain a sudden effusiveness and garrulousness, with jerky movements, elbows clenched in tight to his sides, and compulsive turnings and bendings at the waist.

[*Postscript:* Toni was killed by ambush in the late fifties; two weeks later his two older sons killed two of those held responsible. One of these sons was, in turn, shot and killed more recently.]

5. BONI

Bonifacio Calles Caso was born in 1917, at the height of the Mexican Revolution and at a time when the agrarian movement was starting to crystallize in Naranja. The hard life of his mother at this time was described in the life history of his half-brother, Camilo. Boni remembers that he was *muy racquítico* (weak and undernourished), and, in jest, he claims that many times the central strip of his shirt with the button holes was the only part left. In contrast to Camilo, Boni studied only two years in the primary school before going to work as a cowhand, riding herd on local cattle and in other parts of the region.

Boni grew up in an extended household based on a core of women: his mother, Nana Ana, "took in" two of his maternal aunts, with their sons. The household thus included his maternal grandmother, his mother, her brother (Scarface) and two of her sisters, his half-brothers (Camilo and later Aquiles), and, finally, three first cousins: Juan Nahua, Sebastián Gabriel, and Héctor Caso. These six men all grew up together, except for Juan, who did not enter the household until he was ten. The three half-brothers actually called Scarface "Father," and, as they advanced in years, Nana Ana repeatedly told them that they must "fight for their uncle." The combination of shared residence, economic interdependence, the cultural bond of the uncle-nephew relationship, and, finally, the compelling effect of the father-son kinship terminology all operated to forge a kinship nucleus of men who supported their uncle Scarface; it is very true, and not infrequently said, that Scarface can depend on no one but his nephews when the chips are down. Village politics, in Naranja or any other Mexican pueblo, can be understood only through an analysis of the role of the bonds of blood and marriage. Boni has always fought for his uncle, and many of his acts have been motivated by a desire to "defend my uncle" (respaldar al tío).

For these reasons Boni's extraordinary career as a peasant gunman merits scrutiny. In 1934, at the age of eighteen, Boni waited next to the wall on one of the dark, unlighted side streets of Naranja and shot dead a member of the night watch as he came around the corner. The victim had formerly fought with the hacienda, and then, like many conservatives, had aligned himself with the Ocampo caciques. It is difficult to know the definite reason for such homicides but in this case it seems to have been motivated by a hatred for a former "reactionary White Guard" who was fighting with the men who desired to kill Scarface. In 1937, once again, Boni killed a man by assaulting him at night as he rounded a corner. The victim in this case was a prominent agrarian, one of Primo's fighters, who had sided with the Ocampos and then affiliated himself with the faction of Pedro González. In addition to the immediate factional dispute, this killing was motivated by one of the deepest drives that intersect and complicate Naranja politics: blood revenge. The man had participated in the lakeside assassination of Boni's uncle Tomás Cruz, the immediate successor of Primo Tapia. Three months later, in June 1937, Boni dispatched a third Ocampo by assault; although the Ocampos had been effectively defeated by the Casos, the grudges engendered during this period continued to work themselves out as men like Boni ambushed unpardoned foes. A year later, in April 1938, Boni killed a member of the González faction while both were drunk, later throwing the body in a ditch outside town where it was found seven days later. These four killings, all committed before his twenty-third birthday, served to surround the young gunman with an aura for "valor" that remains to this day, and with some justification, since it must be remembered that, for every achieved assassination, Boni and his sort participated in a half-dozen skirmishes. Boni was himself assaulted, like Toni, but managed to fight off his assailants, or to beat a successful retreat. The degree of valor in Naranja culture is measured by the amount of homicidal intent, by the convincing quality of aggressive acts, and, finally, by the manner in which someone "does not let himself be killed." Boni participated in many shootings and some killings during the last years of the struggle against the González faction, including the ambushing of two men by Casos in 1945. Boni, Juan Nahua, and Bones Gómez have each caused twice as much bereavement as any other man in town, with over eight homicides apiece. On a hot June afternoon, after only four months in the field, I once asked Boni to explain to me the difference between killing by ambush and by assault. The question was ironical and produced a roaring guffaw, followed by a detailed and objective description, as told by an expert.

Boni, comparatively tall (5'10") and rangy, often makes a relaxed impression; a tourist seeing him slouched on a bench before the town hall, languidly twirling his lasso and only occasionally uttering an even-toned phrase, would surely think, "Now there is one of your sleepy, easy-going Indians!" On the other hand, he characteristically moves with purposeful vigor and fast reflexes, whether striding out to the ejido or playing pool. Boni's decisive bodily comportment can be partially accounted for by his athletic experiences. In 1937 and 1938 the Naranja team won the state basketball championship and in 1937 went on to defeat the state champions of Jalisco at a play-off in Guadalajara. Boni and his cousin Héctor were star players for this extraordinary combination (extraordinary in light of the fact that Naranja was a very small indigenous community). In the case of Boni and others, we discover that success in such "civilized" activities as basketball, which we associate with law-abiding, "clean-cut" American boys, need not inhibit a salient role in the pistol politics of a Tarascan agrarian town.

During the late thirties Boni was drinking heavily, and by 1940 he had developed into a serious alcoholic, acquiring the reputation of being an "ugly character," shooting up the town when in his cups, backhanding bystanders, and—says the opposite faction—abducting or assaulting desired women. Boni told me about his alcoholism once as we were walking out into the ejido, and I think that this fascinating conversation is worth citing in full. "I used to drink a great deal, lots!" flinging up his hand with a typically volatile gesture, "but no more now!" And why did you decide to stop drinking? "I used to drink a lot formerly. I would begin drinking one day and continue for a whole month. I used to buy a case of beer and a bottle of brandy before going to bed, already drunk, and would wake up at midnight and drink three or four more beers and a glass of brandy and then go to sleep again for a while. About four in the morning I would wake up again and drink again, and so I would continue for a whole month. Then I would stop for a week, and then start again." Why did you use to drink so much? "It was the vice which had seized me. And finally I began to feel very bad, very sick. When I was like that any sort of sound would scare me, a very weak sound would frighten me and I would turn around like this!" (pivoting around fast on his heel as though he had been surprised from behind). "I felt bad in the stomach because I seldom ate while on a spree. I lived on the alcohol.

"I began to have to stay at home, and many times I would remain lying on the bed all day, hearing everything, feeling everything, but with my eyes closed. And when Aquiles' children—I was living with Aquiles then—dropped something, it sounded like a clap of thunder. My head used to go around and around and I used to see little animals and insects flying and circling next to the ceiling. I began to tremble a great deal. Once I told my mother to make me some orange leaf tea and when I crouched down to pick up the cup I was trembling so that I spilled all the tea on the floor. My face swelled up and got all puffy."

The delirium tremens were becoming intolerable. He summoned a doctor from Zacapu who "cured" him in three months with injections, pills, and vitamins. Since 1948 he has never touched a drop, except once when "they were trying to rub out my brother" (Camilo), when Boni started out at night with his pistol in order to assault a certain party, was dissuaded, and, returning home, downed a whole glass of tequila, which made him vomit. I have watched him refuse a drink several times, and the fact is that he is seldom invited. "When I see a drunkard I feel sick in my whole body. It frightens me!" The alcoholic history of Boni, like that of Bones, would indicate that the inner life of the peasant gunman is not an entirely happy one.

Boni's "defense" of the interests and person of Scarface has been motivated primarily by the early influences previously sketched and by Boni's fixed position as one of the nuclear princes. There is little if anything like a natural, lasting, or spontaneous affection between the uncle and the nephew. In fact it would be more accurate to say that Boni has supported his uncle *in spite of* a deep-lying, rancorous hostility of over twenty years' standing; they have occasionally been off "speaking terms" with each other, and in 1940, when Scarface was municipal president, Boni called him down into the Zacapu plaza and began to swear at him and heap imprecations on his head. This hostility derives primarily from personality differences that redound to Boni's credit, but these have been consistently aggravated by the fact that Boni cannot stand his uncle's present wife. Boni was about to be set free after a full year in the Morelia Penitentiary in 1947, his suspicious uncle having made little effort to secure an earlier release. At this time the obese and insinuating wife of Scarface suggested to him and Juan Nahua, as follows: "And now they are going to release Boni. What can we do to prevent his return here, to *eliminate him?*" Despite such provocations to treason, it was Boni, his brothers, and Héctor who stuck by their uncle after his near assassination in 1945 and who followed him everywhere in 1953 when the "new party" under Juan Nahua appeared to be toppling the Caso hegemony. The material reward for Boni's loyalty has been an ejido parcel, allotted in the late thirties, and several pieces of *tierra indígena*. Like Camilo, however, Boni has never held any political office in the Naranja community. His recent appointment as county police chief may represent a new trend, but is more probably an instance of the "nephews supporting their uncle" during the intense internecine struggle within the national party. As in other kinds of authoritarian government, control of the police force is often the key to victory or defeat.

Boni's personal history has been colorful, and princely in the Naranja sense. Like most of his fellows, he began at fourteen to familiarize himself with the lipstick and permanent waves of the Zacapu brothels. During the 1930s he formed various transitory unions with Naranja women, mostly older widows, and then for over ten years he cohabited with the mother of Liborio, a minor prince only seven years his junior. Boni's alcoholism was intimately connected with "women," by Boni's own confirmation. The large number of widows created by the homicides in Naranja made until quite recently for a normal pattern of union with older women on the part of the sexually active bachelor or the young spouse looking for additional outlets. Boni has had several children, but it has been hard to identify them with certainty, aside from the three who are living with him now, offspring of Liborio's mother. His children are well clothed. Several years ago he abducted the wife of a minor prince and kept her in a house in Zacapu for six months, allegedly against her will. Her husband took her in again on her return. "Didn't he do anything about it?" one asks. "What can you do? It was Boni!" Two years ago Boni began cohabiting with a squat, very Indian woman. They live in the large house that used to belong to Juan Nahua, next door to Héctor, and across the street from Scarface and Camilo. Boni also maintains affairs with two other Naranja housewives.

After what has been recounted above, the reader may be surprised to hear that Boni is the only prince who could be described as *simpático*. His swarthy features and very large eyes are frequently illuminated by a broad and unaffected grin, breaking the usually stern and brooding expression of his face. When working, he dresses in a Tarascan garb of huaraches, colored serape, and so forth. On fiestas and as police chief, he dons soft leather boots, poplin jacket, and a white shirt, making a good impression, enhanced by the pistol in its dudish braided leather holster. Unlike his half-brothers, Boni is extremely courteous and always attentively observes the forms, shaking the lady's hand and saying a few words. For these reasons and others, Boni seems pleasing to women. Three American women reported independently such positive reactions as "what a fine looking man," or "very handsome," or "but he's so polite!" Boni's courtesy leads us to classify him as one of the less acculturated princes, as do his dress, his Tarascan speech, and his brown-skinned paramours.

The most salient feature of Boni's character is his sense of humor, a natural waggishness that contrasts with his otherwise rigorous and determined manner. Boni's humor is not responsive to wit or verbal play, but rather to certain situations which strike him with a fun that he can communicate to his companions. I have already reported his saying that he used to wear only the buttonholes of his boyhood shirts. This is the Indian humor, at first so disconcerting, which causes uncontrolled general laughter when the pot breaks and the festal chef d'oeuvre spreads slowly over the dirt floor. At times Boni seems to be a great roaring madcap, a sort of Pistol. His jocosity and his sudden outbursts of laughter—at such things as the deformed fingers of the village freak (p. 216)—reflects, of course, deeper currents in the man's nature.

One is struck by Boni's love of masks and costumes in what has been described as a masked culture by J. Gómez Robleda, a psychologically trained Mexican doctor and social scientist. Until three years ago he was an eager participant in the Tiger Fiesta. The highlight of this ceremony is a two-hour butting, wrestling dance by men and boys attired in spotted coverall outfits and headdresses of deer horn. Any mention of masks and costumes tends to elicit an immediate, positive response on the part of Boni, and he loves to describe "negritos," "tigers," and various "monos," grinning openly, or laughing (see his Rorschach responses, Psychological Appendix B).

Boni is one of the persons in Naranja who live by the anticlerical principles of radical agrarianism. There used to be many such as there were in Tiríndaro, but most of them have died or have reverted to a minimal acceptance of certain outward forms, such as baptism. Most men now accept the folk religion, although few actually support the clergy. The principles of Primo Tapia are still alive to some extent, but nowhere so much as in his nephew Boni.

The following conversation (not "interview") was suggested by "Death," clad in a sheet, with black stripes to simulate bones, and by the vermilion "Jews" with their lances. Boni and I were sitting on a bench in Tiríndaro, during Holy Week.

Boni: "Have you read the scriptures?"

"Yes, so what?"

Boni: "I have read them, all of them, and other books and pamphlets too, and I like to do it very much, to read everything like that, because there it says that the priests are still the same, and that if Jesus Christ returned to the world again, they would want to kill him again. That is why they are bad, the priests."

"Then you don't think that Jesus Christ was the Son of God?"

Boni: "No, he was like me, and he had a human body too."

"Then you don't believe in God either?"

Boni: "I believe that there is a God who created the world and who began everything, and no more!" Here he swung around toward me, somewhat leaning forward, and making a DaVincian gesture with the large brown index finger of his right hand. "Because all that about the soul is wrong. There is no other world after this one!"

"Then I suppose we won't fly with wings and play the harp," I answered, laughing.

"No. When we die they will put us in the soil and there will be no more. Because we are like animals and we die like animals, thus," and Boni stamped down hard with his heel, as though squashing a bug. "An animal never goes to another place. We are the same. And if there were a God" (and here came the interesting point), "I would go to Paradise, because I never blasphemed against Him, I never deprived Him of honor, as those do who go to church all the time, and cross themselves and pray. If there *is* a God, there is *one God* and no more and it is a God whom one doesn't see and whom one cannot see. He is here and no more," pointing to his head. "I think about Him. I imagine Him, and then I don't need images. The thing is between me and God. All that about the priest and the church diminishes His glory.

"I never pray. When I lie down at night, I . . ." (making a piston-jabbing motion with his right fist) "and go to sleep. I never got married. Civilly, yes, but never in church. I never go there. Only when I used to get drunk they used to take me to some baptism, but I never went there with a sound mind."

I told him that some of those books and pamphlets must have come from the Protestant missionaries, to which he replied, "I don't know about that, but I have told you how I think." He grinned his broad grin and sat back on the bench, seeming very secure in himself. I noted that he did not participate as an onlooker in the Easter Passion Play that night, but remained outside the plaza talking with his policemen.

[*Postscript:* In 1956 old Calles returned to Naranja after more than forty years of absence and silence. He proposed to the septuagenarian Nana Ana that they "join up" again. She refused, after a short period of hesitation. But Boni took in the old man and, at the time I left the field, the father and the son were frequently to be encountered cultivating the land side by side in the ejido or the *tierra indígena*. By 1984 Boni had left his then wife and their unmarried daughter and was living with another woman in a nearby city, where he ran a business while using his Naranja lands to grow alfalfa.]

6. MELESIO

The first patches of data on Melesio Caso gave me intimations of a severe and sanguinary man. An elder member of the fallen party reported once in a hate-filled whisper that Melesio had been a principal actor in a notorious political killing, he and Juan Nahua shooting their victim in the face eight times as two others held him up against an adobe wall in the "Street of the Dead." Their victim was a former friend and comrade-in-arms, a gunman for Scarface, who had incurred the wrath of the ruling princes because of political deviations toward the other faction. Next I read in one of the propaganda pamphlets composed by the fallen party that Melesio was one of Scarface's leading gunmen and had been rewarded with an ejido plot for his services. These and other tidbits caused me to fix an examining eye on the slender, nut-brown, buck-toothed man who hurried nervously to the front of the ejidal assembly one morning in 1955 to take office as head of the Committee of the Watch.

Through subsequent investigations and personal friendship I established the fact that Melesio is one of the nuclear princes in the Naranja oligarchy, his inner position being partly determined by kinship, as the nephew of Scarface, and considerably reinforced through ceremonial kinship and friendship with many of the nuclear princes, such as Bones and Gregorio; he associates primarily with princes. In terms of institutional indices, Melesio's role may be measured by his tenure as mayor of the town when he was still very young and his election as ejidal treasurer during the difficult period of 1941–1943; in addition, he is an eager and invariable traveler on such political expeditions as the picturesque campaign tours of his uncle Scarface. Melesio's economic strength consists of six acres of rich privately owned land as well as his ejido plot, a fine black mare, two donkeys, and numerous pigs and chickens.

Melesio's present position is the result of a long ascent from economically desperate beginnings. One Christmas night when very drunk Melesio told me that his father had died in the United States when Melesio was eight years old. "I suffered a lot. I had to work herding the cattle in the hills and we didn't have enough to eat. My life has been very hard. We used to eat just tortillas and beans." He was an only child. He now looks ten years older than his actual age of thirty-five. Melesio married at seventeen. They scraped together enough financial support to throw a big wedding and dance the traditional *kúpera*, his wife attired in a new blue skirt and wearing many-colored ribbons in her braids. But she and their first child died shortly after the baby's birth the following year. Melesio was married again a few years later to a friendly, attractive woman with a broad, flashing smile, with whom he has had seven children, two dying in infancy. Their family life is a pleasure to observe. The children are always running around, smiling, teasing each other, and generally provoking only half-hearted admonitions from their parents or from Melesio's grave and dignified mother.

Melesio is modest and reserved. Perhaps it is these qualities which make him liked by many other people. His modesty and reserve prevent him from speaking forcefully and directly. His words are inhibited. But, most important, Melesio's speech is the most salient aspect of a deep-going inferiority complex that made him stress his own lack of education and frequently accuse me: I would "write to the others but never to Melesio." Melesio's personality is most like that of the least acculturated princes such as Toni and Bones. His feelings of inferiority do not in any way restrain his intense political ambitions, his desire to always be with the other leaders, to participate in the political fiestas, and to hold political office.

There is a chipmunk quality to Melesio, created by the buck teeth in the round, brown face, but also by the quick furtive way he has of moving his body. And he can be droll. Often during an ejidal assembly or a general conversation something will strike his idiosyncratic sense of humor (maybe because of a double entendre when translating into Tarascan); at such points he will smile fleetingly or chuckle, sometimes buckling down and clapping his hand over his mouth, or pulling his hat down over his eyes in a very amusing gesture. On the other hand, he seldom contributes to a group chat or to stock response guffawing.

Though much younger than Ezequiel and Bones, Melesio is definitely the least acculturated of the nuclear princes. His full-blooded Indian race is matched by adherence to the Indian peasant culture. All the evidence shows that he feels awkward and foreign in mestizo surroundings. Tarascan, his mother tongue, is still the idiom in which he feels secure and fluent and which he uses exclusively within the home when conversing with his wife and mother (but *not* with his children!). Once, when drunk, he asserted, "We, the Porépicha [using the native term for "Tarascans"], have a mastery of two languages, Tarascan and Castilian; we don't know Castilian very well, but even so . . . and this is our pride, to master two tongues . . ." and he slumped down against the adobe wall, pulling his hat down over his eyes. Despite these reservations, Melesio writes and types Spanish and has a stronger tendency to read newspapers and periodicals than any other prince except Aquiles.

Another index of Melesio's Indianness is that the financial surpluses from the sources cited above are not expended on movies, clothes, permanent waves, and other mestizo attributes, but are solidly invested in land and animals. His ownership of a mare and his pleasure in riding about through the streets and fields is also a criterion of his identification with older values. Many villagers independently related or vouched for a curious story about Melesio. Until 1953 he continued to wear the old-fashioned Tarascan array of white cotton shirt and fold-in pants with a colored sash, and was by far the last prince to discard this dress (which many men in the village still use for working). "Melesio used to be ashamed to wear pants with a belt," the speaker will say, laughing. Once in the 1940's he went to the United States very briefly as a "wetback," dressed at the outset in his beloved manta and blue sash. According to several companions, he was mercilessly ribbed by Americans and American-born Mexicans. They kept inquiring whether it was really true that Tarascans wore their neckties not around their necks but around their groins! Such ridicule eventually forced a sartorial adjustment to blue denims. But Melesio was not so quick to finally desert the symbols of his cultural heritage and, as he was arriving home, he alighted from the bus in Tiríndaro, changed into white manta and blue sash, and, so attired, walked the rest of the way into Naranja de Tapia!

[*Postscript:* Melesio and his family moved to a large city several years after the events described above; he was said to be earning good money as a "guard." By 1984 he had built a modern, two-story house along the highway and was farming his ejido and private lands through relatives, although living most of the time in Mexico City where he and some sons and nephews ran a successful establishment.]

Let us now turn to the political life study of Aquiles, pretty much as written in 1956–1957, but substantially edited for style and the like in 1985.

7. AQUILES, MAN OF "SENTIMENT"

Introduction

Ana Caso joined in common-law marriage, her third, with an out-of-town shepherd who, although he "used to sleep in trees," proved to be a faithful and hard-working husband. In 1923 this temperamental woman bore Aquiles N. Caso, and just one year later he was riding slung on her back as the agrarian women of Naranja streamed out across the black earth of the ejido to retrieve the harvest from the landlords. In those days of the heroic struggle, people often stayed up all night because of some excitement or event. Women like Nana Ana were on the move, helping with the field work, hurrying off to political meetings in the evening, and, of course, arguing, gossiping, and being jealous and ambitious about their men. Aquiles today appears, like his brothers and cousins, to have inherited from his older female relatives a full measure of animosities and a social network of affections. Even more than his brothers, he has inherited the emotionalism of his mother, or, as he calls it, the "sentimen-

tality." This personal quality of sentimentality, together with "dynamism," motivates the man and constitutes the dominant value in his
particular system of good and evil.*

Boyhood and Early Manhood

Aquiles' infancy was probably like that of almost everyone else in Naranja
at the time, marked by frequent illness, protracted and tight swaddling in
a sheet for much of the first year if not longer, weaning on beans and tortillas with considerable discomfort, and constant bodily contact with the
mother and other girls and women during the first years of life. From
about two on he would have been playing in the extended household in
the presence of his mother, aunts, grandmother, brothers, and cousins, as
already noted above for Boni. As a boy he is remembered as very mis-
chievous, a "wild one," physically hyperactive, and sociable.

His own first memories provide us with an ample picture of the sort of
experience that helped form the mature individual. Once, when about
five, he was playing tops near a group of older girls and he saw how other
boys would occasionally run up and pull their pigtails. Suddenly, as if he
had wanted it, his top spun away and in between the girls' legs. He
dashed in among them and, yielding to an impulse, yanked a pair of braids
and fled madly. The girl, however, tripped him up with her *rebozo* shawl,
bringing him to the ground with such violence as to injure his collarbone,
which has been "bad" ever since. "I cried, but did not return to the attack. Rather, I thought the top was guilty because it had led me to the
girls. So I threw it into the fire and burnt it up. That's the way children
are" (laughing). The collarbone continued to hurt for weeks. Finally Nana
Ana, desiring to take him to a circus in Zacapu, asked "an old man" to fix
it, which he did by yanking it so forcefully that his patient immediately
fainted. "After that there was no circus, no nothing!" The memory of this
pain is still vivid, as is suggested by the words I have quoted or closely
paraphrased above.

The majority of his early memories concern the struggle with poverty

---

*No English word or set of words corresponds well to *sentimiento*, and so forth
that occur in Aquiles' speech and elsewhere in the discussion below. In certain
cases words such as "emotion" and "feeling" would have conveyed more precisely
the nuances of the original, and would have avoided the high-literary and English-
sentimental connotations which Aquiles' speech (and thought) actually lack; in
other words, while Aquiles uses *sentimiento* a lot, his meanings lack the sentimental flavor of "sentiment" in English. Instead of several or even a half-dozen
context-specific equivalences, however, I have chosen to use the conventional
translation words, and I hope that in the course of the life study below the reader
will acquire a sense for what this point in the semantic field means to Aquiles and
how he feels about it.

and pain, and brief, childhood bonanzas. "We were very poor, my pants were torn, patched." Today he claims, "I remember that I used to go home from school along the wall, holding my hat over my buttocks so that they wouldn't see"—a story which is reminiscent of his brother Boni's boyhood shirt consisting mainly of buttonholes. Sometimes Aquiles could remedy poverty by violence. "I used to want bread very much, because we always ate tortillas and beans. One day I saw Alberto Serrano. The Serranos have always had enough. They lived well. And I saw him enter the store and buy bread for five cents. Five cents was worth a lot then!" he says, leaning forward excitedly. "And so I thought, 'I'm going to eat bread!' When Alberto came out I rushed at him from one side and tore away the bread . . . and ate half of it . . . and gave him back the other half." These little aggressive acts are a typical feature of Naranja childhood culture, as in many other parts of the world. In this instance, however, a scion of the agrarian Casos was robbing a little member of the landholding and traditionally wealthy Serrano lineage. Aquiles' decision to act had indubitably been influenced by things his mother was saying about the Serranos. Mexican Indian and Mexican peasant children generally inherit a wider and more intense set of human relationships than, for example, the children in urban, middle-class United States culture—wider in that more people are involved; more intense in that passions such as hunger and blood revenge are brought into play.

The boy's problems of poverty could also be solved by theft. Once he stole a peso from the rickety table while his mother was outside bent over the washing stone. "A peso was worth a lot then! I took it and went out and bought a whole peso's worth of candy. It filled the whole front of my shirt. I gave it away to everybody—to everybody! I met a girl who was coming in from [the settlement of] Morelos and told her, 'Listen, will you be my girl? I'll give you all this candy!' And I really gave it to her! But when I returned, my mother asked, 'Where is the peso?' I said, 'I don't know, Mother, I haven't seen it.' And then she really beat me, but hard. That is the only time in my life that she really beat me." Aquiles still likes to distribute "to everybody" when the means come his way; largesse is part of his nature, as of his mother's. But he is also the only prince whom I would describe as honest, especially when it comes to the use of public funds. In addition to the unique trauma of this pain from his mother, the only beating probably also left a mark because of cultural attitudes: mestizo peasants typically beat their children (as well as doing other things like twisting ears), whereas Tarascans prefer to discipline by mockery and the like.

Aquiles' father died when he was eight. "We were left very poor, all of us. Camilo no, because he was already in school and they used to feed him there. But Boni had to work as a herdboy in the sierra, and I went around in rags. So my mother went to Morelia to work in the hospital, and I went with her." They lived in a slum area to the south of the city. "But I didn't like it. I used to cry and cry. So she sent me back to Naranja to live with a cousin, Sebastián Gabriel. Afterward, for the year that I was here alone, I used to eat with my aunts and to change all the time. When they got mad at me in one house, I would go to another house and beg for food. And that lasted a year." This year of his father's death, the abrupt change to a Morelia slum, and then eating around with his aunts must have been critical in Aquiles' emotional development. When his mother returned, he went to live with her because "it is always better to live with one's mother."

His childhood memories are dominated by certain features, most of them associated with pain and deprivation. Most of them (including many not mentioned here) also reflect a socially rich and heavily populated environment: the large extended family (described above under "Boni"); the numerous friends, relatives, and acquaintances; the girls with whom he shared and bantered; and, above all, his beloved mother, who was also the chief disciplinary agent (his shepherd father was gone much of the time even before his early death). Somehow during these years Aquiles acquired his comparatively naturalistic attitudes toward sexual behavior, which, for example, enabled him to state without embarrassment, early on in my fieldwork, "It is customary for boys to masturbate a great deal from twelve to fourteen, before they start running after women."

At the age of fourteen, having completed four interrupted years of primary school in the village, Aquiles was selected—probably through the political influence of Scarface—to be sent to the state agricultural school in Morelia, the same one Camilo had attended. Two age-mates who don't like him remember him as a fair student, but he claims to have received "only eights or nines." More significant for our purposes than his mental adjustment to an agricultural school are the personal repercussions of his transfer out of Naranja politics, where he had been growing up during the sanguinary factionalism between the Casos and the Ocampos (see Chapter 5), his basic attitudes being shaped in an atmosphere that still was thick with radical agrarian ideas and the animosities of feuding relatives. Members of the extended family in his own household such as Boni already were emerging as formidable fighters and "red-boned Cardenistas," and in Aquiles there naturally evolved a strong motivation to fight and side with his uncle. It was during the first fourteen years of his life that there hardened in him the inflexible credo: "No matter what, I stand with my uncle, and Boni, with my own blood." In the vortex of passions and ambitions—in short, of politics—Aquiles became habituated to letting himself be guided by his sentiments.

Aquiles' move to three years of Morelia politics in 1934 was not as drastic as one might expect for other reasons. Then as now the indigenous pueblo was tuned in to state and national politics, and the leaders in Naranja were about as *au courant* as their counterparts in the state capital, then in the political ferment that began with "Mugiquismo" (the radical politics of Francisco Múgica in the middle twenties) and reached a sort of climax in the struggle between "Cardenismo" and "Serratismo" from 1932 to 1934, but continued strong throughout the national presidency of Lázaro Cárdenas (1934–1939). Aquiles jumped into these troubled waters like the well-prepared Tarascan fisherman that he was. He joined a Communist student "cell," participated in demonstrations and street fights, and enthusiastically sang "The Internationale." "We were red in those days," he recalls. He vividly remembers the issues of the Spanish Civil War, and the hundreds of Spanish refugee children who were brought to Morelia about 1937 or 1938. "They were very crazy," that is, emotionally disturbed from being orphaned and otherwise brutalized by their experiences.

After completing school in Morelia, Aquiles was sent on to the Indigenous Institute in Paracho, "the Capital of the Tarascan Sierra," and the two-year course to qualify as a teacher of monolingual Tarascan children within the rubric of "the Tarascan Campaign" (which, supported by Cárdenas and financed through him, was dedicated to the linguistic ideal that children should first be taught literacy in the language they know, before moving on to the added difficulties of the second language). The campaign was then shifting into full gear under the inspired supervision of the great American linguist Morris Swadesh, who is still fondly remembered by his erstwhile students—as much for his dominant physical trait ("The Paunch" was his epithet), as for his outspoken Communism. The intellectual and political stimulation of Paracho made a deep impression on Aquiles and he did finish the course, he says. But immediately thereafter, from 1941 to 1952, he taught in a series of (Tarascan and mestizo) hamlets in various parts of the state. The first three decades of his life, then, illustrate the sort of discontinuities in conditioning discussed by Ruth Benedict, which can either be disorienting or make for a highly versatile individual.

Aquiles eventually ended up in Naranja, then Zacapu. Apparently an excellent primary-school teacher, he energetically organized extracurricular activities in Naranja, although his "night school" there, started in 1947 "to make better princes," as he words it, had to be hastily dropped within six months, when he was accused of "creating a division, of wanting to start a new faction" (*partido*). Nonetheless, the amateur actors and public speakers created by this school still give one or more staged performances a year, and the friendships that Aquiles formed with age-mates whom he "had never known before" form the basis for his subfaction or political group of "effective idealists" (*idealistas efectivos*) who are covertly struggling against what they call the "uncultured group" of Gregorio Serrano, leading scion of the Serrano lineage (and brother of Alberto, from whom the boy Aquiles stole that bread). Today Aquiles is one of the best educated of the ruling princes; he takes pride in writing what in his opinion is correct Spanish and in speaking eloquently at ejidal assemblies. He is one of the persons in town who take a genuine interest in matters of wider scope, such as the personality, if not the music, of Glenn Miller, or what was then felt to be an imminent coup by the Chinese Communists in Malaya; curious about the Chinese Communist government, then only five years old, he often asked me questions about it that I could not answer.

Aquiles and Women

Aquiles exemplifies the norms of the Naranja and, to some extent, the Mexican peasant male, norms that are characterized by aggressiveness and dominance vis-à-vis women, and by certain fringes of modesty. He began visiting the whorehouses of Zacapu and Morelia during his early adolescence and continued these nocturnal visitations during all his years as a student and schoolteacher. The female body attracts him strongly, and he is quick and frank to say so. He responded to a lovely pen-and-ink drawing by Watteau with the following: "This woman inspires temptation in me . . . it is as though she were inviting me . . . this woman would make a man sin . . . this woman, encountering two men, would make them fight until one of them had won her, because men are like that, like lions fighting for a woman, her body." In conversations about adolescent sex life, Aquiles and others picture the young man as a sort of Ovidian lion wandering about, looking for the best female flesh he can find, "be it a widow, or a whore, or the fiancée." (The Watteau, incidentally, was in a little book of *Great Drawings* by Paul Sachs.)

At the age of twenty-one Aquiles, "the lion," took his present wife, María, in conformity with one of the two main patterns of courtship: bride-capture. She, aged seventeen, was emerging from her house "with nothing but her dress on" and Aquiles, who had been lying in wait with a friend, pulled out his .38 Super and, under dire threats, forced her to run away with him, he and his friend discharging their pistols into the air as they dashed down the main street of the town to the house of a cousin. As is also customary, physical consummation followed not long after they entered these sheltering walls. The descriptions of this case of courtship disturbed me since I already knew both of the parties as man and wife. I urgently asked about it in the main store on the plaza. Had it really happened that way? What could the girl do about it? "Well, what *can* one do about it? One has to give in," replied her sister, one of brother Camilo's reputed conquests. For Aquiles, on the other hand, this bride-capture showed how you can be carried away by your sentiments.[7]

The wedding was celebrated with great pomp, and the Tarascan *kúpera* was danced in its full details, the girl jigging with various miniature household articles on her back and Aquiles stomping it out with, successively, a plow, an ax, and a machete over his shoulder. To the tune of native melodies, the bride and groom danced up to each other alternatively, barely scratched each other's faces with a bunch of roses, offered a few sips of brandy from a cup, and, not losing step, returned to their places. After this Aquiles' half-brothers and male cousins and the bride's sisters and female cousins danced across the mat and gave each other clothing, which the bride and groom then donned. And so into the night. Aquiles' wife, incidentally, is a Flores, that is, a member of one of the wealthy mestizo (but Tarascan-speaking) families that controlled Naranja in the decades just before the revolt; his marriage to her crossed the closest there is to a class line in the community.

The lion has continued to wander despite or, rather, in addition to his comparatively happy home life. During the time of my fieldwork I gathered that he occasionally visited one of the younger widows in the town, especially when drunk and in the company of friends such as Jaime Morales. While in the United States, of course (in 1949–1952), he had occasional liaisons like all braceros. Finally, he is said to be carrying on desultory affairs with two married women in town, including the wife of the Serrano from whom, as a boy, he had snatched that coveted piece of bread.

The sort of Naranja machismo sketched above does not disclose some of the profounder feeling which it is necessary to understand before we can fully evaluate Aquiles, Boni, Bones, or the other princes. The patterned aggression toward women, shared in some degree by many of these men, is, in the first place, qualified by a dislike of public female nudity. When asked to pass a judgment on the Watteau drawing mentioned above, Aquiles affirmed that he disliked it "because of the nudity. I like the woman, but not like that, better with a veil, like the Arabs, under a tent in a field. . . . She should have something to adorn her beauty." This is part of the pattern which prohibits female exposure, except in the home or by the pond, and which is presumably connected with the premium on premarital female chastity. Aquiles was delighted at the comment by a mestizo compadre from another town à propos of an old Indian woman just then shuffling across the plaza: "Look at that Indian woman! How she honors us by going about completely covered, and how much better her dress is than the ones which show everything!" (pulling his shirt partly down off his shoulder).

Aquiles' anxiety about nudity was tested very far by an utterly perverse

Grünewald depicting three nude witches flagellating each other. He threw himself back in his chair and exclaimed, "This is immoral (*es lo inmoral*)! . . . I would never tell anyone to do those things! I would never allow a picture like that in my house, neither for myself, nor for my children!" His only positive reaction was a grin and, pointing, "That is always the instinct of the woman. She puts her hand before herself to conceal the most intimate part." He went on to say that the woodcut reminded him of a Mexican porno-mag called *Vea* ("Look!") that contains many titillating pictures that he didn't like; he has not looked at *Vea* a second time. The Grünewald also reminded him of an experience in Morelia during his student years. He had brought a girl student home to her dormitory at night, and, as they stood talking in her room, she suddenly (*de un repente*) began to slip out of her clothes, with obvious intentions. Aquiles fled, with a strong feeling of disgust, even nausea (*asco*), and thereafter avoided her. It would seem that female looseness and initiative can repel an individual from a culture of male dominance and premarital female chastity.

Some related factors bear mention. During his formative years a young man frequently sees women in the nude, but they are mainly kinswomen: mother, aunts, sisters, and cousins; the main exception is at the nearby pond or "Eye of Water" where women often do their laundry naked above the waist. Young men, for their part, have no inhibitions about being seen naked while diving into the swimming hole at one end of the pond or cleaning the many canals that crisscross the ejido, "as they have little shame, and even with the women watching them." Permissible nudity is in fact associated with water. Lovers and spouses seldom see or enjoy each others' complete, naked bodies at the time of intercourse.

Female sexuality is inseparable from cleanliness for Aquiles. He actually bathes two or three times a week, and the first quality he listed when discussing female beauty was that the girl or woman should be clean. He intensely disliked an earthy Daumier drawing depicting a lower-class French repast, the mother giving suck to her baby while herself slurping soup from a bowl. Aquiles' reaction was, "This is no home . . . this is not correct . . . those people are living sloppily . . . that woman is not at all industrious, she is not cleaning things . . . if that woman dropped in at my house I would feel a repugnance." The strength of his reactions may have reflected conflicts within the family involving his mother and his wife.

Another aspect of sexuality is the general silence about homosexuality (though I am not sure whether this applies to the generation now in adolescence). It is almost never discussed, and then only with reference to and contempt for "somebody" in Zacapu, or some mestizos who were run out of town fifteen years ago, or the rumors regarding a prominent Morelia politician. During the campaign tour in 1956 a mestizo politician told us a pretty raw joke about professional fellatio. The ten Naranja members of the "election committee" stared off stolidly at the distant mountains; only Scarface laughed and came up with some repartee. The homosexual and scatological reference of mestizo jargon in Zacapu, especially in the factory, is generally lacking in the Naranja billiard hall, where the salty language of men among men involves fornication, adultery, and incest. Take another instance: Rorschach Card VI, which is relatively phallic, caused Aquiles to block, as did a drawing by Michelangelo of a male nude (see Psychological Appendix C). Bodily contact between men is normally avoided, especially by the more conservative such as Bones and Melesio, whose feelings are expressed only by the delicate, minimal Tarascan handshake. Aquiles and some of his friends, on the other hand, display a relatively mestizo style with occasional slaps on the shoulder or taking hold of the interlocutor's jacket or shirt sleeve during a conversation. In play as at work, all Naranja men associate with each other frequently, and, in the case of someone like Aquiles, this includes gaming, drinking, political discussion, and even an occasional movie together. To a considerable degree the patterns of diffuse, positive, and manifold association between men result from a culture, that is, a universe of values and attitudes, which, granted exceptions such as certain widows, makes it ambiguous or awkward to entertain friendly, informal relations with a woman outside one's immediate family or household—and sometimes extremely dangerous (see Homicide Appendix).[8] Concomitantly, women outside the domestic unit keep primarily to the company of women. Social distance between the sexes in the public domain does not preclude a certain amount of banter and often stylized joking, as I noted above for Bones, and it does work synergistically with the way many men, partly because they farm less than half the year, spend a great deal of their time within the familiar confines of their households with their womenfolk and their women's close friends and visitors.

Aquiles en Famille

The consistently sentimental streak in Aquiles is nowhere more sharply delineated than within his family home. Like many Naranja brothers, he grew up in an extended, essentially matrifocal family, as was described in Boni's life history. Also like many Naranja brothers, he attempted the humanly taxing institution of the "joint fraternal household," and, as happens with many brothers, the effort failed after a while. At the time of this particular effort, Camilo's second and present wife, a mestiza, was having a good deal of trouble integrating Camilo's first children with her own family—to say nothing of adjusting to the volatile and earthy Nana Ana. The second brother, Boni, was then living with the wife who was ten years his senior, and carrying on his notorious career of alcoholism and homicide. Some disagreeableness and fighting between the three sisters-in-law and between each of them and their mother-in-law would have seemed predictable and did in fact seeth constantly and erupt not infrequently, according to Aquiles and non-family. Since they were forced to cook in the same lean-to and often sleep in the same room, there was little rest for the peace-loving and weary. "Who was going to give whom the order? And with whom should the son side?" During these trying years the brothers remained loyal and friendly to one another. "It was a question of women!" But after several years Camilo decided that his wife was not going to be bossed around, and departed with his family; relations today between Nana Ana and her oldest son are comparatively cool. Boni's wife was the next to go, albeit without hard feelings, and Boni has recently set himself up as a household head, with another wife. The only son to remain with Nana Ana was thus Aquiles, and this because "The mother is always right. Whenever there was a fight between my mother and María I always told María, 'No, you are wrong, you must listen to my mother and do what she says. She is the older and in charge of my house.' I sometimes said this when my wife was really in the right. We brothers never fought, but sometimes they would side with their wives against our mother. That is impossible, and they had to go." Devotion and obedience to one's mother-in-law, then, outweigh the rights and wrongs of a particular dispute. This is sentimentalism, as Aquiles himself stresses. Needless to say, Aquiles' position was often onerous to María, but, since the departure of the other daughters-in-law, she and Nana Ana have worked out a fairly or at least overtly harmonious modus vivendi.

This family history also illustrates Aquiles' generally clear-cut conception of the locus of authority and the obedience that must characterize certain human relations. Even more than most Tarascans, he places a high value on respect within the family, the larger kin group, and, to a lesser extent, the village and the world at large. Lack of respect, which often means lack of obedience and understanding, is considered to be the principal cause for disturbances within the family. Respect in varying degrees toward various persons is also essential to the maintenance of the basic ideal of communal solidarity. The clash in values between the demands of respect and the lust for power can cause acute suffering in the ambitious and sentimental Aquiles.

Aquiles intensely loves his four living children, ranging from a one-year-old boy, whom he often carries around, to a fourteen-year-old girl now attending a Morelia high school (two of his offspring have died). On seeing a drawing of a fine horse in my little book of masterpieces, he exclaimed, "Ah, I would like two steeds like that, one for myself and the second for a son of mine!" He thinks of his sons as Casos and feels sure they will be princes; while he did not transpose his patronymic and matronymic last names like Camilo, he does often sign himself Aquiles N.

Caso, thus proclaiming his Caso status. His feelings for his daughters are of a passion that perhaps typifies a culture where the bride elopes most of the time, when she isn't abducted, and the father, in either case, is expected to be "mad." I should stress that he is not a severe father and that his children are comparatively spoiled. He usually has to repeat a command four or five times, and then the children obey slowly and non-chalantly—probably because the real authority at home is Nana Ana. The situation, in any case, contrasts with the stricter obedience to their fathers of other Naranja children.

Aquiles as a Worker, and at Play

Aquiles is fairly swarthy, has a thick, wide-based nose similar to his uncle Scarface's, and when tickled by something breaks into a roguish, toothy grin; he impressed several Americans whom I took to Naranja as "a pretty tough character." His eyes are blue. At five foot five, he is the shortest of all the princes and physically slight and gracile, although well-proportioned and athletic. His diminutive physique and comparatively weak hands and back are compensated for by the fast reactions and superb coordination that enabled him to win "firsts" and top money in tough competitions among migrant workers in the California harvests. They also enabled him to captain the Naranja basketball team for five years when it was still of state-championship quality. Once, before an important game with the city of Pátzcuaro, he came down with a high fever. "I was lying on a cot, hot and coughing. I thought I was going to die. Then Mani came in and said, 'What's the matter with you?' I was seized by sentimentality (*me agarró el sentimiento*). I got up and played like a maniac and we beat them, we ran those fellows into the ground!" Similarly, the profuse sweating followed by cool mountain air laid him low with a week-long fever the one time he played during my fieldwork; in fact, he has forbidden himself the game because it (that is, the psychosomatic intensity of it) endangers his health. But I could see then that he excels in this game of tall men ("tall" here meaning over 5'10") by virtue of close dribbling, flashy ball-handling, versatile passing, and fancy underhand and backhand shots. His sometimes fierce sentimentality today finds its expression—aside from politics—in the aboriginal game of *palillos* or "little sticks," which is played on Sundays by large groups of men in back yards on the south edge of town. Aquiles, one of the best players, is very proud that his town can always beat Tiríndaro, to say nothing of Zacapu. As the game progresses he grows more and more excited, absorbed, and tense until sometimes he is "seized by sentimentality" and bursts into tears of rage or joy.

Hard, manual labor filled the middle third of Aquiles' mature life. In 1949 he broke his lengthy career as a schoolteacher and, desiring higher pay and a change, obtained a job as a construction worker for the Zacapu factory. He soon became deeply impressed by the factory's size and efficiency and by the American engineers and mechanics who were his bosses. He was shortly promoted and spent the remainder of his time in industry operating a road roller. The factory so enthused him that he decided to go north and see the Great Civilization, although he had "never, never wanted to before." For the next three years he toiled in numerous orchards and truck farms all over California, Oregon, and Washington, returning once, only to leave again almost immediately with Jaime Morales and three other age-mates. The years as a bracero left a profound imprint on the man. The industrious, industrialized, and very "advanced" people he found there convinced him that the United States was the ideal for Mexico to follow. The high value placed on material improvements in his radical ideology fit perfectly with what he saw as an accomplished fact in the Pacific states. In addition to efficiency and energetic behavior, Aquiles was struck by the cleanliness of it all. In this he was typical of returning migrant workers, who invariably comment that their villages are dirty (*sucio, feo*) and who often make a fetish, by village standards, of washing and keeping their clothes clean.

While in the United States Aquiles became especially fond of Filipinos and socialized with them much of the time. Aside from his own Filipino-like looks and the shared language, Spanish, his strong attraction toward this ethnic group was due to certain qualities of the West Coast Filipino men, on all of which he expatiates freely: habits of hard and regular work, male dominance, and a predilection for a neat house and good clothes. The sartorial influence on him was pronounced and he brought back several suits, vests, and colored shirts, all in excellent taste. Today he often discusses his plans and hopes for going north to educate his children to speak English, and to complete the modernization of his Naranja house, which already contains mosaic floors and store furniture. On the other hand, since setting up again in Naranja he rarely engages in physical labor. "He doesn't work; yes, he *can* work, he *knows how to work* (*sabe trabajar*), but he doesn't."

Language, Culture, and Personality

Nana Ana speaks Tarascan most of the time, exclusively so with her many old cronies, but she has always tried to use Spanish with her children, with the result that neither Camilo nor Aquiles is fluent in Tarascan. Aquiles now speaks very little, although he claims to understand "everything," and he seems willing to continue to forget although, as he says, "It makes me ashamed not to know Porépicha." I found many other men expressing this conflict between shame at forgetting their mother tongue and the prestigious appeal of Spanish. In this regard Aquiles' speech is very interesting and makes him an ideal subject for a study of the relation between language, culture, and personality. His Spanish is comparatively articulate, and, as has been said, he speaks well in public. On the other hand, I have to add that he frequently stammers, hesitates, and blocks verbally, often over proper nouns, or words that actually are the subject of the conversation in progress. At such points he will, for example, say, "This . . . this . . . this . . . building," or he may, by circumlocutions, evade the naming of what he is talking about (an instance of what linguist Roman Jakobson would call incipient substitution aphasia). I had been noticing this facet of his speech and character for some time, and had even been taking fieldnotes on it, when I was utterly surprised one day to have him confide in me that he had sent away to a "Clinic of Specialists" in Mexico City for medicines which he had already picked up in Zacapu. Why? "Failure of memory, Pablo. Many times I can't concentrate on something, or I can't remember something a few minutes later," and he cited two striking examples. I suggested that his recent heavy harvest-time drinking might be the underlying reason. His answer was: "That is why I want to get out of here, because the indolence causes all the vice" (i.e., drinking). This was the nth time he had repeated this wisdom about indolence and the bottle, but now he went on as follows, "I have been troubled by this forgetting for the past three years." I thereupon presented him with a very simplified version of Sigmund Freud's psychology of the errors in everyday life, especially slips of the tongue. He emphatically agreed. "That's it, that's it! It is the tiniest things, the simplest things that don't mean anything, that I keep forgetting!" I then suggested tactfully that certain "bad ideas" might keep surging up to interfere with his thoughts and his memory. He concurred, saying, "That is why we drink, and why I want to leave [i.e., for the United States], so as not to think things one should not think." He had muttered this same sentence in a conversation with some friends a few days before, and I had been meditating on it. Before the reader leaps to a fast, sex-focused conclusion, let me hastily add that the "bad things" here refer primarily and probably exclusively to political relations, and dreams and daydreams about politically connected acts of violence, to political envy and strong ambition. Whatever the particular source or mechanisms, the overt, habitual forgetting is a troublesome fact of life. His brother Camilo displays a similar failing with regard to appointments, dates in the past, and so forth, as does Scarface when it comes to dates and personal names.

Their problems of memory have wider ramifications. Aquiles, like Bones, Toni, Camilo, and Gregorio, often behaves in a way that suggests a species of double existence in the mind. On the one hand, they will participate in daily affairs with vigor and an occasional broad smile, but, if you catch them unobserved, their faces as often as not are covered by a pensive grimness that presumably masks an even darker interior. This is just a special instance of the Tarascan tendency to wear a (stoical) mask, and their explicit consciousness of masks and the masked quality of life (as comes out in Boni's Rorschach). My impression tallies with those of two perspicacious American visitors and is of psychological significance despite the lack of the familiar psychologist's "controls"; in fact, it also corresponds to the conclusions of the Mexican depth psychologist J. Gómez Robleda that Tarascan culture is "a culture of masks." Aquiles stands out because of the contrast between his public front and the stormy, often malevolent cast that his features assume when he draws into himself. His attitudes surfaced in his reactions to the face of agony and fury in Leonardo da Vinci's *A Soul in Torment*, which he rejected even more strongly than the drawing of the nursing mother slurping soup. And, unlike the typical Indian peasant, whose cork-happy imbibing may last for days, Aquiles and some other princes practice fast, hard drinking to get drunk and drop the mask. The masked aspect of Aquiles, the other princes, and even Tarascan culture as a whole is interestingly parallel, incidentally, to the theory of personality in general being a matter of masks, as set forth by culture and personality expert Clyde Kluckhohn: "All of us, even clinicians, are frequently 'taken in' by the masks of the communal and role components."

I have discussed Aquiles' partial loss of Tarascan and some psychological implications of his facial expressions and verbal behavior. The social import of his speech is equally interesting, although less immediately noticeable. His mode of address varies, or better, covaries, rather precisely with the locus in the social structure of his particular interlocutor. To superiors and some equals he will use a slow, carefully enunciated form, with as many learned words and polite phrases as he can introduce without distorting the utterance or sounding pretentious. This first mode would be used toward his uncle or a visiting tourist or an inspector from the Department of Agrarian Affairs. Toward superiors whom he inwardly regards as inferior he uses the same careful mode, but sometimes allows a note of condescension to slip in, and frequently repeats the person's first name. To equals in the full sense, such as Toni, or toward genuinely respected age-mates such as Jaime Morales, he tends to use a forceful, clipped, self-assured mode of speech, simple, idiomatic, and often slangy in the choice of words, all of which produce a sort of comrades-in-arms effect. Toward social inferiors, such as children and maids, he frequently, but not always, adopts a gruff and peremptory tone that sounds autocratic, consisting of only the necessary words in half-completed phrases. In general, Aquiles is respectful and considerate in his own way with ordinary villagers, and contrasts in this respect with his great rival, Gregorio Serrano, of the mestizo Serrano family, who often uses the peremptory fourth mode just described above. From these marked gradations in his speech it is possible to learn a great deal about the informal social structure of Naranja and about Aquiles' personality. For example, he addresses the present mayor in a tone of voice between those of "equals in the full sense" and "social inferiors," reflecting the actuality that the mayor is a political buck private and that Aquiles' patience with him is sometimes taxed while he, officially the town secretary, is executing the duties of mayor. These nuances in speech forms correlate neatly with Aquiles' keen sense for status distinctions that I alluded to above when discussing the values of "respect." Here, as so often, he is unusually revealing and indicative of the complexities and conflicts of his rapidly changing culture. In retrospect, the ideology of Primo Tapia contained a powerful strain of economic and, by extension, social egalitarianism. The Tarascan and circumambient Mexican soil, although fertile, had not been—and indeed could not have been—sufficiently prepared to nourish such radical notions. Today, in 1956, I sense an increasing tendency to slip back to the status relationships of yesteryear—granted that they have changed considerably in content and structure. Aquiles and his brother Camilo sum up in their respective personalities many of the contradictions between agrarian egalitarianism and the recrudescent traditions of a fixed status. The regression to status and that institution so closely connected with status, the Mexican Catholic Church, is exemplified by their mother, Nana Ana, who has made the complete cycle from an anticlerical agrarian female comrade and fighter to a present-day pillar of the church, where she now spends much of her time and money: in her year as *carguera*, in charge of the newly revived religious fiestas, she spent more than anyone else, before or since (Aquiles at the time was sending home fat checks from the United States).

The carping specialist may by this time be wondering why I continue to call Aquiles an Indian, a Porépicha. Let's be rhetorical: is this comparatively educated and widely traveled and indeed experienced individual to be classified with one of your benighted Otomí, barefoot, clad in ragged manta, illiterate, monolingual, and fanatically religious? The answer is: yes and no. Aquiles is unequivocally Indian in terms of the five diagnostic criteria hammered out by the great Mexican anthropologist Alfonso Caso: race, customs, language, community of birth, community of residence, and self-identity. To begin, he is mainly Indian by blood, with straight black hair, high cheekbones, lacking the epicanthic fold, and so forth. Second, his own life cycle has been punctuated by all the diagnostic customs of Tarascan culture, such as infant swaddling, the indigenous diet, and the Indian wedding with its *kúpera* dance. Aquiles does not neglect what anthropologist Pedro Carrasco calls "Tarascan folk religion": his was the most elaborated *posada* fiesta in the Christmas season, with "Little Old Men" dancers barking in the moonlight and the other essential details. And when he dies I am sure his children will bear wax candles and purple flowers to his grave on All Souls' Day. Third, he used to be fluent

in Tarascan, especially in his boyhood and while studying at the Indigenous Institute, and he still understands the largely formulaic double entendres that spice local conversation. Although he doesn't use the language from day to day in the town hall, when he is good and drunk,
moved, and garrulous, the "sentiments" well up in Tarascan form. Fourth,
he grew up and now resides in the indigenous community of Naranja de
Tapia. Fifth, and most significant to me, he regards himself as an Indian
and, when pushed on this in private or in public, he will affirm stoutly,
"No, Pablo, I am Indian. I feel that I am Tarascan, because of race and
customs, although I do not speak it correctly." *(No Pablo, yo soy indio.
Yo me siento tarasco, por la raza y las costumbres, aunque no hablo
correcto.)* A man always is a combination of what he feels he is, what
others feel him to be, and the relations between these two sets of emotions or, rather, sentiments.

Aquiles is also a competent participant in the culture of mestizo, middle-
class Mexico, and takes seriously many of its values. Let us pass the same
five criteria in review. First, mestizo Mexico is mainly Indian in blood,
and becoming more so, and, contrariwise, "pureblood Indians" may not
exist—note Aquiles' blue eyes. Second, his Spanish actually is better, that
is, more articulate and nearer the grammatical standard, than that of most
Mexican mestizo peasants and urban workers, and, indeed, many in the
middle class. Third, Aquiles is perfectly able to play a whole range of mestizo roles in response to such distinct stimuli as a basketball court, a state
political caucus, a county whorehouse, or an American movie or a stray
copy of *The Reader's Digest*. Fourth, while identified with Naranja,
he has lived for many years in non-Indian hamlets, towns, and cities, in
Morelia, and in the United States (being partial to Stockton, California).
Last, he usually refers to himself as a Mexican, that is, as a member of the
national political, social, and linguistic community. So we see that Aquiles, like many schoolteachers and political leaders from indigenous communities, has become a marginal man par excellence, functioning rather
successfully as both an acculturated Tarascan and a sort of generic Mexican citizen to mediate between his tiny village and the larger institutions
of the nation during these years of rapid culture change and disorganiza-
tion. (For the fuller context of these mestizo-Spanish-Indian relations and
classifications, see Chapter 6.)

Cacique to Be: A Machiavellian?

Aquiles' sentimentality has been characterized and illustrated at several
points. The trait reveals itself in an ambition that seldom compromises, in
keen personal envies, jealousies, and affections, and in a ready recourse
to violence—be it in capturing a wife or in an act of factionalism. Or violence against violence: once a fight erupted about thirty yards off and I

saw Aquiles, without a split second of hesitation, streak across that space and spring like a big cat on the back of the larger antagonist, dragging him to the ground and out of harm's way.

Sentimentalism conjoins with the leadership traditions of his family line and what Americans are wont to call "leadership ability" to make of Aquiles one of "those certain elements" who control the agrarian community, even though he has only recently begun to realize his potential. During the final years of the pitched struggle against the Pedro González faction (the late thirties and early forties), Aquiles was back in Naranja as a schoolteacher—with his .38 Super constantly at his belt. He is one of the nephews who assured Scarface the triumph, such as it was. When the latter was nearly assassinated in 1945, Aquiles, knife in hand, chased Martín Valle to his threshold: "I wanted to kill him that night, but he got away." He still wants to kill him. Aquiles is one of the princes who, at secret meetings, for example, have often urged Scarface to have Pedro González bumped off (sonarlo is the idiom), which of course Scarface refuses to allow since this first cousin and mortal enemy possesses a federal safe-conduct and is still "loved by Lázaro Cárdenas," who has enjoined that he be allowed to live out his days.

As for the ethics of assassination, Aquiles drew a crucial distinction one night in the town hall during a lengthy discussion of politics. Speaking of the atrocities against three peons in 1945, he said: "That was not the work of human beings, but of savages. We here, Bones, Boni . . . and I, we have to kill at times, but we kill morally, without speaking to the person, without saying anything to him, only sas-a-sas," making the pistol-shooting motion. "But we never make them suffer too much, torture them." A political killing, from this angle, can be seen as a sort of execution, and the Casos, sure that they deserve to rule, do actually invoke the moral theses of peace and communal solidarity when discussing the liquidation of an opponent. Which reminds me of anthropologist Robert Redfield, both his idealist theses about the communal solidarity (Gemeinschaft) in a Mexican Indian village, and also the fact that his main informant (in Chan Kom) was a most strong cacique. From a more objective angle, I would add that in all the hundreds of written and oral denunciations that came to my attention, none included torture and other atrocities in Naranja—except for the lynching of Primo Tapia, which was, of course, done by federals, that is, mestizos. The strong feelings against such obscenities also reflects the feeling that the village is "one family," and probably a Naranja reaction against the notorious sadism in neighboring Tiríndaro during the hegemony of Severo Espinoza (see Chapter 5), as well as a positive response to the interdictions of Cárdenas and to his well-known humanity.

Aquiles emerged as a major political factor after his return from the

United States four years ago. During the height of the Juan Nahua fission, a friend diplomatically resigned from the post of town secretary and Aquiles was "elected" through the support of his immediate family and because he deceived many people in the new faction into believing that he was on their side. "I went into foul up the politics of Juan!" he now says. This he proceeded to do by depriving Juan of such symbols of power as the town seal and the keys to the town hall, by bribing others such as Bones, by denouncing others such as Melesio Caso as "murderers," and, finally, by being constantly present in the town hall to converse, gossip, and intrigue (as he was still doing at the time of my fieldwork). Juan was isolated after about three months. The coup de grace has already been described; after a decision by the core of the Caso faction, Juan and his law-student son were sprayed with bullets by several mestizo mercenaries from the nearby hamlet of Buena Vista (in retrospect it seems likely that Scarface only told these outsiders to pepper his relatives a bit without striking home—*échenles algunos balazos pa' asustarlos*).

Aquiles' reward for his important role in the defeat of his cousin Juan was continued tenure as town secretary and the ejido plot of a political exile. This means that, in minor violation of the Agrarian Code, three plots are now controlled by one household, since Nana Ana, an ejidataria in her own right, still works the plot of her deceased cousin José Moreno (Tapia's old chum). The three plots must produce almost thirty thousand liters of maize, worth almost ten thousand pesos [which comes to over a million 1986 pesos]. In addition, Aquiles and his mother own over thirty acres of private land, which often produces a huge cash crop of beans, and, of course, many people bring them presents because of friendship or political status.

The celebrated Juan Nahua case, beyond the economic and political rewards, also demonstrates dramatically how the relation between sentiment and principle can become tenuous and conflicted in the mind of Aquiles. Here his first cousin Juan was actually trying to start a renaissance of the constructive agrarianism of Primo Tapia which had largely lapsed during the egoistical feuding of the Libido Dominandi period (see Chapter 5), and in the short space of two years Juan did in fact go far toward organizing Naranja for material improvements and also toward reconciling if not actually reuniting the various factions. A man mainly swayed by abstract principles would have rallied to Juan and worked with him in trying to establish a creative relationship between the new movement and the pre-existing power centered around Scarface and Camilo. For Aquiles, however, the new schism was immediately coded as a means to advance himself politically and, perhaps more important, as "them wanting to seize control and overthrow my uncle" (*derrocar a mi tío*). Both insidious enemies such as Gregorio Serrano and old archenemies such as Pedro

González had, so Aquiles felt, enticed away one of the Caso cousins in order to use him as a leader and a sort of point man to topple the legitimate line of succession. Against all this the right methods were Machiavellian intrigue and, at the end, violence. The first man to desert Juan and switch back to Scarface was the always realistic and opportunistic Toni Serrano (whose life I sketched in the fourth section above). Aquiles took his compadre to see Scarface for the inevitable verbal lashing and then reconciliation, and "as I crossed the threshold to my uncle's house with Toni, I began to weep because of sentiment."

Aquiles was one of the first to give me a clearer idea of how profound and passionate is the lust for power in the princes of Naranja. During an early exploration of political structure, following the assassination of Agustín, he stressed that only the Casos can lead in Naranja.

"Who will succeed your uncle?" I asked casually.

"Camilo," Aquiles said, suddenly very serious.

"And who will succeed him?" I pushed on.

The blood rushed into his face, he slammed back against the wall, pulled in his neck, and said, in a tense, husky whisper, "*I!*"

This discussion grew yet more tense when Aquiles tried to dissuade me from asking any more questions about Naranja politics, and the Agustín case in particular. I refused: "I won't back off" (*no retrodesco*). But as the months passed by, he adjusted to my modus operandi; in fact, at a Christmas fiesta six months later his mother insisted that I get several recipes, "Because Pablo wants to take notes on everything." And my friendship with Aquiles grew, as with Camilo.

Aquiles suffers envy that amounts to anguish because his uncle, outwardly at least, favors his chief rival Gregorio Serrano. After Scarface's election to state congressman (*diputado*), a complicated and bitter struggle began to unfold for the nomination of the new selectmen (*regidores*) in the county. Scarface's goal was to place one completely loyal follower from the peasant sector and two other friends or allies. The other two selectman posts were to be left to the enemy, consisting of the commercial and religious elements in Zacapu and what were actually majority factions in most of the villages in the region. Aquiles' goal was to be the selectman from the peasant sector, and the enemies of Scarface, recognizing this, nominated and shouted loudly for him at the convention. Aquiles, though no political greenhorn, was partly intoxicated by his illusory popularity, and it would have been easy to set him against his uncle, arouse the envy of both, and then defeat and disgrace them. But Scarface, astutely recognizing what was afoot, would not let his nephew be nominated and insisted on Gregorio; by making the latter his "favorite son," he could at once compromise a potential enemy, even co-opt his allegiance, and obviate the accusation of yet more nepotism. A long and bitter letter from Aquiles, describing the above, concludes as follows (December 11, 1956): "I am not disappointed, compadre, no, on the contrary, I am very proud of the fact that the entire region fought on my behalf so that it would be I who would figure on the slate for the peasant sector. My uncle didn't want it, so there's nothing to be done; I will be the same for him, the respectful, loving, and helpful nephew in his career as state congressman."

Aquiles was present at the second convention of Cardenistas that was staged in Pátzcuaro by the supporters of Scarface Caso and the latter's ally, the widow of Francisco Múgica. As was later reported, "They launched me into state politics. I didn't want to enter, but my uncle said, 'Yes!' and so I said, 'Yes, uncle.'" This launching of Aquiles consisted of a speech, the prospect of which was sufficiently exciting to keep our young peasant leader from sleeping for two nights. "All the time thinking, thinking, how can we beat *them?*" How vital are the principles of these younger Cardenistas? What had Aquiles spoken about in his speech?

"I said that we should follow the principles of the Revolution, that we younger men had grown up believing in those principles, and that if the older generations, especially the outside lawyers, now began to betray those principles, what should we younger people think? That's right, isn't it?"

[*Postscript:* Shortly after the life history narrated above, Aquiles embarked on a series of political or quasi-political jobs in various parts of Michoacán, including the "hot country" where his mother used to trek. From time to time he apparently had to stay away from Naranja because of the increased probabilities of getting assassinated by rival factions. For his part, I cannot help but suspect that he was at least partly responsible for the Christmas Eve killing of his hated rival Martín Valle. Then he returned home to his family and to his village as leader, while continuing intermittently in positions at higher levels; he has served as president of the county. The beloved son whom he was carrying around in a blanket once in awhile during my fieldwork was killed in an "accident" that Aquiles feels was a political retaliation.]

Note

The word "princes" (*príncipes*) above and elsewhere is a play on the usual Mexican term "the main ones" (*los principales*), used for leaders or the leading elders in a village. Although a Spanish translation of Machiavelli's *Il Principe* actually was found in the Naranja school (see Chapter 9), and although at least one of the opposition leaders and also the "second cacique," Camilo, had read Machiavelli and even quoted him on occasion, and although the term "princes" was sometimes used to refer to themselves by most of the leaders in the Caso faction, notably Camilo, Aquiles, and Gregorio, and although a careful check in 1986 showed that Naranja politics actually did exemplify most of Machiavelli's advice to the prince—despite all these positive signs, the term *príncipe* was not used by the Naranja population at large and has probably passed into oblivion by this time; the usual terms were *líder* for "leader" and *cacique* for the dominant ones. *Príncipe* is used here as a foregrounding and familiarizing device, and a terminological trope. The reader is encouraged to exercise due restraint in metaphorizing the situation by drawing analogies between "the princes of Naranja" and the princes of Renaissance Italy, that is, the rulers of the cities, and "the princes" of Little Italy and other working class or underclass ghettos. The serious analyst of politics should be wary of metaphors, as Machiavelli himself pointed out. This same serious student is likewise warned against overly intellectualizing the scene by fantasizing some collegium of Mexican peasant philosophers. I make no strong claim for the typicality of these princes, although they do represent much about rural Mexico and even other parts of Latin America.

Fieldnotes Interlude

CHAPTER 2

Political Pragmatics and Practicalities:
Notes on Three Ejidal Meetings

1. Ejidal Elections in Naranja, as Typed August 8, 1956

The convocation notice was posted for a week outside the town hall, following the law, the elections having been requested in Morelia a month in advance [i.e., earlier]. During the week preceding the elections far more ejidatarios assembled at the town hall, as if in anticipation, and a desire to present their loyalty. The princes often absented themselves and were on several occasions observed in twos at night in various parts of the village; presumably they were "making propaganda" and insuring full participation of the ejidatarios.

On the morning of August 8 [1956] the bushily whiskered state delegate appeared and spent the morning sitting on the benches of the town hall, saying little, dressed in a flannel shirt, a towel wrapped around his neck. The ejidatarios began arriving about 9:30 and collected before the town hall or in small groups in various parts of the plaza. About 11:00, after the church bells had tolled a second time, everyone assembled in the town hall, packing it to overflowing out the side and rear doors, the two dozen women sitting and squatting in the front lines, their Indian faces dark and wrinkled with age, stoically impassive.

The meeting was called in order by the delegate, leaning forward bushy and intense over the table, flanked on his left by Gregorio, Aquiles (typing), Mateo, Ambrosio, Anastasio Nahua, and the musician from Morelia (the latter two serving as observers), and, on his left, by Jaime, Martín González, Bones, Scarface, Ezequiel, and several older men. Gregorio then read off the names of all the 214 ejidatarios, checking them off as they sounded off, while Aquiles typed the title (paper?) for the ballot. About 186 were present, those absent including all the fallen such as Martín Valle, Pedro González, Daniel, and Crispín; no public reaction, even facial, greeted the enunciation of these names except for that of Pedro González, when a vigorous middle-aged woman in the front row said, "He is in his house." The role call took about three-quarters of an hour because of the many errors.

The delegate then asked for slates and a short man I have never seen before came forward from way in back and laid a slip of paper on the table. The delegate read the names: Gregorio as president, Mateo as secretary, and Scarface as treasurer of the ejidal commissariat, Melesio as head of the watch. The delegate then asked several times if there were any other slates, or any other suggestions. Toni Serrano suggested that they vote the slate as it was (after being asked about this by the delegate).

Scarface got up and made a supremely unconvincing speech, looking down at the floor most of the time, claiming with a parody of humility that he had already filled so many ejidal positions and had other duties. He wanted to withdraw. Some plant in the audience said to vote the slate as it stood. The ejidatarios as a whole seemed to be passively watching and no expressions of interest or physical reactions could be observed.

Then Gregorio arose and, also looking up and turning frequently to the delegate, made a shorter proposal of withdrawal, pointing out that he had been treasurer during the previous period and felt that he could not bear the official burdens of the presidency. This was followed by a public hush that reeked of unconviction. Just why the princes chose to go through with the caricature of democratic processes and the electoral "draft" must remain an open question; in small, face-to-face government such mockery of the lack of egoism and ambition makes the sore smart more rather than assuaging the pain.

After the delegate had asked several times more for other opinions, Ezequiel got up and made a long address on the virtues of the candidates, their having served the community, and their willingness to sacrifice themselves further for the common cause. This tedious harangue was followed by several more calls from the audience that the vote be taken in a tone of voice that said, "Let's get this over with and go home."

The slate was approved unanimously without a single dissenting vote, and the ayes immediately began to sign or push down illiterate thumbs. Aquiles Caso, still typing the voting list, turned to me with a half-triumphant smile and said, "Now you have seen the democracy of Naranja."

2. Ejidal Assembly Held on September 10, 1955, Typed Up September 11

The announcement was posted eight days in advance, as usual, with the nominal subject of "carrying out investigations concerning the use of the plots" (informally à propos of the "clean-up" [depuración] carried out last year), but questioning produced only half-smiles and "I don't know" [i.e., what it was about—PF, 1986]. The night previous to the meeting most of the Princes were present or dropped in at the town hall and Scarface came around quite potted from having drunk gin all day, and he talked for about an hour, first about national politics being brought into the dispute between teachers and, second, about the first days of agrarianism and Primo Tapia. His relation to Primo Tapia is analogous to that between Stalin and Lenin, with the comparatively uncultured gunman and bureaucrat following upon the real revolutionary leader whom he can praise and extol but never truly imitate; the way he talks about Primo Tapia is a combination of hero-worship and boast, the latter by virtue of his association with the hero.

On the morning of September 10 the ejidatarios began the assembly by 9:30 (Scarface, Ezequiel, Aquiles, Mateo, Gregorio, Bones, and two others), and the assembly began by 11:30. The meeting was called to order by the same delegate, and roll was called by Mateo. The delegate then read a petition by the wife of a recently deceased ejidatario who claimed a plot from two aunts who had been using it. Since the plot was inherited from *her* grandfather and she had all the legal documents claiming legal marriage, the case was quickly settled with "the good will" of the two aunts and a promise by the pueblo "to help them as soon as possible." This case had obviously been set up with the following in mind, since the two aunts had no claim whatsoever to the plot but needed the voice of unanimous promise for what was to follow. The young wife was nervous before the table, but obviously in cahoots with Scarface and the others, to whom she turned for advice several times. At another point a middle-aged ejidataria who seems very talkative, tough, and intimate with the Casos came up and whispered in Aquiles' ear, later went over to Scarface and *knelt* down before him leaning over against his chest as she whispered something. There are about five Caso women ejidatarias who make motions and support actions. On the other hand, it is the *women* who are the boldest at speaking out, as last time when one said that Pedro González was at home and this day when one said, "My friends (*compañeras*) say that before one used to be given lots of corn, and where is it now?" And later: "Everyone is afraid of them" [the Caso leaders—PF, 1986].

The case that followed involved the youngest son of Sebastián Gabriel, a major gunman who had been shot recently by Jaime; this youngest son was representing the family of a younger, unmarried brother and an older married brother who were strongly supported by the deceased Sebastián's sister-in-law (the sister of his dead first wife), who did 99% of the talking, being one of the aunts to whom help had been promised by the previous, unanimous vote. These, the several defendants, had been working the plot since the harvest was collected by the plaintiff. The plaintiff, "Chona, Daughter of Isabel the Midwife," and maid to Luciano, and merry widow [one of the relatively accessible widows—PF, 1986], had lived in common-law marriage (*en estado de amasiato*) for four years with the deceased

Sebastián, and was claiming indemnity more or less equal to the harvest to pay off the debts and the funeral costs. A violent dispute immediately broke out between the fairly attractive mistress, eyes flashing and gesticulating, and the stern old aunt, who pointed with accusing finger. The former claimed to be still in debt and to have the bills (not introduced as evidence), whereas the aunt said the bills had been paid, that the widow had been given a complete harvest (true) after the shooting of her husband, and that her claim had no chance against that of the married boy, *a direct son*, with several other relatives to support (the boy finally came to the front of the hall but said nothing). The chief point of the widow or ex-mistress seemed to be that none of the sons had been working the plot up to this year (because of minority—they were too young).

The *rights* were more or less equal in this case, and the delegate proposed a private settlement ("according to the law one is not supposed to divide up an ejido plot, but in specific cases they can be worked by halves [*a medias*], above all when it's a case of a widow," said the delegate). The delegate urged for a private settlement of this kind, either to let Chona work the land by halves for a year or two, or to give her part of the harvest. The imperious aunt, however, insisted that the plot was all her nephew's, that nothing was owed, at which point Chona burst out, "I have the right, but the whole village is afraid of them" (*yo tengo derecho, pero todo el pueblo tiene miedo de ellos*).

"Of who?" asked the bewhiskered state delegate.

"Of *them*," she replied, clearly referring to the Princes. Scarface looked blank. Thereafter the ejidatarios voted unanimously not to give Chona any indemnity.

This litigation was very dramatic, first because of the glaring hostility between the two women, the ex-mistress and the son's aunt; but at a more covert level the struggle concerned the *common-law wife* (the *amasiato* was a clever legality) of one of Scarface's blackest killers, who had killed González' nephew, among others, and who was finally murdered by one of Scarface's major fighters. The defendant was of course a legal heir too. This case had been decided beforehand against the widow, who will have to depend on working out and doing other things for her support. What would Sebastián have said about this decision? We must recall that Sebastián was killed by Jaime, the special, intimate friend of Aquiles.

During this and other matters the delegate frequently appealed to the audience at large ("what does the assembly think, what is the opinion of the ejidatarios, what do the compadres think?"), but, more often, and more significantly, he appealed to individual Princes: to Don Elías (Scarface), to Toni Serrano, to Gregorio Serrano, and to Ezequiel Peñasco, in that order, and once to Bones, who is as tongue-tied in public as he is

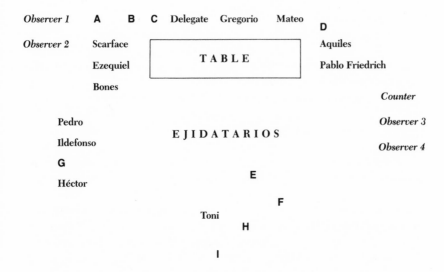

[The letters stand for other, minor leaders. The names of the Observers and Counter were not recorded, but one of them must have been Melesio.—PF, 1986]

EJIDAL ASSEMBLY

trigger-happy in an ambush. These individuals, when called, usually give very short one- or two-sentence party-line answers.

The seating arrangements at this assembly are indicated in the "Ejidal Assembly" diagram. The only important Prince not present was Camilo, who was attending to his county treasurer's business in Zacapu.

Several other important matters were subsequently discussed.

1. The flooding of the ejido by rains due to the bad drainage from uncleaned canals. There was a long speech by Scarface in his hoarse, unconvincing but sinister forensic style, saying that *this* ejidal government would insist on the completion of all ejidal obligations, no exceptions. The old musician arose and asked that all defectors be posted. Then Gregorio read TWO warnings which had been sent to Pedro González about clearing his part of the canal, to be followed by county and state admonitions. Since Pedro's plot is regularly worked and he cannot be killed because of a federal *amparo* (writ of personal protection), we may assume that he is soon to be deprived of his plot "for failure to fulfill his ejidal duties." Since he is old and has no job, this would hasten his demise.

2. Gregorio Serrano said that he would not deal with *medieros* [sharecroppers by halves] in the future; many persons and almost all widows work their land by halves. The delegate then brought in that *accord-*

ing to law, minors, widows, and the aged (70+) have the right to work land by halves, but actually it is recognized and not acted against when others do it "to the point where they are counting furrows."

3. Wagons for transporting the harvest are bought, repaired and managed by the ejido—money is needed for this.

4. A large sum is owed to the ejidal bank because of the crop failure. This should be paid (I doubt if it will be).

5. Any ejidatario working abroad [out of town—PF, 1986] should get an identification card both for himself and for his representative. The delegate reminded the people that anyone who ceases to work a plot for more than two years loses his rights, and that widows and minors must reside in the pueblo.

There followed the most interesting part of the meeting. Gregorio Serrano opened with a long speech (15 minutes) proposing a tax to complete the building of the school [a new industrial school—PF, 1986]. He is not an effectual or very articulate speaker. Then a large, young ejidatario in the audience said, "Why not pay our debts to the ejidal bank first?" Scarface then got up and made a long speech about how long the building had been standing uncompleted, how we should leave something for our children, and the question of sacrificing for the pueblo had nothing to do with paying debts (this several times, and definitely quashing the other man). He also is an ineffectual speaker, leaning back against the wall, glancing at the audience off and on, and talking in phrases broken with the usual interjections.

Aquiles then made a long and very convincing speech, standing near to the audience, gesturing like a boxer and carefully choosing his words and forming his sentences; his was the only address with a beginning, a middle, and an end, and the audience was obviously impressed. The basic themes were *material progress through sacrifice* and *community rivalry*. He described going to see Dámaso Cárdenas [then governor, the brother of Lázaro Cárdenas—PF, 1986] on a personal matter with Bones and encountering the president of Zacapu with delegates from Tarejero, among others, and Tarejero offering 85,000 pesos for the completion of a school, at which Dámaso Cárdenas picked up the phone and began ordering engineers, and so forth. The other communities proposed comparable sums. By contrast, Naranja, which had the first school in the region, before Zacapu, had only 2,000 for new pavement.

One woman [a plant] then proposed one *anega* [100 liters] of corn, and she tried to back out when they wrote her name into the records. The women in the front of the hall did a great deal of conferring. Another one of them then asked, "My friends ask that earlier they gave a lot of money and where is it?" This was a voice of sedition. A man in the rear of the hall proposed one-half *anega*. A woman then proposed that they wait till the harvest to determine their ability to pay. One leader refused to give an opinion! Toni Serrano said only, "Let's vote." *Suspicion and passive resistance* was in the air. Mateo made a short speech saying that the 218 *anegas* would be stored and offered to the governor as such (he really thinks this would prime the gubernatorial pump, although the 8,000 pesos it would yield would be slightly less than half of the 18,000 they need to stimulate the other 18,000 from the government).

The leaders were clearly at an impasse; they sensed that they had lost and lacked the confidence of the ejidatarios because of former embezzlement in which these younger sons would probably not engage. The vote brought 23 for one-half *anega*, 9 for one *anega*. At the former showing, when the 23 emerged, Aquiles and Melesio began to say "majority" and Pablo Friedrich said very loudly, "No!" showing the Thoreau-Luther [see Chapter 9]. The vote of 32 out of 151 was complete defeat for the Princes. They seemed nonplussed until Gregorio Serrano and Mateo began to declare that the majority had not voted. "What do you think? Why didn't you vote?" The delegate said a few words, but the business was officially ended and I left shortly afterward. The princes were depressed, with grim looks on their faces; Aquiles had his head down on his hand (Scarface had left before the start of the debate).

Later that afternoon I asked Aquiles and Ezequiel Peñasco what they would do now. "We'll have to exact it," said Ezequiel. He was mad at the man who had proposed paying the debts and said that all the former construction had been carried out by 85 voluntary workers (this is wrong).

["The effective idealists" had tried democratic persuasion, and it had failed. Now the leaders would go back to force—PF, 1986, summing up a long paragraph in PF 1956 notes.]

3. Ejidal Meeting, Attended February 17 and Written Up February 21, 1956

On Feb. 17 the second meeting of the ejido was held which had been called two days previously by the federal inspector of complaints who had been sent from the Department of Agrarian Affairs to deal with a petition for the restitution of ejido plots made and signed by six men: Florencio Serrato, Emiliano Espinoza, Agustín Galván, Sixto Hernández, Leonardo Sosa, and Miguel González. These were the same six cases which the deceased leader Agustín Galván had, according to Joaquín de las Casas, been "pushing very hard," and because of which Agustín had been eliminated [see Chapter 9 below]. Sixto Hernández and yet another [earlier] petitioner [probably Pilar Garcilazo—PF, 1986] had both died since an earlier petition was drawn up [probably in the 1940s], and their heirs and successors chose not to represent them. Two of the petitioners, Emiliano and Miguel, likewise elected not to appear at the meeting, or represent themselves in any way, deeming it wiser not to irritate the princes but to live in peace hoping for an eventual restitution. The inspector had spent most of the intervening two days in Zacapu, but during our long conversation on the afternoon preceding the meeting it became apparent that he was pretty close to the princes and had already decided that they were in the right and that the plaintiffs were battling for no good. How big a bribe was paid to the inspector?

The first thing the inspector did was to question [one of the two men] who did appear, where the rest were; a two-day period had been set for the purpose of giving ample time to the plaintiffs to make their representation. When the inspector asked this, someone from the back of the hall said, "Ezequiel [Peñasco] says that they don't need land."

Florencio Serrato then burst out, "They haven't come because here they kill everyone who asks" (pedir, to make a petition). At which Bones, who was sitting in the front left corner, snapped back, "And you, who's killed you?" (that is, if they kill all petitioners why have they left you out? do you think you are so brave?).

The inspector then proceeded to name each plaintiff, asking the audience why they had not appeared and why they had been deprived of their plots. The answer was that all of them had "risen up in arms" in 1940–41 as Almacenistas (supporters of an unsuccessful candidate for president), and had left their ejido lands abandoned for more than a year. [Actually the candidate's name was Juan Andreu Almazán, but it appears to have been (folk?) etymologized to Almacén, the Spanish word for "warehouse"—PF, 1986.] This was roundly denied by Florencio Serrato, although he contradicted himself, since at several times he turned around at someone speaking from the floor and said, "You were with me then." [This was not a contradiction: he meant that they were with him in rising up, not in abandoning the fields—PF, 1986.] Finally the implication came to be that the plaintiffs had abandoned the fields for a much longer period of time, at which Florencio burst out, "Listen, listen, I'm not an outsider, I'm from here and I have my plot, there you have it, number 20." [The obvious flaw in the thinking and the case of Florencio and of Leonardo Sosa—who had now come forward to speak for himself—was that they still considered those particular plots theirs, rather than making a general case for restitution; this made the position of the defense much easier because all they had to do was to argue that the present holders had acquired complete rights through cultivation and usufruct. Florencio and Leonardo were attached to their concrete soil rather than being able to think legally—PF, 1956.]

The inspector then began to badger Florencio about no one else having shown up, to which he replied, "WE are all together. If I ask you to lend me your shirt, do you give me a piece of it? No, you have to lend the whole thing" [which was ironic because "the whole thing" hadn't shown up]. At this point, however, the inspector was beginning to build up a case by implication that Florencio had made a false representation to the Department and that he was not actually representing the six men, but only himself. There was also some confusion resulting from the fact that Florencio thought of himself as also representing Pilar Garcilazo in spite of the fact that the latter was not on the federal protocol of the inspector.

The inspector then began to push the question of the reasons for the plots having been taken away. Leonardo Sosa said that "he didn't know the reason." Florencio answered that, "In the first place, because we don't pay contributions, and then because we were Almacenistas," implying that neither charge was founded, but bringing no proof that they were not.

The inspector then opened up with his major point, which he continued to harp upon for the rest of the session. "The majority is against you and you can never fight against the majority. You have to win the good will of the majority, convince them that you are good sorts of people (*buenos elementos*). I have the position, the job of informing myself, of investigating the matter, and nothing more. I don't have the right or the duty to act in these cases. I can't set myself against the majority, the masses, because the duty/obligation (*deber*) is with the masses." We may assume this to be the governmental attitude as expressed by such inspectors, and it means that they try to discourage divisive litigations and try to back the status quo for the sake of communal unity and peace. [The inspector was also repeating the Caso position, probably as per their stipulations—PF, 1986.]

Camilo Caso then spoke for some twenty minutes with considerable effect, driving home the point that under the Agrarian Code the plaintiffs had no possible right to their particular plots, since they had not been cultivating them for over fifteen years (an obsolete case, *caso añejo*) and that on the other hand no one had any right to expropriate the present workers who by the same number of years and far more than the minimum of two had won their titles to the land. The only hope of the plaintiffs was to work in peace and await a favorable decision by the community (i.e., the princes).

The inspector was obviously impressed by this talk, said a few words, and then Aquiles Caso spoke shortly, the gist of which was, "They want to divide the pueblo again and to divide the pueblo is a crime (*delito*). Their actions are filthy and it's a scandal that they are coming here. . . ." This brought a major value into the light and apparently met with the approval of the inspector and the muttering majority. The position of the princes is that they have now secured peace and communal unity and it is a *crime*, punishable by "execution" as in the case of Agustín Galván, to cause division in the town by stirring up complaints at higher governmental echelons. The part to be played by the individual in Naranja, according to the princes, is to be a hard-working citizen and offer help at the town hall, in which case proper recompense will be accorded and consideration will be taken of former rights. To push home this point that justice and land control should and equitably could remain in the hands of the local leaders, Camilo and his half-brother Aquiles cited the cases of four others who had "risen up in arms" as Almacenistas, had lost their plots, and had subsequently been reinstated as ejidatarios when they showed their good intentions (*buena voluntad*). One of these men was cited and came to the front of the hall and confirmed their argument. The ideal, legalistic position of the Princes, based on values of peace, communal unity, and personal loyalty, should not be confused with the actualities in accordance with which kinship, favoritism, and a spoils attitude play an important part.

The inspector then began to push Florencio as to something he had been mentioning frequently, that it was not the majority which opposed him but only a few individuals (*elementos*). Who were these elements, asked the inspector. Hesitating, Florencio pointed back at Camilo, and added, "And your uncle too. Who is your uncle, isn't he here? No, he's, he's in Morelia."

"What's he called?" asked the inspector.

"Elías," said Florencio in a whisper.

"Elías what?" asked the inspector.

"Elías Caso," (that is, Scarface), whispered Florencio.

Florencio would not say who the "third element" was, but he must have been referring to Bones or Toni [in 1956 I crossed out these names and wrote Aquiles and Boni over them—PF, 1985], and fear silenced him because they were sitting just at his left. Toni then got up and, grinning like a schoolboy playing a prank, said, "This lad (*muchacho*) keeps saying that here they kill all those who don't keep quiet. I want to ask: why have they still not killed him? It looks as though he thought he was very brave."

The meeting closed around 8:00, after three hours, but the inspector and some of the princes continued writing until 11:30, and the inspector stayed on until the afternoon of the following day.

The inspector was an able and aggressive young man of about 25 who kept the situation well in hand.

Part Two. Structure and History

I have described nothing but what I either saw myself,
or learned from others of whom I made the most
particular inquiry. The task was a laborious one,
because eyewitnesses of the same occurrences gave
different accounts of them, as they remembered or
were interested in the actions of one side or the other.
—THUCYDIDES, *The Peloponnesian War*

CHAPTER 3

Political Ethnography: "Confidential Friend" and Related Categories [1]

> The third person ending -*mba* (e.g., *pirémba*, 'his/her sister') has . . . a postpositional alternate that is used for compadres, friends (e.g., *amik-hémba*), and the like—it is a morphological symbol for a set of culturally defined primary ties.
>
> —FRIEDRICH, "Tarascan: From Meaning to Sound"

When exploring confidential friendship in Naranja, my lead questions were, "Who are your best friends? . . . friends of confidence?" and the like. Then a pause. "In Naranja?" or "In the pueblo?" Longer pause. "Or in the whole world?" Naturally, these questions varied in content, spacing, structure, and timing. Later the person would be asked what friendship meant to him in general. Typically all these questions were posed in a comfortable, *à deux* situation—sitting on the edge of town, in the (otherwise deserted) town hall, or while walking or working together. The interviewing on friendship was done during the last half of my eighteen-month field trip, so I already knew most of the men well. [Today (1986), thirty years later, the men, in retrospect, seem to have been intrigued as much as anything by these questions and interviews—like an innocuous game. With the advantage of hindsight, I can see how fruitful it would have been to move various steps further and thoroughly question each man about the friendship relations between his friends: how does your friend Jaime feel about your friend Juan? This would have deepened my understanding of transitivity in friendship. I should also have looked more closely at friendship between women.]

The personal discussions were complemented by checking observed behavior, that is, actual patterns of association. A typical file card or slip of paper would contain the following information: Names, Purpose of Association (e.g., a game), Time, Duration, Place, Comments. Hundreds of such cards or slips were assiduously collected. Both the questions and the specific observations had as their context the hundreds of hours of interacting with these men in the fields at work, at drinking bouts, and so forth. The results are discussed below and are also mapped on sociograms which both condense and clarify. (A sociogram is a map or chart of a set of interpersonal structures and/or dynamics in terms of at least one discriminating variable.) The patterns of close personal friendship and their interconnections with kinship and ceremonial kinship demonstrate some of the strengths and weaknesses of the Caso cacicazgo at the time of the fieldwork; an optimum way of getting into the nitty-gritty of politics is to chat with people, especially leaders, about who their friends are, where, when, how, and why.

The structure of friendship moves and preserves social relations in Naranja, and it has political functions that, in general, depend a good deal more on it than it depends on them. One striking discovery in these investigations was the degree of consciousness and explicitness regarding these structures, functions, and dependencies. The average leader is keenly aware of friendship and, with few exceptions, of just who his friends are—almost as if he had the names at his fingertips. There is little variation in the meaning of the term "best friend" or "close friend." The concurrence of definitions on this subject, in fact, constitutes one of the more striking common denominators of value in the community. It turns out that the average person, including the leaders, usually names from three to six friends of confidence, often stopping definitely after the last with an emphatic "That's all, Paul." The range of friends a prince may have runs from none to well over ten, as will be documented below.

What is the meaning of "friend" in terms of indigenous culture in Naranja and in terms of the local language (after noting the etymological curiosity that the Tarascan word for friend, *amígu*, is a borrowing from Spanish)? A friend, first of all, is a person toward whom one feels affection (*amistad*) and confidence (*confianza*), and with whom one wishes to associate in work and play. Friendship reflects psychological factors; it seems to me that it involves an inner attraction, what Goethe called "an elective affinity," that typically develops during maturation in the same village. A friend is also someone who will provide economic aid in the form of money, the loan of a team of oxen, and so forth. Friendship often arises from sharing a cooperative enterprise, and the memory thereof—for example, of having harvested corn together in the sierra and then walked home together drunk. Friendship differs greatly from economic indebtedness, but does interdepend with it.

What is a *confidential* friend? Confidential friendship entails a greater interdependence of feeling, and the inclination or habit of sharing in doings that are often private or intimate. A confidential friend may be someone to whom one can whisper, "Look, I know such-and-such a woman over there. Let's pay her a little visit tomorrow night." Such a "disrespectful" proposition would be impossible between brothers, and, in general, between compadres of baptism.

A confidential friend is also someone with whom one can discuss covert politics, even hatch a conspiracy. I participated in numerous whispered conversations between friends in which the "egoism" and "ambition" of others was laid bare to the bone. Other tricky matters can and should be discussed between friends; as the confidential friend of one man, I felt it consonant with my role to warn him that he had been accused of violating a pubescent girl. A confidential friend is someone who will provide unflinching support in times of danger and duress; it is obviously wise to have a few close friends of confidence.

Structure is meaningless without individual cases to show how it works. Several of the individual responses to questions about friendship deserve special mention here, partly because they illustrate the extremes of variation, partly because they illustrate the mixture of personal and social factors. Martín, in the first case, frowned when I asked the question and, after some thought, affirmed that he had no friends of confidence in the pueblo or in this world. His answer, startling from a man who had spent his life in this small village, was confirmed by my own subsequent observations. Martín was the socially isolated second in rank in the weaker faction whom we saw above fleeing to his house before the knife-wielding Aquiles and who, as we will see, was shot in the back on Christmas Eve about 1970.

Carlos, a second case, is relatively docile and non-aggressive (*pacífico*) and was the only unmarried leader at the time of the fieldwork. He is also one of the most popular and, indeed, fondly regarded men in the village. He insisted that he had only one real friend because the other possible candidate, Aquiles, was too involved in politics.

Crispín, the important opposition leader, illustrates a third situation. In typical Naranja Indian style, he named five leaders in the village. But when asked about the Zacapu factory and the labor union—of which he was secretary at the time—he broke into a broad smile and named at least a dozen "friends, good friends." Thus Crispín is still strongly Indian in his feelings about local friendship, whereas he has adopted the urban mestizo patterns when it comes to his workplace in Zacapu. He participates in both the village pattern of delimited, relatively genuine friendship and the urban mestizo patterns of relatively diffuse and utilitarian friendship—without being particularly aware of the differences, of the degree to which he is bicultural in terms of this vital symbolism.

Fourth, a unique response was provided by the frequently unique Bonifacio, whom we last heard (in Chapter 1) discoursing on abstract religious problems. In answer to my query he threw his arms wide apart and said:

"Everybody!"

"Everybody? But don't you have some who are more intimate, closer?"

"No, I don't. I look on all as equal."

"Why?"

"Because if someone has intimate friends it means they go around drinking. I don't want any of that. I want everybody to be equal. That's why you don't see me wandering around in the streets. . . . I dedicate myself to my work, or go home."

This answer reflects Boni's extreme anxiety about slipping back into alcoholism and delirium tremens, and points to another meaning of "close friend": drinking partner. It also seems to correspond to Boni's concern with masks, comic façades, and the like, as evidenced by his responses to the Rorschach cards (Psychological Appendix B), and so raises basic questions about the necessary relation between various kinds of friendship and the degree of façade or lack of it in an individual or in the patterns of a whole culture. In terms of friendship, Boni, like Martín, is a sociometric isolate.

The fifth case is a group of friends and reminds us that, depending on the culture and the situation, friendship groups can be triads (or more) as well as dyads. Friends are characteristically loyal and affectionate, but it is difficult to predict anything with certainty. Various field methods would lead one to imagine that the friendship between Mateo, Jaime, and Aquiles is highly intimate. The sentimental Aquiles calls the group "the three inseparables." But this friendship has its rubs, especially because Aquiles, the superior in intelligence and status, tends to dominate over the other two. Indeed, that is one reason he likes them. His friendship for them is also based on self-interest: Mateo is well-liked and respected in the town at large, and is courageous, while the brooding Jaime Morales ranks as a dangerous and experienced gunman, the killer of another outstanding gunman, Gabriel. Incidentally, Jaime nurses a generic hatred for Americans because he was abused or tortured in a Texas jail, and it took a while for him to accept that "Pablo is different," as Aquiles puts it.

The surprising strength of the covert tensions between Jaime and Aquiles was clarified one night after "the three inseparables" had returned from a mammoth drinking bout in Tiríndaro (this custom of carousing in the neighboring village reinforces the reputation there of Naranjeños as "badmen"). The three continued to imbibe in the Naranja town hall. Aquiles' face was a grinning, pale, and occasionally tearful mask. Jaime, his pistol visible, jammed into his pants over his belly button, mestizo style, began to direct a long, partially coherent soliloquy in my general direction. All he really cared for, he said, was the good of his pueblo. He would "kill Camilo, and Aquiles, too, if necessary . . ." Such statements, behaviors, and vacillations of friendship through time show that both friendship and political factions are more fragile than they may seem in any given year, month, or day—and suggest that we be skeptical about predictive models, particularly when they ignore time depth and the complexities of character.

Let us now turn to certain specific structural relationships and their political functions. Three such structural facts stand out. The first is the isolation of the cacique, Scarface, and, to a lesser extent, of the second cacique, his nephew Camilo; Naranjeños are aware of this isolation and comment on it. The second fact—not a part of native consciousness, as far as I know—is the general complexity of friendship relations (granted that there are more friendship structures in some other societies). The third structural fact is the clustering of friends around certain focal individuals; people are partly aware of these foci in the sense, for example, of saying that someone is well-liked. Let us take up these empirical generalizations one by one. I should emphasize that they resulted from much spadework in the field and subsequent analysis of data, and sometimes came as real discoveries or "illuminations."

First a prefatory word about the Sociogram of Friendship. I constructed it with elegance in mind, but was motivated primarily by questions of content. Thus, the position of Scarface, at the top because he is cacique; of the older men, to his right and his left because they are his age-mates; of the groups around Toni and Bones, both major leaders; and of the two younger subfactions to the right and the left—all this reflects substantive political rather than formal criteria. The sociogram is actually crude because it conflates behavioral and observational data with the value judgments expressed by the leaders. There ought in principle to be many superimposed and conceptually/graphically interrelated sociograms for the following: (1) each man's first choice of best friend; (2) his other choices; (3) evidence of reciprocity, transitivity, and so forth between the members of little sets; (4) evidence of friendship in terms of play and the like; (5) evidence in terms of work and other, more obviously economic behavior. However, the conflated, reduced model will have to serve here and now as a partly heuristic, partly descriptive device for representing, not a native view of structure qua structure, but a network of human bonds of which the leaders are more or less aware; these men have a fairly good idea of who each other's friends are. This set of bonds also helps to define native categories and is in turn partly determined by their meanings (see also the complementary Sociogram of Ceremonial Kinship near the end of this chapter).

Scarface Caso occupies a prominent and isolated spot in the friendship structure. The ten leaders of the opposition and one or two other Gonzalistas abominate him for what they feel he is: an uneducated cattle rustler and murderer who rose to power because of the support of his nephews, myrmidons, and political connections at higher levels. The less political bulk of the village's population feel a mixture of respect and fear, fear be-

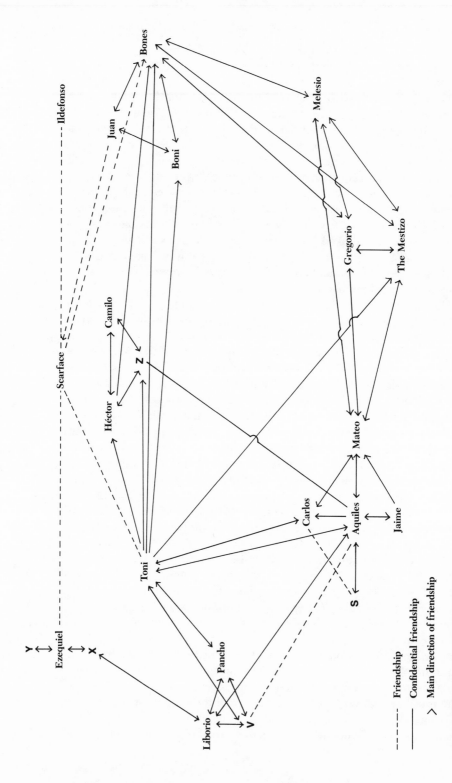

SOCIOGRAM OF FRIENDSHIP

----- Friendship

——— Confidential friendship

〉 Main direction of friendship

cause of the danger to their lives and land if they run counter to his will, respect because of his power in the town and region: several persons have told me that Scarface is the private secretary of Lázaro Cárdenas! But Scarface is not liked by the ruling leaders either. Not one named him as a confidential friend. For most of the leaders he is basically the long-established cacique to whom they are bound through years of shared activities and vicissitudes. His weakness in friends of confidence almost had fatal consequences during the attempt by his nephew Juan Nahua to usurp the cacical status; at the nadir of his career in 1953 only a few nephews and friends held faithful. On the other hand, we must remember that other princes such as Toni and The Mestizo act as his bodyguards and, in that situation, would presumably defend him with their lives.

Scarface's lack of friends grows in part from the peculiar image of him in the minds of the Naranjeños, including their leaders. This image more or less corresponds—as also in the case of his nephew, Camilo—to his own image as the feared and "interminable" cacique. A leader of his genre and mettle should, one gathers, be jocular and amiable in a patronizing sort of way. Scarface intermittently drinks heavily and is talkative in his cups (a useful weakness for the anthrohistorian!). But even at such times he is watching and does not fully relinquish an underlying, stern distance. He is ready at all times to roundly berate a prince and has deserved the reputation of being able to devastatingly castigate truant cohorts. At times his carousing has been followed by moves against his then drinking companion. Genuine familiarity, moreover, might breed contempt and inhibit and reduce the effect of his exercises of authority, which, as things go, rarely downgrade the victim. Scarface is in some ways analogous to what a grand patriarch of the entire community would be; his behavior resembles that of some Naranja fathers within the confines of their homes.

What are some of the bases of his power? Scarface has always stuck close to Naranja, to his political kindred, and to his (formerly confidential) friends, upon whom, as he well knows, his position must ultimately depend. For the long years of his rise to cacique, especially during the thirties, he was a friend of many leaders such as Ildefonso Serrano and Ezequiel Peñasco, in some cases on a confidential-friendship basis. His present, alienated position in the friendship structure is a comparatively recent development, and he continues to be supported through friendship, albeit indirect friendship, with many important leaders.

Scarface illustrates a crucial intersection between the emotional structures of friendship, on the one hand, and, on the other, the larger, impersonal structures of social stratification. His anomalous place in the friendship patterns of Naranja complements his conduct toward "friends" in other parts of the state, particularly Morelia. Here he is all smiles and hearty personableness toward the party functionaries and regional leaders in the state political hierarchy. Camilo acts something like Scarface in these matters. Nephew and uncle, then, with their huge incomes, their Masonic connections, and so forth, have partly moved up and out of village society, even though they continue to live there, to dress like peasants, to sometimes work the fields, and to claim, "I am a peasant, we are all peasants here."

The hail-fellow-well-met brand of association with other políticos outside Naranja is in the case of both men a mask for their characteristically shrewd and jealous understanding of the actualities of these social and political relationships. Scarface had been chatting in typical mestizo style with a young shyster lawyer who was making some of his campaign speeches for him during his campaign tour for state senator. But as the man of law walked up the dirt road ahead of us to help get gas for our truck, Scarface dryly remarked, "That pal will have a fat ass in ten years" [as I realize when copying this in 1985, this is the sort of animadversion that Tarascans make (in Tarascan) when watching mestizos in the towns]. And when their personal careers are involved, both Scarface and Camilo, on the basis of a cunning assessment of the real power relations in question, will blankly and even violently altercate with persons on a high political level. At a major political banquet in Apatzingán in 1956, Scarface refused to shake hands with the national senator and accused him cholerically on several counts.

Pedro González of the weaker, "fallen" faction occupies a position within his faction that is analogous to that of Scarface among the Casos. Pedro is said to act superior vis-à-vis his local supporters. Most of his friends are far-away politicians. His protracted residence outside Naranja (mainly in Morelia) allegedly made him conceited and "egoistical." A complaint or accusation of some of the Caso leaders and some of the villagers is that Pedro "doesn't acknowledge his own people/town" (pueblo). In his case, then, the cacical image has become exaggerated and distorted. [Pedro, incidentally, died alone in his house two decades later, and was only found several days after the fact.]

The complexity of friendship patterning is the second main point, or empirical discovery. Most of the leaders are related by three to six ties of confidential friendship and several additional ties of lesser friendship. This makes for an apparent stability and strength at any one time. Any new factional division will always carry over most of the pre-existing friendships, although, of course, these may be partly changed, broken, or realigned. A crucial discovery during my analysis of fieldwork data was that a majority of the friends of all leaders are also leaders and, moreover, that the most important leaders, such as Gregorio, are confidential friends only with other leaders. Only about 10 percent of the confidential friends of the princes are from outside the circle of major and minor leaders. The princes, in other words, constitute a special subgroup within Naranja that is mostly associated and befriended within itself and is, to a considerable extent, governed from within itself (granted that this relatively inward-directed friendship is complemented by ceremonial kinship, which links some princes outward to ten or twenty *compadres* each, many of them not princes). The structural fact of the comparative introversion of friendship supports my claim, based on traditional political theory, that "the princes of Naranja" should be classed as an oligarchy—granted that it is unstable through time and situated in a society without clearly marked or demarcated classes.

Friendship within the ruling group contrasts dramatically with the situation among the leaders of the weaker faction. The Gonzalistas have few friends: Martín Valle and Daniel León seem to have no confidential friends in the village. The two intellectual leaders and former law students have friends only in Zacapu and the state capital, Morelia. Pedro González himself has only a few friends, and these are outside Naranja. Crispín, the factory worker discussed above, is the only member of the faction who has the balanced friendship ties typical of a Caso leader; significantly, he is also the only fallen prince who is respected and liked by some of the Casos. The simplicity of the González structure, then, derives in part from the paucity of individuals involved. But other forces more germane to our analysis also contribute to its skeletal quality. It is the end-result of the history of the past thirty years and of the personalities of the leaders themselves. Friendship and faction are largely unintelligible when extracted from their local historical context.

Another principal aspect of the skeletal friendship of the weaker party is the manner and quantity of their human associations. They are embittered and disillusioned by the outcome of the factional struggle, and they cannot accept Scarface. They do not even associate with each other very much, nor with the villagers in general, as was shown to me several times when, a week or two after an important happening in the pueblo, the fallen leaders had not received any word of it. They have become isolated and tend to remain in their homes, or are away in Zacapu, Morelia, and other cities (where many have second houses). They are relatively defenseless, and most people avoid them in order not to be accused of "going over to Pedro." Laborers who work for them are in danger of harassment or worse under the Caso "boycott." People who damage or destroy their property generally go unpunished.

In addition to complexity and the isolation of the cacique, a third general feature in the structure of friendship is the way it clusters around key leaders (see the sociogram of Friendship). Immediately below Scarface in authority is a nucleus of three immediate friends, often to be discovered together playing afternoon card games. Camilo, "the second cacique" in some ways, is the leader of this triad. He is followed by his cousin Héctor, formerly an important athlete, who enjoys great influence in the covert politics of the town (e.g., the nocturnal meetings of the Caso leaders). The fact that these two men, two of Scarface's much-accused nephews, should hobnob almost daily with the son of the town's leading corn trader (see Economic Appendix B), is one of those ironies of fate, or rather, conflicts between actuality and ideology, for which Mexico is deservedly renowned. In this cluster, in any case, friendship is strongly reinforced by economics.

A second noteworthy cluster of friends was, until 1954, made up of "the big three in questions of assassination," that is, Boni, Bones, and Juan Nahua. The deeds of these stalwarts have been described in Part I. The cluster is structurally of interest because two of its members are nephews of Scarface and one of them, Juan, is related outward to the large Nahua clan. The popular and lecherous Bones is connected by confidential and ordinary friendship to other princes in all parts of the network—a salient fact in the sociograms and the analysis. By 1956 this bundle of "fighters" had largely disappeared: Juan languishes in exile in a Mexico City slum, while estrangement endures between Bones and Boni as a consequence of their taking opposite sides in the "Juan Nahua Affair." I have included the cluster here because of its significance for almost the entire period from the reform to the present. In addition to overt, behaviorally checkable patterning, political sociometry should sometimes include important relations and clusters that may be mainly a matter of memory or of potential.

The popular, respected, and sometimes roguish Toni Serrano is the center of a third cluster of friends that includes Bones and two Casos, Aquiles and Boni. Toni's friendship nucleus is interesting because he is neither the center of an active subfaction—although a passive or latent one may well be there—nor of a small, exclusive group such as that of the three Tarascan-speaking princes led by Pancho Orozco. Toni, rather, is befriended by a widely distributed circle containing men from all factions, even Gonzalistas. This structural situation, like the others described here, correlates with what one would expect from the man's personality: Toni's cunning opportunism and horse sense preserve him from highly emotional or lopsided affiliations.

There are several smaller groups. One, consisting of older men, centers around the loquacious Ezequiel. These leaders, all influential and relatively unacculturated, have held minor offices and form part of a limited "public opinion" that the caciques do take into account. Another group or cluster consists of five adult Nahuas. Another is made up of the three Tarascan-speaking princes mentioned above, including the ribald jester Liborio and the serious and physically powerful Pancho Orozco.

A friendship cluster of great political significance centers around the able and ambitious nephew of Scarface, Aquiles. It comprises all the younger leaders in the Caso faction, their average age being thirty-one, and includes the gunman Jaime Morales and three graduates of the Indigenous Institute (for bilingual primary teachers) in Paracho. The members of this cluster have joined with the triad under Pancho Orozco to form a subfaction, calling themselves "the effective idealists" (*los idealistas efectivos*); they proclaim a "sincere desire" to work for the good of the pueblo. Under the astute leadership of Aquiles, they may emerge as the winners in a future struggle for power against the slightly older subfaction led by Gregorio. Thus, three decades after the revolt and reform, the "effective idealists" are the most ideological group although the younger Gonzalistas run a close second, as did the failed faction of Juan Nahua. All these factions have very similar ideologies (public works, education, and so forth), and contrast with the Catholic Action group (discussed in Chapter 4).

There is a definite cleavage between Aquiles and Gregorio. The latter leads one of the most important friendship groups. It includes Melesio, Bones, The Mestizo, and several others, with Toni Serrano and even some of the peripheral Gonzalistas in far-flung alliance. These men, in their thirties and forties for the most part, are held together by years of shared experiences in work, play, and politics. The group is not fundamentally loyal to the Casos, and in 1953 and 1954 it swung against Scarface and backed Juan Nahua. Gregorio, although its youngest member, has already held several political offices. His strength and influence derive from his personal friendship with other leaders, his athletic abilities and record, his considerable personal wealth, and, finally, his role as the political representative of the large and propertied Serrano kindred, outstandingly his four brothers and his agrarista father (who, incidentally, is the scion of one of the two mestizo families that ran the town in the days of the landlords). But as functional as these relatively material or at least tangible strengths is the "ineffable quality" of so-called leadership ability which, in his case, also includes a startling sang froid and an impervious sense of security that—according to Aquiles—is currently expressed through "arrogance" toward the lesser folk of Naranja. The political muscle of this group around Gregorio, in any case, led Scarface to make two concessions to his stereotypical role of the established and distant cacique; he definitely treats Gregorio and Bones as equals, the former as a "friend" whose political support he needs, the latter as an "old fighter" and "old revolutionary" with political status and influence in the community.

We can see that friendship is nucleated around a number of key individuals into groups that include other members of the oligarchy, but also some strong or talented men who keep a low political profile. Most of the friendship clusters contain at least one nephew of Scarface. Thus it can be seen that he actually enjoys a broader base in the friendship structure than one would at first suppose. On the other hand, Scarface also exerts himself to attract and retain the loyalty of men at or near the center of friendship groups—as in the case of Bones, Ezequiel, Toni, and Gregorio. Enough comparisons have already been drawn to the relatively weak structure of the Gonzalistas.

It may be concluded that the strength of a cacique is partly a matter of the sheer number of supporting leaders and fighters, particularly talented ones, as well as the complexity and the intensity of the support that his immediate supporters enjoy from their friends. Clearly, such support may be partly or almost wholly indirect in the case of confidential friendship, because to the degree that a successful cacique acquires ties outside the village he will tend to downgrade or even disown his former allies. Finally, the specific lines of friendship nucleation are always a good guide to the general actualities and trends of any ongoing factionalism. On the one hand, political factionalism determines friendship in the sense, for example, that relatively few friendships cross the bitter lines of an active feud; on the other hand, the pre-existing and in many ways more fundamental lines of confidential friendship heavily determine the structure of politics within a faction and the direction of new schisms and fissions. It is in this asymmetrical way that the structure of friendship interdepends with the structure of (factional) politics.

Let us now turn to kinship and how it interrelates with ceremonial kinship, drawing both on the anthropological literature and on several of my own earlier analyses. The additional goal, as already noted, is to show how these two kinds of kinship articulate with those of friendship.

Kinship in Naranja seems to pattern in terms of five units or categories, each with diverse political functions and meanings. The immediate family of parents and children is the smallest familial unit, the one from which the larger entities are built. Fathers, brothers, and sons are supposed to respect one another, and are bound by a personal loyalty that is hardly ever broken: the only cases of brothers being in opposite factions— Daniel and Joaquín de la Cruz (during the revolt) and Bones Gómez and his brother—can be explained on idiosyncratic grounds, that is, Bones' character and, apparently, Daniel's jealousy. When the immediate family gets sundered this way, one or more of its members simply withdraws from politics (Bones' brother) or leaves the pueblo altogether (Daniel moved to Cantabria, former seat of the landlords). Homicide between immediate relatives has, to my knowledge, occurred only in the case of a reputed witch who allegedly helped murder her husband. On the more positive side, any immediate relative is morally obligated to avenge any other and there have been many demonstrations of such rudimentary loyalty. Almost all acts of the vendetta produce political repercussions, and political violence periodically recharges the vendetta.

The father or the most able brother functions as head of the immediate family (*jefe de la familia*), and the nucleus of a cacicazgo always includes the brothers and sons of a cacique (largely a latent or potential rule in Naranja, where the caciques have usually lacked such relatives as available, active males, although, as has been emphasized, cousins and nephews have often figured as surrogates). The cacique gives orders to his nucleus of close relatives but also, at a more symbolic level, plays the role of patriarch to many others in his faction and even to many of the peasants in the village at large.

The second unit is the ejidal family, usually consisting of one or two parents, their sons, and several (or even more) other relatives; the group as a whole calculates its kinship by blood or marriage, usually from a relative of some sort who acquired rights to the usufruct of a plot in the ejido during the agrarian reform (1924) or as a consequence of partitions and expropriations since then. Almost all the 218 ejido plots, which are legally inalienable, are divided among ejidal families and should be inherited according to bilateral descent. Each of these families has a head (*jefe*) who represents it with a vote at ejidal assemblies. The same families predominate at the town assemblies, that is, the ejidal families as a group make up the great majority of heads of families in the town as a whole. Moreover, almost all the men who are active in village politics not only are the heads of ejidal families but also own land in the privately held "indigenous land" (*tierra indígena*); the great part of the latter land is owned by these same men. Some princes, such as Camilo, control both lots of private land and two or more plots in the ejido.

The third familial unit, the household (*casa*), also is bilateral in that kinship is traced through both men and women. The household includes at least one nuclear or extended family living under the same roof, or sometimes in two contiguous houses or huts. The members of a household always share the same courtyard (*patio*) and the same back yard or animal yard (*corral*). Except for a half-dozen fairly wealthy families, the houses and huts of adobe have only one to four rooms, all built over the same floor of earth, which is kept packed hard. Approximately one-third of the households contain families that are extended in ways that seem diverse although they always involve ties of blood and/or marriage. The remaining two-thirds are made up of joint fraternal households (two or more married brothers), a father and his sons, or an extended family built around a mother-daughter line—for example, the grandmother-ejidataria with her three daughters (one a widow, two abandoned by their men). All in all, twenty-nine kinds of familial aggregates were found in the seventy house-

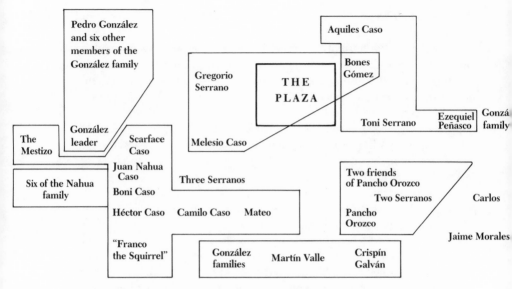

RESIDENCE MAP. Blocks indicate groups whose cohesion may be increased by residential proximity. Most of the blocks are separated by side streets. The national highway (Avenida Revolución) runs through the town from east to west, just south of the houses of Scarface, Melesio, Toni, and Ezequiel.

holds visited in the course of a census. The actual location of the princes and other past or present leaders is mapped in the "Residence" chart; note that most leaders in both factions reside within their respective sections and that these sections are contiguous—presumably reflecting that this was originally a united faction, or "one family." The street names on the Naranja Map, incidentally, indicate the politicization of the town; all but one are names of political leaders or events.

The majority of the households contain at least one ejidal family, with the result that many individuals actually speak as the heads not only of families but also of households at the town meetings, as well as representing ejidal families at meetings of the ejidos. And some households contain more than one ejidatario, because some leaders or sons of outstanding leaders may continue to live with their parents or other ejidatario-relatives even after getting married and acquiring a plot of their own—for example, Aquiles and Nana Ana. In general, however, a household does not contain more than one ejidatario; strong feelings in the village support the principle that the 218 plots should be divided among the maximum number of households, and in this emotional context the categories of household and immediate family are confused when it comes to interpreting the rule in the Agrarian Code that one immediate family should not

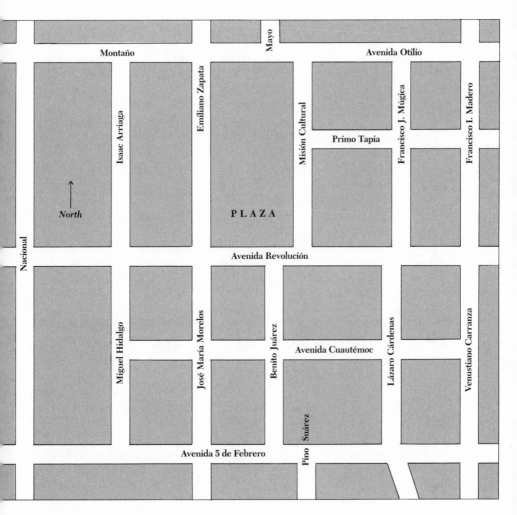

NARANJA STREET MAP

enjoy the usufruct of more than one ejidal plot. The men of a household, finally, are always to some extent tied to each other by shared domestic and agricultural life, and are supposed to back each other up politically. But, in comparison with the immediate family, which is relatively solid politically and comprehensively determines the political path of the individual, the members of a household are more prone to become divided under the strong external pressures of politics.

All three of the units mentioned so far—the immediate family, the ejidal family, and the household—entail relatives, sometimes distant ones, residing close together, usually beneath the same roof. The physical closeness and bonding colors and significantly determines the quality of politics in a little village, as can be seen not only in the conceptual parallels between the family, the political faction (*partido*), and the village as a whole (*pueblo*), but also in the wordings, idioms, and images of the peasants themselves. The emphasis on personal loyalty within the faction, or at least within its nucleus, is to some extent a conceptual and emotional elaboration of the loyalty that is enjoined and also observed between fathers, sons, and brothers; similarly, the ideal that all the ejidatarios are supposed to be equal—"We are all peasants here"—is like an extension of the feeling that brothers should be treated and respected equally within the family. The local tradition of criticizing a cacique with a mixture of respect (*respeto*) and resentment (*rencor*) and the widespread fantasies of assassinating him would seem to be psychologically congruent with the general patriarchy within the family and the deep perturbations that have shaken it during and since the Revolution. The peasants seem to feel that the community is an extension or analogue of the family, or, as they are accustomed to say, "We are all one family here." To repeat Aquiles' revealing wording, "One should kill morally, without making the other person suffer more than necessary, or plead"—that is, family members should not be tormented (this feeling may also reflect a reaction against happenings in Tiríndaro). Finally, the same customs which support the family have their analogies in the ideology of the leaders who appeal to peace, unity, and the autonomy of the pueblo during almost any public assembly. In pointing out these relations between words and meanings in different domains, I am aware that the usage of kinship terms is, like all of language except mathematics, partly metaphorical.

This brings us to the last two kinship categories, both of them large and neither deriving from coresidence. The kindred (*parentesco*) is, in the most superficial terms, the sum of one's relatives. Kinship is traced through both men and women and includes, among others, one's parents' cousins and one's own second cousins. But the kindred also takes in relatives acquired through marriage; for example, the siblings and parents of one's spouse and the parents of a son- or daughter-in-law (*consuegros*); all of these affinal relatives—a bit confusingly in the present context—are called "political relatives" (*parientes políticos*). One should show respect to all these types of relatives, and the peasants generally observe the norm in practice. On the other hand, the composition of these groups varies enormously, and relationships through marriage, not being as well defined as those through blood, can be exploited and neglected in several ways. In any case, it is from this total of fifty to a hundred or more persons that a much smaller number, usually about seven, are selected on the basis of compatibility, neighborhood and neighborliness, and cooperation in agriculture, and it is this smaller number that serves as a sort of protective wall. We have seen that the core of a faction tends to consist of a few uncles, nephews, and the like. It is curious and surely of psychological import that the personal (e.g., political) support groups run to about the same number each—a half-dozen or so, not just the politically active kindred but also intimate friends, the nuclear family, and, as will be shown below, the compadres of baptism.

Of particular interest are the ties of relationship through women, as contrasted with those through men. Despite the patriarchal cast of the culture and the tendency for fathers, brothers, and sons to form extended families, the political kindreds which structure, inform, and vitalize politics may be partly or almost entirely "matrilineal." To begin with, Primo Tapia, the cacique who led the village to agrarian reform, was supported, in the main, by six cousins (first and second), all of them sons of sisters and (matrilineally reckoned) first cousins of his mother. The more recent major cacique, Elías (Scarface) Caso, who more or less dominated from 1937 to 1956, has been doing so mainly through the support of two second cousins and six nephews, all of them related to him through women, three of them sons of his sister—that is, Camilo, Boni, and Aquiles: "When the politics gets hot, it is the nephews who support their uncle," and "nephews" here would be taken to include the sons of female cousins as well as sisters. The untimely death of so many fathers, particularly those active in politics, explains in part the salience of groups that are related, if not strictly matrilineally, then at least through women in some sense, that is, by political bonds mediated through women; neither of the two caciques just mentioned—Tapia and Scarface—had brothers or a father by the time he was an adolescent (Tapia's father had left town). Tapia never had children, and Scarface's sons were too young to figure in the three decades of politics under consideration here. Another motivation for "complementary matriliny" and other alliance through women is that brothers are often involved or at least potentially involved in competition for land or land-connected power, whereas this is unlikely for the sons of sisters and highly unlikely for the sons of matrilineally connected cousins. Affiliation through women, moreover, is a potent basis for political alliance because sons learn from their mothers many of the values and emotional sets that underpin concrete, personal loyalty and also many of the generic values and axioms which partly structure and determine politics. (It should go without saying that when I use the terms "matriliny" and "matrilineal" in this discussion I am not implying some articulated subcultural theory on the part of the villagers; I am simply describing the way things work.)

In addition to the Casos there are several other nucleations of kinship that are important politically although not large enough to be called "political families." With one main exception at least some leaders in each one of these groups are linked to the Casos. The powerful Serranos are tied to the Casos by friendship and ceremonial kinship. Only the Ocampos are cut off, as one might expect, as are three of the families that led the community before the agrarian period (with exceptions that almost prove the rule, such as the wife of Aquiles Caso, who was abducted by him at gunpoint); in fact, few members of these latter families still remain in Naranja. The far-flung ties of the Caso oligarchy partly confirm the claims of its leaders that they are "with the pueblo." The defeated faction of Pedro González, on the other hand, is relatively isolated from the various nucleations of kinsmen and the leaders within each. "Defeat" and "isolation" are, of course, relative terms and subject to the political fickleness of leaders and human populations generally. The fragility of these factions, partly shown by the schisms of 1928, 1936–1937, and 1952–1953, is barely counterbalanced by the continuity of primary group and economic ties. People repeatedly told me that although Pedro's group had been defeated, a few events could change everything and the Gonzalistas would control Naranja.

The last category of kinship or family relationship is the "political family" of persons who share the same name (or a small number of names) as a patronymic or matronymic, plus a perimeter of other allies through blood or marriage, ceremonial kinship, friendship, or economic interdependency. In other words, these are groups with a bilaterally articulated kinship core of sorts, with some emphasis on the patrilineal line. In the pueblo today there are five large political families and a few smaller ones. The political family, like the political kindred, is constantly being compromised and altered through courtship and marriage. Marriage, we recall, is by arrangement between the parents and young people about 10 percent of the time, and the parents and their socioeconomic situation influence the growth of a courtship in various ways; many courtships unquestionably are inhibited or even blocked by factional boundaries. Nevertheless, 90 percent of marriages happen during (often early) adolescence after a romantic courtship followed by elopement or the literal capture and abduction of the sometimes unwilling girl. A considerable fraction of these marriages cross the lines of faction and of political family. All the big political families such as the Casos, Ocampos, Nahuas, and Serranos have at least one member who belongs to the faction opposed to that of the majority of its members. The role of convenient fiction in constituting these groups has been described intermittently above, especially as regards the faction called "the Casos," which after 1920 was made up of the relatively wealthy de las Casas and the relatively impoverished Casos. The groups actually are linked through the descent of some Casos from the prolific ancestral figure, Ambrosio de las Casas, and through the (politically crucial) marriage of Tomás Cruz to a niece of Primo Tapia. The bottom line—about which the villagers are explicit—is that the Casos and de las Casas are two different families in terms of economic background, kinship and friendship networks, and even "culture" in the sense of education and the like, but that they are "one and the same family" politically. The men of this "one and the same family" did in fact remain united until 1937, when they split between the men loyal to Scarface Caso, on the one hand, and Pedro González Caso, on the other. By 1956, after twenty years of factional strife, the village remained divided among the dominant but minority family under Scarface; the opposition under Pedro; at another level, a third family (the Ocampos), most of whose members lived outside the village; and last, possibly, several nascent factions with a familial core such as the group around Gregorio. Many if not most villagers remained uncommitted. Nevertheless, the people keep on speaking of "one family," or of what had been one family.

The political family differs from other categories mentioned so far—the nuclear and ejidal families, the household and kindred—in that its basic purpose, not just one of its functions, is political. The majority of politically active men belong to one of these families, and politics is seen as an interfamily struggle. During the more stressful periods, when politics "heats up," almost any member of a political family can serve as a victim when it comes to vengeance—with the exception that in Naranja (but not Tiríndaro) women and children have been spared. A structure-changing event in the history of Naranja was the exodus about 1934–1935 of over thirty families in the Ocampo faction (see Chapter 5), almost all of them related by patrilineal lines as the members of the large political family that had been responsible for the First and Second Partitions of the communalistic ejido into family plots.

The political family shades off into the political faction. On the one hand, the villagers tend to think of factions in terms of political families. On the other hand, plenty of observed behavior, as we have seen, supports positing the faction as an almost entirely political group that is centered on (the core of) one political family but that also counts on at least one or two other families; in 1956 each faction included at least one person from every political family, a structural detail of no little interest. A faction also counts on the loose affiliation of a fraction of the village that is normally considerable but numbers a good deal less than half, sometimes only two or three dozen nuclear families. In other words, the village usually is divided between two factions, but a large percentage of the population remains fairly uncommitted. The factions are often called "parties" (*partidos*), but we must remember that they differ drastically from real parties because of their local, familial, and even personal character. Nevertheless, ever since the wealthy Torres opposed the agrarian de las Casas, through the Casos-versus-Ocampos period, and so on to the present, the major factions have always been linked clearly to real parties and other formal organizations in the state and even the nation (as will be partly detailed in Chapters 4 and 5). Also, as something of a local, Naranja specialty, the factions have always been informed by an explicit if simplified ideology (in the sense that ideology is defined on pp. 240–241).

To sum up what has been said about kinship groupings: The five kinship groups and the marginally kinship-based factions show markedly different connections to the subsystems of kinship, economics, and politics. At one extreme, the immediate family and the kindred are the most rooted in kinship as defined in terms of blood, the *compadrazgo*, and so forth. The household is defined somewhat more by economics, and the ejidal family even more so. The immediate family and the ejidal family are defined by cooperative labor to a high degree. The political family is mainly political in the sense of entailing factors of ambition, power within the village, and so forth. The political faction, finally, is almost entirely political in its functions and motivation, with many ties into the region and state.

We turn now to the third part of this chapter, and to the third type of important primary bond: ritual or ceremonial kinship. There are four kinds of godparent: of confirmation (*de confirmación*), of the ceremony of the crown (*de corona*), of marriage (*de boda*), and of baptism (*de la pila*). One's godparents and one's godchildren number from ten to forty or more. Godparents have obligations, above all when it comes to contributing to a wedding or taking in an orphan (godparents of baptism). The ties between godparent and godchild have been weakened somewhat since the anti-clericalism of the thirties. In 1956, they were less important than the tie of *compadre* (or *comadre*) that is formed between the parents and the godparents of a child on the occasion of baptism. Such baptismal compadres should respect each other, and they do introduce the term repeatedly in their conversations. The compadre tie is emotional and to some extent sacred. It is stronger than the tie between first cousins. "A compadre of baptism is almost a brother." The prohibition of incest is extended to a man's comadres, and even to the parents and children of a comadre or compadre of baptism. Compadres and comadres, incidentally, are chosen after considerable discussion within the family, the husband, whose voice usually counts for more, being concerned with his compadre; often, of course, a married couple is chosen such that both husbands and both wives are compatible or even good friends.

The system of compadrazgo—a term not actually used in the village— surrounds every adult with about four to eight persons (sometimes more), usually of about the same age, with whom the individual has grown up and in whom he or she has confidence. It is presumed that one needs and desires more or less that number of compadres and that one's political be-

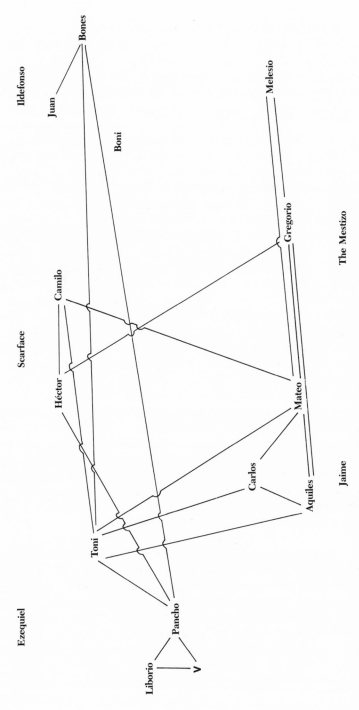

Ezequiel   Scarface   Ildefonso

Liborio

Pancho

Toni

Héctor   Camilo   Juan   Bones

Boni

Carlos   Mateo   Gregorio   Melesio

Aquiles   The Mestizo

Jaime

SOCIOGRAM OF CEREMONIAL KINSHIP (*Compadres de Bautismo*)

havior will be influenced by such relationships. Not one of the fifty-odd leaders over forty years on whom I have information has chosen a brother as a compadre, nor are first cousins (*primos hermanos*) normally chosen. This demonstrates or at least suggests that the institution in question functions to create ties of support and obligatory respect instead of reinforcing or intensifying ties where such behaviors are automatic in any case; my memory in 1986 is that several men in Naranja explicitly pointed out to me, in their vernacular, the "political redundancy" of having a brother be a compadre too. The compadrazgo thus gives every individual the opportunity to complement and patch up breaks in what anthropologists call the web of kinship. In the same vein, in Naranja the compadrazgo is rarely a means for social advancement in the simple sense of allying oneself with someone useful higher up: one does not choose a compadre because he is wealthy or in a higher social category (e.g., more educated), as is common or even the standard in mestizo communities; rather, one chooses someone whose loyalty one can trust. "The mestizos choose their compadres on the basis of interest or advantage (*según el interés*); an Indian looks for someone in whom he can have complete confidence." Naturally, there is an exploitative or utilitarian element more often than this normative quote would indicate, especially on the part of the poor and landless; I am thinking, in particular, of some of Camilo's compadres. However, it still holds that ceremonial kinship in Naranja is comparatively horizontal, organic, and, if you will, genuine.

The compadrazgo has some political functions, or at least implications. Compadres usually vote the same way and display a degree of political attachment that can be amusing. As one leader shouted out once during an ejidal meeting, "Compadre, compadre, do you need your compadre's permission to go to the bathroom?" In any case, a cacique who is planning an act of violence has to take his victim's compadres into account. Since most fighters and leaders have at least some compadres, an attempt to kill one of them may produce a strong counterattack—as in 1939, when the two immigrant mestizo gunmen wounded Bones and were pursued and shot within hours by his friends and compadres. On the other hand, the obligation to avenge a compadre is weaker than that between brothers, and the loyalty between two compadres is often not mutual and can change over time for political reasons (among others). Today at least three leaders in the Caso faction are compadres to leaders in the González faction; Aquiles and Gregorio, ambitious and envious rival leaders of subfactions, are also compadres of baptism; Bones is still the friend and compadre of Juan Nahua. Such conflicted situations can produce tragedy: of the two homicides between compadres, one occurred in 1944; people spoke of it with sadness and condemnation, and the killer has not been seen since he left town shortly after the event. I lack evidence on feelings about the other murder.

The compadrazgo has three other functions that are significantly political and that became, for me, exciting discoveries of a partly covert system. The first of these other functions—now heuristically captured in the Sociogram of Ceremonial Kinship—is that it binds small blocks of leaders to each other. At least two such small blocks—for example, that of Aquiles, Mateo, and Carlos—functioned as discrete political entities in 1956. Such leaders who are compadres follow the pattern of recognizing and reaffirming their tie in conversations. It is rare, on the other hand, for this tie to be symmetrical in that each man is a godfather of the other's child (called the compadrazgo of intensification in other parts of the world). Nevertheless, the three strong leaders in the block that includes Pancho are such reciprocal compadres, and also are friends of confidence and work their lands cooperatively and talk only Tarascan with each other and their wives—who also cooperate with each other in every way, from baby care to cooking to fieldwork; the men are like brothers and their wives are like sisters. The group does not really adhere to any faction, although in recent years it has been going along with Scarface, as noted above, and belongs to Aquiles' "effective idealists." Such small blocks and dyads of compadres have to be reckoned with politically—although the leaders obviously don't think or talk in terms of sociograms and other explicit formulations and representations.

The compadrazgo, in the second place, links leaders *out* of the oligarchal circle, as is enumerated in the Table of Ceremonial Kinship. The popular Carlos, for example, has over twenty such compadres of baptism in the pueblo. The Mestizo is curious in having many such compadres but none within the group (other notorious gunmen—Boni and Jaime—have no compadres of any sort). In any case, many of these compadres in the general population of the village do not participate much, if at all, in politics. The outward-linking function of the compadrazgo is crucial because it can broaden, compound, extend, and also complicate the oligarchal friendship structure.

In the third place, the compadrazgo binds the caciques to other leaders, albeit often indirectly (e.g., the compadres of nephews). The compadrazgo also ties some of the leaders horizontally and vertically upward and outward to other politicians in other towns, and in the state and the nation; the four most powerful men in the pueblo (two in each main faction) have almost all their compadres *outside* Naranja; Camilo, for example, has eight out-of-town compadres, including men from Colima and Mexico City. A leader like this, therefore, has in his ritual kinship as in his friendship moved up into the outside, mestizo world.

Ceremonial Kinship

	A	Bi	Be	Car	E	G	H	Ja	Ju	Ma
Aquiles				✔		✔				✔
Boni										
Bones									✔	
Carlos	✔									✔
Ezequiel										
Gregorio	✔						✔			✔
Héctor						✔				
Jaime										
Juan			✔							
Mateo	✔					✔				
Melesio						✔				✔
The Mestizo										
Pancho			✔				✔			
Camilo							✔			✔
Scarface										
Toni	✔		✔							

Let us sum up some of the politics of ritual kinship. To a significant degree the respectful compadre tie conflicts with political partisanship, and has the least to do with it. Only Aquiles, Gregorio, and Pancho Orozco show the sort of far-flung ceremonial ties to other leaders that one might expect. And one is struck by the paucity of compadrazgo within parts of the oligarchy: Scarface, Ezequiel, Boni, Jaime, and The Mestizo have no compadres at all within the group.

Why are so many of the princes relatively isolated? In part this is because many of them tend to avoid religious ceremonies. Second, some of

Mel	Mes	P	Cam	S	T	Other Leaders	Other Compadres
					✔	2	10
		✔			✔	1	
					✔		20+
						1	3+
✔							Many
			✔			1	
							Many
✔			✔		✔	3+	
							3+
							20+
					✔	4	
							Many outside Naranja
							Many outside Naranja
		✔					

them, notably Camilo and Scarface, are not popular in the town at large and tend to stand aloof. In the third place, leaders such as Camilo have, as noted, moved into the mestizo pattern of forming compadre ties on the basis of interest rather than respectful affection and so are linked to senators and generals. Fourth, the strong respect enjoined by the compadre tie does conflict with political comradeship in some ways—hence the lack of bonds for notorious gunmen ("badmen"). Toni and The Mestizo have, they say, been on the verge of becoming compadres, but always have desisted "because when we get drunk we often call our best friend a cuckold (*cabrón*) and that is all right, but if we became compadres he would get mad and say that I wasn't showing him the proper respect." The normative respect between compadres is often strained in the case of Aquiles and Mateo because of the way they drink together. In sum, the compadrazgo is limited and conflicted in its relations to political structure, at least in the case of the strong cacicazgo in Naranja. It links leaders outward from the village, and it may link them indirectly to some other villagers. It is less important and less functional than kinship or friendship. As one leader put it, "If you make yourself a compadre with another prince, and then the politics changes, *then* what do you do?"

CHAPTER 4

Political Organization

But in political power, its lack of any sense of class or
functional unity and the low intensity of its reactions to
political situations barely allow the rural portion of the
population to hold its own. . . . Obviously, it is not yet
an enlightened proletariat in the Marxian sense, for
its members are not yet aware enough either of the
operation of national politics or their own potential role
in it to act collectively so as to be a decisive force in
determining Mexico's political present.

— ROBERT EDWIN SCOTT,
Mexican Government in Transition

In all Mexican towns which have ejidos, and that would be the great majority, formal government is split and bi-institutional, with powers and
duties divided—sometimes clearly, sometimes fuzzily—between two political groups: the civil arm and the ejidal arm. The civil arm concerns
itself with the administration of the town at large, whereas the ejidal arm
usually limits itself to the affairs of the ejido. Throughout Mexico this
double system actually functions in widely different ways, depending on
the importance of the ejido in the particular community and upon various
local traditions.

In Naranja the formal jurisdictions of the civil and the ejidal arms are
clearly distinguished. The two bodies are of approximately equal importance, and the civil and ejidal officers enjoy similar degrees of prestige:
the financial rewards of the latter are greater, but the former exercise a
more pervasive and often sensitive degree of political control. The deeper
and more controlling fact, in any case, is that in Naranja the two arms of
government complement each other within the system of informal power
that was characterized above via the seven political life studies; in other
words, the informal "oligarchy" runs both of the formal governments.
Comparative data can be found in several of the Mexican community
studies, although most authors have in fact largely limited their discussion of politics to the overt and formal organization. Let us begin with a
relatively overt and normative depiction.

In Naranja a mayor, a judge, a secretary, and alternates for all three should be elected annually by a general meeting of all adult citizens over eighteen, on the basis of slates presented by "parties" or other politically motivated groups. The officers should be of good character, working residents of the community, and at least one of them should be literate and able to handle documents and correspondence. The election should take place in a democratic manner, with submission of slates, a public discussion of the qualifications of the candidates in terms of communal interests, and a final vote by show of hands, uninfluenced by any form of intimidation. Each of these civil officers receives one peso a day. Women, while not excluded legally, have never served as officers, nor did this arise as an issue during my fieldwork.

The mayor is charged with calling town meetings, with administering the usufruct of public lands, and with certain types of economic activity such as calling together the owners of the unfenced *tierra indígena* to decide when the harvest should begin and when cattle should be let in to forage. In addition, the mayor, assisted by the judge, is primarily responsible for representing the community in its relations with larger political units; for the organization of secular fiestas and the fiesta to the patron saint, Our Father Jesus, in its commercial aspects; for assigning public work; for the levying of taxes and dues on land and real estate; and for special projects of various kinds. Finally, the mayor is supposed to take the lead in improving and maintaining the community, whether this means recording the last will and testament of a gasping old woman, or fixing the benches, or getting the lawn mowed on the plaza. He should take the lead in trying to solve the many problems that confront the town in the course of his year of tenure. The mayor should be a man of mature and highly regarded judgment, but he may be quite young.

The principal duties of the judge are to maintain peace and order by dissuading, arresting, or in some other way discouraging persons bent on misdemeanors and crimes; in such duties of law enforcement, signally in dangerous instances where it involves the disarming of an armed and drunken man, the judge is normally assisted by the mayor, and often by the mayor's alternate and his own alternate. The second major duty of the judge is to preside at the sessions of the local court, which consists of the three civil officers. He summons the delinquent parties, solicits testimony, and presides over the confrontation between the principal parties. Finally, he passes judgment after the case has been discussed and negotiated at a session in the back room. More serious cases usually involve the loss of blood, or irreconcilable marital difficulties. These are sent on to the county court in Zacapu along with an explanatory document that has to be issued in Naranja. The judge, ideally, should be a man of considerable experience in the use of small arms and in the forms of physical violence that might be required for the performance of his duties; should have a reputation of being able to enforce the law; and, finally, should enjoy the respect of the citizens as to his probity and ability to pass a just sentence.

The secretary is primarily responsible for generating documents and handling the correspondence between Naranja and larger governmental entities. For this reason a fully literate man is needed, and younger men tend to be preferred for the office. The secretary is also expected to take the lead in all other kinds of "paper work" such as taking or copying the census, recording landholdings and taxes, reading governmental manifestos at meetings and, often, representing the community on the outside on occasions that require a better-educated, politically more sophisticated individual than the mayor may be.

One of the three officers is supposed to be present in the town hall at all hours of the day, including Sundays, and all three are expected to participate in town meetings, governmental and communal endeavors, and the sessions of the local courts. According to circumstances, any one of the town officials can play any of the roles of any other. All civil officials are invited as guests of honor to all communal and many regional fiestas—granted rare exceptions. All officials are permitted to accept gifts from individuals desiring to influence them. They are expected to appropriate a certain portion of the income that is earmarked for the regional, state, or national government, whether from taxes or fines. All officials are to be treated with considerable respect and are often addressed by their name of office (e.g., "Secretary"). In Naranja the alternates are seldom of importance, although, for example, the present mayor took over from his post as alternate in 1955 when Toni went to the United States as a bracero, and he has occupied the position ever since.

Let us now look more closely at "how the system really works"—reminding the reader that in what follows the historical present is 1955–1956. With few exceptions, for over twenty years there has been but one civil slate, prepared two or three weeks before the town meetings at secret conventions of the princes, although also reflecting innumerable informal discussions among the princes themselves and between them and a considerable part of the town's population. At the meeting the single slate is carried forward by a minor prince or some other respected citizen. The nominees then make modest affirmations of their ineptitude, lack of time, and the like. Various major and minor leaders make speeches eulogizing the several qualities of the reluctant nominees. Then they are elected unanimously; the slate has, of course, been endorsed by the cacique and the nuclear princes. Such formal elections of civil officers excite considerable covert interest and detailed analyses within small groups. Many people do not attend these elections, partly because the manner of voting necessarily and literally forces one to show one's hand; the twenty-odd core members of the fallen party are, of course, observing a boycott; the apolitical or uncommitted majority in the town would prefer not to participate so actively in the installment of the formal representatives of an authoritarian political system toward which some of them feel varying degrees of hostility and resentment. Civil elections have been carried out by as few as forty citizens, although threats are frequently employed to force larger participation.

The *literacy* of Naranja civil officials has been in reasonable accord with the norms, and the secretaries, in particular, have ever since the days of Tapia been literate, young, and intelligent men; Aquiles is no exception. On the other hand, the present mayor is well known to have been a gunman for the hacendados during the agrarian struggle and has since regained political status as a result of services performed for Scarface. The illiterate judge, Bones, while satisfying the norms of ability in combat and often referred to in the town with all due respect as "Don Gonzalo" or "The Judge," is hardly renowned for his probity of character and, in fact, is often pointed out or alluded to with sarcasm and resentment by members of the weaker party. Thus the "good character" of Naranja officials must be viewed with the requisite relativity. The civil, as contrasted with the ejidal, officers often are citizens from the town at large and not princes. On the other hand, there has always been at least one major prince on the civil slate since the 1920s, and this is essential for the covert political organization, in order to prevent the deviations and local conspiracies for which the town hall forms such a natural theater.

The single peso a day might indeed cause one to wonder why anyone accepts political office. In actuality, the intake of each official probably averages at least twenty-five pesos a week, and he continues to enjoy the products of his lands, whether they are worked by him in his spare hours or by a son or a hired man. The first source of additional earnings by civil officials is the small gifts of one to five pesos and the many gifts in kind—cabbages, a piece of meat or fabric—that are presented by persons with official matters pending. Second, the officials always take a considerable cut from the large collections that are made for communal projects such as secular fiestas, public works (e.g., construction of the vocational school), and the annual fiesta to the patron saint; in 1956 each of the three officials took one hundred pesos from the proceeds of the latter event. Third, the fines are divided up among the local officials, and, since they run from ten to over one hundred pesos, they represent a significant cash income from "making justice." Fourth, a certain portion of the annual national taxes on land and property is appropriated by the officials, usually amounting to several hundred pesos per man. In general, then, the financial recompense for civil officials in Naranja is attractive, considering the sheltered, prestigious, and occasional nature of the work. It is a welcome change from agricultural toil—or from having nothing much to do.

The nationwide Mexican opposition to re-election, a major and apparently imperishable contribution of the Revolution to public political thinking, has not been adhered to consistently in Naranja since the heroic period of agrarian reform. The idea of "No Re-election," combined with the formal limit of tenure to one year, has frequently been violated by letting the same man enjoy office for a number of years, elections being postponed because "everyone liked the mayor" or because "the politics was hot" or because "Juan was ambitious and didn't want to allow new elections," etc. A leader called Jesús remained in office as judge for seven years, and his father served as mayor for three successive years during the protracted struggle against the Ocampos and then against the González faction. Several other men have functioned as civil officials for three or more years in a row. The present authorities have been in office since 1954, that is, two years, and show no sign of stepping down in the immediate future.

There is great variation in the workings of a given set of civil rulers due to the combination of numerous, diverse duties, widely differentiated personal abilities, the structural fact that any official may play the role of any other at any given time. In the case of the present (1955) government, the initiative for most of the mayor's functions and most of the administrative and organizing work in general has been taken over by the nuclear prince and town secretary, Aquiles Caso, the mayor himself serving as an often present but covertly obedient figurehead and façade. Aquiles calls the town meetings, addresses people (the mayor did not make a single public speech in an eighteen-month period), assigns public work loads, organizes the fiestas, autocratically appoints the members of certain committees, and summons delinquent taxpayers, in addition to handling all the correspondence and the documentary work. The mayor is often present on the bench before the town hall and is treated with deference and respect by the secretary and the other citizens, but few people are unaware that the actual administration and policy decisions are in the capable hands of the nephew of the cacique Scarface. In addition, Aquiles, who is usually on duty, has largely usurped the duties of the judge, who seems content if he gets his cut—with the taciturn participation of the mayor. Once Aquiles emerged from the town hall with a flushed and triumphant look on his face, saying, "I just executed justice (*hice justicia*), you should have seen it!" The official judge, Bones Gómez, hadn't been in the town hall for ten days. Aquiles, in his capacity as functioning judge, is able to exercise and demonstrate his superior "culture" and education (*preparación*) to the unschooled and relatively inarticulate people he is judging. I once watched him arbitrate a pathetic marital dispute between a desperately poor teenage mestizo couple. The real problem was the hostility between the young wife and the husband's mother, but the straw that broke the boy's back was that his disgruntled wife just left a pile of tortillas to cool *on the dirt floor:* "I wouldn't mind if they were cold, but I want them served at least on a piece of paper, not on the floor." This case afforded Aquiles an opportunity to hold forth in full on the subject of female nature and the fact that the relation between mother-in-law and daughter-in-law is the most difficult in this vale of tears. Aquiles generally represents the civil government in the county, appearing at the county court in connection with legal cases, and in regional and state politics (as seen in Part I). On the other hand, the main cacique, Scarface, also participates in policy decisions and the administration of the civil government, although he has held no formal office since the middle 1930s. The present situation affords a typical if slightly exaggerated illustration of the manner in which the formal political organization not only reflects but depends to a great extent on the personality of the concrete men in the government and their status and role in the informal leadership of the community.

The considerable financial rewards of civil office should not obscure the fact that the major attractions of these activities are such things as social prestige and political domination, although the degree to which this is true varies enormously from individual to individual. The pesos involved, although significant, would probably not account for the generally stated and felt desirability of these governmental jobs and the often desperate struggle caused by competition for them.

Considerable political power, in the first place, stems from formal office. A mayor or secretary is perforce an honored citizen in the town and is invited to all the fiestas, where he sits in the place of honor and is given the finest helpings of *mole* (a chile sauce used on turkey), and the first and most frequent drinks of tequila and brandy; if the official is a drinking man, office means great quantities of free alcohol. Naranja, despite the leveling effects of the agrarian reform, is still "status conscious," or rather the parameters of status have been weakened and changed but not eliminated. The possession of little symbols and accoutrements of status such as seals of office and keys to the town hall is highly significant to a Naranjeño; I have mentioned above the importance of the seal and keys during Aquiles' intrigue to depose Juan, and it is noteworthy that the former is still in charge of these symbolically charged objects (see Aquiles' life history).

In the second place, the civil authorities can and do exercise considerable authority over the citizens of the community, often acting as their intermediaries vis-à-vis the county administration, imposing heavy fines on them for "scandals," throwing them into the dark, dank, and filthy

Naranja jail for failures to pay "contributions," or, finally, imposing onerous tasks connected with public works. Perhaps most crucial and penetrating is the role of these civil authorities in arbitrating crimes and torts, often enough of a delicate or explosive nature and reaching far back into time through the chain of resentments (*rencores*) and vengeful emotions and ramifying far out into the community at large as a result of the ties of kinship. During the eighteen months of fieldwork the following cases, among others, were heard: the romantic suicide of a girl whose mother would not let her marry a nephew of Primo Tapia because he, the nephew, was "too Indian"; a case of double incest in an immigrant mestizo family (father-daughter, mother-son, on the same mat);[1] and several bitter litigations over debts. In all such cases the authority becomes privy to some intimate details and is in a position of superior and law-giver; the parties must appeal to him and argue for his favor. Needless to say, such rewards enhance service that is outwardly humdrum.

Having considered the theory and practice of civil administration, let us now examine the other mask of the Janus-faced government, that is, the ejidal aspect. The ejidal administration, the contrast to the civil administration, is characterized both by greater overt adherence to statute law, which usually means the national agrarian code, and by a more colorful combination of covert, illegal, and at times sensational behavior (see Economic Appendix A for a sketch of the main facts on ejido economics).

Every three years, in August, after a printed announcement of convocation has been posted before the town hall for one week, all the ejidatarios should assemble. At the meeting, which must be attended by a delegate of the National Agrarian Commission, a general roll should be taken. If a quorum of 50 percent is present, the slates are requested of the ejidatarios and, after they have been discussed, a vote is taken and the new officers are proclaimed on the basis of a majority decision. A total of twelve ejidal officers are elected: president, treasurer, secretary, a three-man Council of the Watch, and alternates for all of these. They are meant to function as a group. Ejidal officers receive no pay at all. The Commissariat, consisting of the first three officers just named, represents and acts for the ejidatarios either individually or collectively in relation to larger entities such as state judicial authorities, the state governor, and the Ejidal Bank. These men likewise oversee communal activities: they coordinate the harvest, report to the general assembly on the use of ejidal funds, and carry out the decisions both of the local general assembly and of the agrarian authorities at higher echelons. The Council of the Watch is supposed to survey and check on the activities of the Commissariat with regard to the statutes of the agrarian code, the use of ejidal funds, and the calling of general assemblies when they are needed.

In the normal, partly legal practice of Naranja, the effective administrative group has been greatly reduced, from the formally stipulated number of twelve to four: the president, treasurer, and secretary of the Commissariat, and the president of the Council. These four men work together on all matters. The other eight are almost never called upon, and when there is a struggle for ejidal offices, it essentially concerns these four.

All the ejidal offices have, almost without exception, been held by members of the ruling party at any given time; there is no "loyal opposition" in Naranja. Meetings of the ejido are held punctually every three years, and the rule of no re-election has never been broken; in fact, only a few men have held more than one post of any kind in the ejidal administration. At those times in the past when serious and outright divisions existed in the town, especially during the "Ocampo Period," there have been two and even more slates presented to the assembly; these were hotly argued on the floor and were the cause of violence in the side streets of the pueblo. Today, however, with the hegemony of the Caso faction, there is only one slate. This is generally cast up in a provisional manner a month ahead of time by a small meeting of some twenty princes and ten hangers-on, slightly over twelve candidates being noted down by the ejidal secretary. During the two or three weeks following, the candidates on this slate are talked about, mulled over, and variously shuffled by the princes themselves and by the town at large to some extent.

Finally, about a week before the convocation of the general assembly, the nuclear princes and about ten minor princes—actually, about fifteen individuals in 1955—hold a secret night conference, often in the uncompleted industrial school, and make the final decisions about the slate. At these crucial and clandestine meetings the principal speakers are Scarface, Ezequiel, Toni, and Camilo, and there is plenty of evidence that strong differences of opinion come to the fore and are bitterly disputed. In 1955 Scarface wanted to be treasurer of the ejido in order to personally prevent an anti-Caso conspiracy. The majority of the princes were opposed to Scarface's presence on the slate, but, after a lengthy contention, in which the forensic abilities of Camilo were called into play, a vote was taken in which only five men sided with Scarface: Camilo, Ezequiel, Héctor, Aquiles, and Boni, the floor thus being carried on the basis of the superior quality of the ayes, so to speak. The winning slate having been chosen by the oligarchal group, it is presented at the general assembly of the ejidatarios, which, despite what many would call a parody of democratic processes, is generally attended by over 150 persons, or about three-quarters of the total.

After a short discussion and the usual modest professions on the part of the candidates, the slate is elected unanimously, with only a few abstentions. In 1955 there were about thirty absences at the elections which could not be explained on political or personal grounds. The twenty-odd core members of the opposition extend their "boycott" to these ejidal elections, of course, as they do to civil elections. The normally high attendance at ejidal elections and general assemblies of the ejido is to be explained by, first, the widespread public interest in ejidal administration and politics and, second, a certain amount of coercion; if someone is repeatedly absent from the ejidal assemblies the ruling group starts to say that the individual is "going crooked," is "not with the pueblo," or will "soon be with Pedro." Finally, attendance at ejidal elections and general assemblies is legally one of the duties of the ejidatario, that is, of the head of an ejidal family, so that continued absence could, under certain circumstances, serve as one of the grounds for depriving him or her of his or her plot (for the full, vivid details of one such ejidal election, and other meetings, see Chapter 5).

The group of four officers who effectively rule the ejido work together on many of the administrative duties, such as organizing the all-important cleaning of the numerous and lengthy canals that drain the ejido lands (Naranja is sometimes accused by the Ejidal Bank and neighboring ejidos of neglect in this respect). The ejido officers also collect the government tax of 5 percent of the harvest. This collection is greatly facilitated by the fact that harvesting is done with communally administered corn wagons which simply haul the individual ejidatario's produce to the storehouse until his tax and the debt to the Ejidal Bank have been fully paid up; in some cases the ejidal officials compel individuals to pay much of the debt which they owe to the main corn trader, whose eldest son, also the best friend of Camilo Caso, awaits the harvest wagons in his truck parked just outside the ejido lands. It is ironic that this aspect of communal use of the ejido—harvesting, but now geared to enforced debt collection—should have survived from the programs of the agrarian reform! One memorable event in 1956 was when the son of an old ejidataria, whose corn had been wrested away from her in this style, went *loco* one Sunday morning on the east side of town and had to be disarmed by Toni and the mayor, accompanied by the resident anthropologist. In any case, the four officers of the ejido also work together in organizing the harvest, naming the corn pickers and captains of the brigades, and appointing the numerous watchmen who stand guard at intersections all over the ejido after the corn is ripe.

A certain division of labor has also evolved among the ejido officials, somewhat along the lines one would expect. The president generally assists the federal delegate at the important assemblies (see the Fieldwork Interlude above), presides himself at the lesser meetings, and represents the ejido on the outside; in 1956, Gregorio was frequently in Morelia or Mexico City representing the community at political functions and the ejido before state and national officialdom. The ejidal president automatically becomes the official delegate for Naranja at the Ejidal Bank in Zacapu; on the one hand, he represents the community as an associate director of the bank, and, on the other hand, he mediates between the bank and the community on the numerous occasions when the bank officials come to Naranja on official business. The ejidal treasurer is principally responsible for collecting the 5 percent national tax and the numerous special contributions which are levied for the building of a bridge, the improvement of a road, and the like; he also directs the extremely lucrative post-harvest pasturage for fodder in the ejido lands. The secretary handles the correspondence. Finally, the president of the Council of the Watch is usually in charge of the large crew of men who have to be deployed to the many outposts from which they guard the standing corn.

This summary of the functioning of the ejidal government gives rise to some questions. What are the financial rewards for these obviously time-consuming activities? Why has the history of Mexican ejidos been punctuated by assassinations arising from the competition for ejidal office? I was never able to obtain a statement of accounts; the subject is very delicate. A conservative estimate of the annual earnings, based on talking with many people, amounts to a total of about thirty thousand pesos, broken down as follows: three thousand for post-harvest pasturage, ten thousand from the "fund for material improvements" (until 1953), three thousand as graft from government taxes, at least three thousand from bribes, and about ten thousand from the partial or wholesale expropriation of the products of the plots of absent or politically objectionable ejidatarios (some of whom are unable to defend themselves). Although the mean earnings thus amount to about thirty thousand pesos (twenty thousand since 1953), a lion's share goes to the most important man in the ejidal administration.

The ways in which the spoils of the ejido are divided often cause bitter conflict within the ejidal government and may engender long-lasting resentments. At least five thousand of the incoming pesos are actually spent on the needs of the ejido itself, and occasionally a genuine "progressive" such as Juan Nahua makes his appearance and causes a gratifying portion of this capital to be used for some urgent public work. Despite occasional reductions and subtractions from the ejidal pot, it is as a rule so filled to overflowing that a Naranja peasant is willing to risk and sacrifice a great deal in order to obtain some of its contents. The struggle for control of the ejido and the central role of ejidal office in the political life of the village is thus to be explained primarily on economic grounds. The story of this ejido resembles many other stories of Mexico past and present, where political success is the quickest and often the only means to a life beyond bare subsistence. In a town divided against itself, the administrative machinery of the two political branches, the ejidal and the civil, might be expected to be held by different factions at times. In fact this happened in 1927 under the surveillance of a representative of the then National Commission at about the time the Ocampos were winning their short-lived control.

Civil government and the ejidal commissariat constitute the two formal institutions by which local out-of-town relations are regulated and managed, and through which certain statutory and positive norms are enforced by means of written codes, local customs, and various types of force. We shall now proceed to examine the political organization of larger social orbits, such as the Masonic League, and try to sketch or suggest the role of Naranja.

The Catholic movement is weak in Naranja today. Nevertheless, a group of about twenty-five women and five men have for almost ten years been working together as the local chapter of the national Acción Católica. The group is dominated by older women and, specifically, by the wealthy mestiza corn trader Anita Rías (see Economic Appendix B) and by various scions or affinally related members of the mestizo Flores family. Their duties consist principally of helping with the care and upkeep of the church, feeding the priest the one time in the month when he comes to say Mass, and organizing most or all of the several annual religious fiestas. Although the Acción Católica today pursues a mouselike and weakened existence, centering unambiguously on religious activities, it should be mentioned as a political organization because the attitudes of its members and the consequences of its work are strongly hostile to the radical agrarian ideology of Primo Tapia and to many individuals in the Caso political family. The women of the Acción all are conspicuously respectable or are struggling desperately to merit that attribute. They also are what in Mexico are called "fanatical Catholics." I spent Christmas Eve with them, listening to their jests and anecdotes about Scarface.

A second, quasi-political organization is the Freemasons. The Masons of Mexico, now fiercely independent of their Yankee brethren, still profess many of the working principles and the general liberalism of the early Jacobins. Masonry in Mexico was revolutionized by the founding in 1927 of what came to be called "The Cárdenas Lodge" which, after Lázaro Cárdenas' election in 1934, enjoyed a sort of national vogue, particularly in the middle class and among many leaders in the "popular" (e.g., peasant) sectors and in states such as Vera Cruz and Michoacán. This new lodge emphasized national independence, civic responsibility, and "a constructive life based on love, culture, work, and justice" (Brandenburg 1964: 203). In 1945 this lodge was integrated with the Mexican Confederacy of Freemasons. I am certain that Naranja leaders were active Masons throughout the Libido Dominandi period (1926–1956). By the time of my fieldwork, in any case, Camilo and Scarface, "the major elements" in the village, were highly placed in the state chapter of this venerable philanthropic, semi-secret political society; Scarface, when very drunk, claimed to be a Senior Grand Inspector General of the Scottish Rite and a "Number 33" (i.e., in the top rank). [Thirty years later, in 1986, I imagine I still can see him saying "of the Scottish Rite," because it was the only time I ever heard the word "Scottish" in Naranja.] On the other hand, both men were vague and uncommunicative about specifics beyond generalities about "civic responsibilities" and so forth. Their status in the Freemasons would go a long way toward explaining certain "magical" episodes in their careers, and their numerous powerful friends in Morelia and other cities. Much of the covert structure of Cardenista politics is articulated through Masonic lines. In the charmingly dispassionate words of Frank Brandenburg, "Freemasonry is not indispensable; but few educated Mexicans, except for militant Catholics, choose the generally slower path of building a career without Masonic affiliation" (ibid.).

I have already had occasion to mention the representatives of the National Agrarian Commission who preside at elections and at important assemblies. For Naranja this means the middle-aged man we met above (Chapter 2, section 1) with his huge paunch, checked flannel shirt, enormous handle-bar moustaches, and a silver badge as large as a saucer, who arrives the morning of the meeting and reads the official convocation and other documents with such speed that the audience is only able to follow the general drift of their sense. This delegate, an old-timer in agrarian administrations, is often referred to as "dumb" by the villagers, but the fact is that he is very well acquainted with the realities of Naranja political culture; during meetings he is constantly calling on individual ejidatarios to speak up, even if they seldom do; see Chapter 2 for a detailed account of two of these meetings.

A second manifestation of the national agrarian bureaucracy is the inspectors, or "engineers," as they are called, who are sent out by the Department of Agriculture or related organizations to take agrarian censuses, check on land use, make maps, investigate claims and petitions, and the like. These men, usually very intelligent, often graduates of agricultural schools, have been coming to Naranja ever since the early twenties; stories and documents in the archives contain many references to them, as well as, sometimes, their own priceless, factual reports. The engineers are generally treated with respect, with exceptions such as have been described (e.g., in Ezequiel's life history), and they are often bribed in cases that could prove embarrassing for the litigants. One of these investigators appeared in 1956 to investigate the case of the six men who had "surprised" the National Agrarian Commission by appealing the case of the ejido plots of which they had been deprived in 1941. The investigator, a young man in his twenties, dressed in khaki, was probably ignorant at first of the basics of the local situation, but, after two days *in Zacapu*, seemed to have oriented himself and decided to cooperate with the ruling princes. At a high point in the extraordinarily dramatic final meeting in the town hall the young investigator asked in a stentorian tone, "Elías *what?*" (that is, who is Scarface?), the rhetoric of which did not go unappreciated in Naranja; for a full description of the happening, see Chapter 2, section 3.

In the third place, the national agrarian bureaucracy becomes somewhat understood by the successive members of the ejidal administration, who, during their three-year tenure, make numerous trips to Mexico City to carry on negotiations. Usually such intimate knowledge is in personal, personalistic terms: who has the influence? whom must one talk to? whom must one bribe? and how much? In the mind of the average ejidatario, on the other hand, the national agrarian political structure is associated with the national president, federal authority in general (e.g., its custom of brutal suppression of "insurrections"), and the normative structure of the agrarian code. But this average ejidatario also knows that, as an individual, one can reach the larger organizations only through great cost, time, and, often, personal danger; it is wiser and certainly safer to work through the local ejidal commissariat, as controlled by Scarface, or simply through Scarface or Camilo as personal agents.

Finally, the Naranja community has been profoundly affected by the Ejidal Bank of the Zacapu Zone, which was established in 1951 as a response to disastrous crop failures. Although the bank has certain administrative and regulatory functions, it is primarily known in Naranja for its readiness to extend small loans, seldom of over 100 pesos, which, however, add up through the years until they often approach or even exceed the value of a family's crop. These loans, and the inflexible 7 percent interest, are collected at harvest time as described above. As of 1956, the average debt of the ejidatario family is almost 650 pesos and the total debt of the community exceeds 124,000 pesos; three-quarters of the town is in debt (see Economic Appendix A).

Most of the princes are decidedly hostile to the bank because it interferes with their political control, because it forces them to become agents for a rigorous debt-collector, and, finally, because the small loans of hard cash which the bank encourages are all too often spent immediately on food, clothes, and drink; in one notorious case an ejidatario spent most of his loan drinking in Zacapu and then came back in a taxi and had it drive around the plaza until the last centavo was gone. Bank loans to individuals do not in general result in the permanent improvements that would be achieved through investments of larger amounts in livestock or land improvement, and even here there have been gross errors: two or three years ago the wrong chemical fertilizer was sold to some ejidatarios, resulting in an almost total loss of their corn crop. There is at present widespread public resentment against the bank because of the way it enforces payments, in contrast to the more flexible customs of local lenders (see Economic Appendix B).

Men from Naranja have been exceptionally active for the last half-century in larger political organizations and nominally left-wing movements. The successes in such larger arenas of Primo Tapia, Pedro López, and others have already been specified or alluded to in this book and in *Agrarian Revolt;* Pedro González, to take another example, was a CRMDT leader and a state congressman in the 1930s. In 1951 Camilo Caso was elected alternate to the national senator from the state, and in 1956, at the time of my fieldwork, Scarface emerged the victor from a bitter fight for the office of state congressman. Considering the fact that there are only nine state congressmen and two national senators from the entire state, the rate of Naranja participation has been extraordinary. The community and the leaders in the pueblo have always adhered to the wing of the national Party of Institutional Revolution (PRI) which, to a certain degree, is marked by personal worship of Lázaro Cárdenas. The PRI ideology, by the time it filters down to Naranja—or, from another point of view, as it originates in pueblos like Naranja—consists of a bellicose and adamant attitude toward right-wing parties as instruments of "capitalists" and "believers" and a diffuse sympathy with communist ideas and techniques—coupled with a tough practice toward actual Communists in the state of Michoacán.

The role and power of Naranja men in statewide PRI politics is appreciably greater than is indicated by the formal offices cited above. PRI, as it functions today, consists primarily of small local groups of the politically active and intrenched, like those described above. One's success in the party stems not from support from a broad electorate but rather from the nature of one's personal relations with a numerically tiny group, with the "principal persons" in one's town, another dozen or two in one's region, and one or two hundred important men in the state. There are, then, successive tiers of oligarchies that are analogous in size and to some extent in structure and function (e.g., the role of the compadrazgo).

The county politics of the Zacapu region has been controlled or disproportionately influenced by Naranja much of the time since the middle twenties, when the agrarians won the land, and more particularly since 1935, when, with Cárdenas as president and Cardenista state governors, Naranja leaders were elected presidents of the county as well as entering other posts. Today the county treasurer and police chief are both Casos, that is, Camilo and Boni. This strong hold of Naranja on county political life, the latter involving a population over forty times as large as that of the pueblo, is due in part to the long-standing relations and "compromises" with Cardenista politicians at all levels, ranging from the semiliterate agraristas of Tiríndaro to Felix Ireta, former governor and currently the military commander of the Morelia Zone. Such political ties are articulated in terms of personal friendship, ceremonial kinship, Masonic activities, common economic interests, a vague but common ideology, and several other factors, all of which have conjoined to make possible the series of otherwise inexplicable successes in high-level intrigue and the near freedom from criminal prosecution that have marked the careers of the Caso caciques. The political role and influence of these men have, however, also been due to the position of the pueblo in the political organizations that serve to unite the peasantry of the Zacapu region and the state of Michoacán. The strength of these peasant entities has been magnified in correspondence to the major role of agrarian reform in the region.

Let us now briefly review this history, even though it may be familiar to some readers. Joaquín de la Cruz was primarily responsible for the creation of the agrarian committees in the indigenous towns of the Zacapu region. It was Primo Tapia, however, with his sense for organization, who forged the agrarian "shock brigades" of Naranja, and integrated them with the brigades of Tiríndaro, Zacapu, and Tarejero, thus molding an effective regional force for concerted action in agrarian reform. His activities as the elected representative of the Zacapu region between 1921 and 1924 further integrated the region as an agrarian one, both in ideology and in tactics. His activities culminated in 1924 with, among other things, the foundation of the Regional Committee which, ever since that date, has been presided over by Naranja leaders (e.g., by Camilo Caso from 1939–1950), and regularly meets in Naranja. This "Regional Committee of Naranja" originally included only the four agrarian communities named above. Subsequently, however, grants of land were obtained for fourteen additional communities, in many cases during the Cárdenas presidency and always with the secretarial help, political leadership, and, when needed, the experienced "fighters" (*luchadores*) of this "bastion of Cardenismo." Naranja leaders such as Ezequiel helped with the litigations, Pedro and Scarface provided leadership, and Bones, Toni, and others performed invaluable service in the struggles against the last local hacendados and their mestizo supporters. The assemblies of the Regional Committee, generally held every month or two in the Naranja town hall, are presided over by the president and the secretary and their alternates. Both Camilo and Scarface are frequent participants and make long and decisive speeches. One to five members of the commissariats of the constituent ejidos and three or four groups of the largely powerless and vestigial Feminine League serve to make up a body of some fifty peasants. The committee is supported by fifty-centavo dues from all the peasants in the region.

Despite the explosive commercial growth in the county seat and the recently founded labor union at the huge factory of the Celanese Corporation of America, Zacapu was and continues to be a predominantly agricultural area, peopled primarily by peasants and incessantly confronted by the rich black earth of the vast plain with its ejidos. The Regional Committee has therefore assumed an importance in the life of the area and has seized and held on to the role of political intermediary in the numerous cases where an agrarian community negotiates in Morelia or Mexico City, whether about questions of expropriation in the ejido, boundary disputes between villages, petitions for the schools or new construction, or the town's electric light bill. The Zacapu Regional Committee, realistically referred to as the "Regional Committee of Naranja," has been able to exercise a pervasive and rarely remitted control over the extracommunal political and institutional relations of eighteen other towns with ejidos. This power and its exercise partly explain the hostility toward Naranja in some of the towns, notably Tarejero, with its own strong agrarian tradition.

Over and above the Regional Committee in the peasant organization towers the statewide League of Agrarian Communities. The league includes some fifty regional committees that, in turn, represent about eight hundred agrarian communities in the state; the president of the league is the official political representative of the peasants of Michoacán. The league is supported by annual dues of one peso from each peasant and, of course, numerous bribes from interested parties. The elected officials include a secretary, a treasurer, and the secretary general; in addition there are several ordinary secretaries and a hired lawyer. All these officials have their offices in four large rooms on the second floor of a former convent next to the principal market in the state capital of Morelia. The outstanding duties of the league are to represent and speak for the constituent peasant communities before various departments of the government, to investigate and advise concerning land and boundary disputes, and, finally, to work for the granting or restitution of ejido lands in the numerous areas of the state—especially the *tierra caliente*—where reform has still not been effectuated.

The part played by Naranja in the League of Agrarian Communities has always been totally out of proportion to the size of the village. The League was founded by Primo Tapia, its first secretary general, and during the twenties and thirties some secondary offices were filled by Scarface and others. Pedro López held on for three years as secretary general of the Revolutionary Michoacán Confederation of Labor (CRMDT) after it replaced the League. In 1955 Scarface, then treasurer of the re-created League, became its secretary general. The influence of Naranja has obviously been greater than is indicated by formal office, and men such as

Scarface have frequently participated in its policy decisions as honored if informal guests.

Above the League in the institutional structure of the peasantry there rises the National Peasant Confederation, or "Campesina," located in a large building in the heart of Mexico City. The Campesina is the predominant organization within Mexico's agrarian sector, and the agrarian sector is the largest in the land (Hansen 1974:103). Its duties and jurisdictions at the national level are analogous to those of the League in the state of Michoacán, and it is to some extent the political organization that corresponds to the administrative organ known as the Department of Agrarian Affairs.[2] The institutional details of these two units, however, are not actually known by the Naranja leaders, with the partial exception of several princes, and would, in any case, take us beyond the goals of this book. Suffice it to say that the Naranja Commissariat, the Regional Committee, and several of the Caso faction enjoy inordinate influence in the Campesina, due in part to their long-term personal connections, in part to their ability to use the surplus income from the Naranja harvests to grease the wheels of bureaucracy. The principal claim of the Naranja agrarians, however, rests on the historic role of Primo Tapia in the formation of the antecedents of this National Peasant Confederation: its major official delivered the keynote speech at the Primo Tapia fiesta in Naranja in 1956, stressing the importance of Primo's organizational work, his appeals on behalf of the landless peasants attached to the haciendas (*acasillados*), and, finally, his personal affinity with Ursulo Galván of Vera Cruz, one of the founders of the national entity.

CHAPTER 5

Political History: *Libido Dominandi* and the Rise of Elías (Scarface) Caso (1926–1956)[1]

That was no longer the struggle for the lands. That was
nothing more than politics (*la pura política*) . . . the
split that brought death, orphans, and widows. We
entered a time that was bad, bad!

—JUAN NAHUA CASO

1. Economic and Political-Historical Overview

Naranja has lived through an extraordinary number of transformations in this century that were saliently economic, but also social, cultural, and religious—particularly in light of the feedback among these factors. In the 1890s the villagers were cut off from what was probably their main source of livelihood (e.g., through fishing with seines and butterfly nets) by the drainage of the great marshlands. This economic and social cataclysm was followed by the establishment of landed estates where many of the villagers worked for low wages in order to produce cash crops for the national markets; otherwise, like young Scarface, they trekked south to toil as migrant laborers on the sugar plantations. In either case, most of them were transformed into a species of rural proletariat while their village was controlled by mestizo caciques in league with the new landlords and the clerical establishment.

The villagers and their culture, that is, their values, symbols, and beliefs, were possibly just beginning to adjust to these incipient and novel realities when things again were altered by the lynching in 1926 of Primo Tapia, the leader who had been denounced many times to national authorities for his pro-Communist ideology. There followed a breakup of regional cohesion and of the agrarian faction in Naranja, and then the partition of the new ejido land into ejidal plots in 1928 and again in 1931. The plots were, it is true, associated with families in a relatively familiar way but in terms of an unfamiliar overall context: the land was owned by the nation but deeded to the village to be worked, in part by the commune as a whole, in part by the ejidal families who enjoyed the usufruct and harvest of plots. Each family, however, was represented by an individual: the ejidatario. Other forms of this semi-communalistic enterprise were new, as was the welter of regulations, laws, and statutes. The constant growth of regulatory apparatus, governmental structure, and bureaucratic context and of the economic and political values associated with these forms was matched and, if anything, complicated by the simultaneous growth of factional (and anticlerical) violence, intra-village authority, and extra-village expansion through the next three decades, that is, the one-generation time span of this book. I do not have sufficient grounds to argue a unidirectional causal chain that would run from economic-political change to new values and forms to violent and expansive authority, although this was much of the story. What I can do is inquire: what were some of the main features and implications of the new politics—or, more exactly, of the new political history and political structure?

To put the basic point bluntly, politics in Naranja exemplified certain Mexican patterns—most of them universal patterns in Mexican form— but to a degree that made the town atypical and hence peculiarly edifying as a subject of study. Naranja's leaders and fighters were atypically tough, astute, intelligent, and experienced—and numerous. And they were, to an exceptional level, ideologically sensitized and committed, espousing a combination of public education, material improvements, anticlericalism, women's rights, and agrarian reform in the sense of expropriating landlords (as contrasted with, for example, improved land use). They continued to work significantly on all these fronts after the death of Tapia in 1926. Indeed, under Lázaro Cárdenas' presidency (1934–1940), the revolutionary struggle for additional expropriation of larger landholders and for redistribution to landless peasants in their region of Michoacán was to a large extent led and managed by the stirred-up agraristas of Naranja, which, as noted earlier, had a telephone and five typewriters in the town hall at this time.

But the fight for land reform also carried beyond reform, that is, expropriation, in the usual juridical and administrative senses. Naranja's new leaders and fighters were almost all from landless families. Many had, for example, lost their fathers early in life, and all of them had seen not only the success of the revolt but also how power, violence, and state-level intrigue can win big. The expropriation of the landlords thus had many implications for their understanding and for our own understanding of the psychology of cacical politics. The main implication, probably, was that the expropriation whetted the inbred peasant hunger for land in a way that was to perdure and even thrive as a driving cause throughout the three decades under study (1926–1956). Obviously, deprivation (e.g., of land) does not produce agrarista sentiment unassisted, but, when conjoined with other factors such as familial traditions of leadership, it can become a powerfully moving material cause of such sentiments and the ideology to go with them.

Increasingly after 1926 the land that you fought to obtain was in the hands of your fellow ejidatarios, and to that coveted land was tied the rich booty from cash crops, forced loans, and the graft and embezzlement that were assumed to be part of your office. The struggle among the peasants for each others' land in the thirties and forties was punctuated by events that had or came to have major political significance even though the actual amounts of land or money involved were often small in terms of the total land holdings and the cash income from them: 70 acres in the Second Expropriation out of 1,300 in the ejido. In more extreme cases, the amounts involved were almost purely symbolic: "thirty pesos" in the 1937 altercation between the caciques' wives. In partial interdependence with these ever changing economic realities there evolved a revised *libido dominandi*, that is, a lust for power as such, for the symbols and ego satisfactions that stem from dominating over the other peasants in your tiny pueblo, or from winning influence in the region and the state.[2]

This lust is pervasive and endemic in Mexico, and perhaps in much of the world; what was new was the degree of its intensity and, if you will, the drama of its enactment and realization. The methods and attitudes of the heroic period of agrarian reform turned into an exhausting factional struggle that was most condemned locally in the case of the many-on-one murders by Scarface and his associates and the out-of-town assassinations where physical clout was exchanged for metaphorical clout, or influence (*jalón*). But almost as destructive were the alcoholism, indebtedness, absenteeism, and local violence that reduced the number of peasants working the land in a meaningful way. What had begun mainly as a struggle for land for the people and a working of the land by the people evolved into what was mainly a struggle for power to the caciques during the Libido Dominandi period. Similar changes took place in many other parts of the country, but they were probably accelerated in this case by the death of Tapia.

2. An Interpretation: The Cacical Process

"Libido Dominandi" is a metaphor that refers to irreducible psychological facts of emotion and motivation and, just as much, to empirically analyzable facts about social system and process. Libido Dominandi can be seen as materializing in three interacting ways, two of which are outlined in the table below.

First of all, there is a tendency for cacical systems to become more centralized and extreme, partly because the ruling group or leader tends to lose support through disaffection, envy, and the like; this was already a problem for Tapia in 1925. The man who is the chief cacique tends to arrogate to himself, or to others whom he controls, an ever increasing number

Two Fundamental Cacical Processes (1900–1956)

Dates	Alternating Salience of the Two Basic Processes	General Period
1900	1. Centralization under mestizo caciques 2. Fissive tendencies under Indian leaders	Pre-Agrarian
1920	1. Centralization under agrarian Indian cacique, Tapia 2. Fissive tendencies led by Ocampos	Agrarian Revolt
1926	1. Following death of Tapia, acute fission between the Ocampos, led by Juan, and the Casos/de las Casas led by Tomás Cruz and Pedro González	The Ocampo Period
1932	1. Centralization under the Ocampo caciques 2. Fissive tendency led by Pedro and Scarface	
1935	1. Centralization under the Caso caciques 2. Disintegration and exodus of the Ocampos	The Rise of Scarface
1937	1. Fission between the Caso caciques	
1940	1. Centralization under Scarface 2. Fissive tendency led by Pedro González and Martín Valle	
1945	1. Fission and open opposition between the Casos under Scarface and the Gonzalistas under Pedro and Martín	
1946	1. Recentralization under Scarface 2. Fissive tendencies, unfocused	
1952–1954	1. Fission between Juan Nahua and Scarface	
1954–1955	1. Recentralization under Scarface	
1956	1. Autocratic centralization under Scarface	Absolute Cacicazgo

of political roles and prerogatives until he reaches the maximum that Scarface did in 1956. This first process of *autocratic centralization* may be met with passivity or various kinds of active opposition. The centralization is autocratic in that it tends toward the total, personalistic, significantly arbitrary control of a town or region by one man; the cacique, to cite the male-dominant metaphor, wants his pueblo "under his eggs."

Persons who oppose this first process can be absorbed, suppressed, or even expelled physically. However, opposition usually engenders the second, contrary process of *contentious fission*. This fission may materialize as armed, legal, and political conflict between more or less matched factions and may last several years, or even decades, in part because it is entangled in the interdependent processes of blood vengeance. In the history of Naranja, examples include the Ocampo period between 1928 and the mid-1930s, then the González opposition to Scarface between 1937 and 1945, but still going on after that, and a number of other contentions, notably the Juan Nahua fission of 1952–1955. All of the recent fissions have drawn on the residues of the Ocampo opposition. Fissions often involve the political function of fairly unpredictable or not obviously "political" factors, such as the almost categorical association of the Ocampos and later the González faction with music. Fissions generally come and go, and any given faction is rarely totally terminated.

Third in the tripartite process is *expansion outward* into control over neighboring areas, such as mestizo villages in the Zacapu valley, or the Cardenista networks in the state. Such expansion can be an active, integral part not only of autocratic centralization but also of contentious fission: a contending cacique such as Pedro González, whether rising or falling, will tend to look outside for collateral support. The rich details in this book, incidentally, reflect but a small fraction of Naranja's role in the huge network of political exchange, in Michoacán in particular. Naranja is quite extraordinary, even in the national context, for its degree of expansion and extra-village power generally, whereas the first two cacical processes were exemplified about equally and more or less simultaneously in their operation in neighboring Tiríndaro and Tarejero.

What I have called the cacical processes are of course nothing new, are older, in fact, than the Upper Paleolithic, and have been philosophized about in, for example, the early phases of Greek and Chinese civilization; in other words, autocratic centralization, contentious fission, and outward expansion are vital processes in practically all societies, even in all families; they are universals and, like all universals, probabilistic generalizations. What is new is the way I am examining these processes in their local-level reticulation with the changing availability of land and the extraordinary quantity of crops and crop-derived cash. The caciques, notably Elías and Severo, evolved toward ever greater centralization, with a concomitant, extraordinary rise in power until each was not only the strongest but the wealthiest man in his pueblo—perhaps of his region in the case of Elías (Scarface). One does not get much sense of personally or societally imposed limitations on power—overthrow or death being the sole terminus. Similarly, contentious fission was motivated, not only by avarice and egoism in the case of the caciques, but also by a desperate and desperately felt need in the individual peasants to obtain and hold on to an ejidal plot. While my anthropological history focuses on and even foregrounds the leaders as the visible protagonists, let us not forget that each of them as well as all the ordinary, rank-and-file peasants represents a small group of women, children, and usually other men in a household, family, or ejidal family for whom he feels obligated to fight and risk his life and who, in various ways, remind him of his obligation.[3] At one level, then, the basic process is twofold: (1) a struggle for surplus profits and power, both internal and external, on the part of one to several caciques; (2) a struggle by peasants for enough land for a family's subsistence. This simple binary picture is complicated by the presence of a number of relatively wealthy peasants, thirty or forty or more families, or about one-tenth of the total population, whose main concern is neither cacical power à la Caso nor minimal subsistence, but creature comforts such as custom furniture and social and intellectual goals such as higher education for their children. The caciques generally belong to this group, as do most of the princes, but many members of this group, particularly in more recent times, have not been leaders and probably do not want to be or simply lack leadership ability. This local "upper class" of sorts corresponds roughly to the national middle class, but, not named or recognized as such, it is a class only in terms of behavior and statistics: economic groupings, by the same token, are a matter of degree. From the Naranja point of view, in other words, every member of the ejido is still a peasant. The main exceptions are two highly educated leaders in the opposition and the regnant caciques, Camilo and Scarface, who are also more than wealthy enough to be called "rich" (*rico*)—surely a fundamental semantic category in all parts of Mexico.

The primary processes within the village are reticulated—incipiently in the case of Joaquín de la Cruz, notably in the case of Primo Tapia, Pedro López, Pedro González, and, of course, Elías (Scarface) Caso— with a struggle (*lucha* is the usual word) to extend power and influence beyond the village. At first, control over neighboring villages and the increase of one's contacts in Morelia are mainly means to greater power within the pueblo, and they may never amount to more than this for a cacique such as Severo Espinoza (of Tiríndaro). But as time goes by, power in the state tends to become the leader's primary goal and a primary drift of the socioeconomic process of which he is a part. Local wealth from cash crops and local power—in the shape, for example, of exportable violence—come to be valued as the means to getting elected alternate to the state congressman, in the case of Camilo, or, in that of Scarface, of rising to the exalted rank of Senior Grand Inspector General in the Scottish Rite of the Mexican Confederation of Freemasons. Thus psychological factors such as "egoism" and avarice and Scarface's relation to his wives not only set the tone for a period in the pueblo's history but also have to be seen as fundamental forces that interact, as parts of some more general historical process, with the obvious economic and political forces that I have emphasized above. With these theoretical considerations in mind, let us turn to the specific facts *cum* interpretation of the local history of Naranja over one generation.

3. Caso versus Ocampo: The Acasillado Question

All of the Zacapu Valley agrarian communities had strong leaders, but none of the others could match the talent, local prestige, and statewide reputation of Primo Tapia, whose death in April 1926 precipitated the breakup of regional coherence that already was fragile and troubled. Each of the four ejidos in the valley now followed a more independent course in a condition not uncommon in rural Mexico: local leaders vying for power within their pueblos are related more or less directly upward to the state and national networks without the mediation of regional leaders.

Naranja was controlled largely by Casos: the principal cacique, Tomás Cruz, with Pedro López and the dynamic político Pedro González as a sort of second tier. The mayor and secretary were also both cousins of Tapia, as was the president of the ejido; several Ocampos were in minor offices and the Ocampos were in loose alliance generally. The man I call Agustín, assisted by his brother, was a major figure in town politics. Among the other cousins in the Caso clan or "political family" was a flat-faced young fighter who had left Naranja in 1921 under dark circumstances, but then returned again in 1926, on the eve of Primo Tapia's assassination; he was welcomed and made an ejidatario. This somewhat sinister but jovial individual was to emerge as the dominant and symbolic figure of the ensuing decades, as will be demonstrated below. His tough energy, greed, and varying degrees of cunning and Machiavellian intelligence epitomize much in the at once embittered and flamboyant factional politics that the little pueblo was to endure.

The Casos were rough and able. But they were confronted by an equally rough (*duro*), able (*listo*), and much larger group which centered on the huge Ocampo lineage or political family of over thirty adult men. These Ocampos were led by six closely related and intrepid (*valiente*) agrarians: Juan Ocampo Caso, the immediate disciple of Joaquín de la

Cruz; then his son Miguel, said to be an astute intriguer and all too quick to order a killing; third came Juan Ocampo Huante, a stern (*severo*) and sanguinary leader; then his brother, the tough and strong Leopoldo, and his other brother, Hercules, Tapia's former right-hand man; and last, their father, Nestor. These Ocampos are described as full-blooded Indians in terms of race (*la raza, la cara*), swarthy of skin and generally short and stocky in build. Many of them were monolingual Tarascans, and, curiously, as will be detailed below, almost all of them were musicians in the famous Naranja band; an Ocampo had introduced modern instruments in 1885, the Naranja band played a vital role in Primo's orchestration of the agrarian revolt, and up to this day (i.e., 1955–1956) there are Ocampo musicians and band leaders scattered all over the Republic of Mexico. "We were all musicians," says one survivor.

The Ocampos, supported by numerous friends and relatives, had been kept more or less cooperative by Tapia's intelligence, charisma, and, in some cases, strong-arm tactics. But after his death their widespread, latent hostility toward the Casos changed into a more open opposition. The rugged (*fornido*) Hercules returned from exile, and within months this political family was well on its way to controlling the town. Late in 1926 the stern Juan Ocampo Huante secured appointment as chief of the Zacapu regional militia, the most obvious physical force in the area at that time. Early the next year, 1927, Juan Ocampo Caso was elected president of the ejido, an achievement not unconnected with his kinsman's office. In this new confrontation the Ocampos were befriended by men in the upper levels of state politics, albeit less so than the Casos, who were closely allied to the more radical leaders. Notable among the Caso allies were the faction of Francisco Múgica in the League of Agrarian Communities; Enrique Ramírez, the pro-agrarian governor of the time; and the future governor and radical socialist Lázaro Cárdenas. Both Tomás Cruz and Pedro López, through their work with Tapia, could draw on many political connections at high levels. Thus 1927 witnessed not only a stand-off between factions that were relatively equal in power, but the institutionalization of that equilibrium: Agustín Galván, then with the Casos, was elected mayor, whereas Juan Ocampo was still head of the ejido. Different factions controlled the two arms of government.

A definite break between the two factions was delayed by the so-called Cristero Uprising, a series of dangerously large but sporadic and ill-coordinated—or totally uncoordinated—outbreaks by "reactionaries" (*reaccionarios*) in Michoacán, Jalisco, Colima, and other parts of Mexico, mainly in 1926–1927 (although repressive action against them continued until 1929 in some regions). These Cristeros, crying "Long live Christ the King" (*Viva Cristo Rey*), were often inspired or led by armed Catholic priests. There was no such uprising at first in the three Tarascan villages, for obvious reasons, although the movement was supported in the county seat of Zacapu by the former agrarian and comrade of Primo Tapia, Ramón Aguilar. After temporarily neutralizing Aguilar's Cristeros, the Zacapu Valley Tarascans and their mestizo allies took part in campaigns in the "hot country" to the south, sometimes acting as scouts and guides for the punitive expeditions under Cárdenas and other, less distinguished generals. In 1927, an army of over four hundred Zacapu Valley Tarascans, together with two hundred soldiers (with three machine guns), was marched to southern Michoacán and Jalisco (south of the Río Balsas) under the command of Leopoldo Ocampo. There was one battle, but in general the action consisted of wiping out small groups of several to a score of desperate Cristero peasants; often these campaigns became pretexts and the texts of local radical violence against "Catholics" in a very inclusive sense, or simply middle-of-the-road peasants wary of the emergent state. The Cristero Uprising or Revolution had the effect, among other things, of directing the "revolutionary passion" of local agrarians outward against obvious or apparent enemies, or even confused former agrarians, thereby obfuscating many real problems.

The personal ambitions and the familial feuding in the Tarascan pueblos were not long, however, in finding expression in a matter of ejidal politics and deep-going ideology. These were, in turn, articulated with profound practical and ideological (including ethical) differences in the state and nation. Villages like Naranja were partly microcosms of Mexico.

The government of Plutarco Elías Calles pursued a conflicted course that reflected antagonistic ideologies. On the one hand, his administration, containing many agrarians, began with revolutionary zeal to redistribute land on a large scale, with vigor sometimes amounting to recklessness—eventually almost three million hectares, more than any president until Cárdenas. On the other hand, many of the Callista leaders had always been hostile to radicalism, particularly Communism. Calles himself had the relatively entrepreneurial outlook of a North Mexican agriculturalist and of the revolutionaries who became large landholders and ranchers (as did Calles himself in the late twenties—also a financier). About 1925, his government, consonant with these conservative, capitalistic, and individualistic attitudes, began to promulgate laws that were designed to counteract the more collectivistic features of the ejidos and to convert the ejidatario into a sort of small-patch farmer (the analogy to the Juárez Reforms of the 1860s is clear; compare *Agrarian Revolt*, pp. 12–13). Thus large-scale expropriation was being legally bled of its communalistic consequences even while serving to co-opt the support of landless and radicalized peasants. The total complex of laws, decrees, principles, legal measures, and political stratagems lies beyond the scope of this book, except for mentioning some of the key aspects: limitations on the size of land grants, on the size of ejido plots, and on the size of estates that could be expropriated; limits of time allowed to persons processing petitions for land; and increased use of the injunction (*amparo*) to protect individuals (e.g., landlords) and to block or at least delay land claims. The altered national policies, in any case, were spelled out legally in the critical Law of Ejidal Patrimony of December 19, 1925 (Simpson 1937:89 et passim; Mendieta y Nuñez 1946:243): the ejidos could be broken up into inalienable family plots with the title to usufruct vested in the individual ejidatario as the head of an ejidal family, while the land continued to be governed by the community and, ultimately, owned by the nation. The new law was also intended to correct serious abuses of power on the part of the so-called village Executive Committees; the internal workings of the village authorities were to be further controlled and regulated. At the grass-roots level of Naranja these changes in rules and policies boiled down to the numbers of meters of furrow in one's specific plot, the number of family members sharing a plot, and the control and use of the surplus profits expressed in taxes, "loans," and the like. Each faction had to take a stand on repartition that would, in turn, influence the size and nature of its support among the villagers and among the políticos in Morelia.

The Ocampos seized on this new legislation: the ejido should be partitioned because the Caso caciques had exploited the ejidatarios and embezzled funds. They also appealed to the urge of the individual peasant and his family to—at least in some sense—possess a definite plot of land, and to the resentment of many against the abuses of the collective operation under the Casos. They soon enjoyed the support of the majority in the pueblo, if, indeed, they had not enjoyed it already. The more "bolsheviki" Casos, by contrast, held that fully collective usufruct was the only truly revolutionary method and the only one which would enable the community to mobilize funds for material improvements and the like. They enjoyed greater support among the higher-level agrarian politicians in Michoacán. The ideological and practical issue of applying the Law of Ejidal Patrimony thus crystallized the local factions, with a resulting outbreak of sniping and fire-fighting, and a deepening of bitterness and rancor. During April 1928, the Ocampos, in control of the ejidal committee and the militia, were able to push through what has since been called the First Partition, according to which every beneficiary acquired rights to slightly over ten acres of the black soil. Although, legally speaking, the charter for this was the "First Agrarian Census" used by Tapia in 1921, several Caso agrarians were cut out and several Ocampos were included although they had not figured in the heroic revolt, nor even in the first census.

The Casos then and ever after accused the Ocampos of being "reactionaries," even though many of the latter had also fought with Tapia and were "red" Naranja agraristas, if less so than the Casos. In October 1928, Leopoldo Ocampo was elected mayor. The Ocampos now controlled both the civil and the ejidal arms of government.

The Casos fought harder as their faction became increasingly outnumbered. And 1927 witnessed another key political development that was to exercise a decisive influence over subsequent history. A burning issue had long been the *"acasillado* question," that is, the agrarian rights of the sharecroppers and hired men living around the haciendas. Large colonies had formed in the Zacapu Valley, partly as a consequence of the draining of the Zacapu marsh in the 1890s; two such colonies of mestizos lived next to Naranja and others lay beside Tarejero and Tiríndaro. The *acasillados* were recognized in diverse laws and edicts of 1925 and 1927, but since most of the land in the valley had already been distributed, were the *acasillados* to get any and, if so, from whom?

The Ocampos and the Casos again moved into opposite corners. The former were more Indian in this conflict (*pleito*) of politics, as they were in their degree of Tarascan speech. They were prejudiced against the neighboring *acasillados* simply because they were mestizos (*de razón*), and they felt vengeful because most of the mestizos had sided with the landlords, sometimes killing Naranja agrarians. The Ocampos' position was that the community should remain united and keep the most possible land for itself. Many such as the "stern" Juan Ocampo Huante argued that the "Black Ones" (*turisicha*) should be driven out with fire and pistol, just as they had been in Tarejero after Tapia's death in 1926 when the autocratic cacique Juan Cruz de la Cruz enjoined his Indian agraristas "to dress themselves in the blood of man," as he put it, and drive out fifty (many say one hundred) mestizo families from the adjoining settlement called El Pinete. When interviewed by me in the field Juan still showed an unusual degree of ethnic hostility, referring with hatred to the mestizos and Spanish (i.e., as *gachupines*).

The Caso position stemmed from Primo Tapia, early defender of the right of the *acasillado*. Tomás Cruz and Pedro González argued that the mestizos should be given plots in the ejido, taking land from Naranja if necessary, because the Naranjeños at that time were having to hire great numbers of immigrant laborers to work their new possessions. This ideology was to win for the Casos the support not only of agrarian leaders such as Cárdenas but also of the growing agrarian factions among the mestizos in the valley. The immediate consequence of the intensified Ocampo-versus-Caso division about this time was compromise: the pro-agrarians in the hamlets (*ranchos*) of Morelos and Buena Vista were allocated almost token plots of one-half acre each. But the long-range consequence was a grass-roots shift in the sources of local politics itself: after about 1927 the minority faction of Casos maneuvered and fought in alliance with the often desperately poor mestizo wage-laborers, not only of these two hamlets, but of the region in general, against the majority, more Indian (*indígena, indio*) faction led by the Ocampo family. Many of the firefights and some of the killings since then have involved these *rancheros*. Salvador Rangel of Morelos emerged as a courageous and consistent backer of the Casos, especially Scarface. The astute Caso strategy of finding a weaker, outside ally to defeat a stronger opponent within the village meant a profound shift away from the ethnocentrism of the united Naranja that had converged collectively against mestizo hooligans in 1912, and then fought together in the agrarian revolt against the resented mestizo landlords and their supporters in 1920–1924. The *acasillado* question at its Naranja terminus illustrated a revealing intersection of factors of land tenure, ethnicity, political faction, and ideology, and several Machiavellian moves, notably that of allying oneself with and bringing in a weaker, not a stronger, party.

4. The Shooting of Tomás Cruz

The struggle between the Casos and the Ocampos was bonded outward and upward to another large issue: the gubernatorial election of 1928. The Casos typified the support enjoyed by Lázaro Cárdenas: a village minority habituated to violence and radical ideology. During these last months of 1927 they were heartened by the likelihood of legal protection (*garantías*) and political favor (*jalón*) after the election of their man. During 1928 they became more aggressive and offensive. But the Ocampos were just as determined (*resueltos*), and more numerous, and did not surrender the political and military offices that they held in the village and the region. Their main caciques could not tolerate the forceful leadership of Tomás Cruz, and on October 22, 1928, a quick sequence of historical accidents led to his assassination.

We should cast a brief but direct look at some of the details in this turning point in the twentieth-century history of Naranja. Tomás was not only a distant cousin of Primo Tapia but also a brother-in-law of Tapia's sister (still very much alive during my fieldwork, and meriting her reputation as the villager with the best memory). He had sojourned in the United States as a migrant worker, standing with Primo during some Wobbly episodes; some say that he participated in the strike in Bayard, Nebraska, others that he had already returned to fight in the last years of the Mexican Revolution. Back in Naranja by 1920, he survived in the forefront of the agrarian revolt, representing the pueblo in Primo's absence and participating in numerous skirmishes; once the landlord militia strung him up by the neck "to scare him" (*para asustarlo*). Tomás was thin and unusually tall, and, I infer, part Caucasoid in ancestry. All the villagers and other contemporary witnesses concur that he was not only literate but a reader and "very serious" (muy serio). He ranks with Pedro González, and only below Primo and Joaquín, as an outstanding local and regional leader of the period. Having already had experience in office at the state level, it is quite possible that, had he lived, he would have figured significantly in the new Revolutionary Confederation of Labor of Michoacán (CRMDT); he had helped Tapia pioneer its agrarian component. His shooting generated a large dossier—one of the few not to have disappeared mysteriously from the state legal archives in Morelia—which contained a wealth of depositions and other witnessing by Cecilio Valle and dozens of others and from which the following witness by vicarious eye could be inferred (presented below pretty much as it occurs in Cacique).

Tomás was killed by the Ocampos. He and two comrades were drinking in one of the dusty taverns on the outskirts of Zacapu early on the afternoon of October 22. Suddenly they spied Cecilio Valle and three other members of the Ocampo faction passing on foot, heading for Naranja. One of Tomas' friends, Epifanio, jumped up from the rickety wooden table, ran through the swinging doors, and grabbed Cecilio by the neck, shouting drunkenly, "They say you're one of the ones Juan Ocampo keeps around him as a brave gunman, but I say you're nothing but the son of the fucked one . . ." and other things to the same effect. Cecilio, a fairly typical Naranja agrarian, was twenty-four, of swarthy yellow complexion, short stature, low forehead, and wearing an embroidered serape. Epifanio's obscene insults might have triggered the passionate, homicidal response encouraged by the culture—at least in contexts such as this—but Tomás Cruz came dashing out and told Cecilio not to pay attention to the drunken Epifanio. So Cecilio and the Ocampos continued on their way toward Naranja. They were soon overtaken by Tomás Cruz and his group, and Epifanio began to swear again, saying, "They say that Juan Ocampo takes you for a fighting cock (gallo), but I say your mother is the fucked one . . ." They altercated a few minutes. Then Cecilio picked up a large rock from the stone wall to his left and hurled it directly into the drunk man's face, knocking him flat. Cecilio then ran away, soon catching up with Tomás Cruz, who had gone on ahead and was already approaching the willows around the pond outside Naranja, the green, idyllic "Eye of Water," where Primo Tapia had been captured two years earlier. Cecilio's companions had run ahead to Naranja to get firearms.

As Cecilio trotted up, Tomás turned on him and asked, "Where is Epifanio? You bumped him off!" (ya lo fregaste). At about the same time Tomás' other companion, who was still with him, pulled a .45 pistol from his pants and shot at Cecilio, saying, "Here you come!" He missed. Then Cecilio yanked a sawed-off .30-.30 rifle from inside his pants. Tomás grabbed at Cecilio and was shot through the stomach. Tomás' companion then shot at Cecilio again with his .45 pistol, missing again because he was drunk. Cecilio turned on his assailant and shot him through the side. The drunken Epifanio came running up. He had regained his senses from the blow inflicted by the large stone, but blood was streaming over his face and shirt. Cecilio waited and shot him as he came in with his knife. Cecilio, the Ocampo agrarian, was in a state of rage (*coraje*). Three drunken agrarians, including the ablest leader in the village, lay wounded and dying in the dust next to the "Eye of Water." Tomás rolled into the water. The whole thing had lasted only a few seconds.

Eight of Cecilio's companions came running and riding from Naranja with pistols and rifles. They finished off Tomás Cruz. As Cecilio ran away into the tall corn of the ejido, he shouted back, "Follow me, you sons of the fucked one . . ." Primo Tapia's sister arrived on the spot a few minutes later. She saw one of the slain men lying in the arms of his beloved. The corpse of Tomás Cruz was being lifted by two of the leading agrarian women. As the third man lay dying he said to his sister, "Ay! my little sister, now it's happened, what they talked about so often . . ."[4]

The incidents following the killing of Tomás illustrate some more of the connections between politics and law. At first no action was taken because Leopoldo Ocampo was mayor and Juan Ocampo was head of the regional militia. However, Cárdenas was governor. Within a few weeks Juan had been expelled from Naranja on a twenty-four-hour gubernatorial ultimatum, and Cecilio, apprehended by the municipal police, was convicted of murder and sentenced to the (then) maximum of six years in prison which he served out in full. Pedro González, Elías Caso, and Agustín Galván seized control in Naranja. All this while, the federal and state (mainly Cardenista) authorities were trying in various ways to prevent bloodshed, insisting that representatives of both factions be on the ejidal committee, and the pending war was reined in during the beginning of the new governorship; Cárdenas was a great peacemaker; there were only about two homicides a year at first. From among the Casos, nonetheless, the subsequently storied fighter Juan Nahua Caso stepped into the local chronicles, shooting a fellow Caso in a drunken brawl. Surviving "reactionaries" kept becoming casualties. Sacred images were dismantled from the church and publicly burned, the gold and silver being appropriated by the agrarian chiefs. Catholic activities of any kind were persecuted, Pedro González distinguishing himself in these fervent pursuits.

5. Cardenismo in Region and State

Let us look briefly at other towns in the region. In Zacapu, conflict persisted between agrarians, often supported by Naranja fighters, and various shades of "reactionaries," Catholics, and Cristeros; in 1929, for example, a firefight (*zafarancho*) there had an output of over twenty dead Cristeros. Elsewhere the fact that radicalism (e.g., anticlericalism) enjoyed a heyday during the Cárdenas governorship did not, as we have seen, prevent the radicals from fighting with each other. A fundamental issue continued to be whether to ally oneself along the lines of Tarascan Indian identity, or in terms of some sort of non-ethnic class. In Naranja the relatively Indian Ocampos allied themselves with the Indian agrarian faction in Tarejero under Juan Cruz de la Cruz, who, because he was a personal friend and ex-cavalry officer under Calles, enjoyed significant financial and political support from the powers in Mexico City. Tarejero was administered somewhat like a Russian *kolkhoz* (collective farm): tractors, threshing machines, and new breeds of livestock were purchased; ejidatarios punched in on cards, their hours were kept posted on a bulletin board, and they were paid wages. Other Tarejero men supported the ejido by sending home money from the United States, where they were working as braceros. Thus Juan and his cohorts were able to institute what was, depending on your point of view, an absolute cacicazgo or "the model ejido of the Mexican Republic," as it was put by Eylor Simpson in his definitive study (which included Tarejero as one of the cases). [5]

In Tiríndaro the inauguration of a more or less unrestrained Cardenismo contributed to a variant of agrarian caciquismo that achieved considerable notoriety, even infamy. Severo Espinoza, the cacique whom Tapia in his day had managed to subordinate, had seen to it that a mere 108 families were admitted to the ejido by the simple expedient of making renunciation of the church a categorical prerequisite. The relatively large size of the population (over twice that of Naranja), the relatively large size of the new plots (five hectares), and the relatively and absolutely large number of landless families, many of them mestizo and/or fervently "Catholic," all worked together to produce extraordinary pressures on the land, hostilities, and violence. There were killings every month. In 1929 Severo and a group of his Tiríndaro cohorts pulled an opposition family from its adobe home after midnight and dragged them up into the sierra, where they butchered them all, including two children and a hired man, hacking them up with machetes. The pregnant mother was cut open alive, the fetus extracted, and her body stuffed with pine cones. For this atrocity Severo and several others, notwithstanding their "red-boned Cardenismo" (*cardenismo a hueso colorado*), were sentenced to the maximum of six years, which they began to serve in the Pátzcuaro penitentiary. This sort of atrocity, almost unknown during the historical period under study (although daily fare in parts of Latin America today), still inspires horror in the people.

Let us now glance, more comprehensively, at the onset of relatively institutionalized Cardenismo in the state as a whole. As in the Zacapu Valley, radical fanaticism rose to a crescendo as conservative individuals and even sections of the population were repressed, attacked, and killed, typically in connection with anticlericalism. The above-mentioned Revolutionary Confederation of Labor of Michoacán was set up as an experiment—a fairly successful one, as it turned out—in uniting workers, peasants, teachers, and other sectors of the population with "radical" potential into one statewide organization. The leaders in the CRMDT were able to influence or even control the appointment of judges, county presidents, and other officials all over Michoacán. In general, the regional leaders in the CRMDT inspired and engineered much of the local violence. But the extremism of Cardenismo was matched by its complexity; after 1929, strong tactics were used against leaders in the Communist Party, which was then forced to enter a semi-underground phase, some of its leaders concentrating on infiltrating the CRMDT (Embriz and León 1984:147).*

In the state of Michoacán, Naranja was rivaled for radicalism only by such communities as La Piedad, Vista Hermosa, Villa Jiménez, the Eleven Pueblos, and, of course, Tarejero and Tiríndaro. It was only natural that Naranja's able and ambitious leaders should follow the examples of their kinsmen Joaquín de la Cruz and Primo Tapia in regional and state politics. This came to mean the presidency of the county, command of the regional militia, or the post of state representative or even national representative (or alternate to the same). In addition, the Radical Agrarian Socialist League of Primo Tapia, always headed by Naranja men, eventually had considerable impact on the region. The Regional Committee of the League of Agrarian Communities was headed by Pedro González in 1926–1929, by Elías Caso in 1929–1931, and thereafter by Naranjeños (and the allied mestizo, Salvador Rangel). In 1929 Elías was made head of a minor commission in the CRMDT, and Pedro González became a secretary in the same body. Approximate contemporaries, including politically informed persons in the state capital, remember Pedro as "very tough," "a red-boned Cardenista," "a killer," while others say that he was "very energetic, lively, conversed a lot, explained things, very smart" (muy enérgico, vivo, platicaba mucho, explanaba las cosas, muy listo).[6] Be this as it may, the singular power of Naranja involved tenure in formal office, considerable political sophistication, and scores of experienced fighters, some

---

*These "strong tactics," attested by many authoritative sources, were part of a decades-long policy shared in various ways and with varying scope by Calles, Cárdenas, and, indeed, all Mexican presidents and most governors and other leaders and officials; as Hansen puts it, speaking of the sixties, "certain political challenges from the left will not be allowed" (1974:123); the means of not allowing such challenges include assassination, jailing, and similar violence. At one level, both Agrarian Revolt and The Princes document this process.

of whom could function as individual hit men, all of whom contributed to what were correctly called "the strong and fighting agrarian organizations of Naranja, Tiríndaro, and other towns" (Anguiano 1951:31 [writing of 1929]).

Conflicts in the pueblos and the state capital, in any case, were but part of conflicts in the entire nation; President-elect Alvaro Obregón was assassinated in 1928 by a fanatical Roman Catholic. As for agrarian reform, in the sense of expropriating landlords, the preceding president, Calles, as already noted, had been slowing things down since about 1925, and entered an increasingly complicated and contradictory course of action that compromised a basically anti-agrarian ideology with ad hoc alliances with pro-agrarian leaders whose power he needed. Thus, after calling for a new national party in September 1928, he led in creating, in March of the next year, "an amalgam (called the Party of National Revolution) of local political machines and of various other agricultural, labor, and other associations, backed by the silent but ever-present force of the military" (Scott 1964:122); the "machines" of course included that of the agrarian military caudillo of Michoacán, Lázaro Cárdenas. In 1929 Calles, national strong man and kingmaker, supported the moderately pro-agrarian Emilio Portes Gil for president, but the next year he supported an anti-agrarian and began implementing a decision to halt agrarian reform across the board; the governors in eleven states complied, and those in three who didn't were "quickly and effectively disciplined" (ibid.:123). This architect of a new party, the tapper of presidents and the paradigmatic strong man of Mexico, was actually institutionalizing a structure whereby he could be defeated, both legalistically and in terms of power politics.

Let us return to the ejidos of the Zacapu Valley. During these years of the late twenties, pressure on the land kept mounting as sons grew older, as fugitives from the violence of the agrarian and Cristero revolts returned home, and as formerly neutral or even anti-agrarian peasants became acutely aware of the enormous advantages of harvesting about two hundred hectoliters of maize a year (as an ejidatario). The result was strong and widespread demands for a new partition of the existing plots through a second application of the Law of Ejidal Patrimony. In Tarejero two partitions were carried out within a short space of time, transforming that ejido from a model collective farm into a community of almost three hundred ejidal families, each enjoying the usufruct of less than four acres. The power of the autocratic cacique Juan Cruz was greatly weakened. In Tiríndaro, on the contrary, the intransigent allies of Severo Espinoza and his brother kept on liquidating and terrorizing any peasant with the temerity to agitate for partition. [I noted at the time of fieldwork that anyone agitating seriously for a partition in Tiríndaro "would certainly be killed," and no one has divided up the plots since then either, that is, as of 1956 (and probably 1986).]

In Naranja, however, the still powerful and entrenched Ocampos succeeded in pushing through the Second Partition of 1931, on the basis of a Second Agrarian Census: the size of the individual family plots was reduced from over ten acres to slightly over five—still well above what was needed for subsistence; concomitantly, the number of ejidal plots was doubled from 109 to 218. These partitions were turning points in social and political history. In Naranja they strengthened the Ocampos and in Tarejero they predictably undermined the autocratic cacicazgo of Juan Cruz. In both pueblos they meant that the usufruct of the land was actually in the hands of the great majority, and that civil and ejidal government was by ejidatarios, although much of the surplus profits and some additional redistribution of plots remained in the hands of an agrarista minority.

The Second Partition in Naranja also entailed that many families entered the ejido who had avoided or even opposed the agrarian revolt and the agrarian cause in general. By helping these families, some of them devoutly religious, to a small fraction of the ejido, the Ocampos further buttressed but also complicated their position as the majority party. Both of the Caso leaders, Pedro and Scarface, opposed the second Partition, like the First, on the grounds that it was "antirevolutionary" to deal out land to "reactionaries" and "White Guards," and, not least of all, because they did not want their plots and those of their kinsmen and allies chopped in half. At the last moment Pedro acquiesced to the partition in order not to estrange himself even more from the majority. But after 1931 the Casos redoubled their denunciations of the Ocampos as reactionary and thus reinforced the cooperation they had been getting from the radical, Cardenista leaders and bureaucrats at the state level.

6. Contentious Fission: Serratismo

By the end of 1931 the conflicts in Naranja were becoming yet more open. As so often happens, the necessary propulsion was provided by a shift in the political alignments in the state as a whole, centered in the capital. Cárdenas—the state cacique—surprised almost everyone by not finding a successor among the able and fanatical leaders of the CRMDT, nor the radical lawyers and políticos in Morelia. On the contrary, he looked to distant Monterrey and informally invited the Michoacán-born but comparatively little known general Benigno Serrato to accept the candidacy for the governor's term that was to begin in 1932. He was importing an outsider who would depend on him in preference to his own adherents whom, despite their ardor, or perhaps because of their ardor, he trusted less. People frequently claim that "Cárdenas must have memorized Machiavelli," which has some, at least metaphorical, truth, but here he was following a pattern that is common if not typical of strong-man politics in Mexico; while he was the cacique in the Zacapu region Scarface often sought out county presidents who were not native to the region. Cárdenas also was swayed by the fact that as governor he had pushed an often costly radicalism, and now he required a less radical successor to allow for some retrenchment (just as he later tapped moderate Manuel Avila Camacho to follow him in the presidency). Serrato, a courageous man with the ability for the job, still hesitated for a while before accepting.

In 1931–1932 almost every village and city in Michoacán had been divided between two or more factions (*partidos*), sometimes radical versus conservative, but often radicals divided among themselves, as in Naranja. Bloody encounters had taken place. Soon after his nomination Serrato began to surround himself with persons actually or potentially hostile to the state cacique (or caudillo). By the middle of 1932 a more or less open rift had developed in Morelia and most of the state between Serratistas and Cardenistas. When Serrato became governor all the more-or-less anti-Cárdenas factions (many of them conservative) swung to him, so that by the end of 1933 he enjoyed the backing of factions, often majority ones like the Ocampos, in the bulk of the state. Ever since, Serrato, like the Ocampos, has been branded a reactionary, and this is a deceptive oversimplification because he was a revolutionary general with "good principles" (*buenos principios*), to use a typical Cardenista phrase. But like most political leaders he was primarily the creature of political and historical processes outside his control: here, that a cacique's second in power, or the man he taps, normally poses the greatest threat, as a likely "puppet" whom opponents will strenuously seek to win over.

In 1933, at least some of the Cardenistas held firm. "Only some leaders of the CRMDT like Mora Tovar, Mayes Navarro, and Pedro López, and others [e.g., Gabino Vázquez] remained faithful to him and kept up the fight against the government" (Anguiano 1951:77). Cárdenas managed to convey faith and dry powder to his beleaguered cohorts. He visited his state several times during 1933 and 1934, often avoiding Serrato in Morelia or entering from the west or the north and passing through agrarian communities such as Tanaquillo or Naranja or La Piedad on his way to his home in Jiquilpan. Communications between Cárdenas and Serrato became more and more faulty, and local and state Cardenistas became more belligerent; during 1934 many such as Vázquez and López openly refused to cooperate with the governor; they led or inspired a series of bloody demonstrations in several communities. Assassinations were frequent. All this reached a head during the Fifth Congress of the CRMDT, which had been convoked to elect new officers after the Cardenistas had refused the Machiavellian suggestion by Cárdenas that they divide the posts on an equal basis (he knew they wouldn't). The streets of Morelia were flooded by thousands of Serratista peasants in white manta (some claim eighteen thousand) and Cardenista peasants with red and black banners (some claim five thousand). The outcome of all these demonstrations and speeches was that the standing Cardenista officers of the CRMDT remained in power, with Tapia's old comrade Pedro López of Naranja as the Secretary General (1932–1935); in good Bolshevik style, they claimed to represent the majority of peasants and workers. Curiously, in my fieldnotes of a long interview with Pedro I wrote that "by the look in his eyes" I could see that he thought of himself as a "Bolshevik." On the other hand, it is possible that one of Pedro's roles was to block or even help eliminate Communist Party members . . .

The Serratistas, by contrast, formed another confederation with *its* officers. A few months later Cárdenas passed through Morelia on his presidential tour and (the same?) five thousand peasant fighters, including, I assume, many from Naranja, lined the streets up from the railroad station. These political "acts," if nothing else, steel the ambition and vanity of the leaders and harden the solidarity of at least some of the rank and file.

The hard-core Cardenistas also held in most if not all their bastions. To the west of Naranja, mestizo Chilchota went over to the new faction, but the famous agrarian cacique Ernesto Prado of Tanaquillo, supported by the military commander in Zamora, did not alter his course (Sáenz 1936:268). Zacapu itself, with its many conservatives, Tarejero, with its pro-Calles, anti-Cárdenas tradition, and most of mestizo Tariácuri to the north were mainly in favor of the new governor. A crucial problem for these "traitors" was sheer (i.e., military) power: Cárdenas enjoyed the support of most (or all?) the zone military commanders, as in Zacapu, Zamora, Morelia, and Uruapan.

Naranja was plunged into the period that has aroused the most profound and enduring hatred and grudges. By the time of my fieldwork, decades later, caciques such as Elías and Hercules could only speak of it with agitation and, somehow, embarrassment. Specifically, Miguel Ocampo was elected mayor, and the other leaders in the faction tried to control the town under a tandem of caciques, Hercules and Juan. The Ocampos enjoyed some legal guarantees and political protection from Serratistas at the state level, as well as the support of the majority in the pueblo, many of whom owed them their ejido plots or eagerly awaited the revival of the traditional fiestas. Thus, in the thoroughly polarized context of state politics, the Ocampos became Serratistas and hence, because structurally allied with conservatives, "reactionaries."

The Casos, on the other hand, probably constituted the toughest minority in any pueblo in the state. They had lost Tomás, but Pedro González had become a regional cacique and a state politician in the CRMDT. Locally they were led by the singularly endowed Scarface Caso, who, largely because of the influence of his sister, enjoyed the support of no less than nine nephews. He also was also ably helped by his wife, Guadalupe, a feminist activist who influenced many women through her use of the Feminine League (founded by Primo Tapia). And he was backed by a cousin, the ambitious Guillermo de las Casas, one of the heirs of agrarianism, who served as head of the Regional Committee from 1932 to 1939. Another cousin (and Tapia's old chum), José Moreno, rounded out the leadership and provided sage advice, particularly when it came to reconciling personal differences. Somewhat more ambiguous was the support of Agustín Galván and his brother, who were relatively independent and in touch with the Ocampos.

In terms of firepower, Scarface could reckon with the most prolific gunmen, two of whom, Bones and Boni, are described in Chapter 1. The third was Juan Nahua Caso. A half-dozen other proficient-fighters figure in the homicide record and are mentioned repeatedly in the denunciations, notably Sebastián Gabriel. Finally, there were at least thirty rank-and-file "soldiers" in Naranja's "powerful and fighting organization"; at least fifty Naranjeños had campaigned against the Cristeros just five years earlier, and a larger number would help lynch Víctor Aparicio and his Cristeros in 1935. Also, it must be remembered that the Casos were backed by the federal troops under the regional military commanders, who remained loyal to "the man from whom all emanates." Never again did the Ocampos succeed in doing in an important Caso leader or fighter (although many were wounded). As one old Ocampo reported, "After seven in the evening there was a dead silence. People sat in their houses listening for the shooting."

Tiríndaro was special, even in the context of Serratismo. The faction of the incarcerated Severo Espinoza hewed staunchly to Cárdenas. But toward the end of 1931 the large, landless, and largely Catholic majority in that town began to inspire the leadership of a well-to-do and well-read mestizo, the owner of a soft-drink and candy factory, several large houses, and an automobile. With the encouragement of Serratista and former Cristero elements in Zacapu, this man, Víctor Aparicio, organized a conservative agrarian party, arguing, with considerable logic, that there was no necessary connection between renouncing Catholicism and having rights in the ejido lands. It had already been seven years since that land had been won under Tapia, and people were forgetting or choosing to forget that the Church and the conservative peasants had opposed land reform—whereas they could not forget the horror of Severo's atrocities.

Aparicio and his Christian agrarians, as they called themselves, were one, local articulation of the reaction that was taking place all over the state. Within two years Aparicio had won the support of a majority in the town, and when elected mayor in 1934, he carried through a number of impressive material improvements and was well on his way to winning a claim for a second partition of the Tiríndaro ejido. But several flaws weakened his chances. For one thing, the most able fighters were on the side of Espinoza's Indian agrarians, and they were determined not to divide their plots with the "Christians." Repeatedly one notes in Michoacán politics that majority support and convincing principles are never enough: the winning factions are those with organization, the strongest fighters, ideological fervor, and the support of Cárdenas and his network.

In Naranja and Tarejero the conflict between Cardenistas and Serratistas likewise hinged on questions of land. In the former of these towns agrarian feeling continued to grow among the mestizos of the adjoining hamlets, Morelos and Buena Vista, leading to the complete expropriation of the landlords in question. The pressure otherwise being exerted by these mestizos was both toward an enlargement of their holdings in the black soil of the Zacapu Valley and toward the expropriation of several hundred acres of land in the foothills to the south. The Casos of course supported this, whereas the Ocampos claimed, as before, that Naranja should be given more land in both areas and that the former "White Guards" should be driven forth.

Let us pause briefly to touch ground with another reality. A political history tends to focus on the leaders, and one goal in this study is, quite explicitly, to understand leadership. However, I have also dealt with what agrarian factionalism could mean for the population as a whole. For one vignette of what it could mean to a relatively little man let us turn, as a sort of interlude, to "The Miracle of Alberto Espinoza," a minor Ocampo leader of religious conviction ("a White Guard"), who courageously opposed the desecration of the church by political "functions."

1933. In the corn warehouse of Naranja I was attacked by some opponents to the top men (*unos contrarios a los primeros*). I resisted them. But there was another one of them behind me, he doubled my arms, they tied me and took me to Tiríndaro and in the prison they put a rope around my neck and looking at myself in those final moments I asked Our Father Jesus to free me in those moments of death. I made an effort and managed to get my hands under the rope of my neck and so I passed the whole night. the next day they took me to Cantabria where I was going to be shot (*fusilado*), they thought of Tarejero, and finally took me to zacapu, where I obtained my freedom. and so already free I went back to my land and in quinato someone came out on horseback to kill me, but didn't hit the mark (*en mi persona*) because the horse didn't stay still. i went onward. in ortega i had another attack. not a single shell hit the mark. i went forward and by the mercy of god saved my life and as an act of gratitude (*gracia*) I am making this miracle public. Naranja of Our Father Jesus.

12 March 1946

ALBERTO ESPINOZA

This report stood scrawled on an eight- by twelve-inch sheet of tin, hung on one of the inside walls of the church and depicting the details of the ordeal. The men who tortured Alberto in Tiríndaro were uniformed troops. The men who shot at him as he staggered home were roving agrarians. In 1946 Alberto was elected mayor. In 1956, in his eighties, he was still alive and tilling the soil with his two sons.

The local disputes described above were part of the national problem of the *acasillados* and, more generally, landless agricultural workers without traditional communal rights, that was reaching the breaking point. In 1933 at the major PRI convention in Querétaro a group of agrarian politicians connected with but partly independent of Cárdenas pushed through a series of epoch-making resolutions that eventually took the form of the new Agrarian Code and the so-called Six-Year (Sexennial) Plan; *acasillados* were given rights to a land grant (*dotación*) in all cases of demonstrated need. At this same convention, Lázaro Cárdenas emerged as the candidate for president chosen by the national strong man, Plutarco Elías Calles. Cárdenas had appeared to have been relegated to the political penumbra as chief of military operations in Puebla, when in fact he had been laying the groundwork for his nomination as the next Calles "puppet." As organizer and past president of the national "Cárdenas Lodge" of Freemasons, and with a record of exceptional courage and astuteness as a field (cavalry) general, zone military commander, state governor, and national-level bureaucrat (e.g., head of the ministry of Gobernación),* he was hardly a likely "puppet"; perhaps his greatest astuteness was in making an experienced politician like Calles think he would be one.

On December 1, 1934, Cárdenas took the oath as president of Mexico. His followers back in Michoacán exulted. The Serratistas, on the other hand, had seen the hopelessness of their position; a delegation of them went to the capital to congratulate the new incumbent. Cárdenas was, as always, polite and friendly, and accorded them a half-hour interview, but

---

Gobernación corresponds roughly to the ministry of the interior: in charge of the police, the control of dissent, surveillance of many kinds, the administration of elections (e.g., quashing of opposition that will not be tolerated), and many of the relations between local, state, and national government. It is probably the most important and certainly the most powerful of the ministries. By a decades-long tradition, presidents of Mexico since Cárdenas have first served as chiefs of Gobernación.

the next day, December 2, Serrato unfortunately died in an airplane crash en route home. Other Callista governors were deposed during the months that followed, mainly through the actions of agrarian Portes Gil, who had been given much authority in this regard.

7. Cardenismo in the Saddle

The nation began to shake from a series of events, the details of which, dramatic and fascinating as they are, lie outside the scope of this study. Cárdenas, exercising his extraordinary talents, exploited the political process that had so debilitated his control in Michoacán: powerful interests pledged their support and he encouraged them while keeping Calles from growing too suspicious, or taking action. In the national parliament the famous "left wing" was formed under the brilliant leadership of Luis Mora Tovar, the lyric poet and Michoacán socialist who for a time had fought by the side of Primo Tapia. Eighteen Callistas were permanently expelled from the House after a gun battle on the floor of that body resulted in two deaths. Later in 1935 Calles was flown to the west coast in a government plane, and later yet out of the country. Cárdenas had seized control of the body politic. But let us get back to the agrarian villagers and their point of view.

Cacique Juan Cruz fled Tarejero early in 1935 and stayed away where he was relatively safe, first in Mexico City and then in Morelia, until about 1951. Severo Espinoza was sprung from the Pátzcuaro jail and, returning home, began to suppress and liquidate Cristero agrarians with ruthless dispatch. Aparicio, their enlightened leader, withdrew into the hills with some friends and waited for others to follow. But the Christian majority did not move. They huddled in their houses, as someone put it. Severo and some of the leaders in Naranja, Tarejero, and Zacapu mustered a posse of over three hundred which captured Aparicio and his comrades in their sierra retreat and lynched them near the mestizo ranch known as "The Eagle." The six bodies, one of them mutilated, were tossed naked on the porch before Aparicio's house on the plaza of Tiríndaro the evening of the following day. The houses of these Cristeros were sacked. (Víctor's son, then still a boy, witnessed much of this and told me about it.)

For the next six years Severo Espinoza was to hold his village, first in the grip of an absolute cacicazgo, then in the sanguinary confusions of a falling cacicazgo. His faction of Indian agrarians, now larger, grew increasingly restless, divisive, violent—and alcoholic. They were "united" and kept the pueblo united in part by driving out dozens of opposing families, in which they enjoyed the legal protection of Cardenistas in the state government. Severo, like Scarface and Pedro González, was "a very good friend" of the new national strong man.

Severo was fairly tall and strongly built, with a desperate streak. To him must go most of the credit for organizing the agrarian movement in his pueblo during the Revolution, starting in 1911, long before Tapia; he often could survive only by hiding out in the sierra. He with his brother Félix led the Tiríndaro agrarians during the regional revolt as envious subordinates of Tapia; he, by all accounts, ordered the slaughter of prisoners after "the taking of Tiríndaro," for which Tapia later paid the price. Now he was at the zenith of his power.

Some material improvements were effectuated, as they had been in Tarejero: tractors and threshing machines were purchased, or received as gifts outright from Cárdenas, and a large maize warehouse was built. But much of the money from taxes and extortion—the so-called "loans" (prestamos)—was squandered on brandy and the like or expended by the leaders on livestock and privately owned land; Severo became the biggest landowner in town (and still was at the time of my fieldwork). Fanatical anticlericalism was converted into a surrogate religion: any activity smacking of "Christianity" was persecuted, and egregious "believers" were dragged from their homes at night and murdered or driven from Tiríndaro. The trigger-happy men in Espinoza's faction envied each other for their lucrative ejidal positions and private land, and some coveted each other's women enough for this to influence politics. The quantities of land and the economic surpluses available exacerbated the fissive potential inherent in any cacical system, as did the presence of a large and landless majority: the ejido was still in the hands of less than a fifth of the population.

Severo began to change. In 1936 he ordered the assassination of one of his chief cohorts, who had sided with Aparicio and then sided against him, and who, Severo understandably imagined, was now initiating an opposition faction. The following year he arranged for the rubbing out of several leaders who seemed to oppose him, including his own cousin. He was manifesting megalomaniacal and paranoid symptoms. One of his gunmen seen conversing with a supposed Cristero might be ambushed the next night by his own comrades, under orders to kill. Severo was seen talking and gesticulating to himself, and he became more and more suspicious of his myrmidons. Then gradually between 1938 and 1941 he was overthrown by a faction led by a brother of one of his victims. After more realignments and many fatalities the lead was taken by an ally of Scarface (who was still dominant at the time of my fieldwork). It was this period in Tiríndaro history, the late thirties and early forties, which, more than the events in Naranja, earned for the Zacapu Valley the epithet of "the slaughterhouse of Michoacán." Granted the economic basis for the intensity of contentious fission, it was Severo's sadism and ruthlessness which stamped the pueblo's politics. By the time of my fieldwork he was wizened and partly senile, with a determined, cruel line to the thin lips that ranted against "enemies."

Over in Naranja, Scarface was elected president of the ejido early in 1935, and Miguel Ocampo was forced to turn over the office by the direct orders of the Zone Chief of Military Operations. Bones Gómez got the job of town judge. Given these and other circumstances, families of Ocampos, remaining "Catholics," and Serratistas began to leave the pueblo by the dozens, settling in Zacapu, Cherán, Morelia, and elsewhere. This second great exodus (the first being toward the end of the revolt) was accelerated by what it meant for the Casos to enjoy complete "legal guarantees" and military protection. Religious persecution now reached a sort of climax under the fanatical Pedro González; for example, women discovered getting their children baptized, often in distant towns, were denounced and threatened with expropriation—or worse. Religious icons (*santos*) in people's homes were burned on the plaza and property was confiscated under anticlerical slogans. The church was closed for religious services from 1934 until 1945 (according to law, a priest had to have a quorum of parishioners, so intimidation was used to keep the actual number below this minimum).

The main upshot of the Cardenista resurgence was two questions of land tenure. The first involved a legal claim for an additional grant (*ampliación*) which had begun in the early thirties if not earlier under Ocampo leadership amid the conflicting, rival claims by mestizo villagers and a crisscrossing of rules and decrees about due process in such cases. In August 1935 and in April 1936 under the leadership of the Casos this claim was provisionally resolved; 395 hectares of hill country (*monte*), 25 percent of it arable and, I gather, very productive, went to Naranja.

The second major upshot of the Cardenista resurgence was the expropriation in 1937 of the so-called First Group of ejidatarios: fourteen of them (actually two sets, of six and eight), so the Casos charged, had not cultivated their plots after deserting the village during the exodus; they were also accused of being or having been allied with the Cristeros in Zacapu (under Vicente Carillo) and with the "Christian agrarians" in Tiríndaro. Favorites of Scarface were awarded plots in their place, and Caso fighters, in grim confrontations between armed groups out in the ejido lands, debarred the desperate original holders from their titles for the necessary minimum of two years (thus, according to the Agrarian Code, legitimating the new occupants as the de jure ejidatarios); this reallocation was not officially confirmed until 1942. Other plots and much private land changed hands in these years since a total of about thirty Ocampos and Ocampo-allied families left town and numerous rank-and-file Ocampos lost their lives (see the Homicide Appendix).

The dominance of Cardenistas and the expulsion of the Ocampos

The Expropriated Groups

1937 "First Group" (actually two subgroups)		1940 "Second Group"
A	B	
Esteban León	José Sosa	Agustín Galván*
Cayetano Ocampo	Hilario Jiménez	Florencio Serrato
Elpidio Téllez	Eustacio Orobio	Leonardo Sosa
Pascual Ramírez	J. Jesús Espinoza	Sixto Hernández
Hipólito Ocampo	Blas Ramírez	Pilar Garcilazo
Felipe Serrato	Santiago Ocampo	Emiliano Espinoza
	Prisiliano Velázquez	Miguel González
	Florencio García	Luis Ramírez*
		Sabino Gabriel*
		Rafael González*

*These four were assassinated (see Homicide Appendix).

brought in its train the solution of another land question. Mestizo *acasillados* in and near the Zacapu Valley quickly won definite grants of land through the guidance and political connections of experienced Naranja agrarians such as Ezequiel Peñasco, Camilo Caso, and Gonzalo de las Casas. Many of the villagers in Morelos, Buena Vista, La Mojonera, and several other hamlets had long been siding with the Caso agrarians, sometimes drifting into Naranja at night, but also providing a hideout to Scarface on the many occasions when he took to the hills. These relative newcomers to the agrarian cause were now reimbursed with large grants of land in the foothills and the mountains, much of it land which actually belonged to Naranja and Tiríndaro and which could have been retained by the Indians. In 1937 a large group of the last anti-agrarian mestizos, in this case former *acasillados*, "rose up in arms" (*se levantaron en armas*), that is, they retired into the Tarascan sierra and waited for others to join them. They were soon attacked by the rural militia of Naranja and Morelos directed by the doughty mestizo agrarian Salvador Rangel. The anti-agrarians lost six men. The next day almost half the families in Morelos left for distant parts, and their homes were ransacked, burned, and literally torn down stone by stone. After 1937 the mestizo peasants in the Zacapu region played an increasing role in politics, but always under the hegemony of the Caso caciques.

Let us now contemplate the "revolutionary passion" and "Cardenismo without blemish" of the Casos and of the radicalized peasants of Naranja who supported their caudillo loyally throughout the period of Serratismo. They adhered, with relatively great commitment and consistency, to a radical ideology of anticlericalism, material improvements, women's rights, and land reform in the sense of expropriating large landlords and "reactionary" (e.g., non-Cardenista) peasants. We have seen their consistent stand on the question of land rights for the *acasillados*. During the Cárdenas presidency Naranja continued to be "the soul of agrarianism" in the region and to affect the course of events in contiguous regions; the town hall was a center of correspondence, communications, and control in the politics and litigation of agrarianism. Thus Naranja could be said to have done its share in the national program whereby almost 18 million hectares (45 million acres) were expropriated and redistributed to ejidatarios— more than by all previous presidents combined. A huge and expensive corn warehouse (*bodega*) was constructed (for controlling the harvest to the advantage of the leaders, it turned out; it had fallen into disuse by the time of my fieldwork).

The cultural side of rampant Cardenismo also strikes the imagination. I described earlier how the ejido subsidized the publication of Apolinar Martínez Múgica's original biography of Primo Tapia. The primary school staff was expanded to the extraordinary number of ten (some say fourteen) teachers; two of these, incidentally, became the second wives of Scarface and Camilo. Special instruction was provided in manual arts, public speaking, theater, agronomy, and athletics—a sort of Colegio de Agrarismo. In the late thirties, as noted above, the local team, containing several fighters and fighters-to-be, won two state basketball championships.[7] Several Naranja youths, including future princes such as Aquiles, studied in the Indigenous Institute for Tarascan-speakers in Paracho under the gifted, Tarascan-speaking, and politically sympathetic (i.e., Communist) American linguist Morris Swadesh. Dozens of local children and adolescents were studying in good preparatory schools and colleges in the state and national capitals. On the other hand, local teachers were shot at a number of times by resentful Caso fighters, and one of them was stripped and beaten with a stick for allegedly philandering; by the late 1930s, almost all the teachers had left.

The triumph of Cardenismo also meant the satisfaction of individual avarice coupled with Machiavellian egoism. Pedro González' history of aggrandizement through anticlerical confiscation has been recounted in part. Scarface, squarely in Naranja or the adjacent sierra throughout these years, ripped off the lion's share, as follows. While he was president of the ejido (1935–1937), his graft is said to have run to five-digit sums every year (at four pesos to the dollar). He habitually took a sizable reimbursement when ejido plots changed hands, as, after 1937, from the expropriation of the First Group of fourteen, and later, in 1941, from the expropriation of the Second Group; he and his henchmen eventually arrogated to themselves the entire crop from the land of eight of the Ocampos who were expropriated in 1935—a substantial value, particularly in light of the higher yield in those days. Often in the documentation and oral testimony there are claims that he would ask for "loans" of two or three hundred pesos when drunk at a fiesta, or when meeting someone on the highway. Finally, Scarface and other Casos, some of them nephews or cousins of Tapia, took over parts of the private land of the Ocampos or rustled their cattle and horses. By the mid-1940s, possibly, and certainly by the 1950s, Scarface was one of the wealthiest men in the region, possibly the wealthiest [the reader is reminded once again that scores of thousands of pesos in the 1930s are equivalent to millions in the devalued currency of 1986]. In the national context, however, Scarface Caso's use of politics for personal enrichment or, better, his synthesis of a political and economic struggle for power was but a local manifestation of standard practice at all levels; presidents were becoming millionaires almost as a matter of course (Hansen 1974:167).

Scarface's economics and politics were connected with his marriage to the handsome feminist-activist whom I have already had occasion to mention; she seems to have kept him happy and comparatively honest. Judging from his subsequent marriage, he had become relatively dependent on her psychologically. But in 1936 Guadalupe passed away, and this, as far as I can judge, precipitated a personal crisis beyond what is to be expected in such cases. On the one hand, Scarface caused a conspicuous mausoleum to be constructed over her grave in the Naranja cemetery with an emotional epitaph where I was able to read about his "faithful companion in the struggle" (e.g., who had helped him "control the feminine sector"). On the other hand, he is accused by his enemies of pocketing the substantial funds of the Feminine League (of which Guadalupe was president when she died), and he did eventually take over the corn mill that Lázaro Cárdenas had donated to the entire community. Some persons, looking back at all this, emphasize that Scarface had been "a good guy" (buena gente) before the death of Guadalupe, but then grew "egoistical," drank more heavily than before, and led in several many-on-one murders of buck privates in the opposition.

Early in 1937 the expropriated Ocampo ejidatarios again tried to enter their plots and get some of their harvest, but were repulsed by Caso fighters. In April one of the bravest Ocampos shot and killed, in the sierra, a fighter dear to Scarface. Scarface, who was Chief of the Defense, was enraged (lo agarró el coraje), and, taking counsel with some friends that night, decided to murder a young and politically insignificant peasant of the Ocampo faction. On the morning of the following day the selected victim, Rodríguez, went forth with a companion, an Ocampo, to look for his oxen in the stubble of the harvested ejido. What happened after that can be reconstructed from the depositions.

"His mother told us not to leave the house because she knew that they were spying." Rodríguez answered that "They had nothing to fear because he hadn't done anything for which they should injure him." On the way to the ejido they saw one of Scarface's fighters, who immediately got up and ran away toward the center of town. "Why should he want to run away?" asked Rodríguez. On approaching the black soil of the ejido they met a woman from another town who said, "Don't go into the ejido, because they want to kill you." They continued. At the end of a street on the edge of town the pockmarked Scarface suddenly stepped out of a house, accompanied by the fighter who had seen them and run away. Behind Scarface came the town judge and another fighter (a strange, tall man whose face [in 1955–1956] was always covered by stubble). Scarface, with his pistol already in his hand, said, "Draw your pistol because this is where you're going to bite the dust (*porque aquí se los va a llevar la tiznada*)" and immediately fired on Rodríguez, who fell to the ground. Rodríguez' friend leapt over a stone wall and made his escape. Rodríguez' wife reports that she "heard a shot from the place where he had gone, and, worried, I ran to see him and attend to him and ask him what had happened." She learned that Scarface had shot her husband "without any motive whatever" (*sin ningún motivo*). Rodríguez eventually was brought to a corn truck and then to a doctor in Zacapu, where, since the .45 slugs had entered his groin, he did not die until 4:00 A.M. the following day. Scarface actually was arrested but was released almost immediately through the influence of Pedro González and the local military commander.

The murder of Rodríguez was never accepted by most of the village as "that's politics" and so forth. Perhaps the difference was the youth and helplessness of the victim, assaulted by four experienced fighters, or the fact that he was on his way to work; there is a feeling against killing someone en route to work or actually tilling the fields. Ever since, speaking of this and similar events, enemies have accused Scarface of killing "for pleasure." In larger terms, the killing symbolized the decadence in the agrarian struggle, a fall from fighting for traditional lands to a struggle for power within the framework of factionalism and vendetta obligations, to an expression of pure egoism, even pleasure, or venting one's rage against a weak opponent.

Political egoism expressed itself in other ways. Pedro González, who had been active in the CRMDT, now entered the lists as pre-candidate for state congressman. But he was rivaled by tough and powerful leaders in other parts of the Tarascan area, particularly another pre-candidate who had been president of Zacapu County the preceding year. He was shot down, allegedly by two Naranja fighters, while plowing his ejido plot in neighboring Tarejero. (By the time of my fieldwork twenty years later there was still no intermarriage or other sharing between the two pueblos. There was deep enmity in Tarejero against "those of Naranja," and, more particularly, deep resentment at the difficulty of getting through to higher levels of government without the mediation of Naranja.)

A yet more serious obstacle to Pedro's career was the agrarian hero and cacique of San Juan Tumbio, an indigenous but mainly Spanish-speaking village in the sierra southwest of Pátzcuaro. Early in 1937 this man was assassinated, allegedly by another young fighter from Naranja. Thus violence had come to include leaders in distant villages who were also Tarascan and radical agrarian—more radical, I think, than those of Naranja, more radical than Cardenismo would tolerate in the state. (A realistic history of the role of the Tarascans in Cardenista politics would dispel the false realism of those sophisticates who accuse "Tata Lázaro" of "romantic nativism" [indigenismo]. It would be worthwhile to scan all the Michoacán regional newspapers between 1929 and 1960 for items on the assassination of [pro-]Communist leaders and on firefights between leftist factions.) In 1956, in any case, the widow of Pedraza, the assassinated agrarian cacique, ran against Scarface and accused him and his town of crimes against her pueblo. When I accompanied ten Naranja stalwarts and Scarface on his campaign tour for state congressman, our long truck ride—interrupted by mechanical trouble—was crowned by finding the plaza of San Juan Tumbio deserted except for a mangy dog asleep in the dust. The villagers had not forgotten the fate of their leader and a few weeks later voted for the party that his widow espoused: Communist (Partido Popular).

Perhaps the most extraordinary event in the eventful year of 1937 was the invasion of Cherán, a largish town of some three thousand Indians living in wooden houses. Cherán had vast and very inequitably divided fields that produced large crops of wheat and corn. Although a hard day's walk away, its boundary abutted on Naranja's, and, as always between adjacent Tarascan towns, there had been bitter boundary disputes. Moreover, the political, particularly the proclerical conservatism of the majority in Cherán was an aggravation in the midst of the Cardenismo in so much of the area.

On Maundy Thursday several hundred agrarians from the Zacapu valley and the Eleven Pueblos suddenly appeared on the outskirts of Cherán, with women to make tortillas and many horses, mules, and wagons; this was the first time since the anti-Cristero campaigns, incidentally, that these two hotbeds of agrarian radicalism had cooperated this way. The "super-red agitators" were making a show—literally a sort of fiesta—of anticlerical force, and had brought along several bands, including the famous ensembles from Naranja and Tiríndaro: indigenous tunes (sones) were heard. Then an open meeting in the church. Violent speeches. Black and red banners with the hammer and sickle. But many people of Cherán thought that the invaders had come to carry away the crops, not just to help the local Cardenista faction to divide the lands. At the moment when a certain Hernández, leader of the Cherán agrarians, began to hoist the black-and-red in the square, the numerous men who had been assembling beyond the periphery of the fiesta opened fire on the visitors, precipitating a firefight which lasted through the night; when the agrarians retreated the next day, some were intercepted in the mountain passes. Depending on your witness, the total fatalities ran from forty to over one hundred. This sanguinary episode had a precedent in the "taking of Tiríndaro" by the Zacapu Valley agrarians under Primo Tapia in 1924. It illustrates the evolving strategy of agrarian caciques of helping local Cardenista factions with physical force and may well reflect the organizational work of Elías Caso, who spent much time in the sierra in the late thirties.

[It may also have taught Elías to use federal troops in such cases, so that any opposition can be branded "a rebellion, rising up in arms," and dealt with summarily. This actually happened in the large, 100 percent Tarascan-speaking town of Azajo in the 1950s; the "rebels" were led forth on a rope chain of nooses by the federals, and Elías' faction took control of a "united" Azajo. The Cherán episode was reported with essentially the same details by Naranja participants, by the political historian Anguiano (1951 : 49–50), and, from a Cherán point of view, by a shopkeeper whom I interviewed. The generally superb anthropological community study by Ralph Beals (1946) is, at best, inconclusive at this point. One learns that there was intense conflict between agrarian, Catholic, and other factions, that there was a major shootout in 1937, and that ethnographing politics in the Tarascan area is not easy: "The people of Cherán are very reticent about conflicts in the town. Efforts are made to convince the outsider that the town is a harmonious unit, and it is very difficult to secure data to the contrary. The impression, after many months in Cherán, is that a great deal of hostility underlies the apparent harmony. . . . Any efforts to pick up the small leads occurring in conversation were usually adroitly countered" (1946 : 114).]

8. The Most Tragic Fission: Caso versus "González" (i.e., Caso)

By 1937 the Casos pretty much controlled their pueblo, but, many now insist, Scarface lusted to reign as the sole cacique. His most serious obstacle to this was Pedro González. Many aver that he and Scarface were friends as well as cousins, and it certainly looks as though they collaborated politically in dividing the labor of internal, village-level politics—

Scarface's turf—and external politics in the state networks, where Pedro had been operating successfully. Many aver that their wives were good friends, following their husbands everywhere and working together on feminist questions, and this seems to me to have been the case. Two villagers claim that Elías' first wife, Guadalupe, was to blame for the new fission, but she, as I have noted, had died the year before. Others point out that the basic issue was the rake-off from the second Partition and that the role of the wives has been exaggerated. What we can be certain of is the overweening ambition of both men, the great economic stakes, some rivalry between the wives, and the strong tendency of a faction to split shortly after it wins.

At a secret meeting of the Naranja ejido, so the story goes, Elías' new wife, Elvira, an ambitious and manipulative schoolteacher for whom he had vied with Pedro, accused the latter's wife of embezzling "thirty pesos" from an expense fund for the Feminine League. This story is given some credibility by what I saw of Elvira, by 1956 the town's leading usuress and prone to set her husband Scarface against his nephews and cousins to the point, in two cases, of suggesting their "elimination." Pedro's wife, on the other hand, was at that time Secretary General of the Feminine League in the whole state or at least some large section of it, and hence was alienated ("disconnected from the pueblo") and vulnerable in the same way as her husband. Moreover, it seems likely that Pedro's wife would not have gotten along with Elvira, granted her friendship with Guadalupe. There was a bitter argument between the two women before those gathered in the town hall; Pedro tried for a reconciliation, but failed. The break had come. Thus the so-called "question of skirts" and the onset of Naranja's bloodiest if not bitterest fission.

The new faction, although dubbed "the opposition" to the Casos, was in fact led by members of the "Caso family": Pedro González de las Casas, Pedro's brother-in-law Agustín Galván, Agustín's brother, and an heir of Joaquín de la Cruz who at the time was heading the Regional Committee and showing great promise. The new faction was supported by most of the Ocampos, many of the more peace-loving villagers, and some landless peasants in Naranja and the adjoining mestizo hamlets to whom Pedro had promised plots in the ejido. Agustín, strong and experienced, had been prominent locally (but never regionally), and some claim that he rather than Pedro was Scarface's main rival although in my opinion he was trying to steer a middle course between them. After the "question of skirts" episode Scarface first tried to force this man's cooperation and was even on the verge of killing him one night. Agustín agreed on the spur of the moment but then turned around and refused the next day. He had been the ejidal president and now, as is more or less customary, was claiming a large share of the graft. Scarface, later in 1937, accused him and another man of embezzling the cash value of the crop of the recently expropriated ejidatarios and, due to the Caso cacique's clout with the judges and military, both the accused were tried, convicted, and jailed, Agustín serving three years. The next year Agustín's brother was assassinated by Scarface's orders.

In the developing factional struggle Scarface was backed by some of the ejidatarios, many of whom were indebted to him for their plots, by no less than nine nephews, and by most of the outstanding fighters; in the three years of 1937–1939, twenty-three certain political homicides and many more reported and inferred exchanges of gunfire rent the little town, much of this directed or at least encouraged by Scarface and carried out by young Caso fighters against insignificant Gonzalistas or former Ocampos. Scarface's main argument to his constituents was that Pedro, in Morelia most of the time, was conniving at the expropriation of many ejidatarios. Neither of the new factions enjoyed the support or even the collusion of the new state governor, incidentally, and Cárdenas was equally attached and indebted to both of his two old friends and comrades-in-arms.

In another major event of the year 1937 the national east-west highway from Mexico City to Guadalajara was built as part of the Cárdenas Six-Year Plan so as to pass through the heart of Naranja (as also through cacique Prado's Tanaquillo in the Eleven Pueblos, whereas Severo Espinoza had it bypass Tiríndaro). This paved highway and the consequent buses and trucks and even tourists did more than anything else to "open up" the pueblo and speed its modernization, particularly the loss of Tarascan speech.

In the nation at large the entire political structure was reorganized by the Cardenistas. The peasants were combined with the industrial workers in a new structure which then, because of its massive potential, was divided, the peasants being grouped under the National Peasant Confederation ("La Campesina") which integrated new peasant leagues and most of the pre-existing state-level leagues of agrarian communities. La Campesina rapidly thereafter became the major organ for the peasants, promoting expropriation, combatting local officials who obstructed it, and giving the peasants a channel of communication to the capital. ("Peasant" here essentially means ejidatario; all ejidatarios were enrolled in La Campesina [Brandenburg 1964:85 et passim].) These reorganizational preliminaries of 1936 were followed in 1937 by the formal dissolution of Calles' old Party of the National Revolution (PNR) and the creation of a new Party of the Mexican Revolution (PRM), with four sectors, the peasants, obviously, coming under La Campesina. Many peasant leaders from ejido communities such as Pedro and Elías were included in this new, more representative party (from one point of view this meant the cooptation of peasant leaders into the bureaucracy and a weakening of land reform). The following year, 1938, by direct orders of Cárdenas, the CRMDT back in Michoacán was dissolved and replaced by a re-created League. In part this was due to the CRMDT's opposition to the then governor, Gildardo Magaña; he was pro-agrarian, but he too had been brought in from a distant place (Baja California). More basically, it was part of Cárdenas' policy to divide and weaken the extreme left, particularly the Communists (some of whom had infiltrated the CRMDT).

Nineteen thirty-nine was the third year of "bad times"; inter alia, eight Naranja peasants were shot by Caso fighters (see Homicide Appendix). By the end of the year Scarface had practically won and his nephew Camilo had become head of the "Regional Committee of Naranja," thus further reinforcing the tradition of direct access to the upper echelons of peasant and/or Cardenista politics, now often via officials in "La Campesina" (e.g., during my fieldwork time Scarface was once driven to Mexico City in a taxi at the cost of some upper-level ally).

This was also the year in which electrification was introduced as part of Cárdenas' national program for material improvements. This second material change, like the highway, profoundly affected the quality of village life, not only making the streets safer to walk in by night but also increasing the use of radios (with their news broadcasts) and other machines.

In 1939, finally, the Cárdenas national faction or personal party, as it were, openly and decisively broke with international Communism, mainly over the Stalin-Hitler pact of that year and the activities of Soviet agents in Mexico—national integrity, which had legitimated the expropriation of American and other foreign oil interests, being a crucial factor. But beyond this is the argument that "For decades [i.e., as of 1964], the Communist strategy in Mexico has centered on the peasantry and agrarian reform" (Brandenburg 1964:122), and for years Cárdenas politics, partly radical but also essentially representing the middle class, had been focused on variously dividing, diluting, persecuting, and stealing the ideological thunder of the Mexican Communists. The manifold conflicts between Communists and Cardenistas already alluded to constituted a most critical political text and subtext of the thirties, and significantly motivated the creation of La Campesina and many other moves by "the master Machiavellian." The conflicts of these years and those of the early 1950s, when the Communists and allied radicals again tried to form a united front of sorts, account in large part for the keen awareness of local leaders such as Scarface, Pedro González, Camilo, Aquiles, and others of many details of the Trotskyist position, Soviet Communism, Marxist doctrine, and so forth, and their emphasis that "the Communists are our greatest enemy in Michoacán," as Camilo put it. The same background accounts for the keen Communist sympathies of several villagers, including the member of the Nahua political family whose nickname is "the Communist."

Communism was basic in the presidential election of 1940, one of the bloodiest in Mexican history. The Cardenistas were opposed by three groups: the relatively conservative followers of Juan Andreu Almazán, the anti-Trotskyites of organized labor (including many Communists), and the supporters of Francisco Múgica, the Michoacán agrarista who had led the agrarian revolt in the Eleven Pueblos, collaborated with Tapia, and recently declared in favor of Trotsky. The split over Trotsky may have cost him the nomination; Cárdenas tapped middle-of-the-roader Manuel Avila Camacho. In Michoacán the governorship, to which Luis Mora Tovar and Cárdenas' brother Dámaso and yet others had aspired, went to another import, Félix Ireta (later to become a compadre of Scarface). In Naranja, the Casos under Scarface predictably supported Avila Camacho, but some twenty opposition members allegedly "rose up in arms" and retired into the sierra; later, when some of them lost their ejido plots, they were accused of having been "Almazanistas." In neighboring Tiríndaro the faction referred to above, supported by Scarface, continued to wrest power from the declining Espinozas. In Tarejero a new, mestizo-led faction, also supported by Scarface, seized control during this period. Two years later, however, despite Scarface's hegemony or at least great influence in the region, the formerly dominant faction, guided by Juan Cruz in Morelia, killed the leaders of the new faction after a day-long firefight said to have involved over one hundred men and burned down their main house with the women inside (the children survived by hiding in a large oven); fifty families of mestizos were driven forth from their colony, and Tarejero moved out from under the control of Naranja (with a corresponding loss of access to power in the capitals). These several histories, incidentally, illustrate some long-term consequences, pro and con, of Tapia's original strategy of alliance with mestizo peasants—at first *acasillados* and then, increasingly, mestizo peasants of any kind—a strategy predicated, not on the ethnic autonomy of the Indian pueblo, but on the putative solidarity of the (landless) peasantry.

The year 1940 witnessed the installation of piped water as yet another component in the Six-Year Plan: one-third of the houses in Naranja now had running water, and there were faucets at many street corners. This third, simple material change had among its many deep consequences a sharp reduction in the traditional pattern whereby women, particularly young girls being courted, toted water in large, painted, earthenware jugs (*cántaros*) from the "Eye of Water" outside the village to their several homes.

From 1940 on Scarface rapidly centralized his power. He was elected president of the county that year and tightened his control in many towns of the region. Bones Gómez was elected president of the ejido, with Ezequiel Peñasco treasurer and Melesio Caso secretary. This election was followed by the expropriation of the "Second Group" of ten ejidatarios and, eventually, two sons of the original agrarian Joaquín de la Cruz. Then, having served the county, Elías wanted to be state congressman and was elected alternate to the agrarian hero and cacique of "the model ejido of the Pátzcuaro region" (Arriaga 1938). Several people allegedly warned this man, Tulaveri, in the Pátzcuaro railroad station that Scarface felt the post "belonged to him." Tulaveri was later assassinated, allegedly by a well-known gunslinger and marksman from Naranja, and alternate Elías Caso took over; the analogy to Pedro's election in the 1930's is obvious (see pp. 161–162). Locally, the now regnant Casos initiated the construction on the plaza of a large vocational school which, despite government subsidies, stood unfinished at the time of my fieldwork (it had become a political football).

The years 1944–1945 presented the first concerted challenge to the now established cacicazgo—a challenge connected, as is typical, with the gubernatorial nomination of 1944 and the anti-Cardenista moves of the governor the following year. In Naranja, the election of Elías' ally Ezequiel as president of the ejido was followed by the dramatic repulsion of the Second Group, first from claiming its harvest out on the lands, then politically and legally when the Naranja authorities "openly defied presidential orders," as related in Ezequiel's life history. But 1945 witnessed the election as mayor of Martín Valle; he had been a loyal supporter of Scarface until he was framed for mail fraud in 1940 (or, worse, caught redhanded and not bailed out) and sent up to the penitentiary for two years. Now he took charge of a new opposition alignment with the pre-existing leaders: Pedro, the de las Casas brothers, and Agustín and his brother. In fact, a weakness in such a new faction was that it contained accretions of former oppositions (Cristeros, Ocampos, Gonzalistas) and so lacked cohesion. One of their moves was for eight men, led by Agustín, to murder three mestizo laborers while they were working for Scarface in the sierra. The murders are said to have been carried out with machetes (a puros machetazos), and one of the victims was an old man, another an adolescent boy. Again, as in 1937, Agustín was convicted and sentenced, serving three years. The desperation of the new opposition and its lack of fighting power were illustrated by the attempted assassination of Scarface, as follows.

One evening Scarface had been in the town hall conducting business. About seven o'clock, as the gloaming was darkening into night, he left the office there and began walking home along the right side of the street, that is, westward. Suddenly, while approaching the home of his nephew Melesio (see Residence Map, Chapter 3), he noticed a group of "enemies" from Buena Vista (the nearby mestizo hamlet) holding rifles and grouped suspiciously on the next street corner. He recognized that this was it, but that it would be death to turn and run. He also became aware that a car was approaching fast from behind him. So he slowed down a bit and walked a few steps more. As the car passed him and the headlights began to shine directly into the eyes of the five "assassins," Scarface dropped to one knee and reached for his .45. But at the same moment the assailants opened up with a volley, wounding him five times in the chest, side, shoulder, and, most important, in the wrist of the right hand. Dropping his pistol, Scarface managed to stagger into his nephew Melesio's compound and bolt the door. The men from Buena Vista, hirelings of Pedro, dashed up and began to force open the door. At this juncture, however, another nephew, Juan Nahua, had heard the noise and began to edge his way up the street, firing at the would-be assassins. They fled. Scarface was badly wounded and lay groaning and covered with blood on the dirt of Melesio's yard. A bit later a third-class "Red Arrow" bus shot into Naranja from the east bearing Martín, who had left town for the day as is customary for caciques when a killing has been arranged. He was returning in comparative security that the "interminable cacique" had finally been dispatched. But as he alighted from the bus yet another nephew of Scarface, Aquiles Caso (as described in his life history), came rushing around one side of the bus, knife in hand. Martín raced around the front of the bus and sprinted for home. Scarface was hospitalized in Morelia and visited by Lázaro Cárdenas. Martín was arrested for his part in the killing of Scarface's hired men in the sierra and spent a year in the Morelia penitentiary before being released through the efforts of Pedro González. Pedro moved to Mexico City, where he supposedly lived on an outlying ranch belonging to Cárdenas until he was able to return in 1949, protected by a federal injunction.

Having scrutinized what it means to become a cacique, let us conclude by shifting angles and briefly listen to the voices of the peasants in the opposition during these years—all contained in letters written to the Agrarian Department.

From a letter dated December 5, 1946: ". . . we feel no gratitude to the assassin Elías Caso. We even enjoy the advantage that when we go to the authorities to tell them about the crimes he has committed, they answer with energetic words that we should not be rebellious, that we should get to work and not get involved in upheavals. . . . that it is materially impossible to go to work, that many lands of this group [the Committee for the Defense of Society and the Ejido] haven't been cultivated for some time because of the fear that we have of being assassinated . . . everything remains in mystery (*en misterio*)." Another such letter is signed by thirty-eight persons "affected by the blackest cacicazgo in Michoacán." In a letter of October 15, 1947, they report that the inspector Juan Vielma, "because he wouldn't let himself be taken by surprise or bribed by the majority of corrupted leaders, COULDN'T ACCOMPLISH WHAT HAD BEEN ORDERED BY THE AUTHORITIES."

"We live in an era of 'terror' instigated and led by the leaders Elías Caso and Camilo Caso, and whoever doesn't bow down to their caprice pays with his life for daring to claim his rights. . . . The terror which rules in this place has an output in deaths and assassinations so that it makes one afraid to speak of them. The inspector from the Agrarian Department was on the verge of being assassinated . . . all the preparations had been made to assassinate him if he inspected the plots that should be returned to us. The leaders cited had ordered to toll the bells, they had collected the pueblo . . . to not obey any order EVEN IF IT COMES FROM THE PRESIDENT OF THE REPUBLIC is the demagogic attitude of Elías Caso and Camilo Caso." I would add that these words sound as though they came from the eloquent or at least rhetorical pen of Pedro González.

9. Autocratic Centralization: The Apogee of Scarface Caso

We have seen Elías, that is, Scarface Caso hardened by his experiences as an exploited laborer on the big estates of the Zacapu Valley and the "hot country." He claimed to have served in one of the Carranzista (i.e., Constitutionalist) armies during the Revolution, although his enemies deny this and I would say that he was lying about the Carranzista part when he talked to me. He claimed to be not only "a revolutionary without blemish" but also "a companion of Primo Tapia in the struggle," but there appears to be no historical record of this whatsoever. On the contrary, all but his close relatives and adherents agree that he shot one of Tapia's trusted fighters in a drunken brawl in 1921 and thereafter quit the pueblo, working in Mexico City as a hired gun or a bodyguard for Francisco Múgica (the two roles are not mutually exclusive, obviously). In any case, he was back in Naranja "on the eve of Tapia's death," as it is often worded, and was welcomed by the victorious agrarians and made an ejidatario with a share in the ejidal profits. Some idea of potential problems is conveyed by what two of his bitterest enemies reported: "In July of 1925 Elías was drunk in Morelos, celebrating. Primo Tapia joined the group and led Elías from the house. Elías began calling him names, hit him in the face, and tore his white shirt. [Tapia always wore white shirts.] The two men began wrestling and Elías shouted, 'Not just this way' (*no solo así*), and pulled his pistol and shot twice. They were separated by Crispín Valle and Salvador Rangel." Incidentally, I think that this happening is improbable but far from incredible and merits mention here as part of the texture of ambivalence that was indeed an ultimate reality.

Thirty years later Scarface was not someone who stood out in a crowd:

short-to-medium stature; beefy-to-paunchy physique clad in khaki; cheap, peasant-style sombrero jammed down over a square, pock-marked, scarred face with stubbed nose, turned-down lips, and intelligent, hard, watchful eyes. But this unobtrusive body housed "the blackest cacique in Michoacán," as is partly conveyed by the following inventory:

1. He was Secretary General and Treasurer of the statewide League of Agrarian Communities.

2. He was State Congressman from the second Electoral District.

3. He was Treasurer of the Naranja Ejido, and one of the richest men in the Zacapu region.

4. One of his nephews (Héctor) was President of Naranja Ejido.

5. Another nephew (Camilo) was County Treasurer in Zacapu.

6. A third nephew (Boni) was the County Chief of Police.

7. A fourth nephew (Aquiles) was Secretary and de facto mayor of Naranja.

8. A fifth nephew (Melesio) was President of the Committee of the Watch.

9. One of his men was a President of the Regional Committee.

10. Another of his men was County Selectman for the Peasant Sector of the Zacapu region.

11. Another of his men (Bones) was Judge of Naranja.

12. Scarface and his nephew Camilo were both high officers in the (national) Masonic Order, to which they made large and frequent financial contributions.

Another way of establishing and illustrating the power of Elías' cacicazgo is through some all-too-brief fieldnotes on regional and state politics, as follows:

"On October 31, 1956, a meeting was held of all the presidents and most of the other officials of the ejidal commisariats of Mich. (24 committees in all in the Liga [i.e., in Morelia]) assembling in the afternoon and sitting in assembly about 8:00 P.M. When the gov. delegate arrived, with Romero and others, Elías Caso made a half-hour speech ôn 'the course (*proyectoria*) of the League,' stressing the founding role of Primo Tapia, with mention of Ursulo Galván, followed by allusions to his own activities and the general importance given to the league by Lázaro Cárdenas as governor and as nat. president. L. Cárdenas made the League the strong base for his support. Apparently his speech was effective—he didn't speak as a politician, but as a peasant, as a man with simple words.'"

"Elías Caso, who gained nomination as Secretary General [of the League] in January, after the deposition of BB for misuse of League funds (for political purposes) is continuing now to work hard consolidating his position and prestige, while retaining a double function since he is also treasurer. . . . His present support of the PRI-imposed local delegate, widow of Gral. Múgica, is partly being played in order to create the additional myth that he was 'close' to Múgica and partook of his ideology." [He was of course close in the sense that a bodyguard is close—PF, 1985.]

"On 11/31/1956 at the internal convention [in Morelia], during the formal nomination of FR, Elías Caso was one of the three vice-presidents representing one of the three 'social sectors'—that of the peasants of the state, who are, of course, the most important sector for PRI in terms of votes. As a member of the executive board (*mesa directiva*) he stood at the front of the hall and his name was frequently called out over the loudspeaker."

"At a Plenary Session of the Zacapu Regional Committee, the widow [of Múgica] visited briefly, brought in a new car in the company of a Pátzcuaro politician, AM, but stayed outside while Elías Caso, BB, and Camilo Caso addressed the ejidal representatives. Camilo violently attacked BB for not calling a plenary, for pretending to represent the Committee independently, and for renouncing this responsibility. Elías spoke trenchantly, if evasively, about the treachery of ER (then county president) and the necessity of remaining united (against ER and BB) in order to avoid division 'which earlier brought us to the point of killing each other.' This was in part a prediction of what would happen if ER were brought in, in part a threat" [fieldnotes dated March 16, 1956; they are of particular interest because they illustrate the close collaboration between Elías Caso and the widow of Múgica, who lived in a palace/fortress-like structure just outside Pátzcuaro, playing Michoacán politics and supporting herself in part by renting bungalows to American tourists].

10. An Interpretation of the Apogee

The reasons for the outstanding successes of the main cacique under study were numerous and complexly interrelated. Most immediate and concrete was the support of many of his relatives, including some women—typically because they owed him their ejido parcels. Also crucial was the armed support of his many nephews, due mainly to the influence of his sister (i.e., their mother or mother's sister), although, as shown repeatedly in the first chapter, they either disliked him personally or disagreed with him violently on questions of ideology and/or practice. This concrete kinship support worked together with his personal ability—despite a lack of charisma—to win the support of some key leaders and, perhaps diagnostic, of practically all the most "valiant" fighters, many of them his nephews; these "fighters" were for the most part young men who could be recruited to ambush members of the opposition, usually at night. Scarface had a sense, sometimes "passionate," sometimes cynical, for the uses of homicide and intimidation, not only for his own material ends, as when extorting a "loan" of three hundred pesos, but as part of a consistent and unswerving Cardenista politics, the main components of which were, or at least had been, anticlericalism, anticapitalism, women's rights, local "material improvements," and the expropriation of landlords and peasants opposed to Cardenismo. His rough and ready ideology worked together with his growing network of personal relations—for example, as a compadre or a fellow Mason—to powerful men in the army and professional politics. But extra-village politics was based soundly on personal wealth in land and livestock and symbiotic relations with the four main money-lenders, all of them women—one his wife, one the wife of his most powerful nephew, and another the mother of that nephew's best friend. Not least important among these relatively specific causes was the fact that, unlike his main opponent, but, as Machiavelli would have advised, Scarface lived and acted continuously in Naranja throughout almost all the three decades of his increasing power—except, obviously, for political trips to the big cities and the many weeks when he hid out in the sierra or cultivated Cardenista factions in the villages there.

Psychological causes are equally relevant to understanding his rise to power. I would emphasize his personal cunning, astuteness, sagacity, and, in general, intelligence, his political resourcefulness and flexibility, his overweening ambition, and his realistic perspective on situations (often conveyed via humor or an apt and pithy phrase). A second angle on his character is achieved through some sketchy fieldnotes: "Watched for fifteen minutes in Tiríndaro while: (1) he scolded and directed Ignacio Ruíz [the cacique he controls] who took it like a little boy, seldom replying ('You have to command here, you should be on the lookout . . . this shouldn't have happened . . . impossible,' etc.); (2) fleetingly described various power relations at the state level: 'These are secrets that BN [the insubordinate mestizo he had put in as head of the Regional Committee] doesn't know . . . many say that Dámaso [Cárdenas, Lázaro's brother] doesn't count because he's going out as governor, but that isn't true, on the contrary, he'll have more power,' 'I as Secretary General of the League in the whole state . . . couldn't accept a position as the alternate to a woman.'"

A third angle comes from combining his cynical state politicking with his unchallenged record as a faithful husband: neither during my fieldwork nor regarding his first wife in the thirties did anyone level the (Mexican) standard charge of sexual improprieties. He seems always to have been a devoted father and a loyal husband, a family man. By 1956 he had become uxorious, notoriously dependent on his avaricious second wife.

A fourth angle takes into account several paradoxically combined attributes and behaviors. On the one hand, he was, as shown in Chapter 3, a sort of "sociometric isolate," without close friends in Naranja. On the other hand, he had many non-confidential friends (*por interés*) at many levels outside the pueblo and somehow inspired an affection (*cariño*) which many people told me they used to feel for him in the old days before the break with his cousin Pedro. Some still felt such affection for him, even when they were living as expellees in Mexico City. He had real *bonhomie*, a talkativeness to the point of garrulousness, a strongly affective quality. His warm friendship with Lázaro Cárdenas and other, lesser politicians remains enigmatic and fundamental, as do the almost innumerable reports of his jealousy and envy of rivals and subordinates in the village, region, and state—so many cases of treachery and suspected treachery, of accusations of disloyalty, of attempts to win someone back, or of achieved punishment. He was an inveterate drinker (referring to "my thirty years of boozing" [*borrachera*]), and he would wax effusive in his cups, drinking and joking with cohorts and with a man he was already planning to kill, and he would beg forgiveness and pardon of people during a wake; one of my lasting memories was of how he would watch you while you chatted with him. And these ambivalences about violence and loyalty worked both ways: in 1950 one of the men who had helped kill his three hired men in the sierra in 1945 appeared at his door, down on his knees, begging forgiveness ("Perdóname, perdóname . . ."). Finally, this cacique had much physical courage, and a Mexican death humor to go with it, but also the weakness, not only of alcoholism and extorting "loans," but of impulsively or deliberately gunning down unarmed and outnumbered and typically much younger victims "for pleasure." In terms of the metaphor of the mask, which pervades this book, the main components in the cacique's mask were sociability, friendliness, and "revolutionary [Cardenista] principles."

In a more historical sense, however, the role of the cacique had been to mask the gradual loss of his pueblo's autonomy—a politicoeconomic autonomy which had been recreated by the agrarian revolt. The loss was masked, perhaps most concretely, by the way he and his relatives and dependents ostensibly fought with the hired guns (*pistoleros*) of what he was always calling "the reactionaries," although over 95 percent of the killing involved persons within Naranja, many of them further to the left, or local peasants who simply opposed his power or his person more than anything ideological. More systematic, perhaps, was the way he excluded, manipulated, or in some way controlled the participation of the (highly political) legal and military power in the state and nation—as illustrated by the Caso control of regional military commanders and judges of the lower court (*de primera instancia*). More subtle perhaps was the way he managed to get himself heard and obeyed, as the representative of the Indian and the peasant, by políticos of vastly greater education with all sorts of middle- and upper-class social connections: the grass-roots Cardenista could act as the legitimate spokesman of the basic principles of the Revolution such as "Land to the Peasants."* Most hypocritical, perhaps, was the way he spouted anticlericalism while getting his children baptized and condoning contributions to the church and the recrudescence of religious ritual.

The most important mask involved outside capital. On the one hand, the Casos publicly criticized private banks, outside money-lenders and corn buyers, and the national government's Bank of Ejidal Credit (see Economic Appendix A). To the extent that they actually blocked these outside powers they helped to perpetuate an archaic system of old-fashioned horse-and-oxen family-plot agriculture, of locally based credit and lending, much of it by barter (Economic Appendix B), and, in general, an economy in which the surplus profits (i.e., income beyond subsistence) were used for acquiring livestock, food and other consumer goods, and, outstandingly, paying for the education of one's (often many) children in boarding schools and colleges in the cities, particularly Pátzcuaro, Morelia, and Mexico City; such capital investment was mainly limited to about forty families, which, as already argued, constituted a (behaviorally defined) economic upper class that corresponded roughly to the middle class of the country at large. Most relevant for this analysis, the surplus capital was used to shore up the village's traditionally great political influence and power, which, in return, was often lucrative. But underlying this defensive mask of communal autonomy and what we would call the corporate solidarity of the Indian peasant was the fact that Scarface, Camilo, and their allies were personally close to the local money-lenders and corn buyers, and cooperated with those from Zacapu and other centers, and to some extent with the Ejidal Bank (e.g., helping with the enforced payment of loans; the average ejidatario's debt to the Bank is about a fifth of the cash value of a plot, but the average indebtedness of any kind would be a much higher fraction). Finally, these local entrepreneurs banked in Zacapu and even other cities.

By the late 1950s, with the explosive growth of industry and capital in Zacapu, the complexly mediated and masked boundaries between the village and the rest of the world were becoming more and more vulnerable. The odds against our cacique had reached a new level and his countermeasures against the non-Cardenista opposition became correspondingly

---

*The problems of agrarian reform and equitable distribution were very far from solved by Cárdenas or the pro-agrarian presidents who followed him: by 1960, 2,053 agricultural units held an *average* of 2,331 hectares of cropland, despite agrarian statutes that set the maximum at 300 hectares; 1 percent of farm units occupied more than 50 percent of the total cropland in Mexico (Hansen 1971:78). In these terms the radical agrarian position championed by the Naranja caciques continued to pose a threat to landlords in the private sector.

extreme, as I hope to have shown by the itemization of his personal support system above. *

11. Terminus?

In the early 1960s a man from Zacapu shot and killed Scarface as he was coming out across the threshold of his two-story house on the main street. The story in the papers and elsewhere was that the killer had paid the cacique 5,000 pesos to arrange his entry to the United States as a migrant worker—for naught. He was sentenced to twenty years.† This shooting coincided roughly with the death of Camilo Caso, "the second cacique." After ups and downs, however, punctuated by the assassinations referred to here and there above, another scion in the same line was still ruling in the early 1980s, according to two authorities, that is, "the last of the caciques" had not died (Agrarian Revolt, p. 134, to the contrary notwithstanding). In socioeconomic terms the village had again been profoundly transformed, with three-quarters of the land worked by rented tractors, 38 percent of the ejido plots controlled and represented by women, and much of the population earning wages in Zacapu (Mummert-Zendejas 1983:109).

---

*The "heating up" of politics in 1955 and Scarface's extreme measures, including the assassination of Agustín, were connected with a general threat to the national PRI party that year: the conservative PAN party (very strong in Zacapu) won 36 percent of the national vote, and the combined votes of the opposition parties outnumbered PRI in the senatorial race in Michoacán and some other states (Scott 1964:195). Regionally, this was reflected in the "betrayal" of the county president and of the head of the Regional Committee and all the intrigue and rhetoric that took place during my fieldwork.

†For a long time I coded the tale of the gulled, would-be bracero as a coverup by Zacapu commercial elements, statewide political enemies, and the media for the politically motivated assassination of an "interminable cacique." Then, in the spring of 1985, after discussing the matter in a class and with friends, I recalled an episode that I presumably had suppressed because it was one of the few unpleasant encounters in my fieldwork with people in Naranja and Tiríndaro. In brief, having obtained from a friend the name and address of a wealthy Texas rancher who needed workers, I, in all innocence, sent out word in Naranja for villagers who wanted such employment. I had all too often been asked to help in this way (no me ayudas pa' ir al norte?). In very little time I had the names and addresses of over twenty men; young men kept appearing whom I had not seen before; excitement was in the air. Then two of the princes, including Toni, came walking up, tight-lipped, hard-eyed, and tense in their bodies, and asked me, courteously, to stop "recruiting for the North," because Scarface had heard about it and was "very angry."

Part Three. "Political Economy"

Spinoza had earlier inspired me with a hatred for
absurd final causes. Nature and art are too great to aim
at ends, and they don't need to either. There are
relations everywhere, and relations are life.
—J. W. VON GOETHE (Letter to Zelter, January 29, 1830)

CHAPTER 6

Political Economy, Oligarchy, and the Leaders

The feature of personality development that perhaps goes deepest in explaining the princes is that almost all of them experienced a troubled, economically deprived, and sometimes drastically disturbed childhood. The older generations spent the first twenty years of their lives in the confusion and poverty that followed the desiccation of the swamp by the landlords, and the younger men were formed during the hectic days of the agrarian struggle and agrarian factional politics, often witnessing violent scenes. The great majority of the princes were born into families that were poor even by Naranja standards of the time, that is, precisely into that margin of the population that was most exposed to the deteriorating transformations in the economy and the total culture. Childhood and adolescence under the changed conditions of the society made them relatively aware of death in terms of their own death-conscious culture. These men inherited a network of vengeance-filled, hostility-ridden, and economically tense human relationships that are impossible to live down and forget—that, in a sense, can only be perpetuated.

Yet more, almost all the princes were the victims during their early years of a personal catastrophe of vast implications: more than 80 percent lost their fathers by the age of ten, and many, such as Camilo, in the earliest years of their lives. This meant that they were bereft of the economic support and moral guidance and "showing the way" of their fathers. But it also meant partial liberation from the often oppressive sanctions and inhibitions of a patriarchal system and world view. Some of these men were brought up by godparents, but most of them lived with their mothers in a family situation that differs greatly from that obtaining when the Tarascan (or mestizo) father is alive.[1] They were nudged or thrown into the world of adult responsibilities and adult behavior at an age that was generally young for their culture, where many boys start accompanying their fathers to the fields at age six or seven and learning the ropes. They had to help support their mothers and their younger siblings. They received a maximum of "independence training." The psychological import of this shared experience is not vitiated by the fact that many other Naranjeños have also been orphaned and thrust into life as fledglings. On the contrary, this particular experience, when occurring in various combinations with various subsets of other experiences, is part of what sets off the more important princes of the nuclear group.

The princes themselves are unusually aware—even self-conscious—of the hardships of their childhood and, when conversing on familiar terms, will often spontaneously begin to speak about the loss of their fathers and the like. Camilo is typical in stressing that "We had only squash" or "We had only tortillas." Aquiles once proudly asserted, "We, the Indians, are accustomed to hunger and inclement weather (*la intemperie*)." Often indeed I heard from them the ethnic boast, "The Tarascan can walk two days *and two nights* without eating *and without drinking!*" On the second day that I knew him, during a long walk in the sierra, Héctor told me of how it had been to herd cattle in the mountains when he was only ten, and of how once he woke up from a nap on a hillside and saw a huge grey coyote sitting only ten feet away, staring at him silently. The typical prince is an ex–have-not, with painful memories of his origins and the long uphill fight.

The personality development of the princes has also been marked by a high degree of cultural and economic discontinuity. The culture of the individual has often been greatly altered in the course of a single generation; the dress, manners, diet, language, and ideas of many people and families are markedly different from what they were in 1925. Many have been increasingly exposed to the mestizo culture of Mexico, and to the United States. [The rapid change in Naranja, incidentally, has continued into the present of 1986.]

Finally, as has been shown, the culture of the community during the generation under discussion contained an unusual number of contradictions in its norms which, together with economic problems, contributed to the political history we have been dealing with. There was a generalized tendency toward disintegration between norms and goals that sometimes, as in 1937–1939, seemed to amount to a state of anomie. The discontinuities and conflicts were, in fact, so great that, as a consequence, many Naranjeños, far from resolving these conflicts, live today by various combinations of dogged toil, frequent indolence, alcoholism, and, often enough, social and political passivity.

A detailed description of these at least potentially disconcerting discontinuities in Naranja culture was provided early on in the study of Primo Tapia (*Agrarian Revolt*, Chapter 4). His cultural experiences afford an extreme example that is particularly fascinating because of the degree to which his pragmatic, personal integration was spliced to a more abstract, ideological one. But he has been paralleled by many of the princes, and leaders in general, who have had the requisite strength, flexibility, intelligence, and, as it were, realism, to be able to sort out the values of their disturbed culture and patch together a workable integration—integrating conflicts in the sense of entertaining and at times exercising contradictory values and options. Particularly relevant parallels, which also entail intersections with ideology, as in the case of Tapia, have been depicted above in the life studies of the half-brothers Camilo, Boni, and Aquiles, all nephews of Tapia as well as of Scarface.

Almost all the two dozen or more princes of Naranja spent the first five years of their lives in Indian homes that differed little from what (in *Agrarian Revolt*) I inferred for the indigenous culture of 1885. Salient traits of this milieu were infant hunger and mortality, protracted and tight swaddling, weaning on beans and tortillas, and constant bodily contact with the mother and other women and girls. The Indianness of this boyhood was deepened by the fact that—as in Indian Mexico generally— Naranja women have always been ten or more years behind the men in their stage of acculturation to Spanish and mestizo ways; today the majority of women in Naranja still speak Tarascan, if not fluently, then at least as their first, mother language. All but three of the two dozen or so princes treated in this book were brought up and socialized by such traditional Tarascan women.

After their Indian boyhoods, the princes were increasingly exposed to mestizo patterns as a result of school, residence, and work in mestizo areas (especially the Zacapu factory) and, finally, the enormous changes that have been transpiring in Naranja itself. In some cases they began to learn Spanish from older males as they began to work and play outside their immediate families. Many princes, notably Ezequiel, Carlos, and Aquiles, have worked for long periods in the United States, visiting many cities, observing exotic patterns, and talking with Americans and peoples of many other nationalities, notably Italians and Filipinos. They, like Primo Tapia and Pedro López, returned to Naranja with their heads full of new ideas, foreign impressions, and vague impulses to exploit the economy or to improve their own culture. The princes have been molded and twisted by the same forces of culture change that are making Mexican history today. Some of them, such as Melesio, have resisted in speech and dress, while others have largely switched to mestizo ways. Most of the princes embody in their personalities a strange synthesis or at least a composite of the indigenous patterns of earlier decades, the fast-changing, complex-ridden mestizo culture of Mexico, and finally, various elements of the American way of life, so inspiring and yet disconcerting to the migrant worker.

Let us look now at the salient traits of character shared by these men. One is a desire to dominate, to command others, to possess office and the symbols of economic and political power. This lust for power comes in three forms of psychological-cultural symbolism: (1) ambition (*ambición*), in the struggle for status and property (essentially land and livestock); (2) envy (*envidia*) toward individuals who threaten one in this struggle; (3) egoism (*egoismo*), which always sets the interests of the individual above those of others and the solidarity norms of the pueblo. Men such as Camilo and Aquiles exemplify these three, interconnected passions of *libido dominandi* and their material contexts and meanings, as is amply documented above.

The princes are also characterized by an unusual personal energy, a physical and psychic hardness and *élan vital* that sets them off from the average Naranjeño and the average Mexican peasant. This tough vigor has impressed other observers and probably characterizes peasant leaders in many other parts of the world which have gone through rapid stages of progress and local struggles for land. When nuclear princes like Scarface or Aquiles are doing something, whether typing out a census or cultivating corn, they observably concentrate on it and do a fast and efficient job. When they walk they seem to be moving with purpose toward a goal. It is an unforgettable sight to have seen Toni's keen sickle blade flashing in the setting sun as he goes down through a strip of yellow wheat, leaving his fellow workers far behind. The princes gesticulate with greater animation and precision than most Tarascans, whose hand movements typically are small in compass and restrained. The visible energy and drive of the princes, partly psychic in genesis, is also fueled by diet: these men have been eating well for years, as will be detailed below. The princes consciously value their qualities of toughness and dynamism and are explicit about them (*ser duro, dinámico*).

The perceptive and astute leader Hercules Ocampo once remarked during an interview in Mexico City, "The great majority in Naranja are like a herd of sheep, docile and peaceful." This is an exaggeration, even a caricature, but there is some truth to it too. The prince, on the other hand, while not a wolf, is relatively active and prone to violence. Among the likely preconditions for this I would suggest their typically fatherless boyhood, their extreme physical deprivation during infancy and childhood, their witnessing of violence during maturation and getting drawn into it, and, above all, the models and exemplars of violence in the adult world. Violence may reduce to a single political decision—for example, to order an assassination. Or it may mean one's personal participation in more or less calculated homicides as has been described above. Violence, finally, may mean the eruption of blind, uncontrollable rage (*coraje*) that is often justified or even dictated by the culture in terms of economic conflict (e.g., the theft of one's cow) or personal obligations.

A case of this third type of violence occurred early in 1956 and well illustrates the genre. The Mestizo is an important gunman today, and one of the politest men I have ever met. He was sleeping in his house late one Sunday afternoon when a boy rushed in and blurted out that The Mestizo's best friend had been badly mauled by another man, with a stone. The Mestizo's friend had indeed been badly pummeled, but by a large crowd outside town that did not include the accused. The Mestizo is not the type to call for legal proof when his friend is lying bloody. He jumped up from his bed, still half-asleep, dashed out half-dressed, and, crossing several back yards, soon reached the home of the accused lad. He knocked down a section of the stone wall, instead of stepping over it, and then, rushing up to the back door, found himself confronted by the lad's mother, who was interposing her body in characteristic style. He immediately attacked her, ripping off her rebozo and most of her blue blouse before he was able to hurl her backward and pounce into the room. He shot, the .45 bullet passing through the hat brim of the young man, who was standing, trembling, in the corner. Camilo, unofficial judge of Naranja, decided that The Mestizo was not guilty, since he had been given cause for rage. The Mestizo is, of course, an important Caso fighter. The boy who had come in and mistakenly accused the young man was forced, by Camilo's legal logic, to pay the damages for the injuries done to The Mestizo's friend!

A fourth character trait of the princes is their apparent security and the absence of signs of anxiety. In part this further illustrates the reserved, masked quality of personality in the Tarascan area. In part it would seem that courage and mental callosity are prime prerequisites for leading peasants in such agrarian pueblos. A man should not show fear, partly as a matter of face; courage (*valor*) is assumed and, among Tarascans (as contrasted with mestizos), is seldom discussed as such.[2] A man also should not show fear as a matter of practical use, and Tarascans, whether or not they are princes, seldom seem to. The ingrained reaction to great danger is fatalistic resignation ("Kill me, once and for all [*máteme con una vez*]," when trapped), strong and swift counter-aggression,[3] or problem-solving flight. Some princes are simply cocksure in the face of danger. Others joke about danger, accidents, injury, and death itself—as is typical of Tarascans and Mexican peasants generally. The leaders of the weaker or fallen faction display not only security but even a certain serenity that is impressive, considering their precarious position. I once asked Martín how he felt about going out alone into the fields and even into the hills. His answer was, "They could kill me if they wanted to, and maybe they will, but I am going to keep on working." Here, as elsewhere, we note that the act of working seems to be invested with a certain sacredness, albeit not inviolability, which makes a man feel immune—and, on the basis of the record, he almost always is. The dangerous places are the side streets and the outskirts of town, during the evening.

A fifth feature of these peasant leaders is their astuteness or cunning. Astuteness is a partly intuitive ability to size up a human problem and be able to manipulate one's followers and to outfox one's enemies. It often entails a relatively great awareness of larger issues and contexts and also a degree of suspicion and a willingness to violate social norms. *Astucia* is tested critically in political intrigue and in the competition for land and followers. The princes speak of it with high regard.

A final trait of these leaders is acquisitiveness, centered mainly on land. Land and material needs have been the basis of the agrarian and factional struggle and the agrarian ideology, and it is land and the desire for land that continue to move Naranja politics. To some extent this agrarian orientation has been communal, communalistic, even Communist—as in the case of the harvest brigades that still survive from the twenties. But for the overwhelming majority, political activity has to a significant degree been the means for bettering the economic position of oneself and one's family, and the princes have been driven by precisely such urges—notwithstanding curious exceptions such as the profligate Bones and Primo Tapia himself. The prince, like the average Naranjeño, is aware of the typically Mexican interdependency between politics and property, and the present paragraph would, for him, be belaboring the obvious.

Turning from less strictly economic considerations, we note that the so-called "race" (*la raza*) is felt by Naranjeños to be an essential criterion of "Indianness." Indian blood, in my impressionistic opinion, actually heavily predominates in the leaders although only a few, such as Ezequiel, strike me as pure Indian. Only two of the oligarchy look relatively Caucasian, and one of these—Gregorio—is from a family that "has always lived here." Most of the princes are of medium stature although some, like Aquiles, are short and others are tall by Mexican Indian standards. They tend to be slender or fairly well-built, but never fat, with the partial exception of the paunchy Scarface. Skin color ranges from dark yellow to an almost chocolate brown, with the majority decidedly on the swarthy side. Black hair and black to brown eyes mark the group, with significant exceptions such as the grey eyes of Bones and The Mestizo and the blue eyes of Aquiles.[4] Racial homogeneity of sorts integrates the oligarchy and distinguishes them and their pueblo from, for example, the mestizo lawyers in the state and national capitals with whom they have to deal. While interviewing in the Zacapu factory, which has attracted workers from many other parts of Mexico, I noted a lot of friendly ribbing of one Naranjeño as *indio*, "Indian" (*por la raza*), and as *matón*, "murderer."

Language, such a distinctive feature of culture, also serves as a sure index of culture change and of ethnic-economic boundaries. In Naranja, as in many communities, the events of the past decades have produced a surprisingly clear-cut gradient of linguistic acculturation. The total population, including the leaders, is divided into three rough levels, or acculturation age-grades. Persons above forty-five generally have a fluent command of Tarascan and speak it at home. These men passed their formative years in a community that was still essentially monolingual; many women in this bracket still hardly know Spanish. The older princes, such as Bones, Toni, Ezequiel, and Pedro, belong to this age-grade. For them speaking Tarascan is a political symbol; as we have seen, Camilo and Scarface do not use the language at home, with their big-city wives, obviously, but they do profess it to mestizos on the outside, particularly to fellow políticos.

The next age-grade in cultural and linguistic change includes Naranja men born between 1910 and 1930, from twenty-five to middle-aged, and therefore the majority of the leaders. The linguistic aptitude of this group, which includes most of the princes, ranges from a fair passive knowledge of Tarascan, as in the case of Aquiles, to a command of both languages, as in the case of the former schoolteacher Longinus. Three of the mestizo princes speak practically no Tarascan (Gregorio, The Mestizo, Jaime). On the other hand, the triad of confidential friends and compadres led by Pancho speak only Tarascan with each other and with their wives. Until a few years ago one member of this special set, Liborio, held the undisputed title as the best wit in the large "circles" of ten to thirty men who used to meet on Sunday mornings and compete at telling "colored stories" and passing a joke from man to man with cumulatively elaborated double entendre (mainly involving derivational morphology). He was seconded by two renowned gunmen: first, Gabriel, the basketball star who since has been shot by Jaime, and second, "Franco the Squirrel," who is also Naranja's best singer and poet of amatory verse. Thus we see that the majority of the princes occupy very diverse transitional positions, with Spanish as their principal means of communication, but that extremes of complete ignorance and virtuoso-like fluency in Tarascan also are represented.

The people in Naranja display ambivalent attitudes, reflecting their conflicting values and goals. On the one hand, most of the women in the middle age-grade are fluent in Tarascan, and a man like Liborio is publicly praised. People assert that they know Tarascan *too*, or express guilt when their language is faulty. On the other hand, monolingual Tarascans from Azajo are scoffed at, and many people avoid using the indigenous tongue in the streets for fear of being mocked as "Indian." Most of the Naranja population would agree that it is ideally better to know both languages, but that it is practically more advisable to speak only Spanish to one's children. The youngest age group consequently displays a poor knowledge of Tarascan and will often jeer about the subject (although within a significant fraction of families small children still learn Tarascan from their mothers or grandmothers). Basically, it is the limited or even negative value of Tarascan in the struggle with the mestizo socioeconomic system that accounts for the weakness and decline of the language.

Demographic incursion affects acculturation in obvious, quantitative ways. Since the agrarian reform hundreds of people have immigrated; by 1956 there were in-dwellers from no less than thirty-nine outside communities, more than half of them non-Tarascan, including two women from far-off Guanajuato. The oligarchy has been affected by these movements. However, it is striking that only two princes were born outside the village and that both of these were brought in before their fifth year and grew up in complete adaptation to local patterns. Both are married to Naranja girls. One of them, the brooding, pistol-carrying Jaime, acts like any minor prince and fighter. The other outsider is The Mestizo (whose monicker, "Turis," simply means "Non-Tarascan" in Tarascan). Both The Mestizo and Jaime are felt to be part of the town, fondly by some, but both are ubiquitously classified as mestizos on the basis of language, birth in a mestizo community, and, above all, the fact that they do not consider themselves Indian. We have noted the egregious way they remain outside the system of ceremonial kinship among the princes.

The great majority of Naranja's mestizos came and survived as laborers, or married local people. Eight of the two dozen or so princes have espoused mestizas, especially from Zacapu; their tendency toward exogamy reflects cultural attitudes and the simple fact that they have far more contacts outside the community. Only five important princes in the ruling faction married Naranja Indians, and all five of these men are fluent in Tarascan (Toni, Ezequiel, Boni, Bones, and Melesio). Thus in their marriage choices as in their language, the princes reflect the entire range of variation.

The fallen faction is marked by a higher rate of exogamous marriage and, unlike the Casos, by foreign origin. Only half of the ten leaders spent their formative years in Naranja and only three have actually grown up with the town; the rest have either immigrated or spent long years in other parts of the country. Still more striking is the fact that only one of these fallen leaders is married to a Naranja Indian, the rest having selected their partners from the outside. Women play an important if secondary part in the informal political control; the faction of Pedro González displays lack of integration with "the feminine sector." Such facts of birth, residence, and marriage are frequently brought up by the Casos to show that their opponents are "not with the pueblo." Lack of demographic and affinal roots in Naranja is a principal reason for the fall and continued weakness of the González group; many of the immigrant, landless mestizos who supported Pedro have since been driven forth.

We turn now to the domestic economy of the princes. In a nutshell, political position and power correlate in part with wealth, and all of the oligarchy live well by Mexican standards (and those of most of the world, as far as that goes). Almost all are ejidatarios, and in addition many of them own four to six or more acres privately, or work even larger amounts as renters. The wealthiest enjoy the usufruct of twenty or more acres of land, some of it very fertile (Scarface, Camilo, Ezequiel, Gregorio, Pedro, and perhaps Martín). Several possess other sources of income such as stores, corn mills, and livestock, or enjoy, temporarily, the income from political office (as detailed in Chapter 4). The wealthiest of these men thus earn over thirty thousand pesos a year, although the majority have to be content with half that much. Thus the agrarian reform created a de facto or "behaviorally indexed" class of sorts of forty or fifty families of peasants (some of them survivors of the earlier, wealthier class) with considerable if varying margins of purchasing power that permit such satisfactions as store furniture and a college education for one's son. These economically middle- or upper-class peasants contrast dramatically with the dozens of poor families that have no land; about forty women are still earning a pittance by following one of Naranja's traditional crafts: braiding straw for hats.

How has the new income of the princes been expended in more general terms? All the princes now own houses of adobe, often substantial units of three or more large rooms, with floors of tile, brick, or cement. Scarface and Ezequiel possess ostentatious two-story structures on the main street. But these dwellings always retain the Indian base of petates, low stools, open-air hearths, and the like. In addition, they often enough include a complete set of bedroom furniture, numerous chairs and tables, radios, sewing machines, and lurid commercial calendars.

The diet likewise is built on an indigenous base of corn, beans, and chile, with some squash. But it also includes impressive quantities of meat, milk, vegetables, sugar, tropical fruits, rice, starches, coarse wholesome bread, eggs, and yet other items to round out the fare. The typical prince has cocoa, a roll or a sweet roll, and tortillas and beans for breakfast, although these often are divided between a very light early snack and a heavier breakfast proper. He consumes a substantial afternoon dinner of tortillas, beans, and chile, supplemented by, for example, noodles or rice, a cabbage soup with chile sauce, and, finally, some fruit. For supper he may partake again of coffee or cocoa, small amounts of rough bread, beans with cheese, and a few warmed-over tortillas. His children get about two glasses of milk a day, as well as candy and fruits such as oranges. In addition, people often consume great quantities of variegated foods on special occasions such as the fiestas, with their chile sauces and rice, or the month of the broadbean harvest when a typical family often eats several pounds of beans a day. Naturally, there are striking variations to these patterns: Camilo eats "only meat and milk" (just about true), and his brother Boni eats only once a day. The diet of Naranja's better off, which includes the princes, is, in any case, extraordinarily good compared not only to rural Mexico but to the United States (in terms, for example, of minerals and vitamins, low levels of sugar, fat, cholesterol, etc.).

The wealthier Naranjeños dress well, as was clear in the life histories above. This fact reflects a combination of the income from the ejido and the older indigenous cast to Naranja culture that showed up in the well-ironed manta and brilliant serapes of the turn of the century. The people of Tiríndaro still accuse the Naranjeños of dressing like dudes instead of improving their houses. Actually, these peasants tend to alternate between two kinds of clothing. For work they don crude boots or huaraches, serapes, large sombreros, and clothes of manta, khaki, or denim. In this attire they look like the "typical Indian." On festive occasions they dress in black shoes or short soft-leather boots, well-pressed pants of poplin or black wool, fine cotton shirts, and jackets of khaki-colored poplin or white cotton, or leather aviator jackets. Some go hatless; others wear narrow-brimmed straw sombreros or hats of grey or tan felt. The younger men often sport brilliantly colored shirts, ranging from dark maroons to Hawaiian designs in which blue-green predominates. Although he doesn't have any suits, the wealthier Naranjeño (and hence all the princes) dresses as well as the average American farmer on a Saturday night.

The younger women often make a sloppy or unkempt impression compounded of untended permanent waves, cotton dresses in garish colors, and ill-aimed attempts at make-up; they have far more work per day than the men, since children and tortilla making are invariable, time-consuming daily occupations. When dressed in their best to go to Zacapu they look either like representatives of the urban lower classes or like shiny Indians with a mestizo veneer.

The middle-aged and older women still wear braids and something approximating the traditional Tarascan attire, but they stand in sorry contrast to the comparatively unacculturated women of Cherán and Azajo, who continue to integrate brilliant ribbons woven into shining, clean hair with an embroidered blouse, a heavy, pleated black wool skirt, and a brightly colored apron. Both men and women fall rather clearly into the three acculturation age-grades mentioned previously. The men have largely made the sartorial adjustment, alternating variously between the two dress styles described. The women display a sartorial vacillation that may well reflect the confusions of their rapidly changing culture, particularly the economic conflicts entailed by the high cost of indigenous female attire and, on the other hand, the socioeconomic pressure to dress like the mestizo women in the Zacapu markets and similar venues.

Let us turn now to "customs" and their economic implications, matters of which the villagers are well aware. The princes, considering their status, participate little in the local fiestas because of the anticlerical heritage, agrarianism, PRI ideology, and, more concretely, their opposition to the priests and the huge payments the latter try to obtain. The princes actively discourage religious fiestas, to the point of sometimes intimidating citizens who talk about reviving the passion plays of Holy Week; we saw in Camilo's life history how the three Caso half-brothers shot up a religious procession. The general boycott and opposition by the princes makes particularly significant such exceptions as Boni's dancing on "Tiger Day," and the fact that Liborio is the best "Little Old Man" dancer and mimic of voices and gestures. It is possible that the princes will soon switch to supporting the colorful pageantry of local "customs"—which could be done without readmitting a priest by distinguishing between local folk religion as against the clerical, national religion. Almost by way of compensation, in any case, the princes tend to spend lavishly on the personal or individual fiestas of baptism, marriage, and burial; a curious index of the degree of individualism is thus found in the contrast between avoiding communal religious fiestas and largess when it comes to those of the life cycle.

The preceding data should have demonstrated that the princes are a highly acculturated group that nevertheless is still Indian by the best definitions, although someone used to a sierra Tarascan village would stress the marginality of their participation in the areal culture. To me the most convincing criterion of acculturation is attitude: both the Indians of Naranja and the mestizos of the adjoining pueblos emphatically and unanimously agree that the Naranjeños are indigenes. As a matter of fact, there exists among the princes a certain nativistic sentiment, fragmentary but clearly visible in its outlines, that finds its expression in the long-standing expeditions, usually led by the younger princes, to excavate Tarascan figurines from the nearby burial mounds (compare the figurines and statuettes referred to in Boni's Rorschach). Most of the reading Naranjeños are enthusiastically interested in prehistory and Tarascan legends.

In a community where land is king and work means agricultural work, one finds, of course, a common denominator for all males, including the princes. I have purposely and repeatedly stressed that the politically motivated members of the Naranja community, despite divers "vices" and illegalities, have always been and today remain working Indian peasants above all else; even Scarface and Camilo qualify in terms of their past, although both are now often classed as "rich" (*ricos*). But when men are working together in groups there always arises a critical, competitive spirit that is generally articulated through favorable or invidious comparisons as the case may be; workers rank each other on the basis of their aptitudes and their production (just as American farmers are constantly comparing each others' machines and mechanical abilities). This practically universal pattern operates to a pronounced degree in Naranja: all men are located somewhere on a hierarchy depending on the extent to which they, not work, but "know how to work" (*saber trabajar*), a phrase that often crops up in men's conversations about each other (it is just as common in Tarascan as in Spanish). Some of the princes, such as Toni and The Mestizo, are rated "best workers"; anyone who has seen the former harvest wheat with a sickle or the latter rapidly load heavy sacks of corn on a staggering mule would tend to concur with the communal evaluation. The majority of the princes such as Camilo and Ezequiel are rated as "good workers" or, in the case of Aquiles, as men who "can work very well when they want to." On the other hand, some of the best workers in the town are nowhere close to being in the oligarchy of princes, and some princes, such as Jaime, are not highly regarded and are minimally capable on the rare occasions when they put their hands to the sickle. The primal jobs such as reaping or picking corn never occupy more than a few months of the year and are interspersed with rest periods of days, weeks, or even months. These rest periods have combined with the exigencies of an archaic technology to place a high premium on working fast for short periods—both in the sense of short seasons and in that of getting through one's row or furrow as rapidly as possible, then resting briefly. The prestige deriving from one's ability to work fast and expertly, while not essential to becoming a prince or even a leader, will enhance the chances of an individual who, consciously or unconsciously, is seeking to enter the nuclear group.

Industrialization creates an unusual kind of work and constitutes a trenchant index of acculturation in the present case. About sixty men from Naranja have worked for the thirteen-hundred-man Celanese Corporation of America factory outside Zacapu, and by 1956 twenty-two were still employed at an average wage of eighteen pesos a day. Most of the princes under forty have worked in this textile factory, either on construction, as in the case of Aquiles, or within the massive entrails of the plant itself. Several, such as Crispín, the leading younger man in the fallen faction, have more than five years of experience as "spinners" in the (to me at least) nearly asphyxiating acid fumes of the vast "coagulation halls"; conditions were so bad that some developed pulmonary problems and withdrew. Some have become labor leaders; Crispín has served as first secretary of the union. In all cases this industrial experience has affected the younger princes, exposing them to a fast brand of mestizo culture, to the rhythms and regularity of factory life, and, finally, to the materially improved style that results from a factory paycheck and the incentives expressed by one's fellow workers.

Besides agriculture and the factory, two other specialties are crucial to Naranja's political economy: politics itself, of course, and then music. Music has always been a major preoccupation ever since Juan Ocampo introduced modern instruments in 1886: except for a few years following the exodus of most of the Ocampos in the middle thirties, the band of this little pueblo has served as tutor and example to many other Tarascan communities (which, in general, export a great deal of music to the mestizos around them). In 1956 the twelve-piece band performed twenty-two times in seventeen different communities. The year before that, moreover, the band leaders organized a svelte, fourteen-piece orchestra that was playing in cities all over the state, averaging 1,200 pesos per performance, and over 4,000 pesos for Independence Day; it ranked second only to the professionals of Morelia. One would not recognize the one-time "Apaches of Naranja" in the members of this artistic ensemble, gleaming in their turquoise-blue bow ties and jackets and buff slacks, as their chromed saxophones and brassy trumpets unite to produce the imperious rhythms of "The Widows of Cha-Cha-Cha."

Music correlates with and clearly symbolizes the politics in Naranja de Tapia. The band even figured crucially in the agrarian revolt, as in the anecdotes reported by Pedro López (*Agrarian Revolt*, p. 109). But ever since the great fission in 1926 and the killing of Tomás Cruz in 1928 the leading musicians have always been anti-Caso, first as Ocampos, then as Ocampos within the Gonzalista faction. The ongoing tendency today is for persons to go into music who are either neutral or hostile vis-à-vis the Casos and for the Casos to abstain from music. And corresponding to music in politics there has been a great deal of politics in music, notably in the Joe Hill style of song in the agrarian period. The size and success of the Naranja bands and orchestras have, in any case, long rankled the egoism of the ruling Caso princes. They feel that the existence of a powerful and independent interest group menaces their authoritarian control over the community.

By conscious plan and/or the expression of an uncontrollable envy, the Caso princes decided to force the musicians to play in Naranja on Independence Day, thus depriving them of the one hundred pesos *per man* that they had been earning by practicing their art in larger communities. Daniel, a swarthy and indomitable artist, bluntly refused to obey the authorities, and managed to offend the vain and domineering Gregorio in the course of the argument in the town hall. Later, during a drinking bout, Gregorio waxed bitter and exclaimed that "Daniel is bad, very bad." The authorities, led by Aquiles and Gregorio, functional mayor and president of the ejido, respectively, then proceeded to call in all the other members of the band and to interrogate them as to whether they were "with Daniel" or "with the community," implying then and later that those who sided with Daniel might lose their land or that "something might happen to them in the sierra." The minority that stuck with Daniel all turned out to be Ocampos or Gonzalistas, but they are also the best musicians. A meeting of the entire town was then held, at which the authorities read off the names of the musicians, denouncing those who stood with Daniel as "not wanting to cooperate with the community." An old musician arose and made a pathetic plea to the effect that Daniel was trying to "do something beautiful, that the money involved wasn't the most important thing." At this Aquiles stood up and declared that "we are not interested in beauty or anything like that. Clear out of here with your beauty (*váyanse con su belleza*). All we want is a few tunes on Independence Day." The result of this typically coercive action on the part of the autocratic princes has been the hoped-for division among the musicians. The poorer, the weaker, and the inferior players are "with the town." The best musicians are not going to play for Naranja, preferring to pay Independence Day dues like ordinary citizens. They are now throwing all their energies into bettering the swanky orchestra. As Daniel said, "We are trying to create something new, with beauty, and they can't stop us from playing. Anybody has a right to make music, doesn't he? Most of the time I work in the fields as a peasant, so if they want to find me, they can!" Whatever one may think of "cha-cha-cha" music, the fact is that the perfect, clear tones of Daniel's trumpet are recognizable at a great distance— during, for instance, the late hours of a fiesta—and would assure him a job with the best American orchestras.

In Naranja, as in rural American towns, athletics functions to forge political leaders, and athletic success remains in the public memory to influence relationships throughout the rest of the individual's life. Most of the princes of Naranja have been athletically outstanding in some way. The older ones such as Ezequiel and Bones distinguished themselves in the equestrian arts during the early days of the mounted militia. Basketball has been the primary sport in the town since the early thirties, and many of the stars have become princes, notably Héctor, Boni, Aquiles, and Gregorio. The recent diversions of the red brick poolroom have added homely laurels to such princes as Camilo, Aquiles, and Mateo. The final sport of note is the Indian game of *palillos* or "little sticks," that, we saw in Chapter 1, inspires the sentiments of the *very* sentimental Aquiles. *Palillos* is played by one to three groups on Sunday mornings in the refuse-littered back yards south of the town. The men who display the greatest expertise in bouncing small polished sticks off a flat rock are, aside from Aquiles, the (now deceased) gunman Gabriel, the doughty

Pancho Orozco, and that likable composer of Tarascan love songs, "Franco the Squirrel." Not only do athletic successes like these inspire lasting respect; the type of decision-making and the personal manner bred by athletics are a more fitting training for leadership in a small agricultural community than the rational, intellectual qualities that are encouraged by advanced education. Two important leaders in the fallen faction are the son and nephew of Pedro González, both former law students; neither enjoys much rapport or even contact with age-mates. The only leading Gonzalistas who have starred in athletics are now in their fifties and, so to speak, on the bench. The Caso men have all been good athletes, and in this significant respect they are "with the pueblo."

Violence has been discussed psychologically and as a basic factor in the economic struggle. It also calls for discussion in cultural terms. Some of the main causes of violence at this level have been (1) the indigenous patterns of self-help, (2) the ever-present network of personal loyalties and vengeful animosities, (3) the obvious interdependency between effective force and legal-political control, (4) the breakdown of social norms and the over-excitation of the struggle for land, that is, mainly, ejidal plots, and (5) the specific accretions of the Revolution and forty years of agrarian factionalism. Violence has been inspired by the human relations and the generic state of partial anomie existing ever since the early twenties. The leaders tend to employ violence, and individuals prone to violence become either leaders or myrmidons.

Let us look at some of the specific ways that a propensity to violence is reflected in political roles. At present most of the princes either are gunmen—notably Boni, Bones, Melesio, Toni, and Scarface—or are prone to violence and pack a pistol on occasion, as would hold for Camilo and Aquiles. Several minor princes are reckoned dangerous gunmen: notably, the temperamental Mestizo and the taciturn Jaime Morales. On the other hand, some important gunmen, often mentioned in accusations, are not leaders at all; for example, the recently deceased Gabriel. And many actual or potential leaders, whether or not they are called "princes," have not, as far as I know, committed any violent acts toward anyone, although they may have acted violently in self-defense: Mateo, Carlos, Ezequiel, Ildefonso, Gregorio and his four brothers, Pancho Orozco and his two close friends. The salience of violence among the leaders in the Caso faction is part of the extremity of the cacicazgo of Scarface Caso.

The González faction contains only two gunmen, and both are, as it were, mediocrities. In December 1955, one of them suddenly drew a .45 from under his red-and-brown serape and fired point-blank at Jaime as they were standing together in a peacefully conversing group in the gloaming outside Toni's general store. He missed and was immediately disarmed by Mateo. No overt disciplinary action was taken, although, of course, the attempt at homicide has been recorded mentally and may contribute to some future happening. Many of the leaders in the González faction are clearly not prone to violence, which is presumably one reason Pedro González has intermittently hired mestizo gunslingers from the outside—with backfiring results, as we have seen.

It would be easy but inappropriate to fall back unselfconsciously into American usage and the rich connotations of words like "hired gun, gunslinger, desperado, hit-man, hood," and so forth. It would be still worse to simply equate the Naranja "fighter" (*luchador*) with the urban, mestizo hired gun (*pistolero*) or professional killer (*asesino, matón*), although there is obviously some overlap in meanings and behaviors and although the second set of terms are used in published and spoken accusations against men correctly named by the first set of terms. What— before we get more pedantic—is meant by an epithet like "fighter" (*luchador*) in the contexts covered by the foregoing paragraphs and, indeed, this book and *Agrarian Revolt*? Above all it means a peasant and otherwise normal member of the community who habitually carries a pistol in times of political stress and who, for reasons of temperament or ambition or political or kinship loyalties, will engage in the killings by ambush or direct assault that characterize the ongoing struggle between factions and "political families." What might be called the empirical indices for such a fighter or gunman include the following: (1) the number of men he has killed or tried to kill; (2) the circumstances under which he carries a pistol (fighting knife, sawed-off shotgun, etc.); (3) his work as a defender of a cacique; Toni, for example, always packs a loaded and sometimes cocked .38 at his belt when forced to walk about at night. During the politically tense situation of 1956 it became increasingly dangerous for Scarface to go about, in Morelia and elsewhere, on his business as congressman-elect and head of the League. Naranja gunmen-fighters were called into action and shadowed him for months, and they were Bones, The Mestizo, Boni, Jaime, Melesio, and Toni. The attitudes of Naranja leaders toward killing and other violence are curiously ambivalent, two-faced. On the one hand they are fully aware of the grim realities of death and the attendant hardships for widows and orphans, and they frequently invoke these realities in their political pronunciamentos. On the other hand, they often voice a callous attitude, as in the case of Camilo and others whose biographies are given in Chapter 1, or, as noted, they may take an irresponsible, devil-may-care position, as expressed by one individual following a speech I gave on Independence Day:

"You could be a leader here, Paul, you could order killings!"—without any compunctions on his part that this should be a criterion for local leadership.[5]

The dominance of Naranja in the political economy of the region has never depended solely or even largely on the use of violence within the intrigues of the Cardenista political network. Ever since the days of Primo Tapia the political leaders in this pueblo have been characterized by a level of intelligence and "mental preparation" that is considerably higher than that of their counterparts in other pueblos such as Tiríndaro, Zurumútaro, or Tanaquillo. By level of intelligence I refer simply to my personal evaluation of such things as verbal ability, consciousness of culture patterns, awareness of the surrounding environment, and the ability to reason and solve problems. Many of the princes are actually rather fluent, even wordy, in the context of the conversations in the awkward and incorrect Spanish that marks these bilingual communities. In terms of verbal aptitude the leading princes are Scarface, Camilo, Ezequiel, and Aquiles, but they are inferior to at least four members of the weaker faction: Martín, Pedro, Pedro's son, and Juan Mejía. The stereotypical anthropologist, trained and habituated to anticipate people with a "subconscious acceptance of unarticulated themes" (or to sentimentalize an informant as "the wisest man I've ever known" and the like), would probably be unable to handle the degree of sophistication and self-awareness shown by many of the princes, notably Scarface, Pedro, Camilo, Aquiles, and Juan Mejía. This articulate self-awareness stems from a combination of family tradition and extended exposure to other cultures, especially urban mestizo Mexico, and, in some cases, to secondary or even legal education and protracted residence in other, distant parts.

But the principal cause for this political sophistication is the special local tradition of thinking through and figuring out thorny political problems; the leaders of both factions manifest an understanding of regional and state politics that contrasts with that of their counterparts in neighboring towns and areas. Many experiences impressed me in this respect, some of which have already been set forth on preceding pages. Late one afternoon I entered into a long conversation by the willow trees that line one of the canals next to the ejido. After a bit Juan Mejía shifted to politics with the proposition that "We develop an objective analysis (*un análisis objectivo*) of the politics in Naranja"—which we then proceeded to do. At another point I asked Camilo why the Caso leaders had relaxed their anticlericalism. His answer was: "Political expediency, Pablo. Our principal enemies are the Communists," a statement on which he then elaborated, finishing, as on other occasions, with a reference to Machiavelli. Naranja political refugees, or at least emigrants, in Mexico City spend countless hours discussing and analyzing their own vicissitudes and the fortunes of the Caso cacicazgo. The average citizen of the town partakes to some extent of this specialty; after the first six months of fieldwork there were few interviews that were not interrupted or terminated by the inevitable subject: politics. Political savvy is a local intellectual hypertrophy—granted that some villagers are indifferent, or avoid engagement as much as possible.

The average prince is more generally aware of the surrounding environment than is usual for Mexican peasants and their leaders. This ranges from Carlos' historical research on Don Vasco de Quiroga to Longinus' witticisms about "pleonasms" and "philippic speeches." The princes tend to answer difficult questions on agriculture and politics with comparative speed and decisiveness. Men such as Toni and Gregorio are remarkable for the quick closure with which they respond—or flatly assert their ignorance or inability.

It is almost paradoxical, as I have said before, that a town as small as Naranja should contain or at least have produced so many able and often educated leaders. In part this reflects the community-wide enthusiasm for intelligence and higher education. A striking instance of the Naranja Renaissance is Juan Mejía, who was a top student in the Morelia law school until his father was killed and he had to return to the village to work as an ejidatario and support six female relatives; the frequent products of his poetic fantasy, to which he "dedicates himself," have been published in several national newspapers. He spends his afternoons and evenings reading excellent foreign novels and histories of Mexico because "one must never stop studying." But he too is possessed, not obsessed, by the local *libido dominandi:* "I cannot leave this town because of the politics," he says.

[By 1984, however, this courageous and brilliant man had been gone from his town for a long time and was living in a distant city. I could use a tape recording of our "objective analysis"—PF, 1986.]

By Mexican standards the educational level in Naranja is high. Today 60 percent of the town is literate and the educational average is somewhat above one year of schooling. The educational average of the leaders is five and a half years, and all except Bones are literate; the group includes six ex-schoolteachers and three former law students. Five of the leaders regularly read books and magazines, and some people in the town at large read comic books, *The Reader's Digest,* "romances," and chapbooks of popular songs. Aside from Juan Mejía, the indigenous autodidact Martín Valle deserves special mention because of his unusual historical abilities and his hobby of privately recording events year by year.

But the present level of education and even intelligence is inferior to that of the core under Primo Tapia. No one in Naranja, as an intelligent leader, would be a match for Tapia, who was able to elicit the following of a dozen able and gifted men—even after the assassination of Eleuterio Serrato and the defection of Hercules Ocampo. Factional politics and the rise of Scarface, with his complexes about not being "cultured," have led to the death, exile, or political nullification of over three-quarters of the most able leaders. Some of the rulers today, notably Toni and Bones, are anti-educational, envious of their educated rivals, and even willing to persecute schoolteachers.

Forensic ability might be regarded as an index of intelligence, although this would depend greatly on the orientations of the culture. Most of the best public speakers are also political leaders, but of these only two, Camilo and Aquiles, belong to the ruling group. The majority of the ruling faction are actually rather ineffectual as orators. Oratorical ability is by no means essential for success in local politics and may in fact arouse the envy of others without convincing the rest of the population; and, even if convinced, the "masses" are apt to remain ineffectual before the violence and higher-level intriguing of the princes. Naranja peasants are comparatively laconic and short on words, expressing themselves inadequately even by Mexican rural standards. In part this reflects the difficult times of a town halfway between the resources of Tarascan, rich in puns, and the extensive vocabulary and wealth in proverbs of the Spanish language. Many persons in the linguistically marginal communities of Naranja, Tiríndaro, and Tarejero complain that they know neither language (see discussion of bilingualism earlier in this chapter). But the broken and unfinished quality of much Naranja speech may echo deeper chords of cultural anomie that also is symbolized through alcoholism, depression, and aggression.

In Naranja de Tapia, formerly of Our Father Jesus, the economic and political ideology summed up under the phrase "radical agrarianism" continues to dominate the rationalizations of the leaders, and this despite the fact that only one of the four "old fighters" belongs to the ruling faction of the Casos. Nevertheless, the leaders in the town still subscribe officially to the ideology of Primo Tapia and Lázaro Cárdenas. The functional significance of this ideology is illustrated by the behavior of Scarface, who constantly tries to create the myth that he was Tapia's right-hand man, who reiterates an unmitigated left-wing ideology, and who is secretive about baptizing his children. The leaders seldom enter the church, and then only for such innocuous ceremonies as the Christmas Mass. Nor do they support the communal or the religious fiestas, although they may participate in them. In light of all the qualifications and compromises, it should come as no surprise that the only consistent anticlericals are Bones, Boni, Pedro González, and a few others in the González faction.

The other aspects of Primo's heritage were material progress, education, women's rights, and land reform. The pattern of united community action in recent years for purposes of material improvements is impressive by Mexican standards. During the past four years (1952–1956) the following material projects have actually been carried out: the construction of a road to the ejido lands, the lining of that road with stone walls, the construction of two cement bridges in the ejido, the paving with asphalt of the street around the plaza, the laying down of mosaic tile flooring in the town hall and the main school building, the building of a large pink-stone bench in the plaza, and several lesser achievements. These sorts of activities are intriguingly connected with the processes of factionalism: rivals compete with each other in showing that they "want to do something for the pueblo," and destructive envies usually prevent them from accomplishing as much as they could do or set out to do. In the end, the ruling oligarchy decides to promote an attractive project, often with the hope of being granted supplementary funds from the government, and the lethargic and disillusioned mass of the population is coerced into paying contributions and providing labor. This pattern of partly coercive public works or "material improvements" led by a motivated minority stems, in particular, from the days of Primo Tapia, but certainly has antecedents reaching back into the remote past. Many of the major and minor princes are keenly aware of the things that could be done to improve the community and not infrequently start to talk about the subject in tones of accusation and self-reproach. Many leaders, such as Aquiles and Jerome Nahua, are acutely aware of the ideology of Tapia and Cárdenas, "of what Primo wanted for his people." Yet it is of note that the two main caciques, Scarface and Camilo, although in a class by themselves in terms of upper-level contacts, are also conspicuously inactive when it comes to providing leadership for the numerous public works of which one hears so much. Scarface is mainly concerned with personal aggrandizement and political status; Camilo and the lesser leaders are blocked by the envy and suspicion of Scarface and between each other: as soon as one of them starts a move to "improve the pueblo," others claim that "he wants to organize a faction and divide the pueblo." The same set of factors operate at the state level: Cárdenas has a monopoly on reform. The urge for material improvements in the way of life, as a result, is expressed primarily through individual or familial initiative—as is to be seen in the comparatively good housing, diet, clothing, and education of the leaders and their families.

It is in clothing and educating their young, in fact, that the leaders in the community have displayed the greatest progress: over thirty-five children are in primary schools, high schools, colleges, and professional schools in Morelia, Pátzcuaro, and Mexico City. The urge to education, part of a profound national aspiration, was able to integrate the radical ideology, the new incomes from the ejido, and the individualistic drift in the culture. Camilo's seven children in schools in Mexico City, of whom he is understandably proud, provide an extreme but representative indication of the passions and beliefs that are focused on education. Many Naranjeños feel that most of their problems would be solved if they were more educated. It is the level of education, and consequent intellectual explicitness, synergistic with the high economic stakes, that has created the peculiar intensity of Naranja politics.

The final aspect of the official ideology, land reform, can, of course, find no direct outlet since the land has already been expropriated from the landlords and partitioned. This strictly agrarian plank is partly conserved today through feelings of gratitude toward Tapia, through more or less justified affirmations that the agrarian reform was a success, and, finally, through some degree of adherence to the codes, laws, and edicts of the national agrarian organizations. Despite numerous lesser abuses, the ejido is administered with comparative equity, and the lands are inherited or transferred in accordance with something like the agrarian code. Unlike the multitudinous cases of thoroughly corrupt ejidos, the Naranja ejido is worked and the products are enjoyed by the overwhelming majority of the ejidatarios. This last dimension of princely behavior is due to a combination of factors: (1) taking ideology seriously (e.g., "the effective idealists" mentioned in Chapter 3); (2) the increasing vigilance of the national administration, which frequently sends out inspectors and delegates; (3) the corrective, monitoring effect of the criticisms and denunciations of the weaker faction under Pedro González.

To sum up: I have described and to some extent analyzed the political oligarchy of the princes in terms of about thirty concrete dimensions, such as diet and degree of bilingualism, that interdepend with one another and are to some extent mutually implicatory. One overall pattern that has emerged is the complexity of the group's functions and roles within the community. A second is the gradual, continuous, and probabilistic nature of the features that define their relations to one another and to the town as a whole. A third pattern is the way diverse internal processes such as the drift toward individualism and a mestizo life style have been interacting over time with continuities in factional structure, housing, and so on. Fourth, in terms of comparative peasant studies, one must single out as typologically extraordinary the degree of surplus capital available, the degree of local violence, and the degree of formal education and political sophistication of some of the leaders and their relatives. In other words, the products which Naranja exported during the three decades in question were, in alphabetical order: corn (and profits from corn), music, political leadership and ideology, and political violence. Finally, perhaps the most fundamental pattern is the complex feedback between the character, attitudes, and political cerebrations of the leaders and, on the other hand, the workings of factors which are mainly or at least marginally economic—such as the black earth of a coveted ejido plot, or the bribes and rewards of office, or the agrarian ideology, even if it is partly vacuous, or a legal education for a son with its possible consequences of keeping the pueblo "under one's eggs."

Part Four. Experience and Methods

The activity of these people interested me only as an
illustration of the law of predetermination which in my
opinion guides history, and of that psychological law
which compels a man who commits actions under the
greatest compulsion, to supply in his imagination a
whole series of retrospective reflections to prove his
freedom to himself.

 —L. N. TOLSTOY, "Some Words about *War and Peace*"

CHAPTER 7

Fieldwork Categories:
Sources of Shattered Bits

The simple immediate facts are the topics of interest,
and these reappear in the thought of science as the
"irreducible stubborn facts."
—A. N. WHITEHEAD, *Science and the Modern World*

1. *Participant observation* entails, first of all, the researcher's presence
and to some extent active participation in the individual life cycle (e.g., a
wake), the annual cycle (e.g., of religious fiestas), the daily cycle (e.g.,
making tortillas), and all other recurrent and patterned phenomena such
as town meetings or communal harvests. Witness the exigencies of harvesting wheat.

Fieldwork Datum No. 1: Harvesting Wheat with Toni Serrano
*[Fieldnotes, May 5, 1955, coded under no. 24, Agriculture, Human Relations
Area Files.]*

I tried cutting wheat a lot more and found it heavy going, sort of like cutting
corn [as I had on the farm in Vermont] or asparagus [as on farms in Massachu-
setts], but a lot more pull on the withers, and of course the sun is oppressive.
The group tends to work about as fast as I can, taking only five-minute breaks
from time to time, until it gets through with an *avesana* [a cubic measure of
grain], which takes about an hour, and then rests ten or fifteen minutes. The
grain is tough and requires a strong pull of the arm to cut a handful. There is
hardly any talking among the workers while on an *avesana*, and while sitting at
the end of a row they only occasionally converse in a desultory fashion. They
seem to be conserving energy for the hard work.
    Some men eat breakfast at home and start to work an hour or so later. The
majority hit the field by five or six in the morning and work as hard as they can
till eight or nine when one or more of the women brings out breakfast and sits
with them in the field while they eat (today this consisted of one large [rough
ground] wheat roll, flat, rather sweet, and delicious, about four inches across,
and a glass of milk) . . .

These intensely visual and otherwise physical experiences, their description in fieldnotes, and their analysis and personal internalization are

indispensable to one's understanding of the general culture—as should go without saying. But they also are important to one's understanding of politics: political history, factionalism, leadership, and political culture generally—for example, the claim that a given leader "doesn't know how to work."

Let me give some more examples to counteract the illusion that political anthrohistory is a bounded compartment. To begin, my careful study of local child-rearing practices, stimulated partly by my own fathering experiences and partly by questions in the *Outline of Cultural Materials*, added critical input to some of the political life histories—information which few historians would have known, discovered, or exploited. As a second example, my study of and participation in the annual Holy Week pageantry in neighboring Tiríndaro provided indispensable input, not only to the meanings of this fiesta in Naranja, but also, politically, to how Primo Tapia worked with and made symbolic use of this fiesta during the agrarian revolt (e.g., he played the part of Lucifer). It also provided input to gauging the religious and antireligious attitudes of the princes of Naranja in 1956—as illustrated by Boni's theological discussion (Chapter 1) and, on the other hand, the generous support to religious fiestas provided by the mother of antireligious Boni, Camilo, and Aquiles. Incidentally, my attempts to capture in writing the whole colorful gestalt of the fiestas was crucial in getting going the synthesizing process that led to *Agrarian Revolt* and the present book.

Fieldwork Datum No. 2: Tarascan Midwifery
[Fieldnotes, June 26, 1955, after interviewing Isabelita, aged seventy, Tarascan-speaking, outside her home.]

Some mothers are very sensitive and don't want to eat, and vomit because the foetuses are sensitive. There are various potions. [Four listed] . . . the usual causes for abortion are: (1) a fight with another woman, don't want to support another child, anger or fear. . . . The first birth is the hardest and many are afraid because they don't know what it means to have a family; they don't cry or shout but the pain is great. . . . The placenta is buried in a corner within the house because the mother would have pain if it were buried outside. . . . Babies are buried in the cemetery. . . . If the baby is born a little bit dead (*"muertito"*) they cover its head with a bowl and blow in cigarette smoke—successful in two cases.

This is one of four interviews with midwife Isabelita, resulting in about 600 words of notes (added to about 1,200 words from other people).

Political anthrohistory calls for continuous residence in the town or locality for a year or two, not only for such general patterns but—and this is just as vital—so that the student may catch on the wing the revealing, accidental happenings as they constitute recent history. It was the assassination of Agustín, one of the original agrarian fighters, on the highway outside Naranja in 1956 that opened up the political vendetta and agrarian politics for me: what had been "patterns of culture" in a dusty and peaceful pueblo, à la Redfield, turned into masks for a political dynamics of consuming interest. To take another example, during a so-called civic fiesta, a flare exploded prematurely in the hand of the gunman who had ignited it. Not only did he give little sign of pain, but the leaders with him hardly broke their stride, nor did they evince concern beyond casually suggesting that he ought to have a doctor remove the splinters. This gives one insight into attitudes toward violence and also illustrates the commonsensical proverb that had been cited by one of those leaders, Scarface Caso, before the parade: "The generals live and the soldiers die." On another such occasion I attended a wedding in Tarejero that, so it turned out, included people from opposing factions—most of them carried concealed weapons, that is, pistols hanging inside the front of their pants, over the groin.[1] Many of the fiestas, incidentally, featured heavy drinking of rum or sugarcane brandy, chased with beer.

I resided in Naranja almost continuously for one year, although I went to the state capital most weekends to see my family and spent some full weeks in Tiríndaro and Zacapu. Then I resided continuously for half a year in Tiríndaro with my family. Having a family along increased participant observation, partly because my two-year-old daughter Maria ran around visiting many families. On most of the days during this last half-year in the field I walked over to Naranja to carry on as before. I ended up participating in almost all recurrent patterns and hundreds of non-recurrent and revealing happenings in Naranja and Tiríndaro; comparing two villages always yields insight. I was dreaming a great deal about Naranja in these months or lying awake nights in Tiríndaro thinking about Naranja politics. To gain further comparative perspective I visited two dozen other Tarascan towns or mestizo towns with a Tarascan dimension—from Tarecuato, where a Naranja faction had settled in the last century, to Tzintzuntzan, seat of the preconquest empire, to Cherán, where I could talk with the major Tarascanists Max and Lisa Lethrop.

All participant observation is to some extent active, that is, is participation, but some is relatively more active; I taught English (for six months to a dozen Tiríndaro adolescents), helped medically, drafted documents, became several kinds of ritual relative with dozens of villagers, gave a speech at a fiesta—or a helping hand at a fight. The memorable wedding in Tarejera just mentioned above began with drinking of rum and beer. About halfway through I found myself in the half-lit patio struggling with my host, trying to wrest away his .45. I failed and we both returned to the party. About an hour later I went outside and watched three men from each faction standing in the street with their pistols drawn, talking things over. After another hour the host's cousin, who was leading the rival faction, began to get aggressive toward the host. Two kinswomen of the latter fell on their man and dragged him away. I pinioned the cousin's arms from behind and walked him to the door. Then the party wound down, although a few of us sat around for a while, drinking.

All my fieldwork, incidentally, was done in Spanish, which I began using in an interview on my second day and which I spoke fairly well after six months, and correctly and fluently after a year—in terms of what was heard and said in the Zacapu Valley; most of the people I dealt with were either bilingual or Spanish-speaking. I also read some Spanish-language literature, especially some anthologies of poetry and, near the end of my field stay, *Don Quixote*. Many of my fieldnotes and extended observations are in Spanish, and I wrote long business letters in the language. My thesis was in some sense co-drafted in Spanish and, years later when checking and reworking the translation, I felt that it had been written to be translated.

I learned basic Tarascan, both through systematic study and from the group I was teaching English to in Tiríndaro. Eventually I was engaging in a lot of desultory chitchat in Tarascan, and I carried out an ambitious census in the 100 percent Tarascan town of Azajo. A decade later, in 1966–1967, I decided to live up to my local reputation and turned to Tarascan full time, using it almost exclusively for my last year of mainly linguistic fieldwork in another region of the area.

2. *Direct witness*, normally eyewitness, is uniquely interesting because it is related to the anthrohistorian's own problems of memory and seeing. If a happening is dramatic, physical, or traumatic—and many political events are—then recall may be heightened and there may also be high consensus decades later. An attack with spears and slings on some drunken mestizos in 1912 was remembered this way. On the other hand, there may be great variation in the reports of persons claiming to have witnessed the same event when it comes to dates, motives, and political associations. A special type of extended eyewitness account is the autobiography, and the anthropological historian should collect dozens of brief autobiographies, even if only two or three pages long, as well as more intensive documentation. "Autobiography" in a general sense comes naturally to most peasants (and probably to most people anywhere), since it is a sort of extension of talking about oneself. I collected hundreds of eyewitness accounts and dozens of autobiographies, seven of the latter eventually written up as sections of Chapter 1 in this book.

3. *The key informant*, an inheritance from classical social and linguistic anthropology, has a new and distinctive significance in political anthropology. This is because, unlike the linguistic structure of a natural language such as Tarascan, which is known intuitively by all speakers, a political

history is known only in idiosyncratic pieces and patches which must be internalized and synthesized by the anthrohistorian. To give an idea of the actualities of this issue, I will list a few of the two dozen absolutely key, semispecialized individuals, the star witnesses:

(1) Two aged brothers (the Espinozas), who had led the radical agrarians in neighboring Tiríndaro in the twenties and thirties.

(2) A cousin, friend, and major follower of Primo Tapia, that is, Pedro López, who also filled important state offices.

(3) The renowned leader of an earlier agrarian revolt in the Eleven Pueblos, and cacique there in the thirties and forties.

(4) A schoolteacher who had grown up in the neighboring mestizo hamlet and knew a massive amount about Naranja politics in the thirties and forties.

(5) A son of the initiator of agrarian reform in the region; this son had resided continuously in the town ever since.

(6) The main surviving leader of the large Ocampo faction that had largely departed in the late thirties.

A half-dozen other key witnesses, such as Scarface, Camilo, Nana Ana, and Ezequiel were frequently and intensively interviewed, and their information and opinions worked into the study. Several of the most knowledgeable people had to be tracked down in the most diverse sections of Mexico City.

Most of my interviews lasted one to two hours, although a few took only half an hour, and many individuals gave me five or more hours of informative conversation. No one was ever paid, with one exception: an impoverished mother whom I asked lots of questions about child rearing. This not paying, which became established from the start, partly reflected my own poverty (with a wife and two children on $90.00 a month), partly the practical habit of moving from friend to friend and contact to contact, thus depending on friendship and kinship patterns and the willingness of people to help (see "Interviews and Conversations" under "Sources" at the end of this book).

4. *Gossip* gives insight into the political and moral codes, and how leaders are evaluated. Some gossip may be heard from only one person and yet fit well into the mosaic of a history. The majority consists of what I call "consensus anecdotes," some of which are mainly figments in the imagination of older women, but all of which give one insight into politics. In some cases the boundary line between anecdote, history, and myth becomes exceedingly fuzzy; for example, there was general agreement that the Casos fissioned tragically into two new factions, about 1937, due to accusations of bribery and a public altercation between the wives of the two caciques, Scarface and Pedro; but the exact details and the general meaning of this historical "question of skirts" remained somewhat murky

to me. A second "consensus anecdote" told of how 109 signatures were collected in 1921 for a petition to expropriate the landlords; half the signatories were actually anti-agrarian proclericals who had been duped into thinking the petition was to obtain a new priest—a hoax which still provokes laughter. This bit of gossip was partly confirmed by records in the Department of Agrarian Affairs, where I actually found the list with 109 signatures. By an added irony of fate, it was the 109 signatories who became the heads of ejidal families after the First Partition in 1928, which was contrary to the communalistic principles of the original agrarians. Such bits of "great gossip," or at least "consensus gossip," can live on for thirty or more years, often because they have been reduced to a skeleton and then clothed with a symbolism from the deepest values in the culture. I heard hundreds, maybe thousands, of anecdotes, and recorded dozens of them.

5. *Common sense* occasionally took the form of imported Spanish proverbs, but more frequently was expressed in succinct generalizations that are appropriate to many contexts, such as, "One has to fight the fight" (*hay que hacer la lucha*). The leaders of the town, particularly Scarface and Camilo, were given to embedding their common sense into their conversations and I think that common sense is part of political judgment and that much political action is judged more realistically and perspicaciously by the native—be it a Tarascan peasant or a Vermont farmer. The role and validity of the native's common sense is one thing that differentiates politics from myth-making, language structure, and much other cultural life. An appreciation of common sense and the interpretations of the peasant should play a fairly large part in local history or micropolitics—not as a governing model or framework, but partly as a leavener and partly as a stabilizer. That is how it figures in *The Princes of Naranja*.

6. *Personal letters* are priceless because of their frequent intimacy and succinctness, and their simplification of political values. I probably found and read between seventy and one hundred letters, including the thirty-two that I found in a wooden box in Primo Tapia's sister's hut—in which, for example, Pedro López was mentioned often enough and with enough affection and detail to overwhelm the allegations by the dominant Caso faction that he had not been a close companion of Tapia and a major leader in the revolt. At the other extreme in their content were the letters already published in Martínez' important, pioneer biography of Tapia, which bear telling witness to many of the more imaginative and poetic aspects of Tapia's life.

7. *Personal documents* are psychologically slanted or at least informed interviews, intensive discussions of family life and other personal matters, and the output of specific elicitation procedures, such as the Rorschach interview, that stimulate the person to project his/her values and the

symbols of the culture as a whole. The Rorschach, like the *Outline of Cultural Materials*, has been condemned by some anthropologists in the name of phenomenological or symbolic approaches, but I found both of these instruments to be extraordinarily productive of insight in terms, precisely, of the values for which they have been tossed out.

Fieldwork Datum No. 3: Rorschach Cards and Politics

[The first part of Camilo Caso's reaction to card I is given in full in Psychological Appendix 1. When asked to trace the card, he limited himself to the winged figure. His second set of responses went as follows:]

"Yes, it is like a bat, or a butterfly, depending on the shape. I also see a body, a human body with feet, the thighs would be here, here the hips," leaning forward, apparently excited by the discovery. "And here still more the thorax, all covered with a veil, and here the hands extended," throwing his arms wide apart. Camilo went on for some time elaborating on these reactions: the white parts in the center were important to him for his identification of "the bat." [The same procedures were followed for the other nine cards, of course.]

The Rorschach cards and their interpretation lead one into or at the least give one intimations of a special, interior universe of personal, local, and cultural symbolism that is significantly connected with political symbolism. With the exception of "stalagtites" and "stalagmites" on a later card, Camilo, like the other princes interviewed, drew his interpretation mainly from his Tarascan world. Like his half-brother Boni he often referred to masks, veils, and similar disguises, which may be what the psychologists call "a persona response," but also, as already noted, reflects what a psychologist working on the Tarascans called "a culture of masks." A mask orientation is clearly crucial to the political culture in question and to its interpretation. Moreover, the psychological anthropologist Raymond Fogelson did a professional analysis of the responses and concluded that Camilo was "more introverted than extroverted, that his thinking is interior and relatively slow, that he doesn't give way to affective aspects of his environment, and, above all, that he is extremely realistic and pragmatic." While I would argue about Camilo not yielding to affect, the point about realism and pragmatism corresponds excitingly to what was seen in Camilo's precepts and practice. Finally, the process of administering a Rorschach normally creates a bond between the fieldworker (at least this fieldworker) and the respondent that manages to be at once intimate and innocuous, and conducive to politics. The interview with Camilo, as noted in Chapter 1, led to a feeling of mutual warmth and one of the most interesting shared analyses of my fieldwork sojourn.

Such psychological documentation should be understood and interpreted in the light of religious ritual, work, politics, family life, and other contexts in the culture of the respondent. It should, in principle, include a broad sample of the population such as children, adolescents, women, and the elderly, and both immigrants into the community and refugees from it. In a political history or ethnography it will naturally focus on the leaders. I gave Rorschachs to nine leaders and also devised a provocative "thematic apperception test" of sorts from a little book of line drawings by thirteen artists: one by Grünewald of three naked witches flagellating or at least switching each other was particularly suggestive, as was Michelangelo's "A Damned Soul" (see "Aquiles" in Chapter 1).

8. *Local chronicles* come into being when someone records names, dates, events, and the like in a diary or town record book or just makes personal notes. Such written chronicles are indispensable for pinning down the actual years in which events took place (one kind of fact for which the peasant memory is typically poor)—but such documents should be enlarged by having the authors of the chronicles provide their own annotation and interpretation. I obtained such elaborations of the list of homicides from an elderly, peaceful man and from the bitter and perspicacious Martín Valle. Taking him for what he was, a sort of natural historian, I elicited his specialist's chronicle of the homicides, most of them political, that had been committed over the preceding thirty-five years. I checked his list with other villagers and then rechecked the whole with him (see Homicide Appendix). To Martín's credit be it noted that he included homicides by members of his own faction, though he justified them in terms of revenge and similar legitimate motives, whereas many of the killings by his enemies such as Bones, some of them reported by his enemies, were attributed to drunkenness, murderousness, and rivalry over women. A comparably tortuous procedure of elicitation and cross-checking yielded a chronicle of the seizure of ejido plots by successively dominant factions and, in particular, of the three expulsions carried out by the Casos. Here I was helped by a genre that is priceless and falls between the chronicle and gossip or slander: the printed or at least typed political denunciation, many in files in Mexico City, many against Scarface. These denunciations often contained lists of expropriated individuals, the numbers of their ejido plots, the names of the persons who acquired the plots, and, often enough, some of the reasons or attendant circumstances; on the fullest of these lists, nine of the twenty-two cases dealt with involved killings or a role as a gunman. Chronicle, then, one of the more rudimentary forms of history, can be, like biography, a natural component in the most sophisticated historiography, and it seems to generate reasonable, intriguing, and natural questions for both the antrohistorian and the villager—despite the fact that few people think in long sequences of events ordered by a rigorous chronology; on the contrary, many villagers, when discussing what happened in the past, will move

from one subject or event to another in terms of thematic or emotional associations.

9. *History*. Published biographies, political, economic, and military histories, and collections of historical documents such as memoirs are critical sources of information and may be numerous when the localities have mattered in the national economy and polity. In the presence of such documentation, the anthrohistorian is in a position to interconnect local, state, and national levels of discourse. While in the field I frequently read county, state, and national newspapers, and these sometimes proved invaluable, not so much for the "facts" as for the attitudes and interpretations; for example, *Vision* (December 9, 1966) dealt in an interesting way with a judicial-political institution that is "as Mexican as the *piñata*" (and practically ignored by anthropologists to date), namely, the *amparo*, or judicial safe-conduct (which played a fateful role in the cases of Joaquín de la Cruz and Primo Tapia). Other, more strictly historical resources were the main biography of Francisco Múgica, whom Scarface allegedly served as a bodyguard in the twenties, but who also was a general, an agrarian leader in the Eleven Pueblos, and, briefly, governor of the state of Michoacán. Even more helpful for *The Princes* were several biographies of Lázaro Cárdenas, personal friend of Primo and Scarface, but also, again, a general, a radical governor in the state, and eventually the president of the country. There were occasional relevant articles in regional and state newspapers. But even such a rich and atypical set of published sources was rarely concerned with the Zacapu Valley, much less Naranja, and one had to sift out priceless details, sometimes finding only a few phrases in an entire book: for example, one general history of Mexico wrote deviously about Calles "whittling away the strength of local chieftains" (e.g., the lynching of Primo Tapia); a general book about Cárdenas had one gem of a phrase about "the powerful and fighting agrarian organizations of Naranja"; an excellent book on the ejido in Mexico had no less than a third of a chapter on the neighboring village of Tarejero; another history included a fascinating appendix, attributed to Múgica, on how to get elected by hook or crook, mainly crook. And so it went with the mosaic. By the time I wrote my two-volume thesis I had sifted through dozens of books and articles on modern Mexican history and politics and, indeed, often lectured on these subjects at the University of Pennsylvania. Since those years, of course, an entire library has been created, not only on recent Mexican history but on agrarian problems in particular and the specifics of Michoacán agrarian history; at least three books or doctoral theses have been produced about Naranja.[2]

10. *Numbers* arise from many sources; a large part of peasant conversation is about numbers in some explicit or implicit sense (compare Sol Tax's

Penny Capitalism). Just as valuable as "peasant numbers" are local records and the practical statistics in government offices at all levels; I would particularly single out the reports of surveyors and inspectors. A good example of numbers that proved critical for analysis was provided by the Ejidal Bank—the local (Zacapu) branch of a mammoth government credit and finance organization. Its employees were totally cooperative and gave me many facts and figures on land, land use, the use of fertilizers, the financing of irrigation, and so forth, and, perhaps most relevant, on the exact debts of each ejidatario (see Economic Appendix A). I had to copy out the facts in longhand.

Other numbers have to be inferred by, for example, doing a lot of pacing and measuring; my circumambulation of the town's boundary called for two days of hiking, much of it in the high sierra (and many parts of it with political connotations). At another level, I did a house-to-house census with thirty numerical questions, some of the answers to which figured in the appendix on diet in *Agrarian Revolt*. Yet other numbers are inferred by watching and asking; for example, the number of tortillas actually eaten per day, as compared with the number desired by the peasant. Some numbers remain inaccessible or indefinite, or at least not directly accessible. I was not encouraged to visit the so-called "Cayetano Ocampo Purchase," a huge bean and maize field deep in the sierra, because it had been wrested from the Ocampo faction and was still being disputed; as a result, I had to figure out the essential statistics from a politically balanced set of individuals representing various persuasions. This led to a full list of the meters of furrows held by everyone in thirty-four named fields of non-ejidal land. The obtaining of these facts still seems like a considerable achievement.

Fieldwork Datum No. 4: Seven Categories of Descriptive Statistics

(1) Diet of 29 Naranja families (15% of the town), with precise figures on bread, beans, and 19 other food categories.
(2) Debts to the ejidal bank in 1956 of 172 ejidatarios (crucial because of the anti-bank posture of Scarface and Camilo).
(3) List of 56 towns represented commercially at Naranja's main fiesta, to "Our Father Jesus," with a map of the market-plaza, and an itemization of the products in each booth.
(4) List of 88 persons holding non-ejidal lands in about 34 named fields in terms of the numbers of meters of furrow; and 800-word analysis of the meanings.
(5) Table of the Naranja workers in the Celanese factory in Zacapu: name, age, birth and residence, years and type of education, languages, land holdings, number of dependents, number of visits to the United States, livestock and other property, work experience, and political status.
(6) Vital statistics; for example, from deaths (1940):

19/9 Antioco Rosas   45 years   wounds from a cutting weapon
8/10 Antonio Perez   2 years   diarrhea
9/11 Trinidad Jiménez   2 months   inanition
(7) Cross-checked list of homicides since 1920, with names of victims, assailants, date, place, and, often, the circumstances (which were usually political), for example:

    35. Hermenegildo Ocampo   Juan Nahua Caso   3 July 1935
        MV: because of the Ocampo feud; both were drunk
        PG: to take away an Ocampo plot
    36. Francisco Pérez Ocampo   Wenceslao Martínez   11 Feb. 1936
        MV: part of the Ocampo feud
        PG: because he was an Ocampo
    37. Luis Obregón   Caso   November 1937
        MV: to avenge Tomás Cruz
        R: Who knows? LO was also linked with the Casos
    38. Wenceslao Martínez   Leopoldo Jiménez   14 Mar. 1937
        MV: the Ocampo feud; Jiménez was avenging Francisco Pérez
        R: the Ocampo dispute; WM was killed in the sierra
        X: Scarface ordered it; both victim and killer were Casos
[See Homicide Appendix for 76 homicides between 1926 and 1956.]

In one way or another, numbers are obtained on vital statistics, diet, ritual, debts, boundaries, livestock, houses, incomes, prices, crops, and many other things—in fact, any and all matters where the peasants feel that numbers matter, and practically all intelligent peasants are keen microeconomists.

I have purposely been using the word "numbers" for what might be called descriptive statistics, and as a fieldworker I have an enormous appetite for them and collect them prodigiously; such statistics are, among other things, a way of getting a provisional grip on political or other cultural complexities. Copious numbers of this sort are, furthermore, a prerequisite to an adequate political anthrohistory, partly because they are so integral to the native point of view, as just noted; partly, as in the present case, as a counter-weight to the personalities, the flamboyant ideologies, and the so-called poetry of revolution; and partly, last of all, as a leaven or grounding for the two-inches-off-the-ground mentality of the theoretically *sophisticated* symbolic, hermeneutic, and/or interpretive anthropologist. I have not, on the other hand, been referring to analysis with chi-squares, slide rules, computers, and statistical theory, and did not use these things, although, I hasten to add, the facts in my fieldnotes would lend themselves to sustained study in these terms and would probably result in a monograph several hundred pages long.

11. *Legal files* at the county, state, and national levels may be fragmentary but may include concentrations of eyewitness accounts that,

"Rashomon" style, give many angles on the same event, such as a land seizure; they may contain denunciations of each other by local leaders. Legal files are fragile in that many get destroyed or discarded, or may be closed to the anthropological historian (as the vital Gobernación files were to me). In a couple of spooky cases, legal files had been removed when I went back to check something.

When luck was with me, I was able to walk into an office dressed, as usual, like a peasant: sombrero, white cotton shirt, khaki "chino" pants, and huaraches (sandals made of car tires). After modestly introducing myself as a person from such-and-such village, or as a visiting student doing a bit of fieldwork (*trabajo de campo*), I would usually be given the run of the files as a matter of courtesy by an indifferent or unwary secretary. This is how I got the crucial information on the shooting of Tomás Cruz and of young Rodríguez (see Chapter 5). I probably gained access to two or three hundred pages of legal files, possibly much more (and many more pages of files in the Department of Agrarian Affairs); as already indicated, all the information had to be copied or abstracted in notes (a blessing in disguise, since I was forced to think about their contents, which would not have happened over a Xerox machine). I also had and sometimes used letters of introduction from the Yale Anthropology Department, the National Indigenous Institute, and the bishop of Morelia.

As an example of what can be done with such legal files I repeat here an excerpt from "The Shooting of Tomás Cruz."

Fieldwork Datum No. 5: The Death of Tomás Cruz

Eight of Cecilio's friends came running and riding up from Naranja with pistols and rifles. They finished off Tomás Cruz. As Cecilio ran away into the tall corn of the ejido, he shouted back, "Follow me, you sons of the fucked one. . . ." Primo Tapia's sister arrived on the spot a few minutes later. She found one of the slain men lying in the arms of his beloved. The corpse of Tomás was being lifted up by two of the agrarian women. As the third man lay dying he said to his sister, "Ay, little sister, now it's happened, what they talked of so often."

12. *Laws*, such as the state and national criminal codes, local statutes, and regulations and decrees pertaining to land reform and administration, should be studied carefully by the anthrohistorian (although they are typically totally neglected by anthropologists of Mexico, and probably of other areas). Such material is public and accessible, but a substantial amount may have to be abstracted and analyzed for inclusion in local history. In Mexico, to an unusual degree, the Agrarian Code has functioned as a cause of local revolt and reform, whether as a constraint or a catalyst, and it often impinges on local history. It is known in part by some villagers, such as Pedro, Camilo, Ezequiel, and Aquiles and may become part of the way of life; particular statutes, referred to by their specific

numbers, can become the legalistic charter for bloody contests over small plots of land, and so the numbers end up as household words—at least among the more articulate peasants. For such reasons there is repeated reference to the Agrarian Code in this book. On the other hand, Mexican laws, both criminal and agrarian, are also ideologically and philosophically serious statements, as is illustrated by the following from the penal code of Michoacán:

Fieldwork Datum No. 6: The Penal Code of Michoacán

. . . a penal code should be imbued with an eminently normative and practical character. Someone has said that idealism lives on a dearth of imagination. And indeed, to think that reason can solve the problems posed by reality, by making use of a certain number of ideas, is nothing else but absence of imagination. . . . The principle that there are no misdemeanors but only delinquents should be supplemented by a formulation that maintains, "There are no criminals, only men."
Crime is mainly a contingent act, resulting from antisocial causes.

Most of the foregoing dimensions involve memory. By the time of field-work, for instance, the agrarian revolt was already thirty years gone by, but the many survivors could recall many parts of it very well indeed. Such local and personal memory is of many kinds, of course. Its validity may be high—in the case of a consensus about the components of a fiesta that is no longer practiced. A life of almost continuous residence in a village may result in a higher accuracy of memory and great consensus about certain kinds of local happenings than would obtain in a contemporary, literate, urban, mass-media-saturated environment; I am reminded of the realistic figure of the old Spanish peasant in Hemingway's *For Whom the Bell Tolls,* who kept daily records in his head of all the vehicles that passed on a road; I was often struck by the memory of villagers for particular trees, other villagers' livestock, and so forth. An extreme case of such local memory among semiliterates was the sister of Primo Tapia, universally regarded as the person with the best command of genealogies. Another extreme case was another old woman, Concha: since she could remember all fifty-six booths at the annual fiesta, and their community of origin, and what they had been vending, I attached considerable credence to her account of how and why Bones accidentally shot a woman. The use of memory is, if anything, enhanced by the presence of opposing factions who correct each other's errors; I was on good terms with many witnesses and participants in both factions, including all the main caciques, who were "star witnesses." But the witness or other evidence of someone with low intelligence, alcoholic tendencies, and a mind half erased is valid when it comes to something like the loss of an ejido plot or the killing of a brother—events nobody forgets. Even a drunken beggar possesses, if not a bit of genius, as Balzac claimed, then at least some shards and remnants of the historical mosaic.

Fieldwork Datum No. 7: A Retarded Villager
[Fieldnotes, Naranja, June 16, 1955.]

1 deformed boy aged 17 sells ice cream. 5' high, stubby fingers 1–2" long, without nails, toes the same, fat, wall-eyed, grotesque lop-sided smile, strange contraction around right ring finger and right leg above knee as if they had been tied every night with an elastic or string, like a tree that has been girdled with a wire. He is definitely "apart" and does not go with the other adolescents. He is often kidded about his body. Explanation: "mother ate venison during pregnancy, or she saw a snake." [Boni liked to joke about this boy.]

To sum up the preceding pages, the anthrohistorian has available— among two dozen sources or more—the following: participant observation, direct witness, the key informant, gossip, common sense, personal letters, personal documents, local chronicles, published history, numbers, legal files, and laws. Naturally, any one of these overlaps with some of the others, but none is reducible to any other. Similarly, to evaluate each source in relation to any other and to show how it interacts with others during the inference and composition of an anthropological history would make a huge article, more likely a book. Suffice it to say that the anthrohistorian works with multitudinous bits and components and keeps them in mind during fieldwork and write-up that involve a complex integration of biography, ethnography, and historiography.

The sheer number of my sources and the plethora of facts and field experiences should not create the illusion that my fieldwork was adequate; nor were my fieldnotes, which vary enormously in quantity and quality. At one negative extreme are, for example, the potentially priceless witnesses who politely refused to talk about politics—notably Francisco Orobio and Ildefonso Mata, both companions of Tapia in the revolt. At another extreme are certain vast zones of potential description that lie totally or almost totally outside my fieldnotes. I naturally acquired the Spanish (and usually the Tarascan) names of the most important plants and animals, but the entire field of so-called ethnoscience, which my classmates from Yale were focusing on, is limited to a scribbled list of twenty-seven Spanish and Tarascan names of illnesses and a slip that runs as follows:

Fieldwork Datum No. 8: Intimations of Ethnobotany

If Luis is a good example, then it may be said that the Naranjeño has an extremely detailed knowledge of descriptive botany. In the course of two all-day walks [measuring boundaries] I asked him the names of over 35 plants and he failed only once, and that was when he had forgotten and just couldn't remember.

In each case except the most common plants he took the specimen and examined it carefully for 30 seconds before coming up with the name; it would be an understatement to say that he knew the names of 150 or more flora (trees, flowers, etc.).

Even this bit of "ethnobotany" was connected with politics because Luis was a scion of the weaker faction and I became his godfather of the crown (a minor form of compadrazgo involving a ceremony with a tin crown).

The middle range of competence in my fieldnotes includes kinship, religious fiestas, and a few other areas with fuzzy edges. Retrospectively, I paid less attention as time went on to less obviously political categories (although periodically sending out fliers in the dark—as when I elicited all the recipes for foods at a baptismal fiesta not long before my return to the States). At the other extreme are the relatively complete (but still inadequate) files on, for example, the life histories, land holdings, and factional politics. I cannot overemphasize that the excellence of such records generally correlates with and reflects one's theoretical concerns and training—here the five courses in anthropological and general economics, the political science described in Chapter 9, and the rereading in the field of a half-dozen political philosophers in cheap Spanish-language paperbacks (e.g., Aristotle's *Politics*). In retrospect, again, I can see clearly that as my work coalesced around politics I relied increasingly on my own very active memory because I realized the impossibility of physically recording and sorting out the wealth of detail and ideas surging in my mind.

After a year in the field I had a grasp of the local political history that was generally better than that of practically all "the natives"—although the latter remained superior in their own egocentric universe of experience. The exceptions, such as the leaders I have dubbed Pedro, Scarface, and Camilo, obviously controlled far more information but were extremely biased through the hatreds of factionalism and the vendetta and actually didn't know lots of things about the faction to which they happened to be opposed. Increasingly during fieldwork the local history became a vast matrix of stored information into which new or confirming (or contradictory) evidence was fixed mentally during interviews and participant observation. During the last six months in particular even one hour of rapid conversation with a key person could contribute hundreds of bits of information, which I rapidly classified en route. That is why I have repeatedly stressed the importance in local history of doing both extensive interviewing of ordinary folk, whose lives have always been affected by politics to some extent, and also intensive interviewing of key, specialized experts, such as the old agrarians I hunted down in the slums and suburbs of Mexico City.

The fieldwork and fieldnotes I have been discussing are analogous to the many-ringed circus of the anthropological field linguist. After years or even months the linguist may have an extensive record of the details of dialectal variation, or an analytical grasp of the phonology or some other part of the grammar that is better than that of any native speaker—although large areas of "language" remain essentially white places on the map. Similarly, the linguist's active, practical knowledge will remain inferior to that of any native—just as the anthropological historian may remain incompetent to seize the helm as a chief, or to fill the shoes of a gunman. But the two situations are not analogous in other ways, notably because, as noted above (section 5), political anthrohistory consists to a greater extent of specific details and because the natives are relatively conscious of politics, whereas they are largely unconscious of grammar.

Fieldwork Datum No. 9: The Day of the Dead

[In my fieldnotes for November 1955, there occurs a creative reaction to watching a solitary girl on vigil beside a family grave on the afternoon of the Day of the Dead. This has been changed below by giving the context first and ending with the inferred "inner speech."]

* 1 *

On the midafternoon of what we call Halloween the Indians of Naranja who have been bereaved within the past three years start to leave their adobe huts and houses and wind slowly across the bottom of the land to a foothill slope rising into the sierra—a long colorful procession of women in blues and pinks and the men bearing great purple wreaths and clay figures covered with orange flowers. Arriving at the cemetery, each family proceeds to its freshened grave, smoothed over with volcanic ash, and the flowers are strewn, the wreaths erected, and many candles lit. Here they sit quietly for about two hours, each gaudy little group by its dead relative, conversing and joking in Spanish and Tarascan. Some are alone with their heads bowed.

* 2 *

By one such grave there sat a thin girl of about nine wearing a dirty, threadbare dress. Most of the time she appeared to be staring down vacantly at the black ash, casting only a furtive glance at those who passed by. The last rays of the setting sun were filtering in over the green shadow of the sierra, hardly warming the evening breeze that made the flame of her three tiny candles flutter and twist in their desperate struggle for existence.

* 3 *

[There follows the inferred "inner speech" of the girl, that is, the gist of her thoughts from that morning until the time I watched her.]

"Why no beans this morning? Mama always says at night, 'Beans tomorrow,' but all we end up with is tortillas. Nothing but tortillas. And my stomach hurts, so dry, like when Mama cried when I was sick before when Papa died. Said God had forgotten us, all of our people, until Aunt Lupe pulled a few cents from the oven for penicillin. Mama says we'll all go to the graveyard when the tortillas run out. . . .

"Now Mama says we should take candles to the graveyard because that is how it is. Once a year everyone goes. Strew purple petals on the fresh-turned earth, and watch over a row of candles to warm the souls. Old Souls. Dead children, the 'little angels,' get orange flowers and big dolls of clay with bread and oranges and candy and bananas . . .

"But we lack candles—and no tortillas—and if I own a dress how can I sell *that?* If this day is for All Souls, where are the candles? Even little wax ones. I could keep them burning in a big storm—even if Mama won't go because of shame. That's what she says, shame. . . . It's good I came to Aunt Lupe's house. It's afternoon already and the band is tooting for the Souls—but there's no fiesta dinner for *us* today, and not even candles for Papa, or my twin, or my little old grandpa! Papa was so tired all the time and then Mama said he was wandering around drunk all the time on his saint's day and then Gabriel killed him on the edge of town. Because he was an Ocampo they said. Why? All that about the Ocampo, I don't understand. . . .

"It's good I came here to my Aunt's. She's gone to the graveyard so now I can get a peso from the oven, in the back, to the left, between the bricks. The oven door is narrow, but I'm little! I was the tiniest in my class that one year I went to school. Now, now the peso! Let's go! My Aunt won't mind because it's for the candles, for my twin too. Is he yellow and puffy still as when he shrieked that last day?

"Late already, let's go, let's go! The sun is setting behind Calvary Hill already and I feel the chill wind. Let's get to the graveyard with these candles. She only charged twenty centavos each, so I'll buy crackers afterwards. The wind is cool. Quick, quick, get a light from those people over there and put up the three candles by the grave. Aren't they nice? Aren't they beautiful? Quick, snatch a few purple flowers from that grave, no one's looking. Now let's watch the grave and the little candles for the souls of my Papa, my twin, and my grandpa. . . ."

Fieldwork Datum No. 9, a reconstruction by the fieldworker of the imagined flow of thought and words in one of the villagers, would seem maximally "subjective," but is in fact warranted for a number of reasons: (1) the fact of obligatory rules in the culture, which can be used as content, (2) the highly formulaic character of most (peasant) speech, so that one can concatenate formulae, (3) knowledge of inner speech, including one's own, is necessarily inferential, as are many prestigious scientific enterprises such as the reconstruction of the laryngeal sounds in Proto-Indo-European (circa five thousand years ago). In any case, the experiment of Fieldwork Datum No. 9 stands at the opposite pole from Fieldwork Datum No. 1, the recording of relatively physical, observed facts.

CHAPTER 8

"Writing It Up"

About the "whaling voyage"—I am half way in the
work, & am very glad that your suggestion so jumps
with mine. It will be a strange sort of book, tho', I fear;
blubber is blubber you know . . .
            —HERMAN MELVILLE (letter to Richard H. Dana, May 1, 1850)

J'ai fini mon travail, maintenant il ne faut que l'écrire.
(I've finished my work, now all that's left is to write it.) —JEAN RACINE

The Experience

As far as pen-to-paper goes, there simply comes a point where the historian or anthropological historian feels that enough is known and felt and
intuited, and s/he starts to put together an integrated synthesis, or at least
the beginnings of one. In my case, two thesis chapters—on Primo Tapia
and Bones Gómez—got banged out in separate fell swoops while I was in
the field, residing in Tiríndaro. I also sketched several outlines of the thesis and projected, thesis-related articles and books during the last half-
year of my sojourn (see the Preface). The rest of the two-volume anthrohistory was written over a seven-month period, four mornings a
week. (Two other mornings were devoted to graduate courses in linguistics and Chinese civilization.) Sundays I relaxed, and, as a means of
staying grounded, reread *War and Peace* in Russian.

The use of fieldnotes varied greatly. The parts of the two volumes that
deal with relatively technical material, such as the Agrarian Code, and
the relatively analytical parts, such as the microsociology and political
ethnography in Chapter 3 of this volume, were composed with fieldnotes
and other documents before me on the table. But mostly I composed in
some sense "out of my head," with, of course, constant subsequent checking back to notes after finishing a few pages or a section; all of the political
life studies (Chapter 1 above) were composed in this way, that is, when
the relevant information had built up in my head. Most of the two-volume
thesis was drafted three times. Of the seven months during which it was
composed, the last four were devoted to the agrarian politics that appears
in Parts I–III of this volume.

The writing of a book is determined critically by concurrent episodes, and in this case the gods smiled on me. For financial reasons I had to grab at an offer to teach even though it entailed not only anthropology but also two courses in sociology, a subject which I had never studied formally or informally—all of this for two-thirds time at an extension of the University of Connecticut. The job called for two rides a week between New Haven and Stamford, one way frantically preparing lectures. The evening ride back was with a new-found friend named Ludwig Schaeffer, then an assistant professor of history, with a traditional orientation: he could rattle off the names of all the kings and queens of England, Germany, France, and Spain, and other countries as well over the centuries—and their loves and political and military exploits. He was an extremely (bemusedly) interested, urbanely critical, and essentially historical listener to my semiweekly conversational presentations, whether of the thesis sections I had just written or the chapters in *War and Peace* I had just read.

The weekly experience of "telling it to Lew" created a novel, personalized oral-history dimension for the enterprise: now, while *writing* it down, I could *talk* it out to a native in the intellectual culture for which it was intended, just as I had been able to discuss all the details with the villagers in the field and, to some extent, with my then wife who had lived with me in the field (Tiríndaro) for six months. "Telling it to Lew" was matched by preparing drafts for my committee chairman, Sidney Mintz, who, about the same time, was writing up for publication the life history *Worker in the Cane;* we sometimes exchanged ideas, and he made valuable suggestions about, in particular, the economic dimension, the life history model, and the anarchists and similar radical movements. (The other two members of my committee were Clellan S. Ford, an expert in the life history approach, and the polymathean and sophisticated Cornelius Osgood; together with an appointed fourth reader, Leopold Pospisil, this was the committee that approved the thesis.)

The experience of writing the thesis *Cacique* was an exercise of the intellect but also an act of passion. A sense of purpose about agrarian politics was laced by guilt at how my little daughters had had to suffer malnutrition, illnesses, and other dangers (e.g., Maria was bitten by a rabid dog; Su nearly died more than once of sudden sicknesses). In that year of write-up the four of us were living in a run-down two-room tenement apartment. Composing the thesis together with two-thirds teaching and two-thirds graduate study left me thirty pounds underweight, racked by coughing fits, insomnia, free-floating hostilities, and fantasies of homicide, alternating with periods of enthusiasm, happiness, and a sense of insuperable strength—the classic manic-depressive syndrome. The emotional commitment grew so violent that, after the thesis defense, my rational faculties told me to veer away and focus on linguistics as a sort of antidote, even to go off to India for a year of teaching and study, and otherwise to acquire some detachment and perspective.

When I returned to the rewriting after seven years of teaching (including courses on kinship and politics), it was shortly after I had left my first wife; the job proved almost as draining emotionally (guilt at having had to leave my daughters and four-year-old son added to the intensity). The rewriting was, once again, intertwined with the study of history, and, to a far lesser extent, the historical novel. Over the same months, as a calculated input, I read or reread Xenophon's *Anabasis*, Thucydides' *Peloponnesian Wars*, many of Plutarch's *Lives* (memorably Alexander and the Gracchi), and T. E. Lawrence's *Seven Pillars of Wisdom* (which is of course permeated with a Greek perspective). I had been teaching and advising in cultural anthropology, but I did not turn to it for models at this point. I read the four works in classical historiography carefully, line by line, lovingly, for the historian's art-cum-science and as a stabilizing intellectual outrigger; they also reinforced certain aspects of style and of my own philosophy of history—for example, the interplay between individual *hubris* and inexorable fate. During the same period of write-up I taught a heavily historical course on Russian culture that included much conventional history and a few highly realistic historical novels such as Aksakov's *Family Chronicle* and Sholokhov's *Quiet Don*. The rewriting of *Agrarian Revolt* also entailed an exploration of principles of English style; at least eight typed drafts underlie every printed page, and some difficult pages were rewritten three times in one day. Sydney Mintz rejoined the effort in this period with some early-on stylistic editing, some good advice, and help with the job of getting presses to give *Agrarian Revolt* a serious look (it was rejected by five presses in 1965, sometimes with ideological motivations disguised by invective: "It contains not one well-written sentence"). In 1966–1967, accompanied by my then wife Margaret Hardin, I did eighteen months of intensive linguistic and lexical semantic fieldwork in another part of the Tarascan area (plus six months of dialectology later, in 1970). I visited Naranja and Tiríndaro several times, briefly, and, without getting systematic, picked up some political information and insights. My political thinking and interpretation of Tarascan politics was furthered by participating in the formative conferences on political anthropology (Burg Wartenstein, Austria, 1966) and on symbolic anthropology (New Orleans, 1969). These crucial conferences and my follow-up reading (e.g., of Victor Turner) and discussions (e.g., with Marc Swartz) drew me away from linguistics and into the then avant garde of two new points of view with a few components that could amplify my own. Also in 1969 I wrote the last chapter, on "Causes," for *Agrarian Revolt* and, after having shelved it for four years, got the book accepted in two weeks.

The recent history of the writing of *The Princes* is similarly not devoid of interest, notably as pertains to the role of chance and order in such enterprises. The decade after the publication of *Agrarian Revolt* was devoted mainly to Indo-European linguistics, mythology, Homeric Greek (resulting in *The Meaning of Aphrodite*), Tarascan morphosyntax and morpholexicon, and other variously related and unrelated matters. Then, in the spring of 1981, Friedrich Katz crossed my path behind the Rockefeller Chapel (I have never seen him there before or since) and urgently asked me to discuss the methods used in *Agrarian Revolt* with Jean Meyer, a French anthropologist specializing in Mexico who happened to be in Chicago for a two-day conference. I agreed and made a breakfast appointment but then, feeling I didn't fully understand or even remember these methods, called the thing off, feeling guilty. The next year student John Leavitt asked me for a course in field methods in linguistics because he wanted "to know how to read a grammar." I initiated a general course which gradually, amid considerable student confusion, drifted into anthropology. I presented my first approximation to what is now Chapter 7 above. I worked on during the summer and fall of 1982, adding the long sections on write-up and personal background (Chapters 8 and 9) and presented the results in various sections and versions to the Latin American Center (two times) and the Anthropology Department (spring of 1983). Although these statements were well received, the 125-page total was too long for an article and too short for a book and hence was rejected by six publishers.

On the morning of February 4, 1984, while running home over pavements with some new ice to fetch my daughter Kanya to school, and a bit inebriated by the Russian grammar and poetry that I was to teach in an hour, I broke two leg-ankle bones (only thirty paces from where I had met Katz three years earlier). The months of convalescence, including a long cast, freed me from on-campus distractions. I concentrated on a crash course in Classical Hebrew, on select readings (notably Emerson and the T'ang poet Wang Wei), and on researching, drafting, and planning publications. Then in June, during another lunch, Katz, responding to my complaints about the betwixt-and-between status of my methods manuscript, suggested, "Why don't you add 100 pages from your thesis?" While I was working on this over the next two weeks I also hit on the right strategy for a second book, *The Language Parallax*. All that summer I wrote on both books alternately; at the point of total inanition, I would go to a Cubs baseball game. As things progressed with *The Princes* I realized that I should include the entire second volume of my thesis, some of which I edited minimally, some of which I rewrote, all of which was typed out by Lois Bisek (who had also typed all of *Agrarian Revolt*). Both books had reached a submissable form by September. *The Princes* was submitted on

September 11. *The Language Parallax,* after some additional work, was submitted in November and accepted in two weeks. Roughly simultaneous with these activities in September I began formulating a plan for a Joint Degree Program in Anthropology and History. My father's death that month gave me additional impetus to institutionalize the relation between anthropology and history as "something he would have liked." In December I circled through the Tarascan area two times by bus, concentrating on the symbolism of place (which resulted, among other things, in the poem "Janitzio"). In January 1985, back in Chicago, I renewed my efforts to launch a joint degree program with the history department. Shortly thereafter the University of Texas Press accepted *The Princes of Naranja* but judiciously suggested that I take my time for revisions. With renewed motivation I therefore instituted a new course on the anthropology/history interface, called it "Anthrohistory: Mexico," and read *The Princes* page by page to the half-dozen students, getting some feedback and doing some rewriting. That same spring of 1985, however, was made strenuous by an acutely infected middle ear (twice misdiagnosed and resulting in permanent damage), a recurrence of an inflamed nerve in the brain, and the near-death of my fourth daughter (e.g., two weeks of intensive care). After somewhat recovering from all this I returned to the drafts of a large set of dreams (potential dream poems) and began to train for a fieldtrip to the Russian Dukhobors of Canada. Jogging along Lake Michigan in July, I retraumatized and permanently damaged the formerly broken ankle. Barely able to walk, I stayed at home and started to randomly retype pages in *The Princes* (a type of quality control that has become a habit). I soon realized that the accepted text was below the standards of *Agrarian Revolt* and even farther below those that I believe in. I worked almost ten straight weeks (i.e., sixty-six days), starting between four and six A.M. after an expresso or two, and eventually retyping and variously and intermittently improving the entire work except for the life histories. In that sixth-story (two-bedroom) nest with my wife and two small daughters, Kanya and baby Joan, I also reread all my fieldnotes pertaining to politics, many other fieldnotes, and read or reread a considerable amount of Mexican history (e.g., Hansen, Brandenburg). The most crucial consequence of this second confinement and of teaching the course that spring was not so much the retyping and rewriting but the reordering of the entire book. I put the biography, ethnography, and historiography first, and put the three chapters on field methods, write-up, and general background second, and internally reordered this now second part (what is now Chapter 9 was formerly 7); as my wife, Deborah, put it, "The Iliad should come before the Odyssey." I also re-created Chapter 5 from a chronological sketch that verged on being a cop-out into a strong and complexly orchestrated anthropological history—the fulcrum of the book, as it should be. Even this hinged on accidents: in September 1985 my wife's mother died after a ten-year bout with cancer. I was torn about whether or not to attend the funeral in Boston but did not go because I felt this was the climax of a thirty-year process of some kind, and did indeed on that weekend write out two key things that I had not been able to say until that time.

I fired off this latest version to Texas and, using my left foot most of the time to accelerate, drove to Saskatchewan for a curtailed field trip. In early November, while going backward and forward over the excellent copy-editing, I developed acute eyestrain but also began to retype and partly to rewrite the three main life histories, making them coordinate with Part II and incorporating the gains in the published versions of two of them. I also partly rewrote Chapter 5. As a final test I set up a repeat for the winter of 1986 of my new course, now called "Anthropological History" and worked through and stitched further on "Aquiles" and "*Libido Dominandi.*" After reviewing the copy editor's many hundreds of reactions to my review of her work, I somewhat reordered and rewrote the final chapter on "Background" in April 1986 (some pages are still fairly new), and added the section that you are now reading on the writing of *The Princes.* Much of the rewriting referred to above, by the way, did not involve style so much as interconnections between deeper levels of meaning and symbolism.

Let me review and sum up. The composition of successive drafts involves positions on style and organization and content that naturally change over time as one becomes more explicit or self-conscious or secure or honest or, more generally, changes oneself. The life studies of the seven princes were shaped by changing concerns with political morality and telling psychological detail. One of them was written in the field, the rest in the post-field year and then, in three cases, in 1965–1966 and very recently. The following, more analytical third of the book, which interlocks complementary approaches, was written and drafted over several periods. The last third, on methods and experience, was first drafted in 1981–1982. (See the chart "A History of Anthrohistorical Writing.") Note that the time interval between the overall review and considerable rewriting of *The Princes of Naranja* (1985–1986) and the original fieldwork (1955–1956) is identical to the interval between the writing of volume 1 of *Cacique,* that is, *Agrarian Revolt* (1956), and the final year of the historical period dealt with in that volume (1926): thirty years in each case. But granted all these diverse origins and shifting concerns, the writing was governed by general principles and explicit guidelines that, although they cannot be sharply differentiated from inexplicit intuitions, can to some extent be spelled out.

A History of Anthrohistorical Writing

Parts	I					II			
Chapters	1					2	3	4	5
Sections	a	b	c	d-f	g				
Dates of writing:									
1956	✔				✔				✔
Winter 1957	✔	✔	✔	✔	✔		✔	✔	✔
1965–1966	✔		✔				✔	(✔)	✔
1981–1982									
Summer 1984							✔	✔	✔
Summer 1985	✔		✔		✔		✔	✔	✔
Winter 1986					✔				✔

Principles of Composition: Structure-in-Process

The basic idea is that symbolic units such as words, clauses, themes, patterns, ideas, facts, and other elements of form and content may be organized or organize themselves naturally in terms of movements, counterpoint, implications, cumulative effect, linear and non-linear order, overture and cadenza, tension and release, cause and consequence, correlation, the fugal interplay of motifs, galaxies of interacting contexts, and—to break the itemization—similar techniques and principles and ideas about composition. The basic job to be done in a craftsmanlike manner is *to write a good text,* but this should not be confused with the interconnected gist of the matter: *to compose a good book* that will allude and refer in the richest and most comprehensive way to the many realities for which any text is, at best, an imperfect diacritic. Let me illustrate this by discussing about ten of the specific tactics of composition that went into the thesis *Cacique* and just as much or more into the revised and edited *Agrarian Revolt* and *The Princes.*

The principles of composition are of four kinds: (1) lexical, involving words, idioms, and similar short symbolic units; (2) syntactic, involving the ordering and emphasis of such symbols and other information within and between adjacent sentences; (3) the gestalt level, deployed over a paragraph, a chapter, even the whole book, and illustrated, in turn, by four subtypes: (a) "partial holography," (b) "climactic integration," (c) "texturing," and (d) "telegraphing ahead." Of these principles, the syntactic, texturing, and telegraphing ones were used primarily in the second

III	IV		
6	7	8	9

(✔)			
✔			
	(✔)		
	✔	✔	✔
✔			
✔	(✔)	(✔)	(✔)
		✔	

and subsequent write-ups. All these principles will be discussed and illustrated in what follows. (4) The last principle involves such strategic considerations as degree of symmetry in exposition as partly iconic with the degree of order inherent in the subject matter. Naturally, there are many other shallow, tactical principles such as chiasmus versus straight derivation within the paragraph (simplifying: *a-b-c-b-a* structure versus *a-b-c-d-e*). And there are many deep principles involving, for example, a fugal relation between repeated, parallel themes. These ideas about composition were not made fully explicit or partly ordered in relation to each other until 1982–1983.

Lexical Level

At one relatively simple level words and idioms serve as fresh notes that must be listened for in fieldwork and set carefully into the composition; to paraphrase the poet Osip Mandelstam, like a chord in a great mass, a symbol yearns for its place in the history. To take another example, some idioms are ideological jargon in Spanish but sound novel to the American reader: "Iberian exploiter" is one; "the Attila of Michoacán" is another. Yet other recurrent words and phrases have more subtle potentials; for example, "eye of water" is a standard idiom for any spring-fed pool or pond but also works to symbolize politico-mythic undercurrents in the scene of Primo's capture and the assassination of Tomás Cruz (in Chapter 5). Finally, the perhaps idiosyncratic idiom "I am not a turkey to die in the gloaming; a man dies at noon" sets the tone for a perilous life and eventual martyrdom. Such locutions are local color and gems to decorate an anthropological history, but they also are symbols that condense, integrate, and incarnate the meanings of that history. I had been made keenly aware of the level of lexical symbol through my work in linguistics and philology, my readings of Suzanne Langer, Edward Sapir, and others, and, above all, through two short conversations with the philosopher F. S. C. Northrup.

Syntactic Level

A second level involves the ordering of information within and between sentences. To create a maximum sense of flow, I almost always avoided *hysteron proteron*, that is, starting with something later in time and, within the same sentence, ending with something that had happened earlier. More generally, I avoided looping back or jumping ahead, temporally. On the contrary, the words within the clauses and also the clauses and phrases within sentences and the sentences themselves in their linear order were made to correspond as closely as possible to the successive points in time to which they referred. The reference at the end of one sentence should, in principle, overlap and connect with the temporal reference at the start of the next sentence. In other words, there should be a maximum iconicity between syntactic order and the external, chronological order. Sentences should not be aligned like semiautonomous stones along the top of a narrative fence, as they so often are in social science, but should be concatenated like the links in a chain. On the other hand, I also avoided the technique of explicit overlap favored by some historical writers, both historians and historical novelists, whereby a key word in one sentence is repeated in the next, and a key word in the next is repeated in the third sentence, and so forth. I avoided this technique because I wanted to minimize this kind of redundancy—although it can be a powerful syntax indeed (e.g., in Tolstoy). In any case, the syntax of words and other verbal elements was made to collaborate with the ordering of information so as to maximize the sense of necessity or inevitability and serve the general metaphysics of fatalism. I was more or less aware of these syntactic principles in *Agrarian Revolt* and still have some notes on them, which were made, however, not during the time of the original composition in 1956–1957, but during the period of rewrite in 1964–1965. They also operate in various ways in the life studies in Chapter 1, but the main analogues to them in the analytical chapters are principles of anaphora and cross-reference which increase (the sense of) systematicity.

Gestalt Level

A more complex principle of composition is that of multiple-angle shots or, better, a partial holography of the same reality. While congruous with and indeed derivative from the multiple contextualization and theoretical eclecticism of the book as a whole, it must be seen as a concrete, even tactical device for organizing paragraphs and the like.

Take the most simple-minded of instances, the weather. I start off (*Agrarian Revolt*, p. 10) with the fact of there being not four but two seasons, thereby inviting the angle or view of the average American reader; then comes a sentence at a meteorological level—hail, precipitation—which is made subjective by the phrase "fierce deluges" and Mexicanized by the national name for the season, "the waters"; two more sentences on mountains and cold are again subjectivized by the phrase "rugged, green" and then entirely relocated into a child's-eye view: little Tarascans shivering at night under their embroidered blankets; the paragraph ends with my own intense perceptions of the weather in the Tarascan sierra and then with a closing, Mexicanizing phrase about the "cold country." Thus the account of the weather is far from being flat "descriptive ethnography" or geography, in the sense of a one-dimensional account by a self-appointed omniscient observer. On the contrary, it is made a constantly fluctuating reality, the beauty of which is implied, as seen through a half-dozen rapidly changing lenses shooting from different angles.

The same principle of historical holography becomes more powerful and enriching when you are viewing personality, politics, and similarly surcharged information, as in the political life studies, in Chapter 1 of this book, outstandingly those of Camilo and Aquiles Caso. Take the personal quality which Aquiles himself emphasized, perhaps overemphasized, when representing and interpreting himself, namely "sentiment(al[ism])" (*sentimiento*). We develop an understanding of what this means by following the words and the idea/emotion through a series of revealing contexts: (1) as part of a boyhood impulse to pull a girl's braids and steal a rival's bread; (2) as a response to his mother's injunctions to "always fight for your uncle"; (3) as a feeling when visiting a bordello or abducting his wife-to-be at pistol point; (4) as an emotion when dancing at his wedding or at the baptism of a godchild; (5) as a reaction of (metaphorical) nausea at a woman's nudity, slovenliness, or sadistic perversity; (6) as the drive to star at basketball or the adult game of "little sticks," and the joy of winning and the anguish of defeat; (7) as the sternness and anger of enjoining obedience to the mother-in-law both in his own home and among those whom he is judging in the town hall; (8) in the chaos when he is losing control over language itself and reverting garrulously to Tarascan when drunk; (9) as his zeal when rushing into hand-to-hand combat to defend a relative or when staying awake all night before a political rally where he will speak. In these and many other ways the violent, emotional meanings of Aquiles' "sentimentality" is added up and synthesized in a psychological holography, and, at another level, the reader is made to share a synthesis of the meanings of Spanish *sentimiento*, which is *not* "sentiment" in the American English sense.

A similar kind of psychological holography governs the representation of what I call Primo's "almost diagnostic predilection for violence" (*Agrarian Revolt*, p. 75). Here the focus or eye shifts from some historical facts to the quoted words of a regional poet, to those of a bitterly rivalrous cacique who was heavily responsible for Primo's death, to those of an affectionate matrilateral nephew; then come some more historical facts; then comes some primordial cultural context, that is, in this case, the Tarascan or, more generally, the rural Mexican child's early and frequent first-hand experience of violence, death, disease, vengeance, and so forth; then I shift to Primo's own desperate fears, melancholy, premonitions, and dreams of death as worded by him in letters that were included in the biography by Apolinar Martínez Múgica; then come key phrases culled from dozens of talks with his contemporaries, particularly female relatives and one of his mistresses: "Primo always used to say, 'They are going to kill me'"; then follows his personal and ideological identification with his mother's brother, also an agrarian leader, also martyred in the cause; and finally, Primo's return to Naranja in 1919 to "step into the breach" (echoes of Prince Harry!) when he perceived "the conjunction of the stars," as I put it. Thus in less than three printed pages the focus of the reader on the subject is made to flow and remain integrated even while the actual focus is shifting a dozen times to give—or at least I tried to give—a heightened sense of the reality of Primo's "diagnostic trait."

A third example of psychological and historical holography comes from the entire present book, which, like the original thesis, could have been called *Cacique* because it is a character study and a sustained analysis of one man, Elías (Scarface) Caso, an analysis and presentation that is perhaps more effective because it deals, not directly and ostensibly, but obliquely and from many angles with what Scarface meant to many others and the way he figured in diverse groups, institutions, and historical events and processes.

To switch metaphors, this psychological and historical holography could, following Goethe, be called a trope of multiple mirrors since the points of view reflect not only realities and imaginings, but also into each other to irradiate the subject matter in question. Call it what you will, the tactical principle of holography pervades both *Agrarian Revolt* and *The Princes*, not only in the biographical studies but in the ethnographic description and the historical reconstruction as well.

A yet more complex principle—because over a wider scope—calls for the climactic integration of the various dimensions within the bounds of each chapter. In two of the central chapters of *Agrarian Revolt* a long series of topics or themes is dealt with successively, paragraph by paragraph, or in sets of paragraphs. Then, in the last page or so, each of these earlier thematic units is referred back to by a condensing series of clauses and sentences. A second device for creating cumulative impact is used in the last two central chapters, where a series of implications, suggestions, and omens point ahead toward Primo's doom—toward his sense of mission and his own premonitions and, second, toward his actual capture and lynching. Yet another kind of chapter closure is used almost everywhere in *Agrarian Revolt,* including the prologue and epilogue: (1) ". . . there surged the peasants' urgent and implacable demand"; (2) "The black soil was fertile and the seed had been sown when Primo Tapia returned from the north to lead his Indians to the ultimate harvest"; (3) "More acutely than anyone did he discern the conjunction of the stars"; (4) "'They made a luxury of savagery with Primo'"; (5) "Naranja, once the proud 'soul of agrarianism in the region.'" Here the chapters are wrapped up with deliberately figurative, emotional, and, for the most part, conventionally poetic language. The one exception, Chapter 2 of *Agrarian Revolt,* proves the principle since its entire concluding two pages are highly figurative. I was only partly aware of this strategy when I wrote *Cacique,* and hesitated because it might have melodramatic consequences, but then went ahead and used it throughout during the rewrite of the final draft of *Agrarian Revolt.*

Similar climactic integration is used in *The Princes of Naranja.* In Chapter 1, the first six life studies function, in part, to sensitize and orient the reader for the last, more complex characterization of Aquiles Caso. On the other hand, the overall structure of this work is not as chronological or narrative as that of *Agrarian Revolt,* but more complex. Several kinds of political reality are viewed from complementary angles with the goal of building a multidimensional system. By another, kindred technique, the analysis is enriched or intensified by superimposing four levels over a simple chronological base, a horizontal axis of multiple interpretation intersecting with the exaggerated linearity of a reduced narrative line.

Two similar but more comprehensive principles can integrate a history over yet longer time spans. The first of these principles, which I call texturing, can weave together bits of information at every conceivable level. One prime example of this is seen in the names and sociopolitical patterns of the so-called "political families" (see Chapters 3–5). These are sets of persons who share a last name, whether as patronymic or matronymic, plus other persons linked to the family by marriage, friendship, or ritual kinship who more or less work with it in intrigue and factionalism; political families always include allies without the last name, and there usually are a few persons who bear that name but stand outside the family, or even in a hostile faction. The name itself may be a politicized semifiction; the Casos and the de la Casas constituted the political family of "the Casos," although these were genealogically distinct groups which had intermarried only a little. Political families in this sense figure integrally in both *Agrarian Revolt* and *The Princes:* as part of the historical-ethnographic background; in their functions in Primo's life-history; as politically crucial groupings during the revolt and the long period of factionalism that followed; and as a point of orientation for the individual and for small groups in village politics.

Equally complex and pervasive fabrics involve the many meanings and associations of master symbols such as maize: its cultivation by family groups; its cash value to the landlords in the national market; its meaning to children and its potency as a symbol of power, a life symbol; and the sheer physical facts about its taste in fresh tortillas, the beauty of the many colors of *criollo* or Indian corn, and so forth. Like political families and, as it were, politicized maize, scores of other strands of symbolic threads run crisscrossing through the books to weave many levels of warp and woof. Such deliberate texturing, in its pervasiveness, differs from the relatively simple symbols that I discussed at the start of this section.

I was attuned to master symbols during the first write-up because of my work in comparative literature and anthropology (e.g., Melville, Benedict). I was not, on the other hand, primarily conscious of complex texturing during the initial drafts, when the main concern was to get the massive facts and insights of fieldwork down on paper in an organized and coherent form. During the rewrite of *Agrarian Revolt* I carried the master symbol strategy further and greatly increased the symbolic and stylistic cohesion of the text as a whole through hundreds of minor shifts of emphasis in the writing. Such rewriting has not seemed as imperative in the case of the seven life studies in *The Princes*, which, together with the Tapia chapter in *Agrarian Revolt*, constituted the heart of the two-volume *Cacique*—and the parts whose first drafts I wrote with the greatest confidence; for other reasons, I want to communicate the style and symbolism of the life studies as they were synthesized during and shortly after the fieldwork on which they are based.

By a second principle, which I call telegraphing ahead, hundreds of bits of information are positioned so as to prepare the reader for an event or, from a more intellectual point of view, to contribute to the reader's sense of cumulative necessity in the history. One example of such telegraphing occurs in the seven political life studies. Here, as we move through the gallery of princes, the diverse roles of women in Naranja are introduced gradually: as victims or objects of sexual aggression and mocking humor; as ambiguous but powerful figures in the homes and families of leaders (e.g., grandmothers, wealthy usuresses); as dominant mothers and mothers-in-law in extended families and kindreds; as sexually desperate and even promiscuous; as tenderly caring for their own offspring and those of others; as toiling energetically in the fields of corn, or serving on committees for political action or religious ritual. All these roles and the contrast and complementation between them prepare the reader for the tremendous intensity, tension, and also human richness of the relation between mother and wife and, third, the prince on whom the entire chapter actually focuses: Aquiles Caso.

A cognate example of telegraphing informs one strand in the agrarian revolt volume. Here the sequence runs from descriptions and allusions to the backbreaking agricultural and domestic work of women to their roles in kinship and social organization. Then we meet a series of kinswomen, wives, and mistresses of the agrarian hero. Later, when the first harvest has been seized and many of the men locked up, we reach one of the political and mythic cornerstones of the book when the "slaves of the slaves" rise up en masse against the landlords' militia and eventually, after restitution has been legalized, physically retrieve most of the ransacked maize. Near the end of *Agrarian Revolt* it is a woman who runs out to the "eye of water" to warn Primo of the approach of government troops, and, finally, it is five women who walk all the way to the state capital to retrieve his mutilated corpse. The cumulative crescendo and then decrescendo in the role of women in this anthropological history is interwoven with other woman-related themes and interpretations: for example, the contrast between the dozens of loyal peasant women, many of them Primo's matrilateral relatives, and, on the other hand, his succession of mestizo mistresses.

By way of summary it is worth belaboring the obvious point that the ultimate model or, better, strategy is to construct an aesthetic and scientific whole with many interacting, orchestrated levels such as the different arenas of politics, familial structures, and so forth. These levels of content are also levels of style or, more generally, form: the form of a statistical fact, of a ritual speech, of a national law. Intersecting with these many levels and partly defining them are diverse individual points of view and even ways of talking: the scores of pages of direct quotes from sharply characterized leaders, the scores of pages of raw fieldnotes in my voice at that time. Thus just as Part I above can be read as seven variations on several political themes, with a recapitulation and integration in "Aquiles," so the book as a whole is a rough analogue to a complex piece of music with many parts (voices and instruments) and sharply contrasting movements.[1]

Evidence and Relevance

The techniques of composition dealt with in the foregoing sections have to be used and thought of within a larger context of method and concept, that is, within the more comprehensive problems of historiography itself, whether or not anthropological. I take these larger problems to be four in number: first, to have an adequate sample of evidence from the infinitude of what happened ("evidence," of course, including the historian's response to what happened "out there"); second, to state the history in an interesting and persuasive way that, preferably, does justice to its complex multidimensionality; third, to document the history by marshalling many kinds of evidence, at least some of it accessible to the reader for checking and re-evaluation; and, fourth, to have a philosophy of history that includes and, preferably, affirms the historian's practice of historiography, and a more general metaphysics of history itself in terms of such fundamental issues as change, dynamics, and time. Perhaps the most distinctive or diagnostic thing about anthropologically oriented history is that the historian is in the position of creating much of the documentation (e.g., fieldnotes). Let me suggest how these four problems were approached in the present case.

"The data" set forth in *The Princes* are often based on actual, unique experiences—an image, a statement, the sight of a leader's orphaned son, the awkwardness and mockery in an argument at a town meeting. The first-hand quality of some of the evidence may make the anthrohistory more vivid and more valid, at one level, but at another it may reduce the craft in its construction. At least as many pages in *The Princes*, though, represent single-step inferences away from first-hand evidence, as when I decide that two men are close friends on the basis of how they converse on a certain subject, or when a childhood and adolescence are pieced together from interviews with the leader himself and with his relatives. In some parts of *The Princes* and most of *Agrarian Revolt* roughly every complete datum, be it in a sentence or strung through a paragraph or even a longer unit of exposition, is supported by two to five units of evidence—often many more. By "units of evidence" I mean anything from a government census to a personal letter to some gossip by an ancient crone. Such units of evidence, whether historical and highly inferential or based on my own witness, have been classified into about thirty general categories, a dozen of which were discussed in Chapter 7. I would underline, for the historian with a sometimes ritual faith in the published document, that, at least in local history, much of the nondocumentary evidence is more reliable than the published sources. My rule of multiple sources of historical inference was methodologically fundamental in the first draftings and remains so to this day. The exception—of valid evidencing through one source only—is illustrated here and there below and resembles the situation in structural philology where you have an entire paradigm of well-attested, reconstructed terms, and then a near gap which is saved from being total by one textual instantiation.

The canon of multitudinous or at least multiple sources raises problems. For one thing, to footnote and annotate my writings fully would have led to something like a scholarly edition of *The Divine Comedy*, with three-quarters of many pages devoted to notes and hundreds of references to relevant theory. Much of this scholarly coffin construction would involve informants who had died (and hence cannot be consulted) or letters since missing and other inaccessible information. In the same vein, to cross-reference the text to source materials in the dozens of relevant books and other publications would have given a seriously misleading impression of the entire enterprise—and of the evidential status of this published history itself. And it would have necessitated or at least suggested critical polemics with some of the historians in question. A more practical implication is the prospect of trying to publish and get distributed a manuscript of five thousand pages or more that would have been rendered almost unreadable by a partly ritualistic scholarship.

As a result of these considerations I made the drastic decision to give only a fair sample of the evidence for the information in *Agrarian Revolt:* the rate of about three references per page seemed enough to ground the reader and give a balanced impression of the source material. Almost no references are given in *The Princes* (except in Chapter 5), partly because of the same dilemma of multitudinousness, partly because I wanted to synthesize and make coordinate three fundamental inputs: (1) facts and inferences from published history; (2) descriptions based on my first-hand experience; (3) the testimony of eyewitnesses. These minimal but partly heuristic procedures are to some extent followed by many historians and anthropologists, and some of the most illustrious of them dispense with footnotes altogether.

Categories of Description and Analysis

The principles of composition given above are comparatively formal, even stylistic. When it comes to substance or actual material-symbolic content, I have built in terms of eight dimensions of description and, in part, analysis, which also functioned as "causes" in a loose and traditional sense. These eight dimensions are involved at most levels and at all periods of the anthrohistory in question, although at any one point only one or two of them may dominate. The eight dimensions overlap with one another, but no one of them can be reduced to or included in any other. Each dimension has its distinctive basis in data and experience, and each is associated with a body of humanistic and social scientific thought. Some instance of any one of the dimensions can trigger change; for example, the advent of a gifted leader. Any of these dimensions can either channel change or constrain it; for example, the landlord's militia constrained agrarian expropriation, but the agrarista militia effectuated it. All eight of these dimensions are actually invoked and discussed by local leaders, to whom it would be absurd that the revolt or local factionalism was not in some serious sense attributable to economic factors such as poverty, to local political families, to ideologies of reform and revolt, to the use and misuse of violence, and to the leadership ability of men like Tomás Cruz.

The eight dimensions fall roughly into two main types. First are the mainly descriptive dimensions of observation and, to a lesser extent, interpretation, which entail a great number of basic field questions: (1) materialistic factors; (2) political space, and geography; (3) political time, history, and chronology; and (4) overall culture, particularly political culture, that is, the web of symbols in the culture as a whole, a gestalt. The second set of dimensions, on the other hand, are both more specific in terms of descriptive compass and also analytical in the sense of specifying methods and concepts and applying them to penetrate and sharply interpret political language and behavior and their interconnections. These four relatively analytical dimensions are: (1) social and political organization, both local and extra-local, formal and covert; (2) the political functions of primary groups; (3) ideology; and (4) the character and personality of leaders, seen in cultural context. The eight dimensions or categories were not clearly formulated and ordered until the mid-eighties, and the rough dichotomy between description and analysis was particularly late in emerging, but such dimensions clearly underlie the original work, *Cacique*, and the two volumes that have emerged, *Agrarian Revolt* and *The Princes of Naranja*. Let us now turn to the four dimensions that are relatively descriptive.

1. *Materialistic factors.* This term does not necessarily imply a commitment to "materialism," but simply the relevance, particularly for a study of agrarian politics, of such factors as environment, the economics of production, the dietary needs of the human body, public health programs, and what anthropologists somewhat vaguely call "material culture." These materialistic factors are, at one level, relatively observable, tangible, often measureable: you can count the tortillas in your basket and the number of days with frost. Such factors are worth knowing objectively, but at least something about them is usually known and classified by the peasants also, and discussed at least as much as personal relations. In other words, when dealing with material aspects of agrarian politics one must have an abstract and underlying interpretation that is grounded in theory—such as, in my case, was learned during five semesters of economics and economic anthropology. But one must also be grounded on the peasants' ground and, as far as possible, in the semantic, symbolic, and emotional meanings of the peasants, which, in turn, have to be translated, interpreted, and somehow conveyed across the barriers of culture.

2. *Political space, and geography.* Political space means the towns,

roads, mountains, pools, and other spaces and shapes across and within which the political history transpires. In a primitive or peasant area, events have "a local habitation and a name," and many locations and places are associated with an event, often a political one (just as, in Chicago, we have the little "Clarence Darrow Bridge," where Darrow spoke, and the alley next to the Biograph Theater, where Dillinger bit the dust). Political leaders seem sensitive to such political geography and enjoy listing places, talking about place names. The anthrohistorian collects and internalizes all such symbolism as part of the reconstruction and inference of the local or regional history in question. Sometimes s/he can carry a contemporary description back entire into the past, without distortion. To recapture Primo Tapia's seminary days of the 1890s I made a bus trip and could report, "The seminary building of pink stone still stands; its massive columns and arches command a superb view of Lake Pátzcuaro, dotted with islands and often shrouded with mist." The geography of a (political) history is seen as a network of symbols that must be woven judiciously into the fabric and carefully and gradually introduced and explicated to the necessarily alien reader.

3. *Political time, history, and chronology.* This dimension raises profound and paradoxical questions because time itself is to such a large extent an individual and cultural construction. The anthrohistorian cannot take anything for granted about time because, for one, there are several popular and scientific kinds of time in his/her own culture: for example, time as an object or commodity which can be lost, or an abstraction which curves. These temporal prepossessions contrast with the ideas of time held by Tarascans, for most of whom, for example, time is part of the physical environment and inextricably associated with the position of the sun, and time is something that happens to you and about which it is rarely necessary to be exact. In general, multiplicity of temporal models is a given.

Nor can the anthrohistorian ignore temporal complexity when constructing an argument, synthesis, or historical representation. S/he must entertain as serious strategies such alternatives as: (1) a chronologically ordered series with implicit causation of the *post hoc ergo propter hoc* variety; (2) zigzagging along or looping back over a hypothetical time line or segments of a line; (3) going backward through time from the better known to the less known in a progressively retrogressive history; (4) introducing events as they actually or hypothetically enter the individual or collective consciousness (as Gatsby is introduced in Fitzgerald's novel); (5) a fugal or counterpuntal relation between the observing, historian's time and the native's time (which latter may be non-linear); (6) deliberate changes (e.g., decrescendo, accelerando) in the intensity of time as represented; (7) an argument or exposition that, while involving time, is not temporally ordered; (8) shifting embeddedness in different kinds of time, in which, for example, a future is embedded in a past. *The Princes of Naranja* involves a complex temporal model with several interacting kinds of time and temporally different experiences.

4. *Overall (political) culture.* Political anthrohistory must always strive toward synecdoche, in relation to the larger, cultural whole which it also condenses, or at least represents. For this reason one needs an overall cultural view and an omnium-gatherum approach to data collecting: technological, economic, social, religious, ideological, and so forth. The political analyses above—of leaders, friendship, ejidal office, and so forth—have been consistently contextualized in the overall culture of the village of Naranja; in fact, except for religious ritual, an overall cultural sketch could be extracted from the preceding chapters. Overall culture has to be seen and constructed at several levels, each with their complementary terms. First, the local point of view as revealed through standard locutions, typical and/or revealing behavior, patterns, and paradigms, and so forth. Second, whatever can be inferred from a wide range of methods that may or may not correspond to local views: frequencies of social association, symbolic clusterings in the anthropologist's test. A huge inventory of supplementary questions is provided by two anthropological manuals: *Notes and Queries,* and the coding book of the Human Relations Area Files—about a quarter of which I checked out in the field. Third, the overall gestalt can be synthesized in terms of so-called holistic or microsystemic anthropology. My main models for this were E. E. Evans-Pritchard's Nuer work, Robert Redfield's books on Mexico, Martin Yang's *Life in a Chinese Village,* and the fine community studies of Tarascan towns by George M. Foster and Ralph Beals.

More subtle ideas about description came from two quite different sources. One was from course work with the unsung father of what was once the "new ethnography," Cornelius Osgood—hence my attention to the details of what he, following Knud Rasmussen, called material, social, and intellectual culture. The second major input to overall description was the "realistic" American and Russian novel, partly because of the sensitivity with which ethnographic detail is dealt with by, for example, Turgenev and Steinbeck, partly because of the way these works create a pervasive symbolism, a network of secondary associations that, in this case, contextualizes the politics. Holistic, general historiography and synchronic, general ethnography were not, in any case, pursued for their own sake and, aside from a short culture sketch, I have never published on these topics. Rather, ethnographic and historiographic data gathering and analysis were pursued as indispensable contexts and intended inputs to "the history and present structure of politics in a Mexican village"—

just as massive political description amounting to many thousands of pages of fieldnotes was reduced to the condensed statements in *Agrarian Revolt* and this book.

One benefit from holistic general ethnography is that, within the complexity and comprehensiveness of "the whole," there emerge certain salient concerns or activities in the culture which have to be integrated with the dominant problem. In the case of the politics of Naranja, violence emerged as one such focus. Violence and the potential for it figured often in the words of this town of "killers," where many had been involved in knife fights and firefights since their adolescence; even the outwardly peaceful primary-school teacher with whom I lived had several scars from knife fights. Because of all the action in the thirties and forties, in particular, the Tarascan villages of the Zacapu Valley (and Tiríndaro as much as Naranja) were at that time known as "the slaughterhouse of Michoacán" (*el rastro de Michoacán*)—as I have already noted. In addition to these matters of reputation and language, there was a significant amount of violence in the peaceful year of my sojourn. My first two chapters, drafted in the field, sketched the lives of the "colorful and violent" Primo Tapia and of the town's leading gunman, Bones Gómez, and my first publication (in the journal *Psychiatry*) was called "Assumptions Underlying Tarascan Political Homicide." Thus violence meshed with my own latent tendencies (including masochism) and an impulsive lack of physical fear that have been illustrated more recently by several (isolated and foolhardy) attacks on persons initiating criminal acts (e.g., theft, rape) in Chicago. But violence also was conceptualized in terms of some of the theories and methods of the social sciences, notably the melange contained in the textbooks for a course called "Social Problems in America" that I had to teach twice while writing my thesis.

Let us turn now to the four relatively analytical dimensions, each characterized by specific methods.

1. *Social (political) organization and process.* One of the most relevant subcategories of overall, holistic culture is that of social organization in the sense of class and caste, social hierarchies and categories, and, in particular, the organization of political groups or at least of groups with political functions. The processes by which peasants share and compete for power over land and over other peasants are analyzed above in terms of several intersecting dimensions. First, there are the more public, institutionalized, explicitly ordered forms of government, particularly the two local arms of civil and ejidal government; most ethnographies do not go beyond this overt, public system. Paralleling it, however, are the informal processes for winning and distributing power; these particularly involve the constitution and workings of faction, and the techniques (tactics and

strategy) by which leaders, (political) families, and factions compete for office and for power in general. (A good case could be made for setting up "tactics and strategy" as a separate analytical dimension under political anthrohistory, with subsections on rhetoric, techniques of alignment, and so forth.) Both the informal and the formal processes, in any case, articu-late with leadership, ideology, and the political functions of primary groups, as is shown in Chapter 3 above. Analysis consists in discovering and stating such relations.

2. *Primary groups.* Local life mainly involves family, kindred, and ge-nealogical relations and, almost as centrally, the small groups of friend-ship, especially "friendship of confidence," and ritual kinship—the sev-eral kinds of *compadrazgo.* These ties were inferred by ethnographic questioning, by several techniques of so-called sociometry (e.g., record-ing sets of interacting persons on three-by-five cards), and by participa-tion: for example, several dangerous confrontations between siblings, cousins, and compadres gave me priceless insight into the relative power of these bonds: whom do you side with in a knife fight, your first cousin or a compadre of baptism? My study of these primary groups was carried out generally with political relevance in mind: the bonding of leaders, the ac-tivation of kindreds in the vendetta, the genealogies of "political fami-lies," and so forth. In a peasant village even more than in state or national politics—where they are critical too—primary ties such as brotherhood are ipso facto political, and keys to political history; the fifth chapter in *Agrarian Revolt* describes some of the primary ties between the agrarians as these were reconstructed for the early twenties, and the third chapter of *The Princes* details the primary ties of friendship (inter alia) among the leaders in 1956. My precepts for these practices of description came partly from ethnography but more from small group sociology, particu-larly G. C. Homans' brilliant *The Human Group* and a number of books on industrial sociology which I had read during a course with DeWitt Bakke the winter before I went into the field. These methods of small group analysis have since passed out of fashion or developed in the direc-tion of highly formalistic goals, possibly because the leading practitioners did not care to link their findings with other systems of data, systems of analysis, and general theories.

3. *Ideology* is not here a synonym for culture or cultural structure, nor for a society's explicit ideas about culture, language, and the like, nor is it to be taken as the equivalent to the colloquial meaning of a particular po-litical or religious creed such as Jeffersonianism or democratic socialism. "Ideology" is taken to refer to a more or less explicit, verbally formulated set of ideas for talking about values like land and power and for evaluating their pros and cons—all this coupled with some sort of tactics and strategy for changing things in a desired direction or for blocking such change. Ide-

ology, while not as observable or countable as the daily tortillas and their cost, is heard about frequently in conversation, gossip, and speeches and is in its way an empirical, objectively describable matter. Political ideology clearly was overdeveloped in Naranja to the point of becoming a cultural hypertrophy; as has been detailed, many leaders are clear about factional structure, the role of Communism in the state, techniques for gaining power, and so forth, and often discourse about them in a sophisticated way. But Naranja is not all that different from many other communities with a developed or even exacerbated political (self-)awareness, often the result of specific, historical causes. One decade later, in 1966, two days after hitting the field again, I arrived in the homicide-ridden, priest-dominated, large high sierra town of Patamban to discover, during a stroll at dawn, the leaders of the "Bolsheviki" faction meeting in a barnyard and quietly discussing ideology.

"Ideology" raises in acute form the problem of text and textuality. While to many historians and political scientists ideology is implicitly or ultimately a question of texts, in a peasant region only a few leaders have ever read any ideological texts or even derivative discussions, while the great bulk of the population garners almost all its ideas on the subject from oral sources such as speeches, the radio, arguments at town meetings, even what I have elsewhere called "life-changing dialogues." The job of the anthrohistorian is to comprehend both the textual and the oral dimensions, to discuss Machiavelli with the leader and the speech with the peon, and so work out a complex, multilayered model which s/he variously uses to illuminate the analysis. My own sources for the role and meaning of ideology were mainly original texts in classical political theory, such as works by Thomas Paine, or Machiavelli, who figures in Naranja ideology. This was combined with the political science of the time; with intellectual history, notably the magnificent, still standard synthesis by George Sabine (*A History of Political Theory*); and with the ideas of the villagers.

4. *Character and personality of leaders.* The personality, or perhaps better, the character of the leaders was ascertained as a partial by-product of the methods already noted above. The results were enlarged and integrated by an eclectic mélange of ideas from the then flourishing subfield of "culture and personality" (which, like small group sociology, has waned because its results were not reticulated with those of other subfields). For these studies of personality and character I found essential the sorts of theory contained in Ruth Benedict's "Continuities and Discontinuities in Cultural Conditioning"; the sorts of methods contained in John Dollard's *Criteria for the Life History* and Clyde Kluckhohn's brilliant monograph *The Use of Personal Documents;* and the comparative perspectives provided by anthropological life histories.

Equally important were studies of depth psychology through private reading on psychoanalysis, through research for George Devereaux, and through personal communications with William Davenport and a psychiatrist friend, Mildred January; the latter even sent me three volumes of Freud (in German), and I read them carefully in the field. I was not at that time aware of Jungian work, nor had I been nor have I been analyzed.

Probably more contributory than depth psychology, and certainly inextricably intertwined with it, was what might be called humanistic characterology, particularly as in the following: (1) French and Russian novels (including Pushkin), and Chaucer and Rulfo; (2) Greek and French moralists such as Montaigne and Pascal (my favorite college philosophers); while in the field I reread Spanish popular printings of the French moralist La Rochefoucauld and the Greek moralist Theophrastus; (3) biography and autobiography such as that of Benvenuto Cellini. Such are the diverse sources alike for the Primo Tapia chapter in *Agrarian Revolt* and the seven political life studies in this book.

The ideas of personality and character drawn from these sources were integrated with what I found in the local culture. A political culture such as that of Naranja stands out cross-culturally because of the relative salience of its leaders, but also because of the relative explicitness and frankness with which the leaders and ordinary folk discuss and conceptualize the classic issues of all politics—leadership, faction, and ideology—and, perhaps more particularly, such personal traits as egoism and violence. Thus as a fourth input to the synthesis of an idea of personality or character, and to the specific life studies below, we have to include the description and analysis of various local verbal/conceptual categories or classes. These classes include that of the leader—the town boss (*cacique*), fighter (*luchador*), and hired gun (*pistolero*); the categories of primary grouping such as confidential friend (*amigo de confianza*) and compadre of baptism (*compadre de bautismo*); the various groupings of kinship and politics, ranging from the ejidal family (*familia ejidal*) to the political family (*familia política*) to the faction (*partido*); the various kinds of politically charged act such as "to support" (*respaldar*), "to betray" (*traicionar*), and "to be united" (*estar unidos*); the various kinds of emotion with strong political overtones such as envy (*envidia*), rage (*coraje*), and the attribute of "loyal" (*fiel*); and finally the category of politics itself as a partly distinct entity (*la política*). The meanings and the feel of these and many other categories were learned through methods in some calculated sense, but even more through experience, friendship, and identification and resistance to identification. Categories and feelings such as these are explicitly and/or implicitly dealt with in *The Princes of Naranja* and constitute one level in it, but a level that is part of an organic synthesis rather than the particulate, atomistic objects of a semantic analysis.

Diverse psychological foundations protect one from a typical failing of the anthropologist, which is to ignore leaders in their uniqueness in favor of the levels of society and culture. Such foundations also protect one from the equally typical failing of the historian, which is to interpret leaders in terms of his/her own bourgeois and academic values. A comparativist orientation leads one to handle better one's psychological relation to the leaders under study and to more precisely and empathetically construct the views and world views of such leaders.

Conclusions (1)

Let me provisionally conclude this discussion with an anecdote that some may find revealing. My first formal anthropology course was a year-long affair dubbed "General Anthropology": six Yale graduate students sat around an oak table and gave reports on basic writings to each other and the instructor, Wendell Bennett. In the second term it fell my lot to do "the community study" as my major project. By choice I focused on Mexico and, in particular, the work of Robert Redfield, who was then one of the half-dozen dominant figures in a field that was still seen as unified. While fascinated by Redfield's ideas about what he called the "folk-urban" continuum, and even more taken by his precise and literary style, I rebelled most fundamentally against his views of politics, leadership, and political history, both in Mexico at large and his fieldwork community of Tepoztlán. I wrote in my personal notebook in 1953 as follows:

> I wonder off-hand whether or not Redfield oversimplifies the homogeneity, the uniformity, the contentment, and the resignation of the Tepoztlatecos. For example, do all the townsmen have plots for maize and, if so, are they for subsistence? If not, where do they work, and just how does the family live? I should judge that in considering the total culture of Tepoztlán a considerable amount of weight should be accorded to the historical fact that the center of the 1920–23 revolution in southern Mexico was in the state of Morelos i.e., where this town is located. Los Zapatistas.

Although I was only twenty-four years old at the time and very ignorant of Mexico (e.g., my dates for the Revolution are totally off), I was dead certain that I was right about Redfield being wrong. More generally, I was irritated by what seemed to be an American version of the illusion of harmony, order, and cooperation that *might* be somewhat realistic when it came to villages in Illinois, New England, Germany, or Scandinavia, but that flew in the face of what I intuited about Mexico. My objections to Redfield were later stimulated and supported by communications with Wendell Bennett and Sidney Mintz, who were familiar with the contro-

versies swirling at that time and introduced me to some of the literature
(e.g., Oscar Lewis). But my objections to Redfield were also coupled with
some more longstanding objections to the theory and views on political
issues that were propounded by my father. My strong objections to the
ideas of both these strong minds, conjoined with a healthy respect for
much of their work, no doubt deeply determined my perceptions of politics when I got to Mexico.[2]

Conclusions (2)

Beneath the complexities and eclecticism of the approach advocated
above, there is a methodological gist. To recapitulate, a number of methods and approaches, such as participant observation, are present or at
least implicit in most ethnographies and ethnohistories—in most culturally anthropological and anthropologically historical statements—as
standard components of description. This holds for the four dimensions of
description above: materialistic factors; political space and geography; political time, history, and chronology; overall (political) culture. The other
four dimensions, which I call "dimensions of analysis," may possibly be
standard dimensions of ethnography or ethnohistory, but by no means
usual is the way they have been fused with the first four dimensions into
one descriptive-analytic whole. These second four dimensions, to recapitulate, are: (1) *social (political) organization and process*, that is,
the formal and informal processes of politics and government, including
informal tactics; (2) *primary groups*, specifically, the microsociology,
sociometry, and kinship ethnography of intimate, primary ties and the
groups formed by such ties, and the groups that overlap with such groups;
(3) *ideology*, that is, the more or less explicit ideas about real values like
land and power and, more generally, ways for thinking and talking per-
suasively about them; (4) the *character and personality* of leaders, via the
genre of the life history and analysis in terms of cultural values, particularly those of politics and economics. The four dimensions of analysis all
interconnect with one another; for example, the values in an ideology are
always one basis for any political organization, and primary ties such as
those of "friend of confidence" always interact with other bonds between
leaders. For representing the actual interconnections between these (and
other) analytical dimensions, two of the best models are surely the cy-
clical and the historical: the life, annual, and daily cycles, and, as emphasized in this book, the local history and the life history. In this spirit the
four analytical dimensions in question and, by implication, the four descriptive dimensions are integrated with one another above as one superordinate system, structure, or simply universe. This structure, that is, po-

litical structure, is then integrated with the intersecting dimensions of time, that is, here, history, specifically political history. The two major dimensions and their permutations—the history of a structure and the structure of a history—provide a fruitful model for local-level politics and, more generally, anthropological history.

CHAPTER 9

Background: Personal and Intellectual

Jumping Off

With banjo and with frying pan,	An' we started,
Susanna, don't you cry,	Rockin' an' a rollin',
We're off to California. . . .	Long towards the ol' peachbowl. . . .
—AMERICAN FOLK SONG	—WOODY GUTHRIE

My approach to the problem was indirect and fortuitous—in part a series of linked accidents. Desiring continuity with my Soviet and Russian studies, I sedulously constructed a major grant application in the fall of 1953 to pursue anthropological doctoral fieldwork among Turkish peasants and, in a comparative framework, Turkmen pastoralists on the Soviet-Afghan border. Contrary to fond expectations, I lost out. That summer of 1954 I landed what appeared to be the only job in recession-ridden New Haven: old-fashioned, piece-rate labor in an old-fashioned slaughterhouse/meat-packing plant. The classic sweatshop, mainly staffed by East (of the Rhine) European "pigstickers" and sausage-stuffers, got me genuinely interested in the bonds between workers on the job. At the same time I kept hearing that there was no money for linguistic fieldwork; so, with a flexibility lubricated by desperation and sagely guided by the then chairperson Irving Rouse, I shifted to almost the opposite direction: Mexico (near and cheap). As part of the same move I also shifted to a radically different, almost ad hoc, almost opportunistic doctoral problem: industrial anthropology. To allay my total ignorance of the subject I took a reading course that fall with Yale authority DeWitt Bakke and rapidly concocted a project in a very practical anthropology that, by my cynical calculus, would appeal mightily to the foundation men of that time: to investigate the "small group dynamics" in a Mexican workplace and, concomitantly, the patterns of labor migration. I played seriously with doing the anthropological sociometry of Mexican miners deep in their shafts and at one point even found myself being interviewed by mysterious executives (American

Smelting and Refining) high over the Hudson River. But more intriguing by far was a lunch-time conversation with anthropologist Pedro Carrasco, who just happened to be a friend of my advisor. Tarascan Indians, he reported, were leaving their villages in droves to work for a large, newly constructed synthetic fiber plant operated by the Celanese Corporation of America. Armed with a starter grant of $1,500 from the Wenner-Gren (then Viking) Foundation and burdened with the idea of somehow supporting a wife and two infant daughters (aged one-and-one-half years and six weeks), I headed, in January 1955, for the mines of Monterrey and the industry of Mexico City. After about ten days of hectic sightseeing (e.g., piggybacking one-year-old Maria to the top of the pyramid of Teotihuacán) and of uniformly disastrous interviews with businessmen such as John Foster Dulles, Jr., I took the family to Morelia, found a modern ranch-style home for them in an American "colony," and pushed on by "Green Arrow" (second-class) bus for the green Tarascan sierra and the factory in Zacapu.

Fieldwork Datum No. 10: "My First Tarascans"
[First fieldnotes, February 1955]

I was taking the beautiful bus trip from Morelia to Zacapu and we had just passed the sweeping rise along the sinuous road as it runs up over the high hill and you have Lake Pátzcuaro spread out before you like something from a Swiss postcard, the still blue waters surrounded by mountains, the thin stone walls stretching down to the shore through light green fields of wheat where barely visible fishermen are hanging up their nets and then, as a focus for this sun-bathed gem of bluish-rust, there is nestled on a semi-peninsula the town of Pátzcuaro with its low brown and sand-colored houses and the pointed spire of its single church. This view was just receding from our sight as we dropped into another valley of rolling fields and burros picking stubble when I noticed the bus slowing down and a group of three women standing by the roadside flagging us. As they climbed in I noticed the mussed hair and large placid eyes of the babies that two of them had slung in their dark blue-black rebozos. One of these mothers was about forty, very wrinkled in her coppery face, her dusty black hair parted in the middle and drawn back in a small bun, and her gleaming black eyes slightly bloodshot. The other mother was similar in appearance although only twenty-five and she had almost buck teeth and her skin was much lighter. The third was a girl of about fourteen also with large front teeth and her skin burnt almost black by the hot sun of Mexico. She too was barefoot and wore a cotton dress of light blue and a strong rebozo around her shoulders. All three seemed sturdy, serene and self-sufficient. They came back to the part of the bus where I was sitting, the stripling girl passing on to the rear, the younger mother standing next to my seat. The older woman swung her baby down and across her breast and, as she squeezed into the seat behind me I noticed that she wore a sort of skirt hanging down behind her, a piece of heavy pleated black felt. I eyed my neighbors with what seemed the ideal combination of curiosity and discretion but I thought to myself only, "They are indios." This was exciting enough and I had already experienced a lively sensation as the black felt of my neighbor brushed against me when she sat down. Then almost simultaneously it percolated to me that the older woman had not understood the ticket collector and, as the climax and quintessence of all lost aboriginal America, I heard (now through the clatter of the bus) the dulcet and utterly exotic sounds of the Tarascan tongue of the East and far away that gives us Chinese-sounding names like Tzintzuntzan. I turned and looked out of the window at the swiftly passing fields. "So these are my Tarascans," I thought to myself, very happy, "I like your looks."

Intimations of the Real Politics

The Zacapu factory turned out to be challenging in an irritating way and—what with its high-pressure, piece-rate, chemically polluted work in huge gaseous chambers—could conceivably have led to an edifying and even fascinating book. I actually spent several weeks there and visited workers and their families in the villages and completed a detailed questionnaire. But the factory was all too familiar to me, and the mestizo workers who made up the great majority were not what I wanted to devote my doctoral dissertation to. Nor was I drawn to the golf-playing American managers. One, a Texan, kept a large Bowie knife in his office and spent some time explaining that the little trough down the center of the blade was there to let the blood run out while the point went in. The gestalt of the Celanese situation was to some degree absurd and not profoundly interesting.

These negative impressions and reactions combined with the appeal of doing the kind of anthropology I had read about in graduate school: a community study, provisionally, of one of the three colorful indigenous villages nearby, each consisting of fifteen hundred to three thousand peasants living in a few hundred houses of sunbaked brick around a dusty central plaza with its fountain, stores, church, and school. While I was vacillating between the two fieldwork enterprises—village or factory?—two events, one a ritual, the other an assassination, changed my consciousness. The ritual, in which I participated actively, was the annual Naranja fiesta on April 26 for someone named Primo Tapia. Delegations of schoolchildren were bused in from all the neighboring towns and marched in straggling columns around the plaza. As clouds of dry-season dust swirled about and made me blink, many little and adolescent girls recited their poems about Primo. Bands played raucously. I kept hearing about Primo, "a great man."

The second event, a prime example of "historical accident," the unpredictable, unique precipitant, came after I had pretty much decided on the villages for my fieldwork. I had only been in Naranja off and on for a total of two months and, my suspicions of Redfield notwithstanding, had formed a somewhat idealized view of a Redfieldian "little community" devoted to tilling the soil, religious ritual, harmonious cooperation, and the like. It was now June. I had been back in the state capital visiting my family over the weekend. About dawn that Sunday morning the man I call Agustín was shot dead on the highway to Zacapu. When I returned the next day and heard from the schoolmaster with whom I was staying, I began to make inquiries. I encountered reticence but was soon tapping into a deep reservoir of factional differences, personal jealousies, and a history of conflicting land claims which I had found extraordinarily natural.

It turned out that Agustín had been one of the surviving "original agrarians" who had fought the good fight with Primo Tapia, signed the first agrarian census, and received one of the plots in the First Partition. As noted here and there above, he had led within the pueblo between 1927 and 1937, when he was jailed for embezzlement. He was forcibly deprived of his plot in 1941 and jailed again in 1945. He himself had occasionally been involved in ambushes, usually as a victim. There had been scores of homicides and hundreds of shoot-outs and firefights over the last thirty years—in a town that averaged about one thousand souls. For almost two decades, especially before his sharp demise, Agustín had been "prodding the land question" (*picaba la cuestión agraria*), that is, petitioning in the capitals for the restoration of the plots taken from him and others. Recently he had "been walking around with complete confidence, wearing a Texas style hat" (*andaba con toda confianza, llevaba un sombrero estilo tejano*).

I was forced to realize that Naranja exemplified a fascinating and sensitive political situation and that the main protagonists such as Toni, Boni, and Aquiles (see Chapter 1) were people I already knew fairly well—in other contexts. Indeed, my interview with Aquiles in this aftermath-of-assassination context became a "life-changing dialogue," notably at the point when he predicted that he would someday be the cacique and I for my part insisted that I would continue to investigate the politics behind Agustín's assassination (I eventually found more pages of archival material on this in Mexico City than on any other subject). Naranja epitomized an end-point in the informal system of caciques and local factionalism with much attendant homicide that was widespread in Mexico (and still is today in 1986). I kept hearing the name "Scarface."

Obviously, I was being detached from industrial sociology, even from writing up the original interviews and the answers to the questionnaire. At the same time I was drifting in a third direction for which I had longed in the first place: linguistic anthropology. I was tantalized by the verbal morphology of the Tarascan language, specifically the long and complex ("agglutinative") words with their so-called "body-part suffixes" as suggestively discussed in Cherán by missionary Max Lethrop. But after a mere two years of general linguistics and general anthropology I was hardly more prepared to write a linguistic thesis than an anthropological one—at least conventional theses. I eventually did deal with the linguistic (morphological) problems in great detail in fieldwork and write-ups between 1966 and 1970. But back in 1955, despite the allure of the language, I kept sending back notes and overall outlines on ethnography and agrarian politics to my advisor, and he encouraged me to keep on navigating or at least let the winds blow me into the uncharted waters that I had been finding.

All this oscillation between agrarian politics, ethnography, sociology, linguistics, and so forth reflected an eclectic background and a personal habit of maximizing one's options—and also ambivalence and even avoidance. For one thing, I had managed to get a bachelor's degree (with honors) and a master's degree without writing a thesis and felt hesitant and self-deprecatory about the doctoral enterprise.

Tacking into Politics

As politics increasingly surrounded me I found myself casting about for things I was intuitively sure of and could use for constructing what was to be not just the satisfaction of an academic requirement, but a good book, or two. Political anthropology hardly existed as a defined subfield and I had not studied it formally, but I did keep thinking more and more about three kinds of polity which I had read about and felt I understood and which were in some sense analogous to what I was discovering in Naranja de Tapia. These polities included, first, the Greek city-state, medieval and nineteenth-century Russia, and Renaissance Italy, all encountered as part of a general humanistic and historical education. Second came the League of the Iroquois and the Nuer of the Sudan as they had been internalized through reading and discussing Lewis M. Morgan and E. E. Evans-Pritchard in anthropology graduate school. The third island of knowledge was the New England village of my adolescent years and my father's fond but also hard-eyed perceptions; my fieldnotes and write-up contain strong opinions on "democracy" and many (rather simple-minded) comparisons of Naranja with town meetings in New England, that is, implicitly, Concord, Massachusetts. I also looked back at Soviet history when trying to evaluate the Naranja caciques.

A second factor was pure fate. Shortly after the assassination of Agustín I found a cheap, popular, Spanish-language version of Machiavelli's *The Prince* in the Naranja schoolhouse "library" (i.e., a box of books). You could probably spend a lifetime vainly seeking a copy of *The Prince* in the schoolhouse of a small Mexican Indian village. But now I reread the immortal Florentine avidly, the way you read the grammar of a language you have learned or are learning practically through conversation in real life situations. I tried to recall what I had learned about him from my father and from George Sabine's great *History of Political Theory.* The fact that the book was in Spanish, which I was still learning, forced my mind to create many bridges between theory and data. My fieldnotes contain many passages copied out from this great realist, comments on those passages, and provisional formulations for a sort of ethnopolitical theory— mostly written in Spanish.[1] The serendipitous discovery—no matter that it resembled the opening pages of a Romantic-Realistic short story or novel set in the Caucasus or the Canadian Rockies—was decisive.

A more rational reason for crossing the Rubicon into political history and anthropology, with all the attendant problems of competing with my father, was a growing conviction that just about all the research in Mexico (with the salient exception of Oscar Lewis) had been avoiding such things as local factionalism, caciquismo, agrarian and other vendettas, and many earthy and even dirty political problems—perhaps hypertypically in the case of Robert Redfield (see the anecdote near the end of Chapter 8). This neglect still typifies much research today: with the laudable exceptions of Gail Mummert-Zendejas, David Ronfeldt, Frans Schryer, Lila Romanucci-Ross, and probably a few more, there is understandable reluctance among both American and Mexican scholars to spend the Malinowskian minimum of one to three years in the dust, disease, and intermittent dangers of continuous fieldwork in the midst of a local (agrarian) cacicazgo, or indeed any politically hot pueblo. Even when fieldwork of this sort is done, there is a tendency to present the results anemically and bandaged over with professional jargon. Of course, nobody can be faulted for neglecting politics when going to the field with a highly focused, previously demarcated objective such as verbal morphology, ceramics design, or the like.

Another compelling force was literary. During my adolescence my favorite American authors were Whitman (*Leaves of Grass*), Melville (*Moby Dick*), Benét (*John Brown's Body*), and Henry David Thoreau. Moreover, since I attended high school in Concord, I read and reread *Walden* while periodically walking and camping on the shores of Walden Pond. I discussed the pros of it with my father and with a Yankee orphan of my age with whom I used to cut out hurricane timber in the Concord woods. I heard about the cons of it from Irish-American classmates who were incensed at Thoreau's ethnic prejudices. Thoreau's philosophical and action-oriented anarchism fused with the distant anarchism of another author who has been a major influence since I was sixteen, Leo Tolstoy; indeed, I was preparing to write a Harvard Russianist doctoral dissertation on Tolstoy's syntax, but then shifted to anthropology and linguistics at Yale. These interrelated influences, in any case, as well as Isaiah Berlin's brilliant lectures on the Russian anarchists such as Bakunin, and what I read about the Spanish anarchists in Hemingway and the intellectual journals, made me singularly receptive to what I began to hear about the *anarquismo* of the Zacapu Valley Tarascans and other Mexicans.

I also felt predetermined for political history by nature and by background—including the culture of a patriarchal but also variously permissive and suggestive family that made one acutely aware of where one was to go. For our last trip to Europe (i.e., before the Nazi seizure of power) my mother gave me a book of famous battles, and, although I couldn't read, I spent the week on the boat memorizing the pictures and captions. Later I learned to read by memorizing Stephen Vincent Benét's *Book of Americans* (mainly doggerel devoted to historical greats such as Daniel Boone and Sam Houston). When my brother Otto and I were in the fourth grade we wrote a short chapbook on the battles of the Civil War—Antietam, Bull Run, Fredericksburg, and so forth. Names like "Stonewall" Jackson and Miles Standish (the Pilgrim leader) were common household words; memorable family arguments revolved around who was a greater man, Miles Standish or Johann Sebastian Bach, Jesus Christ or Siegfried? In primary school I excelled in "history" and "current events" and related projects like voluntarily (and without competing volunteers) reciting longish historical poems (e.g., "Barbara Frietchie" and "The Charge of the Light Brigade") to my variously bored and boggled sixth-grade classmates. During the summers of these years we played frequently with a newcomer within walking distance who was obsessed with the history of his home state. *Texas History Told in Pictures* was added to the Altsheler novels (about pioneer Kentucky) as one of our basic charters; Davy Crockett, Jim Bowie, "Deaf" Smith, and Sam Houston became our new heroes; and the woods between the Connecticut and West rivers sometimes reverberated with amateurish rebel yells and the click of genuine antique caplock and flintlock rifles (the boy's political scientist father, eventually wrote a definitive book called *A Study of War*). Another local professor, sociologist David Riesman, had been inspired by my father to go into gentleman farming in nearby Upper Dutton; he now says that as boys my brother and I "talked like adults," that we were "homunculi." Such intellectualism worked variously with emotional bonding: one childhood transatlantic crossing, alone with my father, I long described as "the happiest days of my life."

During high school I continued to succeed in history in the conventional sense of military and political history. As if our superb courses in ancient and American history were not enough, I organized an insurgent petition to institute medieval and/or modern European history; the procedures were politically correct but the project was disregarded by the principal. I then set up autodidactic courses (e.g., American Revolutionary Thought), which expanded to world history later on. Aside from an intoxicating freshman sequence with the famous teacher Richard Newhall, and some subsequent work in Russian and intellectual history, I took few history courses in college. But it was history I chose and scored well in as my special field in the Graduate Record Examinations. More basically, history was one of the two subjects in which I saw myself doing better than my more competitive brother (today a well-known editor and the author of several excellent historical works). My incentive to study literary and military history came from my mother (a history major and lifetime reader and discussant of historical literature), whereas my incentive to study political and intellectual history came mainly from my professional historian father. Thus the eventual switch by a fledgling anthropologist to a radically and independently historical approach seems adequately motivated.

Carl Joachim Friedrich

By studying the politics of peasants I was able to identify with my father in several interconnected ways. I am speaking not only of his legendary erudition and scholarly productivity, but of his singular empathy for what he called "the tillers of the soil." The background is worth sketching. Early on in World War I his own father (Paul Friedrich, an internationally known surgeon and inventor of the rubber glove) had died from sheer exhaustion on the Russian front and subsequent heart failure. To help support the large family, adolescent Carl began raising rabbits in large quantities and, trundling his large cart, made scores of excursions to villages surrounding Leipzig to barter them for staples—bread, butter, eggs; this became crucial during the nation-wide food shortage. Coming from an intense, intellectual, half-aristocratic family and already immersed in his beloved Homer and similar authors, he was deeply impressed by the peasants with their distinct dialect and life style and frequent acts of homespun kindness (e.g., putting him up for the night). After the war he was a Saxon Lancer stationed among and often working with Saxon peasants. He became fond of them.

An analogous elective affinity for "the tillers" extended to the relatively alienated Vermont farmers whom he studied and philosophized about while running our large dairy farm during the Depression and World War II (eventually we had fifty head of Jersey cows). After the first years, however, he confined his own tilling activities to our huge vegetable garden (feeling constrained, among other things, by the local perception of him as a gentleman farmer). During the summers of 1942–1944 I, on the other hand, worked for and with these same Vermont farmers (for $.40 an hour, half of which had to go to War Bonds). The almost pre-industrial conditions were the same as those depicted in Robert Frost's poems about not-so-distant Derry: hoeing corn, harvesting corn (often with sickles), pitching and tumbling hay, using horses for most operations, and so forth. There was tremendous conflict and competition between my father's fore-man and his two sons, both my age-mates (their family farm had been foreclosed)—and between all three of them and myself. Within the limits of the notoriously laconic Vermont conversational style, I talked with these and other farmers, including a long string of hired men who inevi-tably quit because they couldn't stand the hard-driving work patterns of our foreman. Summers I shifted to the rural Vermont dialect. I came to understand something of rural poverty and how desperate it is to be forced off one's farm. During the high school years, on the other hand, I often worked on truck farms around Concord, and sometimes went back up to our farm on weekends with my father. We conversed a great deal about farming (e.g., new fertilizers, cattle breeding). He was fond of re-telling how he had exhorted his mother to invest her savings in a farm but she had then lost all in the German Inflation. Thus our (my father's and my) relation to acquiring, possessing, and not losing land was or came to be charged with emotions of taproot depth. In 1951, only four years be-fore hitting the field in Mexico, I went back—regressed in a sense—to a summer farm job in Concord. The same agrarian orientation surfaced in the heavy 1953 Yale course on "African Culture" when I declined to do the questionnaire-based ethnographic sketches that G. P. Murdock strongly suggested to his students (as input for his own statistical, cross-cultural research) and, instead, wrote a long term paper intensely com-paring seven societies and called "Patterns of Land Use in Negro Africa." All these experiences, *mutatis mutandis*, made me responsive in 1955 to a discovered case of agrarian revolt and the subsequent struggle for ejido lands. The way I took to Naranja de Tapia was a renewal and projection of agricultural and agrarian concerns, and exiguous farming under strong fa-therly encouragement and, at times, persuasion and verbal "agreements" that boiled down to coercion.

(Our attempt to farm in the hills north of Brattleboro is captured in my mother's remarkable article, "I Had a Baby" [*Atlantic Monthly*, 1939]. My brother sagely held aloof from farm work [after a miserable winter charged with a flock of intermittently cannibalistic Plymouth Rock hens]. We kept losing cows through Bang's Disease. Then the great hurricane of 1938 heavily damaged our woodlands. I had several nearly fatal accidents. My kid sister Liesel drowned in 1943. In 1945 a holocaust destroyed our barns and forty-two of the fifty cows in our championship herd of Jerseys. Heavy lifting led later to my three hernia operations, one inguinal; I was bitter about the whole thing and at having spent all my high school summers "tilling the soil" [although I remain perennially, vicariously involved in such agricultural matters as the recent devastation of small family farms in the Midwest]. But my father tried to carry on in West Brattleboro. The foreman's oldest son died of TB at nineteen, his younger son shot himself at twenty-one, and his wife left him. My father finally dropped out of dairying but resolutely bought another farm in southern New Hampshire where [an expert beeman] he made honey and became a regional leader in tree farming.)

During our long walks in the New England woods, my loving, compulsive, political-theorist-cum-historian father, his blue eyes sometimes flashing, used to hold forth about political theory, contemporary politics, and American literature as political literature. I responded sympathetically to philosophical anarchism (e.g., Thoreau) and what might be called idealistic or formative Communism—for example, his typical liberal's view of the International Brigades in the Spanish Civil War (1936–1939), or his admiration for the "German Revolution" (i.e., the Communist seizure of power in many German cities and indeed entire regions in 1918–1919). I also acquired a deep hostility toward Soviet Communism, Nazism (especially the anti-Semitism), toward autocracy, authority, and dictatorship generally and any manifestations of the latter such as systematic indoctrination or the use of torture. My father later lost his sympathy for "idealistic Communism" and came to be known internationally as the interpreter of the political theory of authority, a reputation which he achieved by, among other things, a relentless comparison of Nazi Germany and Soviet Russia. In a wider sense he became *the* expert on authoritarian government, that is, *the* authority on or about authority (a peculiar self-reflexivity—compare the logically different "a poet's poet").

As for political science strictly speaking, I had had a number of courses in theory, notably two terms of my father's scintillating lectures in "Gov 1" (those on Aristotle, Machiavelli, Hobbes, the anarchists, and "reason of state" still stand out in my mind). Near the end of college I spent eight months doing fieldwork with Russian escapees in displaced-person camps in Western Germany (1949–1950), collecting short life histories under the direct supervision of a major political scientist, Merle Fainsed, and the distant supervision of Clyde Kluckhohn (perhaps the leading expert on this approach). During graduate school, to support myself, I had worked part-time to a total of over a year with F. Barghoorn, analyzing Soviet documents pursuant to his eventual *Soviet Russian Nationalism*. By the time of the Mexican fieldwork, then, I was about equally a political historian or scientist and an anthropologist, which may be why my first published book, *Agrarian Revolt*, has been of equal interest to the two fields. Both of the Russian studies positions, however, were obtained at the suggestion and through the personal influence of my father, an influence toward which I was becoming increasingly resentful.

I was made hypersensitive to the allure and perils of authority. While (voluntarily) assisting my father in translating Hegel for the Modern Library Series, about 1950, I wrote in my journal, "Beware the fang of fatherly pride—DO NOT CO-AUTHOR HEGEL," that is, accept his suggestion that I be listed as cotranslator. I eventually was acknowledged as cotranslator of the "Philosophy of History," and the work as a whole was dedicated to me.

My scholarly motivation, then, was determined by an intense, complicated, ambivalent, and highly competitive father-son-brother triangle (analogous to the foreman and his two sons), ensconced in an essentially patriarchal family culture. As my mother puts it: "A woman can be honored at three times in her life: as a girl by her father, as a woman by her husband, and in her old age by her sons." I therefore felt obliged and in some sense predestined to do the job on the newly found and rapidly unfolding Naranja cacicazgo, despite the fact that I disliked politics and its study in several ways—and still do—and despite my preference for linguistics and the conviction that my basic telos was toward poetry. The same perduring sense of obligation and lingering identification made me devote the summer of 1985—a year after my father's death—to rewriting much of this book, before doing initial fieldwork among the Russian Dukhobors of Canada and without even getting to the composition of my first long poem.

The dim sense of being locked into a patriarchal triangle and, as it were, doomed to politics, was part of a larger, encapsulating, personal fatalism that began to form in early childhood, between the ages of four and six. Part of it came from my Prussian countess grandmother (father's mother), who lovingly read to me, in German, the entirety of a popular prose edition of the *Niebelungenlied*, with its Germanic vision of doom. I also learned her attendant philosophy of fate. More formative, though, were the sayings and example of my Midwestern, Old American mother, who still believes, not in any divinity, but in fate: "What has to happen will happen." Moreover, a peculiar syncretism of American folk fatalism and Hispanic fatalism had been created by our close reading and discussion of Ernest Hemingway between about 1939, when I first read *For Whom the Bell Tolls* at age twelve, until 1945, when I left home at the age of seventeen for a brief stint at Williams College.

Home-bred fatalism was hardened by the drowning of my sister when I was fifteen, by (sometimes successful) struggles to make high school athletic teams although some of the other players resented (e.g., during World

War II) the German professor's son, by nearly losing my life several times through accidents on our farm, and by tough experiences in the paratroopers. The fatalism was enlarged and rationalized or at least verbalized through critical intellectual experiences at Harvard and Yale—the Russian novel again, Greek tragedy (which I read during anthropology graduate school, as an antidote of sorts), and a course by Perry Miller on "the classics of the Christian tradition" that emphasized Augustine and Pascal. Indeed, it is difficult to disentangle the strands of three interwoven varieties of generic fatalism: a personal sense of impending doom that was and remains simple-minded; what was, theologically speaking, a belief in predestination; and, finally, a scientist's commitment to the heuristic *and* truth value of a dynamic, necessary system of interdependent parts and relations. Various kinds of tension and cohesion among these three points of view—and an artistic intuition of an organic whole—underlie both *Agrarian Revolt* and *The Princes of Naranja.*

The various fatalisms that I brought to the field seem akin to the fatalism of Primo Tapia, Camilo Caso, and the other leaders, and of the Tarascan and neighboring Mexican peasants among whom I have lived for three years. Obviously, a full semantic and conceptual analysis of the Mexican and Mexican Indian peasant's view of fate (*la suerte*) would disclose fascinating differences within that country and between Mexican fate and a more generically Hispanic idea. But whatever my position may be called, the essential point is not that personal fatalism is indispensable to understanding attitudes toward fate, nor that I exported into the field a mélange of ideas from American Calvinism, Germanic myth, Greek drama (hubris), Hemingway, and so forth and so on, but that these diverse experiences sensitized me to the fate that I was to encounter in the villages of the Zacapu Valley.

These fatalisms, predestinations, causes, forces, and influences to the contrary, I was reluctant to give in to my father, that is, to fall back on something I had learned mainly from him. I did not decide irrevocably on political anthropology until, as noted above, I had—each in about two sessions—drafted two highly political chapters-to-be (the life studies of Primo and Bones). This was after a year, near the beginning of the last half-year, when I lived in Tiríndaro with my wife and daughters (then over one and almost three years old). My time spent on participant observations in neighboring Naranja dropped considerably, but I was doing more integrative thinking and writing.

General Theoretical Background

Even before fieldwork my eclectic background made me feel that the general anthropology of the time with its five fields of language, culture, human biology, prehistory, and personality, was too narrow for me. I was led to include, for example, political science and the humanistic tradition in general (my penchant encouraged by the precedents of Benedict, Redfield, and Sapir). Any idea, image, literary model, or even turn of phrase was welcome as long as it helped to illuminate. I drew on philosophical and social science positions that partly contradict each other, of which eight merit enumeration here. Considerable *empiricism* underlies my attention to, for example, amassing descriptive statistics, mimetic studies of people and scenes, and physically experiencing the colors, smells, sounds, and similar stimuli of the villages—the feel of a corncob while harvesting, the taste of a fresh tortilla, the drinks at a fiesta, the sound of popular songs (obviously, it is hard to differentiate here between empiricism and philosophical sensualism). Considerable *relativism* underlies my commitment to setting political mores and happenings in a long-term historical context and to evaluating behavior and attitudes (e.g., of a "fighter") on a cross-cultural basis. Considerable *romanticism*—which, as Whitehead showed, is an intellectual position of coordinate, scientific import—underlies my concern with the rebellious individual and my intuition that chaos roils beneath the rule of law, or at least order (a bit transparent in a town torn by the vendetta-cum-factionalism). Considerable *structural-functionalism* underlies the inference and description of the various primary groups both during the agrarian revolt period and during the three decades dealt with in this volume. Considerable *rationalism* underlies my attention to the role of formal, statute law and my attempt to account rather systematically for the economics of revolt and for the psychological motivation of the leaders. In the same vein, my interpretations in both volumes owe much to *Marxism* in some generic sense—for example, the concern with economics and with the idea of system, just as my interpretation of personality and the dynamics of friendship owes much to *Freud*. I was vaguely intrigued by the possibility of blending salient elements in these two semi-rationalisms in the crucible of an exciting case study of leadership and economic conflict. Yet I viewed and still view with skepticism much of the Neo-Marxism then and now popular in Mexico, as also most brands of Neo-Freudianism then and now popular in the United States. Considerable *phenomenology*, in the last place, underlies my attention to clearly defining or at least giving good intimations of my own emotional and intellectual outlook at this case of politics—like a boy scuba diving or an antique-lover going from shelf to shelf. Some of the life histories of the princes in Chapter 1 are also phenomenological in the sense that you, reader, are meant to be persuaded to turn a corner and enter the personal world of, in particular, Bones, Camilo, and Aquiles. I was familiar with the basic texts of these eight philosophical positions or at least methodologies, notably those of Machiavelli, Descartes, Hegel, Boas, Radcliffe-Brown, and such formative Romantics as Coleridge, but I avoided casting my study in terms of "isms" and "ologies" (with the partial exception of Machiavelli, as seems warranted by his relevance both from the outside looking in and to the national and even local leaders reflecting and commenting on themselves). In any case, I justified my omnibus and in some ways logically contradictory eclecticism in terms of an axiom: the clarification and explanation of the historical case is my primary objective, and the relevance of the case to the theories will emerge naturally and in due course of time and analysis. *What I learned as theories I practiced as methods.* By the same logic, theoretical footnoting has generally been omitted from the body of the biography, ethnography, and historiography above, and from the bibliography. Such a theory, if integrated and explicit, would constitute a hefty third volume.

Within this flux of ideas impinging from the social sciences and the humanities I also, over a considerable period of time, moved into or at least became more sure of a basic metaphysical position. At a relatively intellectual level it came from Hegel, Tolstoy, Saussure, the Marxians, and other, mainly German and Russian, thinkers. Theoretical reality is a system or organization of relations between interdependent, mutually implicatory factors and dimensions—and hence of course of relations between relations. At another level, then, historical phenomena are totally determined, not in the simple, unicausational sense that "Everything has a cause, even a pimple," as one of Gorki's characters has it, but in the Spinozist sense that these phenomena are differentially part of a system of mutual implications. Today I would add that this view which I held in the 1950s saw no sharp line between the level of the system of historical phenomena and the level of ideas and feelings about those phenomena. In other words, ideas and emotions determined phenomena, including collective action, just as acts and deeds determine ideas. The last chapter of *Agrarian Revolt*, on "the causes of revolt," written about 1969, is predicated on this metaphysical assumption, as is Part III above, "Political Economy." But these are just the salient instances of an orientation that pervades both of the books in question.

Such a philosophy underlay the belief—and the desire to demonstrate—that the rich bottomlands *had* to attract persons with the risk capital and technical know-how to acquire them and take advantage of local labor (as happened in other fertile parts of the country); that adequate leadership *had* to arise to articulate the need for reform (indeed, other villages such as the Eleven Pueblos generated similar leaders—albeit perhaps not as fascinating as Primo Tapia and Scarface Caso); that the revolt or other drastic change *had* to occur under the circumstances of the Mexican Revolution and its aftermath (and had already erupted in hundreds of other pueblos); that Primo Tapia, Pedro González, Camilo and Scarface Caso, and other leaders *had* to use their political abilities, economic surpluses, and local traditions of violence to expand their power in region and state (as in parallel situations in Vera Cruz, Morelos, and elsewhere); that the dearly won ejido lands *had* to be partitioned into family plots because of peasant hunger for land and flaws in communalistic administration; that internecine, factional strife was unavoidable and, indeed, part of a Mexican national tragedy; that, finally, Tapia *had* "to die like a man, at noon," as he put it, and that his cousin Scarface too would perish by the bullet or the knife. Determinism merges with fatalism.

Initially such radical determinism justified itself on ethical grounds: the force of ecological, economic, psychological, social, and other factors or "causes" was felt not only to explain but to exculpate the land-seizing, homicidal peasants and their leaders such as Camilo Caso and Primo Tapia, *and* the priests, landlords, and generals who opposed them. Besides, the agrarian cause, in the sense of a social issue, is a just and worthy one. But I increasingly came to feel that the ethical sort of justification, despite its persuasiveness, was not essential to the scientific assumption of determinism which is justified by its productivity or "fruitfulness": one is led to deeper levels of exploration; to searching out contexts, causes, origins, and constraints; to exploiting the available theories of economic, social, psychological, and ecological determinism. My belief in the fruitfulness of radical determinism was reinforced by the demonstrated fruitfulness in linguistics of such determinist ideas as "the exceptionlessness of sound laws." In terms of the tactics of exposition, such a philosophy means setting up the political biography, ethnography, and history so that the reader will be persuaded of an inherent, directional necessity.

A determinist vision of historical processes, presented above with deliberate accentuation, worked as a sort of methodological ideology in those days of fieldwork and write-up—not alone, but together with the looser and more permissive outlook, stemming from a humanistic background, that led me to see and describe or at least adumbrate such things as indeterminacy, historical accident, revolt and faction, irregularity and statistical variation, and the intuited contours of personality and politics (see Chapter 7). Moreover, I was able to empathize sufficiently with the leaders to obtain complex facts that suggested considerable freedom of choice. Salient examples of such freedom were Tapia's varying loyalty toward friends and supporters and persons in greater power; his choice to ally a Wobbly-derived anarchism with international Communism; and his decision to stay on in the Zacapu Valley long after he became a marked man. A similar combination of historical determinism and freedom of choice informs my representation above of the "Seven Princes," notably Aquiles' conflicted allegiances within the complex situations of his household, his political family, his village, and even state politics. From my own point of view, influenced at that time by Pascal, Tolstoy, and the existentialists, above all Kierkegaard and Camus, this freedom of choice and responsibility for one's choice may well have been an illusion of individual consciousness. But such individual consciousness was none the less significant, led to myriad fruitful questions, was the only conceivable zone of personal freedom, and, finally, is no more an illusion than the artificial whole of absolute historical determinism. The "tactics of exposition," to which much of this book is devoted, thus consists of crafting the dialectic and fugal interaction between historical necessity and the countervailing forces of indeterminacy.

Economic Appendix A

The Ejidal Bank and Naranja Ejido Economics

[The account that follows was synthesized in 1956 from statements made by the officers of the bank in Zacapu, from some literature that they gave me, and from statements made in the village; minor, mainly editorial changes were made in 1985.]

The Ejidal Bank in Zacapu, established in 1951, as part of the national Ejidal Bank system, has the objectives of making small loans to individual ejidatarios so that they can buy seed and pay for labor and fertilizers; making larger loans to individuals and communities for major improvements such as the construction of dams; and finally, combating the usurious corn buyers and money-lenders. The bank also tries to take the initiative in organizing and financing larger projects that affect the entire region, such as building canals or major drainage operations. Naranja entered the bank in 1954 as the result of an urgent need for help after the disastrous crop loss of 1953.

Ejidal administration. The Zacapu Bank is staffed by a chief, an assistant chief, and about ten secretaries and technicians, and serves about forty-five ejidos. The president of the ejido in each member community automatically becomes an associate (*socio*) of the bank, participating in its meetings and in policy decisions. Loans are made by agents of the bank to individual ejidatarios, but they have to be negotiated by the president of the given ejido, who mortgages a certain portion of the community as collateral—not particular acres but a general fraction of the ejido. Since much of the privately owned *tierra indígena* is also part of the ejido under the bank system, the number of potential debtors is considerably larger (507) than the number of ejidatarios (217); in 1956, 220 individuals from Naranja were enrolled as debtors [507 appears in my notes, but 240 is the relevant number]. About 17 ejidatarios are absent from the pueblo and do not have the right to borrow money. In addition to the ejidal authorities, the bank operates locally through informal corn buyers to whom it extends credit in order to buy maize in competition with the usurious private "monopolizers."

Ejidal lands. The ejido, as noted, includes two kinds of land. The ejido proper consists of 716 hectares of moist land (*humedad*) that were won in the agrarian reform of the 1920s. Of this, 567 hectares are divided into plots of 2.5 (or 2.6) hectares and worked (e.g., plowed and harrowed with horse and oxen) by the 217 ejidatarios, that is, ejidal families; one plot technically belongs to the school for agronomic uses but is actually exploited by various individuals. About 120 to 130 additional hectares, many of them along the edge of the ejido, are divided among individuals, many of them leaders, although the title is vested in the community. Two hundred seventeen of the 295 heads of families in Naranja are technically ejidatarios, although, as noted, about 17 of these are not in residence and their plots are handled by relatives or friends or are being exploited by leaders. Families have an average of five persons.

The second kind of land, called *tierra indígena*, consists of the following: (1) about 30 hectares of moist land along the edge of the ejido, that is, the part not classified as ejido proper and controlled by leaders; (2) the 395 hectares of privately owned and controlled land in the bottoms and foothills deriving from the additional grant (*ampliación*) of 1935 (described in Chapter 5); (3) additional land in the bottomlands and foothills not covered in my 1955–1956 measurements (possibly 100–200 hectares); (4) a large piece of land in the hills called "The Cayetano Ocampo Purchase." Eighty-eight individuals own land in these "indigenous lands." Ten of these owners own less than 1,000 meters of furrow (I have to resort to this unit since that is the way the information was given to me); 49 own between 1,000 and 10,000 meters of furrow; 29 own over 10,000. Of this last, wealthiest group, the largest landholders are a son of Joaquín de la Cruz, Elías Caso and his sister Ana, the Serranos (collectively), and the Torres (the family of the pre-agrarian mestizo caciques). Much of the land of these wealthiest individuals is taxed in Zacapu due to a special arrangement worked out long ago by the formative agrarian leader Joaquín de la Cruz; as a result these individuals pay lower taxes than the other landowners and Naranja does not earn from their holdings. Most of the *tierra indígena* is worked by the friends and relatives of the actual owners, such sharecroppers, who are usually landholders themselves (e.g., ejidatarios), getting one-half of the crop by the commonest form of contract.

Most owners of "indigenous lands" are also ejidatarios. All the land in the Naranja ejido, whether in the ejido proper or *tierra indígena*, is described by bank officials as "very good."

The following tabulation of land holdings is crucial:

Heads of non-absent families who are ejidatarios
(i.e., 17 are absent)   200
Heads of such non-absent families who only own private land   40

Total   240

Portion of heads of families owning or controlling
land of any kind   240/295

Some facts on production and consumption. The moist land produces about 100 hectoliters (about 283 bushels) of corn per ejido plot of 2.6 hectares, at a cash value of about 3,500 pesos for each of the 218 ejido plots. There is considerable variation in the productivity of these plots, however, ranging from 40 to 90 to 130, depending on the villager speaking, the part of the ejido in question, and the weather and hydraulic conditions in any particular year. It is an accepted custom for ejidatarios to cite about 30 hectoliters less than the real crop, partly to reduce the 5 percent national tax but mainly to guarantee an annual minimum for their own sustenance (about 100 bushels, worth about 1,000 pesos). Even local creditors are chary about collecting this subsistence minimum, although that may happen in the case of debtors who are extremely weak and/or politically inimicable.

Activities of the Ejidal Bank.

1. *Fertilizers.* The black soils of the former swamp have been analyzed, and the principal lack is reported to be calcium, but there are others such as phosphate. Due to faulty analyses and variations in the soils of the ejido which were not taken into account, the application of cheap chemical fertilizers provided by the bank resulted in enormous crop losses for the unfortunate individuals who availed themselves of these services; there was much discussion of this in 1955–1956, and leaders such as Camilo criticized the bank on these grounds. However, one man in Tiríndaro who had his soil privately analyzed was able to increase his crop yield by 30 percent and persons were starting to experiment with crop rotation and the planting of alfalfa and cabbages, with very promising results.

2. *Hydraulic problems.* The administration of the Zacapu ejidos poses enormous hydraulic problems and calls for constant repair and drainage of the network of canals, small rivers, sluices, and so forth (e.g., the Canal of Naranja). The system must be administered, at least in principle, not only by the ejidal authorities of the constituent villages but by some sort of central authority—as in the days of the landlords. There has been serious flooding all over the Zacapu Valley for the past twenty years or more, especially in the very rainy years, when parts of the ejido are knee-deep in water for a time. Flooding seems to be correctly ranked with soil exhaustion due to lack of rotation and fertilizers as a main reason for the constant decline in production (down to a half or a third of what it was in the mid-1920s). Thus the breakup of a regional unity of sorts after the death of Tapia in 1926 also entailed technological and economic problems that

were entangled with the political history (1926–1956) dealt with mainly
in Chapter 5 above—primarily in that the documented weakness of regional control corresponded to an economic decline. The Ejidal Bank, in
any case, now purports to fulfill the functions of hydraulic coordination.
In 1955, it collected sizable contributions from all the member ejidos that
are within or beside the former marshland area and hired an outside company which carried out the drainage of the Angula River north of Zacapu,
which has become clogged. Naranja paid only 20,712 pesos of its promised 32,648, however.

3. *Corn traders.* The bank claims that one of its major objectives is to
compete against corn traders, in both Naranja and Zacapu (the latter have
agents in the villages). Traders buy ahead of the harvest at 30–100 percent interest—except Anita, whose terms differ—and one-sixth of the
ejidatarios sell all their crop in advance this way. In 1955 and 1956 the
bank informally commissioned Camilo Caso to buy corn for the bank at
the standard 7 percent interest rate with an upper limit on his purchases
of 350,000 pesos, but he bought only 25,000 pesos worth. He is seen by
the bank as "a good element," but he is personally too involved with the
Naranja traders, one of whom, of course, is his wife. About half the heads
of families are indebted to at least one of the four Naranja usuresses (who
in three cases are to some extent acting for their husbands). Otherwise,
the bank claims that it has somewhat reduced the effects of corn buyers
and traders in the Zacapu region as a whole.

4. *Money-lending.* Since 1954 the bank has been lending 100–1,000
pesos at a time to Naranja individuals to pay for seed and other costs of
growing crops. Another ostensible purpose of such loans is to reduce the
number of ejidatarios (especially women) who work their land through
sharecroppers (*medieros*). A widow, for example, can hire laborers and
manage all the work of her ejido plot at an annual cost of three or four
hundred pesos, whereas a sharecropper gets half the harvest, or well over
1,000 pesos. The bank, however, has had little success along these lines
since many ejidatarios would rather turn over the whole matter to a
sharecropper in order "to avoid hunting for hired men"; hired men earn
five pesos a day as a flat rate, working from about 7:00 A.M. to 1:00–4:00
P.M., but many earn 12–15 pesos a day during the harvests when they are
on piece rate (and may be hard to find for political reasons). Also, of
course, many renters are on established terms with their sharecropper
that would be hard to break. Finally, since much of the money the bank
lends is actually spent on consumer goods, the benefits have often been
questionable or very limited (as when the food and drink is consumed in a
few days or even hours).

5. *Ejidal debt.* In 1954 the debt was 79,997.01 pesos, and in 1955 it
rose to 85,884.98 pesos. Of the 217 ejidatarios, 172 were in debt, owing

an average of 498.86 pesos. During these years Naranja thus fell seriously into arrears, presumably, in part, because of the refusal of Juan Nahua Caso and other leaders in the insurgent faction to cooperate with the bank in debt collection. By 1956, the total debt had risen to approximately 124,000 pesos with an average individual debt of about 650 pesos, or, as noted elsewhere, about a fifth of the annual crop value. Many members of the fallen faction or, better, the several anti-Caso factions, are refusing to pay their debts, or to cooperate in public works such as canal drainage (see Chapter 2). They send in constant petitions and complaints to the higher authorities, complaining of violence, coercion, embezzlement, rustling, and so forth. The ruling Casos, on the other hand, represented officially by Gregorio Serrano and, since 1956, by Héctor Caso (and, informally, by Camilo and Elías Caso), are forcing some weak or inimicable persons to meet their payments and are claiming to be trying to re-establish the credit of the community.

6. *Indebtedness of leaders to the Ejidal Bank (1955).* Note that this list includes three leaders in the fallen or opposition faction (85, 88, 147).

25. Melesio Caso	556.94
28. Ana Caso (i.e., involving Aquiles)	684.23
85. Juan Mejía (Pedro's nephew)	136.16
88. Pedro's son	697.47
103. Gregorio Serrano	712.13
107. Boni Caso	538.26
110. Camilo Caso	695.50
116. Mateo	654.18
147. Martín Valle	400.60

In addition to these nine, several other minor leaders were indebted. Over half were not indebted at all, but the second cacique in each faction was so indebted.

7. *Conclusion.* The conflicted, sometimes antagonistic, sometimes partly cooperative behavior of the Naranja leaders and the village as a whole was based on an essentially realistic assessment of the situation. As Roger D. Hansen puts it, "The Ejidal Bank has from its inception attempted to organize *ejidos* in accordance with its own interests, and always to the detriment of any aggressive and independent peasant leadership . . . employees of the Bank are more often accused of fraud and corruption than those of any other Mexican governmental agency. And in Mexico, being number one in corruption is a very high fence to ride at" (1971:118).

The History of Anita Rías
(Fieldwork Datum No. 11)

[Recorded about the spring of 1955; only some minor grammatical changes have been made, and some redundancies eliminated.]

After surviving the Revolution, Anita, still a young woman, began, in 1920, to buy, butcher, and sell hogs and chickens. During the 1920s she often oversaw the slaughter of two or three hogs a day, working from three or four in the morning until late at night. [My fieldnotes actually say "slaughtered," but it seems very unlikely that she would have been doing it herself—PF, 1986.] About 1925, after the ejido was formed, she started buying and selling corn and dealing in land. In 1926 she went to the United States and remained for two years to avoid the constant violence between the "Bolsheviks" and the "Catholics." In 1928 she returned to trading in corn and land, tending her store, and butchering, which she continued through the thirties and forties. Her most striking habit in these years, and often commented on, was to go out herself to the ejido plots as they were being harvested, and collect her debts on the spot.

 Corn. In 1955–1956 Anita had 150 debtors in corn from among the 217 ejidatarios and the 295 heads of family. These debtors usually borrow to buy food or to pay other debts. Their loans range between 100 and 500 pesos, with an average of about 200. The terms are "one for two": one liter of clean corn, in the bag, ready to eat, is lent by Anita in the late spring or summer, in return for two liters of the corn that is standing at the time of the contract and delivered, or picked up in the field, unclean and often unhusked. No one pays up in a bad year, or if Anita feels it will cause undue suffering. In 1955, the worst crop ever, no one paid Anita. About 5 percent never pay in any case. In a normal year, with a good harvest, about half will pay in full, a quarter will pay half or more of their debt, and the rest will pay less than half, or nothing. Thus of 200 pesos due to her, for example, she generally collects 150, of which 20 is waste, leaving her a net earning of 30 pesos on a 100 peso loan. Her annual income from corn trading is claimed to be about 15,000 pesos, but is probably much more.

Anita stressed that corn-trading is a risky business and that one can never be sure what one will make (however, since debts are carried over from year to year without added interest, there is always some security since even the people who delay in paying are an asset in good will). She says she never exercises any formal compulsion to make people pay and that the rather high reliability of her debtors is due to the fact that they may have to borrow from her again and it is important to keep their credit standing. [I have seen her literally wrestling in the dust with one emaciated, widowed, and hopelessly indebted ejidataria. They were struggling for the last bushel of maize to come off one of the harvest wagons— PF, 1986.] All those to whom she lends are "more or less friends: I wasn't born here but I've lived here almost all my life, I know everybody and we're friends, there's always something of friendship." She lends out a great deal in one-or-two-hectoliter amounts as a sort of stopgap charity. Many come to her tearfully (*de llorón*), and she lends to them even though she knows they are bad risks. It is clear that Anita's social and economic function is considerably more than being a corn trader. She is a sort of communal corn bank with the following particular roles:

1. She gives everyone a sense of security about very hard times such as the present when there isn't enough even for tortillas.

2. She redistributes wealth by keeping half the fairly poor ejidatarios in debt and getting poorer at her conditions, but also losing a great deal herself in supporting the very poor at a straight loss. She lives unostentatiously for the same reasons. She told me she has never experienced resentment on the part of the town people toward her, which is (largely) supported by my observations and is also due to the common knowledge of her small beginnings and hard work: "She began very poor."

Her winnings from the performance of these functions are not gigantic: at least seven other people make more than 15,000 pesos. Anita is liked/popular among the politically radical and the poor, despite her exploitative, capitalistic role.

Beans. Anita does some small trading in beans at the same 1:2 terms, but this is only for seed, and people don't come to her for beans during hard times.

Land. Anita's dealings in land are important, although not as large and lucrative as her corn-trading. She was reserved about land dealings, and I didn't push it. She has land mortgaged, on collateral, or pawned from twenty or thirty persons, usually for one to three years, and "by halves": she provides the seed and the debtor does all the work (her profit is large on this and she is sure to collect!). Anita says she doesn't deal in ejido parcels but says that many do, even though it is against the law.

Money-lending. Anita also makes some straight loans of money, usually for six months at 2 percent per month, that is, 24 percent per year. She does some (of this) business in the neighboring mestizo hamlets but *never* in Tarejero or Tiríndaro, she stressed, which didn't surprise me.

Only three other persons do any sizable corn-trading: Camilo (i.e., Camilo's wife), María Serrano, and the wife of Scarface.

Corn dealings by Naranja's main entrepreneur are mainly by barter, the total number of pesos exchanging hands amounting to a tiny fraction of the total value exchanged. Despite criticisms of the combination of money-lenders and corn buyers in cahoots with caciques, one result is that most of the materials remain within the village rather than being spent in Acapulco.

Homicide Appendix

A cross-checked record of mostly political homicides in Naranja during the period under study (1926–1955) compiled September 12, 1955, from dozens of sources. Retyped August 1985, reordered more accurately by date, cutting some circumstantial data and the names of the killers and sources. See "Generalizations" below.

1. Primo Tapia. April 26, 1926. By federal forces under orders from the president.
2. Felipe Hernández. July 30, 1926. He was head of the rural militia serving the landlords.
3. Ramón Serrato. October 30, 1926. He was the cousin of another man who was in trouble with the agrarian leaders.
4. Tomás Cruz. November 23, 1928. He was cacique of the leading faction.
5. Pedro Téllez. November 23, 1928. A friend of Tomás.
6. Pablo Espinoza. November 23, 1928. A friend of Tomás. Nos. 4, 5, and 6 killed about the same time.
7. An Ocampo. January 1929. Killed by a Caso fighter in a drunken brawl.
8. Juan Manuel. April 18, 1929. Killed by Caso fighter, also in a drunken brawl.
9. Jacinto Orobio. October 30, 1930.
10. Fidel Cupa. December 18, 1930. A drunken brawl, slain by a Caso fighter.
11. Hilario Reyes. April 10, 1931. Dispute over ejido plots.
12. Cosme Sarco. July 16, 1931. Cosme was a hired man of an Ocampo leader; he was killed by a Caso fighter.
13. Eusebio Espinoza. May 13, 1932. Slain by agrarians, over land or in revenge.
14. M. Delfina Nieves. May 24, 1933. One of two women slain.
15. Silviano Reyes. June 8, 1933. "Because of ambition."

16. Miguel Flores. May 1934. Had visited a Caso fighter and was talking with his wife when the latter came home.
17. J. Jesús Espinoza. June 7, 1934. He had sided with the landlords, then the Ocampos.
18. Cecilia Cruz. December 7, 1934. Trying to break up a brawl involving her husband. Shot accidentally.
19. Braulio Nieves. May 1935. Over a woman.
20. Hermenegildo Gochi. July 3, 1935. An Ocampo, shot by Caso fighter, both drunk.
21. Francisco Alonzo Gochi. January 11, 1936. An Ocampo, shot by a Caso as part of the struggle.
22. Luis Ramírez. March 11, 1937. He had participated in the shooting of Tomás Cruz and was shot in revenge.
23. Wenceslao Jiménez. March 14, 1937. Shot by an Ocampo in revenge.
24. Estanislao Hernández. March 15, 1937. Shot by Caso leader in retaliation for no. 23.
25. Atanasio Téllez. April 20, 1937. Shot by a supporter of the Casos.
26. Victor Gochi. April 30, 1937. Shot by a Caso, part of new fission.
27. Felipe Serrato. June 13, 1937. Shot by a Caso fighter.
28. J. Jesús Jiménez. June 13, 1937. Shot by a Caso fighter, on the highway, because he belonged to the González faction.
29–31. Three mestizos from Buena Vista. February 5, 1938. Shot by Casos.
32. A González member. April 1938. Shot by Caso gunman.
33. Sabrino Gabriel. June 22, 1938. He sided with González; while picking cherries in the sierra he was shot down out of a tree.
34. Otilio Téllez. August 9, 1938. Shot while drunk, an Ocampo.
35. Ernesto Galván. August 30, 1938. Belonged to the Ocampo faction.
36. José Aparicio. August 19, 1938. In revenge for no. 35.
37. Juan Reyes. September 21, 1938. Shot at night while wandering drunk, killer unknown.
38. Miguel Jiménez. October 12, 1938. A González member, shot by a Caso.
39. Pilar Tovar. October 24, 1938. Belonged to Caso faction, shot by two cousins from Uruapan.
40. Miguel Maya. December 4, 1938 (or 1937). Killed by a Caso while drunk in Zacapu.
41. J. Jesús Espinoza. January 18, 1939. Killed by Scarface's men while harvesting in the ejido; had switched sides after accidentally shooting one of González' men. Seems to be a different man with the same name as no. 17.
42. Lucas Guillén. January 18, 1939. Mestizo gunman hired by González, shot by Casos.

43. Jorge (Jesús Espinoza Reyes). January 18, 1939. Mestizo gunman hired by González, shot by Casos. Both no. 42 and no. 43 shot after trying to kill Bones.
44. J. Natividad Orobio. July 29, 1939. Was Gonzalista, his assailant was a Caso and president of the ejido at the time.
45. Juan Romero. August 16, 1939. Killed on the road at night by a major Caso fighter, on orders.
46. G. González. December 17, 1939. Because in Pedro's faction.
47. Gregorio Rodríguez. December 17, 1939. He was with Pedro, killed on orders from Scarface although the assailant was his brother-in-law.
48. Silvester Reyes. 1939. Shot seven times, but lived.
49. González peasant. 1941. Shot by a Caso.
50. Antonio Sarco. January 8, 1942. Opposed the Casos.
51. A Caso fighter. 1944. Killed on highway by an Ocampo fighter.
52. Odilón Espinoza. August 10, 1944. He had been ordered to kill a member of Pedro's faction; was allegedly trying to abuse his intended victim's daughter when the father surprised him.
53. Refugio Vergara. August 13, 1944. A drunken brawl.
54–56. Three mestizo workers from Buena Vista working for Scarface. 1944. Slain by González men.
57. Blas Ramírez. April 27, 1945. Ambushed on the highway to Zacapu by Casos.
58. Salvador Romero. April 27, 1945. Same as no. 57, together with him.
59. Antioco Rosas. September 13, 1945. Rosas, on orders to kill, was grabbed by his intended victim and killed with a knife; one of the few cases of man-to-man homicide (*macho a macho*).
60. Augustín Zarate. January 2, 1946. A Caso pursued this González follower out of Zacapu and killed him on the edge of town.
61. Ignacio Madrigal. January 2, 1946. Killed in Uruapan by Scarface's men; taken to the edge of town in a car and shot.
62. Rafael González. September 6, 1946. An Ocampo, shot while coming home on his donkey; his three-year-old son was wounded.
63. Ubaldo Avila. February 1, 1948. Killer and reason unknown.
64. Fidel Magaña. February 11, 1949. Because he supported González.
65. A. Cuevas. 1949. A partisan of Pedro, killed by Casos.
66. J. Jesús Nieves. January 22, 1950.
67. Genaro Alonzo. February 22, 1950. Killed by mistake by someone who thought he had taken part in the murder of the three laborers working for Scarface (nos. 54–56).
68. Salvador Rangel. March 28, 1950. Not actually a Naranja man, but the leader of the pro-Caso faction in the mestizo hamlet of Morelos and frequently in Naranja. Killed by hired guns while riding on a bus.

69. Odilón Sosa. July 2, 1950. Shot down in the road by a Caso leader.
70. Genaro Aparicio. September 2, 1950. A Gonzalista, shot by a Caso on the way to Zacapu.
71. Miguel Espinoza. September 21, 1950. Held against the wall by two Caso fighters and shot to death.
72. Luis Ramírez. July 17, 1951.
73. Primo Juárez. August 18, 1951.
74. Sebastián Gabriel. October 1952. "A question of skirts"; both were Caso fighters.
75. Elpidio Téllez. April 1953. Killed by Casos.
76. Augustín Galván. June 1955. Killed by Caso fighters.

Generalizations

An imaginative statistician could doubtless do much with the above sample, since it is both adequate and almost total ("almost" because I occasionally run across a record of yet another homicide in my notes—the actual, historical total was probably between eighty and ninety).[1] For the present I will simply list a series of inductions, and some additional generalities, as follows: (1) After high casualties among top leaders in 1919–1926 (de la Cruz, E. Serrato, Alejandro Galván, Tapia, Cruz), and despite serious woundings of Scarface, Martín, and several others, the basic fact during Libido Dominandi is that the great majority of victims have been rank-and-file peasants belonging to weak families, or with few relatives in the village. (2) For every homicide there are more woundings and shootings (e.g., in Tiríndaro for the six months of my residence there were numerous exchanges of gunfire, but no deaths).[2] (3) The stats do not include the role of Naranja fighters as hit men "on the outside" in the service of their caciques, or even of other leaders in the state—a probably formidable record that is no longer accessible, or at least largely inaccessible; their unsung successes on the edges of distant villages and the streets of Purépero, Zacapu, Uruapan, Morelia, and other cities contrast with the unenviable fate of the mestizo pistoleros occasionally hired for similar services in Naranja. (4) Many of these homicides were reported by two or more persons, notably including a desperate, middle-aged man whose real name actually was Refugio. (5) Many of the killings were connected with drinking, and many occurred at night. (6) Killings occurred at all times of the year. (7) The great majority if not all were somehow political. (8) Only three of the seventy-six were actually punished by the law, and two of these lightly (e.g., a night in the county jail). (9) Most of the homicides were by Caso fighters, often young men in their teens or twenties. (10) There were only two or three face-to-face, man-to-man homicides, that is, most were by ambush, or the assault of two or more against one; this is one reason why many emigrants or politically withdrawn persons, such as the three sons of Joaquín de la Cruz, argue that the Naranja fighters are not particularly brave (*valiente*). (11) The town's population during the thirty-year period averaged about a thousand.

Psychological Appendix A

Camilo's Rorschach

[Camilo was interviewed on October 2, 1955, 5:30–7:20, the evening of the "Tiger Day" fiesta, after I found him casting up accounts in the billiard room which he operates. Rorschach cards, presumably familiar to most readers, are ten cards with images that are bilaterally symmetrical because they are made from ink blots; some parts of some images are colored. The person being interviewed is allowed to describe what he/she sees for as long as he/she wants (which is timed, however); then the person traces the cards and produces additional responses if desired; the interviewer may also pose questions from time to time. For the reader's convenience the cards have been given convenient labels in terms of images that are perceived by many persons. For more background on the value of this kind of "projective technique" in anthropological and political history, see the discussion of "Fieldwork Datum No. 3" in Chapter 7 above. For general background, see the excellent, practical book *The Clinical Interaction with Special Reference to the Rorschach*, by Seymour Sarason, which guided me in the field.

To get back to the interview, we first went to the school, which turned out to be too dark, and then to Camilo's home. The kitchen was quiet, with the windows closed, but well illuminated by one electric light. Rapport seemed excellent, as it was with his half-brothers. After a brief explanation of the inkblots, we began with card I, which I will call "The Bat."]

1. "The Bat"

1, Sixty-five seconds of silence, then, "A butterfly, a pigeon," pointing to the central part, especially the white spots in the center.

At this point his younger daughter entered the room, was introduced, and asked for and was given thirty centavos.

2, Next, "In the center, something that resembles a weevil" (*gorgojo*), "What is a *gorgojo*?" I ask. "It is a little creature (*animalito*) that eats (*pica*) corn," he answered, smiling and holding up his fingers about a

quarter of an inch apart. "That is all I find, Pablo, the two sides are equal."
Total time: 3'.

II. "Two Bears"

1 (Smiled a little right after looking at the card), 10", "The center looks
like a screen (*pantalla*)," making a circular movement with his index finger
on the white.

2, "And here two dogs." "What are they doing?" I ask. "They are holding up the same figure" (pointing at its apex).

3, about 1', "That's all I see . . . this red," pointing at the red on the
bottom, "I don't find a complete resemblance." "And even if it isn't complete?" I ask. "No, I don't find it."

While he was drawing, "And these things?" I ask, pointed at the snouts.
"No, that's what I don't find."

Total time: 3'14".

When handing back the tracing, Camilo said, "Only the screen."

III. "Dogs or Cocks and Drops of Blood"

1 (Again he smiled immediately upon seeing the drawing), 15", "Two
men dressed in masks (*de antifaz*)," looking up at me and smiling.

2, "Or better, yes, better, they look like two animals dressed like people
in masks" (drawing his hand over his face as though to describe a mask).

3, Pointing to the bottom center, "It looks like a thorax, or something
like this," straightening up and clapping the small of his back.

4, "These," pointing to the red drops, "are equal to these, the heads,
except that they are in reverse, the opposite," turning the card around,
"No, they aren't completely equal, but almost so."

5, "This," pointing to the red bow, "Equal [i.e., bilateral], nothing more."

While drawing the card, "They are two animals dressed like men in
masks, here the feet, and here the beard very prominent," pointing at the
beak and the eye mask with the eye holes. "This single foot." "Yes, here is
the thorax . . . as if they had cut the pelvis here," gesturing as though to
cut through (his own) pelvis in cross-section, from the back. "And afterward they also cut the breast here," cutting inward on his chest with the
flat of his hand, "so that everything can be seen from above," that is, as
though you were seeing a cross-section from above. He was quite ani-
mated by the idea, and repeated the gestures more than once. "Nothing
else, you can't see the pelvis well . . . the form of a ring with two dark
sides," pointing at the partially obscured ring at the bottom. "And here it
resembles one of the apparatuses of the body . . . the lungs."

Total time: 4'50".

On handing back the tracing, "I didn't draw these things" (the red) "because I couldn't think of anything; on the lower part I drew the part of the ring which can be seen." ("The ring" with the central white hole and the obscured sides was more important to him at the finish than the masked animals.)

IV. "The Turtle"

1 (Puzzled and frowning a little), 1′20″, "I don't find any resemblance here, Pablo."

2, 1′20″ (After covering the left half with his hand), "In one part, perhaps? Yes, in order to represent (*presentar*) the chest of an animal, but this part would be very thin" (pointing to the upper central mass).

3, App. 2′ (smiling, leaning forward and pointing with his finger at the tiny projections, bottom and center), "And these are like the feet of a man."

4, "Very difficult, Pancho . . . I don't find anything" (handing back the card slowly). When beginning the tracing, "I don't find anything . . . this is like a kind of rock, stalagtites, stalagmites . . . but, no."

Total time: 5′.

When handed the tracing paper he ignored the above responses except for the human feet and said, "Here I saw an open chest with the backbone, but not clearly, as if it were still covered with meat." And on handing it back, "I sketched the spinal column, nothing more, and one can't see the bones." (Note: he seems to have begun calling me Pancho when puzzled.)

V. "Bat"

1 (Grabbed the card fast, as if to get at it), 35″, "The center," touching the central core, "and these are like a bat also, but in another shape" (*forma*).

2, "Here," pointing to the right, "a person lying on a wing . . . and here," drawing his finger down the left side, "equal to this side . . . with the arms crossed," straightening up and crossing his arms across his chest.

3, "And they have curly hair and eyelids," smiling with satisfaction to see the parts come out.

With the drawing phase, "Yes, it is a bat, and the human bodies lying down, as already indicated. And here," smiling, "the back parts of the animal" (*partes traseras*), pointing to the dependent legs.

Total time: 3′15″.

vi. "Animal Hide"

1, 20″, "The skin of an animal, right? And this would be the part of the feet, and this of the hands, and here the back" (he seemed relieved at having found all this so quickly).

2, "And here you can see," pointing to the neck, "a human form with a kind of veil, of gauze, with everything," smiling, "the combed hair with the part in the center," pointing at the cleft at the top, "and the wings extended."

3, "This resembles a candelabra (*candelabrio*) with the base underneath and everything holding up the human figure already pointed out." While doing the tracing, "It's the same things I already explained to you, Pablo."

vii. "Dogs"

1 (Smiling right away), 1′, "Two little dogs, here you are, with the neck turned and the little hands going back," straightening up and throwing back his hand.

2, "I don't find anything else, Pancho."

While tracing, "Yes," regarding the dogs. "I don't know the shape of this part," pointing to the bottom squares, "except that they serve as the base for this."

On handing back the tracing he pointed to the absent tails and said, "Two dogs with these cut off because I didn't see anything."

viii. "Animals Climbing"

1 (Looked at me and laughed shortly as I handed him VIII), 20″, "It's like a tree with branches," pointing to the upper part, "and with animals clutching the leaves."

2 (Pointing to the white in the center), "And this . . . this resembles . . . a spinal column."

3, "These animals, it looks as though they were holding up the central part, a sort of pedestal, although they haven't lost the shape of an animal." During the tracing, "And this down below?" I ask. "No, I don't think of anything. It's an illumination (*iluminación*)."

Total time: 3′20″.

ix. "The Candle"

1, 20″, "It's a candle with the light (*iluminación*) shaded (*opacada*) by a glass or a veil" (pointing to the central strip).

2, "Here I see a kind of coat (*chamarra*)," revolving his finger in the bottom central pink, "and here two hands grabbing backward."

3, "Two heads, lying down," smiling, referring to the pink heads at the bottom.

4, "That's all, Pancho . . . that is, you (*tú*), Pablo."

I ask, "What is this Pancho? From what name?" Camilo answers, laughing, "From Francisco."

While doing the drawing, "It's a candle, and farther back a light (*iluminación*) like a kind of hearth. The hearth is farther back," gesturing, "and the candle is more this way," bringing his hand in toward his chest. "This blue part is like a candle."

Later he pointed out the masks of the "Little Old Men" dancers at two points in IX.

x. "The Eiffel Tower"

1 (Leaning forward and looking with interest), 40″, "A rock" (the two red parts).

2, "And here above two animals holding up a pillar" (*pilastra*) (the grey on top).

3, "These yellow things are two animals holding up two things" (the yellow parts on the inside).

4, "A type of mask" (center bottom green).

During the tracing, "Yes, it's a series of animals, as I told you, but I don't understand all of them. Here are bulls and here, look, you (*tú*), with the horns" (upper green). "And here two rocks holding up the blue part in the middle."

On handing back the card, "Here, a rabbit, covering its eyes."

[After the interview we talked about politics for over an hour, and then had supper with his wife and daughter during which he demonstrated that all he eats is meat and milk products. The interview was typed up immediately afterward that night.]

Boni's Rorschach

[Interviewed on October 1, 1955: 4:10–6:30. Typed right afterward, translated 1985. Boni had been encountered before the town hall with two other princes. The interview took place in the main classroom of the school. Rapport was excellent; we are on a sort of joking relationship; reciprocal *tú* (as with all the princes whose life histories occur above).]

First Responses

I-1, B. looked puzzled, then held the card away for 30″, "Although it isn't exact?" Smiling, "Yes, although it isn't exact. What is shown."

2, Giving the card a vigorous shake, "It has the shape of a bat, like this" (pointing to the center), "with the body, and the wings, thus," following them with his finger, "and the arms . . . and the tail too. Like this," throwing his arms far apart.

3, About 3″ later, "Here, like a cloud."

4, "That's it, nothing more, a bat and a cloud."

Total time: 4′35″.

Second Responses (while tracing)

"Because I have seen them . . . a cloud, more and more" (as if he saw possibilities of other things but did not want to expatiate).

[Boni, Pedro, Héctor, and Aquiles are all highly kinesic and accompany any utterance with emphatic gestures, often involving the entire body in a sudden spring to the feet or a grand gesture of the arms. Unfortunately, not all of this could be recorded because I was too busy getting down the words.]

II-1, Smiled. 30″. A violent gesture of slapping his own back,
"Like here, your back, your body,
with the lungs" (feeling up behind
his back, arching backward).

2, "Two bears, like when they're
little and they put their hands
here, in order to fight with each
other."

3, "Because the bear does not
have a tail, but, with the knees
like this," doubling one leg up
close to his body, "like people."

4, "And they also have hands."

Total time: 4′.

"Yes, it's like I told you . . .
those bears live here in the 'hot
country'; they're fighting."

[Note how all the informants ignore blood imagery despite their familiarity with it through animal slaughter and the homicidal experiences
most of them have had. Note also the high frequency of fighting and
masks in Boni's responses.]

III-1, Immediately laughed. 40″.
"They are little monkeys (*monos*)
dancing" (gesturing with his
hands).

2, "Dressed like a *charro* [like a
Mexican cowboy, a standard festival costume], with jackets of
leather, like Zapata!" Leaning forward with a grin, and touching me
on the arm.

3, 4, 5, Made the same movements as above in a sort of dramatic style, often stretching the
card to arm's length.

"They are two little monkeys
(*monos*) dressed in *charro*. Here
they have a tie, look, you," throwing out his left arm in a wild gesture; he held the card for about
1 1/2″ before returning it, then,
with a grim, unpleasant look in
his eyes.

[The reference to Zapata probably derived from a conversation that we
had a week earlier about famous agrarian leaders. I think he saw a lot
more in this card than was admitted, especially in the blood spots. He
would be a good man to reinterview. Note: *mono*, about which he and the
culture have an absolute mania, means monkey, but is also used for image,
doll, and the like.]

IV-1, No behavior to indicate a block or puzzlement, as with the others. 50″. "A part, like an owl (*tecolote*)."

2, "Or the skin of a lamb (*cordero*) or a sheep (*borrego*), or of some animal."

Total time: 2′30″.

"It's like the skin of a sheep (*oveja*), also, in this part here" (drawing his finger down the side).

"Or like a gorilla with the hands like this" (flexing both biceps and laughing broadly).

[This is the first appearance of the owl, also with a tremendous role in this culture; it was a good hit on my part when, as I started to get the facts on political assassinations, I told people that my owl was bringing them in.]

V-1, Grinning roguishly, "A figure/image (*mono*)."

2, "It's a *mono* dressed in a skin of some sort."

3, He turned the card over and inspected the back.

4, After about 1′30″, "It's like a Moor or a Tiger" (both fiesta get-ups dating from the sixteenth century).

Total time: 3′.

"It could be a dead owl, with the wing extended" (stretching out his arms to the left and right, that is, an owl spread-eagled).

"Why is it an owl? Because of the shape of the ears, and because the owl also has ears like that."

[Note: owls, nocturnal ambush, *monos.*]

VII-1, Smiling again, 20″. "It looks like the decoration on an icon (*imagen*)," describing an icon with his hands, "as of angels."

2, "Also a dance by Negroes who are decked out, they are dancing."

Total time: 2′15″.

"It looks like an icon, or Little Negroes (*negritos*) dancing." At this point his face got grim and his voice final. "That's all."

["Negroes" refers to festival clowns ultimately deriving from the Negro Moors of the seventeenth century.]

VIII-1, "A mountain where animals have been born and they are climbing up to wait for the sun."

2, "A fruit tree which the animals are climbing."

"The animals can climb up in order to eat, or to sun themselves."

[No indication of a covert reaction to this card that might be elicited by further interviewing, as in the case of card III, except for the bottom part of the tracing.]

IX-1, 1'20", "The altar of an icon that can be worshipped."
2, "Nothing else."
Total time: 1'10".

"Yes, that's all . . . because many are like that, with the little angels (*angelitos*) below."

[I doubt that further questioning would produce more here, except about the bottom part and the clowns' heads on the top of the tracing.]

X-1, No time recorded. "The backbone of a human being" (indicating the central part).
2, "Here are the lungs," pointing at the red part, "and here is the thigh."
3, "And here are the kidneys," pointing at the yellow part, "and here, and other parts here . . . all" (i.e., all is part of the human body).

"It's a human body, all of it." About 1'30" later. "It's very difficult, I can't do anything here."

[Note: he did not have an inferiority complex, but did much better at the beginning of the test; then his interest declined.]

Aquiles' Rorschach

[Interviewed on October 14, 1955, 11:30 AM–1:55 PM. Rapport good but interview interrupted as indicated below. Typed up after interview, translated 1985. One of the most important interviews.]

First Responses

I-1, 10″, "It seems to be a view of a butterfly."

2, "Or of this part here" (smiling and pressing both hands, first against the groin, then against the pelvis, just below the small of the back) ". . . but of a skeleton, not like this."

3, "A map."

4, Throwing his hands far apart, "Or a skin/hide" (*piel*).

5, "All, no?"

Total time: 2′15″.

Second Responses

"A butterfly that's flying . . . these are drawings which the butterflies have above them" (the white spots).

"A skeleton, which has its seat here" (whacking the small of his back), "and is like this," with his hand to his groin, "but without flesh."

"A map, because it has everything, water, and these peninsulas" (the wings), "and these little gulfs, and these things like lakes."

"The skin extended, the neck, and this cut part, and the part of the hands, and this is the tail . . . they always cut it off."

"And here?" pointing to the antennae, "like here they cut off the tail."

"And here," pointing at the central part, "there is also much of the butterfly."

[Aquiles from the start manifested a "high quantity and quality ambition." First of numerous groin and pelvis responses, against a background of many "populars" (i.e., responses usually given on Rorschachs).]

II-1, 30", "The mouth of an animal." "How?" I ask. "This part," drawing his finger around the dark part.

2, "Are these parts which can be explained together? Just as you see them, then."

3, "Thus, like the cavity of a volcano."

Total time: 3'.

"Drawings of a dog, a bulldog" (indicating the white around the outside).

"The crater of a volcano erupting."

"And these parts" (the snouts)? "For me it's something like the larva of an embryo. Do you know what a larva is?" "Yes, it's the same word in English."

"And these parts?" I ask. "It's part of an animal."

[Aquiles was trying to impress me, often seeking out rare words and in two cases asking me what they meant. On handing back the drawing he said, "The superior mandibula, and here the inferior," pointing to the top and bottom halves of the black part. His reference to all the white around the black, however, makes me think that at first he saw all the black central mass as the vocal orifice, and then switched to a more conventional response.]

III-1, 20", "It seems to be something that's at the bottom of the sea . . . like mushrooms?" (pointing to the main body).

2, "Two unknown beings . . . here are the eyes . . . here a figure that's never been seen."

"Plants which take shape, under the sea" (the two arms).

"Here is a shell, no, a river."

"Something extraordinary, an apparition (un fenómeno), nor is it an animal."

"And this?" I ask, pointing to the bow. After some thought, "A road between two walls, a gate . . . a door, to open it, far away."

"And this?" I ask. "It's like when they pull out the heart, the liver of a steer . . . have you seen that?"

[Fenómeno also means a monstrosity, a malformed thing, neither man nor beast. Note the unusual image for the red bow, and the rare word. The incidence of rare or very learned words is probably a good index of the stress felt by this individual during the test: except for the cascade-river part there is not one popular response among the ones given above.]

IV-1, 30", "Part of a fissure/crack (grieta) . . . do you know what a fissure is?" "Yes, it's like a

"And this?" I ask. He says: "Like little narrow feet . . . and this part is like the tail."

crack/crevice (*rendija*)." He had
me stumped, but I made a good
guess.

"Like when lots of snow forms
. . . a shape, and the shadow
hits . . ."

2, "Thus, as I see it, it's the
head of an animal, the eyes."

3, "Also the view of a hide
doubled up" (smiling as though he
had found something, putting his
hand on the upper side and doubling it to indicate the folded hide).

4, "That's what it looks like
to me."

Total time: 2′20″.

V-1, "For me it's like something
that lives under the sea, these
monstrosities."

2, "A bat."

3, "Or an island."

Total time: 1′45″.

"A bat, flying, or tacked up."
"All of this—earth, and all of
this—sea."

VI-1, After pondering for some time he pushed it away and sat back in
his chair. He had been wrestling with VI for at least two minutes when
interrupted: an official came in from Zacapu with some papers referring to
ejidal affairs and, after discovering that I was an American and saying a few
words in horrendous English, broke into what seemed like an interminable harangue lasting *twenty-three minutes* which began with some experiences in a California fruit orchard and continued from there, wandering
by free association. Neither Aquiles nor I said anything during all this
time; I obviously paid no attention whatever, doodling on a paper and
staring out the window. When this hateful apparition, reminiscent of the
pathological liar in *Dead Souls*, finally took his leave, we continued, Aquiles apparently unbothered, but I in a state of suppressed rage that manifested itself in the one question, "Who is that dope (*Quién es ese tonto*)?"
at which Aquiles smiled and said, "He's not from here."

30″, "Like some pieces of meat,
as if I (whacking side of pelvis)
someone . . . this is what one
imagines" (pointing to the horns).

2, "I no find, very poor the

"I saw little . . . this part here,
but not *erect*" (stressed). (Then he
got up and, turning away from me,
pulled his shirttail out and up,
pointing to his spine and then

imagination . . ."

clapping the small of his back, slightly curved), "Like this now, but *not erect,* thus."

[Note: His disparaging remark about his own imagination, like Carlos. When he handed back the tracing I asked, "And this?" "A being of the sea."]

VII-1, 30", "Another drawing formed by the snow."

2, "As if it was the entrance of a . . . yes, an entrance."

3, "Here in order to scale, what are they called, explorers of the heights."

Total time: 2'.

"Like a shape that the snow forms, thus, transparent, neither dark nor black."

"Mountain climbers (*alpinistas*) climbing to reach the top."

"And this?" I ask. "A fissure."

VIII-1, 15", "A plant of the sea" (pointing at the orange part) "under the water, of the *sea,* to be exact" ("sea" stressed).

2, "A fantasy, yes?" (*fantasía*).

3, "Some things like animals that scale."

Total time: 2'.

"A plant of the sea."

"Parts of an animal, stepping with its right and left hands."

"And this?" I ask. "That is oil, above, and these spots of water where the water cannot pass."

[Note: an unusual response.]

[On handing back the tracing, "What are these lines?" I ask. "The petal of a flower which is called *perito* and that's how it remains after they cut it." Note the great number of aquatic images; Aquiles saw something of the sea when he worked in California, and he may recently have seen a sea movie such as Disney's 20 *Thousand Leagues.*]

IX-1, 10", "It doesn't resemble this part, here" (putting both hands on his groin) "of a skeleton, and it continues in this way in order to form this part" (putting his hand on the base of his spine).

2, "A reflection, the shape of an illuminated fountain."

3, "Or a great depth (*profundidad*) here."

Total time: 1'50".

"This part and here" (the orange) "forms these" (thigh bones).

"A cavity in the depths of the earth."

X-1, 20", "It's something, looking with an apparatus . . . different

"These are the tentacles of the octopus."

beings which you can see with a microscope like this" (putting his fist to his eye).

2, "And this could be an octopus" (pointing to the blue).

3, "And this part is a bone, here" (clapping his shoulder and upper arm).

Total time: 2′30″.

"These are the bones of the seat" (putting his hand to the base of his spine) "here where the bone begins."

"Here are cells."

"And here?" I ask. "These are like worms which are coming out of a larva."

[The second response to II was interrupted by the same odious individual, coming again for three signatures, but spending about fifteen minutes in a lengthy soliloquy which included counting in English from 1 to 100 and then by fives in the same range.

The whole test took about two hours, subtracting the time of the interruptions.]

Notes

1. Seven Political Life Studies

1. The term "fighter" (*luchador*), used locally for men like Bones, means an otherwise normal (e.g., land-tilling) peasant who carries weapons and is relatively prone to use them as a part of politics; at times of stress or similar upheavals a large fraction of peasants may function as fighters. They are sometimes called *pistoleros* by their factional enemies, but this pejorative term, perhaps best translated as "hired gun," is more appropriate for the professional guards, assassins, and so forth employed by caciques and caudillos in many parts of Mexico (see Chapter 6, pp. 194, for a fuller discussion).

2. Sex and politics are linked closely in Mexico, as in most places, in the sense that they often seem to share the same psychological sources, or, at least, that a politically ambitious man usually has many affairs with women and exploits his political power to satisfy what Eric Wolf called his "limitless sexual deficit" (Wolf 1959:239). But the matter is more complex than that: in some cases the leader seems to be satisfying not so much an appetite or a want as expectations of it, and in all cases the sexual aura of village politics makes it difficult if not well-nigh impossible to disentangle a man's actual history and inclinations from the web of innuendo, gossip, and scandal in Oscar Wilde's sense of "gossip made tedious by morality." There is also the problem of the limitless needs for vicarious sexual experience on the part of some anthropologists and their readerships. Frankly, for the sake of discretion, I would rather omit the sexual component from these life histories. But that would woefully distort my purportedly realistic characterization of cacical politics. I have done what I could, and the discriminating reader is invited to take the flesh off the bone *cum grano salis*.

3. Spanish *bravo*, "ferocious, savage, brave, wild, harsh, ill-tempered," is impossible to translate with one English word; it also occurs as an adjective for highly seasoned food and in the idiom for the bullfight, *la fiesta brava*.

4. The material in this and subsequent "postscripts" is, for the most part, based on inference, second-hand information, or brief interviewing, and should be taken as helpful background but not at the same level of carefully checked historical accuracy as the body of the work. While I have profited

greatly from the detailed restudy of Naranja by Gail Mummert-Zendejas (1983), her work was not primarily on politics in the sense that I am using that word here.

5. The word "cacique" (pronounced *kah-sée-kay*) comes ultimately from the Arawak Indian language but is now used throughout the Spanish-speaking world, with enormous variations in meaning. Obviously referring to Mexico, I define *cacique* here as a strong and autocratic leader in local and regional politics whose characteristically informal, personalistic, and often arbitrary rule is buttressed by a core of relatives, "fighters," and dependents, and is marked by the diagnostic threat and practice of violence. These caciques bridge, however imperfectly, the gap between peasant villagers and, on the other hand, the law, politics, and government of the state and nation, and are therefore varieties of the so-called "political middleman" (Wolf 1955). There may be a sole cacique, or two or three co-caciques. Succession is normally within a cacical political family, as will be detailed below. "Cacique" is different from: (1) "fighter"; (2) "leader" (*líder*), a relatively neutral term; (3) "representative of the town," a laudatory term for a generally accepted leader and for the elected or formally agreed upon official who represents the town at the county and other levels; (4) "*caudillo*," the label for a boss or quasi-military dictator at higher levels, including the nation, but usually involving states or large regions; (5) *jefe*, literally "chief," used for the head of a political unit, from the immediate family (*jefe de familia*) to the nation (*jefe máximo*) (Friedrich 1968:246–248); (6) *príncipe*, the temporarily fashionable term used by many leaders in Naranja for themselves (see pp. 73–74).

6. While all the financial facts in the microeconomics that run through this book have been given in the "historical present" of 1955–1956, the reader with the desire to imagine them in terms of contemporary realities is reminded that the United States dollar was then worth 12.50 pesos, so that the peso was worth 8 U.S. cents; whereas by December 1985, the Mexican peso had fallen to 1/5 cent, and correspondingly the dollar was worth 508 pesos; the dollar in the U.S.A. in 1985 was worth less than a third of its value at the time of fieldwork thirty years earlier. A more concrete way of looking at this was that in 1954 and 1984, urchins and beggars were asking for "un cinco," but in the first case that meant five centavos (Mexican cents), whereas in the second it meant five pesos (Mexican dollars). The tens of thousands of pesos referred to in a cacique's income thus convert to millions of pesos in today's catastrophically inflated currency.

7. Although they shouldn't be taken too literally, the language categories are relevant here. What Aquiles and others like him did was "to rob/steal" the girl (*se la llevó, se la robó*), which, in the local semantics, clearly differs from rape (*estupro*) because of the intention to marry.

8. I once resided in a Tarascan village household, where I was served at table, often alone, by the beautiful young (childless) wife. A tangible, mutual attraction was growing. Then, after two weeks, I overheard her husband, with whom I was on good terms, declaring, while drunk, that people were gossip-

ing about Pablo and that if he found out that his wife was unfaithful, and so forth. Although I did not feel fear, it seemed to be in the interest of science and marital harmony to decamp to the next village for awhile.

3. Political Ethnography: "Confidential Friend" and Related Categories

1. In this chapter the foregoing political life studies will be related to the social and cultural structures of kinship, ceremonial kinship, and friendship, focusing on the peculiar, semi-covert institution of confidential or intimate friendship. It should be noted that there is a strong precedent in anthropology for interpreting the social aspect of culture in terms of interacting structures with various complementary and contrasting functions, and that there is a voluminous and sometimes brilliant literature on kinship and, to a lesser extent, ceremonial kinship. It should also be noted that close friendship is essential in most cultures, including political cultures, and that partially effective means for inferring it were devised long ago in industrial and small group sociology. Nevertheless, ethnographies, particularly those held up as canonical, are largely silent on the delicate matters of close friendship. My central goal here, then, is to explore and describe friendship and similar primary structures by synthesizing the currently neglected techniques and insights of small group sociology with those of kinship ethnography, culture and personality, and political anthropology.

4. Political Organization

1. This case came to light as a consequence of the pregnancy of the daughter, a thirteen-year-old schoolgirl, and caused considerable excitement. It was judged in Zacapu and dismissed for "lack of evidence," but the family left Naranja immediately and there was talk of stringing up the father in the portals. The girl made a dazed impression.

2. As general, critical background, the following addenda: (1) By the early sixties only four states were still subject to a regional strong man and in only two of these did that strong man enjoy "extraordinary power" (Brandenburg 1964: 151)—Cárdenas in Michoacán obviously constituted one of these exceptions. (2) Scarface's rank of Thirty-three in the Scottish Rite, the highest possible in the Masonic Order, was attained by five of Mexico's past presidents (Brandenburg 1964: 146). (3) By the late fifties PRI was being financed by 3–5 percent of its members, including "the ambitious officers of farm groups" (Scott 1959: 154), such as Scarface and Camilo. (4) I will quote at length from R. Hansen's succinct description (pertaining mainly to the fifties and sixties): "The members of the PRI's agrarian sector are the passive victims not only of state and local officials, but also of several major organs of the federal government. . . . the Department of Agrarian Affairs [is] directly involved in the administration of Mexico's *ejidos*. . . . There are two kinds of evidence that the Department of Agrarian Affairs does not effectively represent the interests of Mexico's *ejidatarios*. The first comes in the form of the Department's inter-

ference in *ejidal* elections. It has the statutory duty to supervise such elections, and thus becomes the instrument by which those interests outside the ejidos control them for their own political and economic advantage" (1974: 118–119). This would partly explain the intransigence and occasional hostility of the ejidatarios and leaders of Naranja to the visitations of the Department, just as the descriptions in *The Princes* flesh out the necessarily abstract generalizations in this paragraph. In the same vein the present chapter illustrates that the sort of common interpretation given by Scott (in the epigraph) has very uneven truth value.

5. Political History: *Libido Dominandi* and the Rise of Elías (Scarface) Caso (1926–1956)

1. While I have limited my footnoting and in-text scholarly references for reasons given in Chapter 8, I wish to acknowledge, in particular, the valuable historical research of Victoriano Anguiano Equihua, Frank Brandenburg, Arnulfo Embriz Osorio, Roger D. Hansen, Armando de María y Campos, Gail Mummert-Zendejas, Robert Edwin Scott, and Eylor Simpson.

2. The expression/concept *libido dominandi* is part of a long Augustinian tradition (Harry Levin, personal communication), and figured in Renaissance and Baroque psychology. A novel trichotomy was formulated by Pascal (*Pensées*, Series XIII, 545 et passim): *libido sentiendi*, the lust/urge/will/drive "to desire the flesh"; *libido sciendi*, the drive, etc., to know, see, and the like; and *libido dominandi*, the drive/desire to dominate and control ("the pride of life"); the third *libido* is primary or superordinate (*Provincial Letter* 18). Three archetypal incarnations of these primordial emotions and motivations, as elaborated in comparative literature studies, would be Don Juan, Dr. Faustus, and Machiavelli's Cesare Borgia. Thanks to Gail Miller for researching this.

3. An outstanding deficiency in this study and the few others we have on factionalism and bossism in Mexico is the failure to investigate and fully evaluate the "negative" role of women. We know that they are victims—notably as widowed mothers—but to what extent and just how do they instill the values of family rivalry and the vendetta in children, stimulate and even encourage homicide between their men, or incite men to factionalism through gossip and scandalmongering? (Clearly, both the latter activities are also in the male domain.)

4. Among the rich depositions on this critical case was a long one by Ildefonso Mata, a close friend of Tapia, who lived through the revolt and Libido Dominandi periods without injury. In this case, he allegedly kept leaving and re-entering the scene while trotting home on his donkey, and thus witnessed much of the action.

5. There is obviously inconsistency in Juan Cruz of Tarejero (1) accusing Tapia of being a Communist, (2) setting up a *kolkhoz*-style collective, and then (3) later siding with the Serratistas. But each of these and other seemingly contradictory moves was more than adequately motivated; among other things, a constant basis for Tarejero politics has been rivalry with Naranja and

resentment at having to go through "those of Naranja" to get to higher levels. Ideological consistency is not a hallmark of Mexican local politics.

6. At the time of my fieldwork there was still a considerable amount of scandalmongering about Pedro: taking advantage of the women of political opponents (e.g., in connection with the anticlerical violence of the thirties); an alleged predilection for the red-light district of Morelia; seduction of Naranja schoolteachers. His blindness in one eye was supposedly due to gonorrhea. Even when we make allowance for the role of sexual accusations and braggadocio in Mexican politics, it remains that he was probably an egregious womanizer.

7. The ethnographic credibility of this fact is increased by strictly analogous cases; for example, from about 1946 to 1950 the Concord, Massachusetts, high school football team (on which I had played second string during two of the war years) began playing and beating Class B and Class A teams with over ten times its student population, and once it went to Raleigh, North Carolina, where it defeated the local team in an intersectional contest. Similarly, the small peasant village of Heidmühlen (population 600) in the extreme north of Schleswig-Holstein, actually on the Danish border, organized a soccer team which, after six years, in 1982–1983, won the Class A championship and was eulogized in the Kiel newspapers. While documentary evidence may still exist of Naranja's comparable heroics, I cite this as an example of how to triangulate evidence to increase the validity of historical inference.

6. Political Economy, Oligarchy, and the Leaders

1. Widows often remain independent in their original home, especially if they have land enough for subsistence. Or they may be integrated into the larger household of a relative, in which case their sons may or may not enter into a dependent, son-like role vis-à-vis the dominant male in the household. In either case, the widow is likely to entertain sexual relations with one or more men, often leading to permanent unions, in which case the stepson must accept a position that is analogous but not equal to that of a natural son.

2. Tarascan doesn't have an equivalent to Spanish *valor* and its allied forms. The root *ts'iwé-* (infinitive *ts'iwé-ni*) means mainly "to put on a brave or manly front or mask," and is often used mockingly (this is the subtext to Toni's mockery at the end of the third town meeting described in Chapter 2). Otherwise, there is *walór-huká-para-ni*, "to put on a brave front," sort of like wearing your pistol where it can be seen.

3. A major source for some of these generalizations was the depositions of witnesses to homicides that I found in dossiers in legal archives.

4. Attributed, as is standard in Naranja, to the French—i.e., the French expeditionary force under Emperor Maximilian which passed through the area in the 1860s. A woman of 104, whose final deposition I attended with Aquiles, was said to have seen the French.

5. The reader is cautioned against sensationalist conclusions. It is true that the rate of homicide, woundings, and shootings in Naranja was much higher

than in "the Wild West." On the other hand, we must remember the difference between (statistical) rate and cultural value and image. By way of comparison, there were only sixty-five "professional shootings" (face-to-face shootouts) between 1865 and 1924, that is, about one a year, in the entire state of Oklahoma. Similarly, most of the time between 1926 and 1956 Naranja was a somnolent village of hard-working peasants.

7. Fieldwork Categories: Sources of Shattered Bits

1. The "pants" referred to here (and in "The Shooting of Tomás Cruz" in Chapter 5) are the loose, baggy, and capacious Indian variety; the tightly fitted mestizo wear not only emphasizes the genitals but forces one to carry one's pistol on display in a holster; there is an amusing story of a policeman not only losing his pistol in a Tarascan fiesta crowd but having it replaced by a bone of beef.

2. In this connection, I would like to express the wish that scholars would branch out a bit and, when it comes to Michoacán agrarianism, turn to, for example, Zurumútaro or Tanaquillo; similarly, there are many almost unstudied Tarascan towns, such as Comachuén.

8. "Writing It Up"

1. For the idea of history as an analogue to music I am particularly indebted to Hajo Holborn, who was teaching at Yale when I was in graduate school there.

2. Given my intuitive, ambivalent relationship with Robert Redfield, whom I have never seen, it should be added that long after coming to Chicago I eventually (1972–1976) co-taught Homeric Greek (and culture) with his son James, using a "challenge and response" model (I challenged on Tuesdays, James responded on Fridays); the output included, inter alia, a major book by each party to the cooperation.

9. Background: Personal and Intellectual

1. The projected ethnopolitical theory was roughly consonant with but, I think, of greater intrinsic interest than the ethnoscience then being pioneered by Yale classmates and friends. But it was rejected at my second doctoral proposal, which I was asked to give after returning from the field to make sure that my scholarly activities were in order. Instead of the theory I was asked to set my fieldwork in a comparative context and relate it to current work (e.g., comparing Naranja to the Ancient China of the then fashionable Karl Wittfogel, on the grounds, as I recall, that they were both "hydraulic despotisms").

Homicide Appendix

1. The federal inspector who wrote the brilliant report of April 27, 1941, estimated that ninety had been killed by then. In September 1985, I ran across another: R. López, August 8, 1938.

2. Fieldnotes: "On the night of 26 September 1955 a group of young men was singing in the churchyard about 10:00 pm when they were joined by two men, Epigmenio Hernández and Tomás Baraja, both drunk, who, after singing along with them for a while sent for a bottle of *rebolcado*. Then two men approached through the darkness and the leading one, wrapped to his eyes in a *cobija* (blanket), shot Baraja and Hernández through the chest with a Mauser, after which all present scattered on a run. Although no one saw the man, Telesforo Barnabe has been formally indicted, partly because he shot the father of Barajas' *padrastro*. The suspect fled the same night and has not been seen since."

After I began to explore the homicides, people sometimes asked me where I had learned so much about them. My answer, "My owl brings them to me at night," was good for a laugh, and fit with local symbolism. I was on a reciprocal *tú* basis with all the leaders, but Scarface grew noticeably cool toward me during my last months in the field.

Sources

Books and Theses

ANGUIANO EQUIHUA, VICTORIANO
1951   *Lázaro Cárdenas, su feudo y la política nacional.* Mexico City: Editorial Eréndira.

ARRIAGA, ANTONIO
1938   *La organización social de los tarascos.* Morelia.

BARTRA, ROGER (ed.)
1975   *Caciquismo y poder político en México rural.* Instituto de Investigaciones Sociales, Universidad Nacional Autónoma de México. Mexico City: Siglo XXI.
1982   *Campesinado y poder político en México.* Colección Problemas de México. Mexico City: Ediciones Era.

BEALS, RALPH
1946   *Cherán: A Sierra Tarascan Village.* Washington, D.C.: Smithsonian Institution, Institute for Social Anthropology.

BRANDENBURG, FRANK
1964   *The Making of Modern Mexico.* Englewood Cliffs, N.J.: Prentice-Hall.

BURGOA, IGNACIO
1964   *El amparo en materia agraria.* Mexico: Editorial Porrua.

CÁRDENAS, LÁZARO
1972   *Ideario político.* Mexico: Ediciones Era.

CARRASCO, PEDRO
1952   *Tarascan Folk Religion.* New Orleans: Tulane University Press.

CLINE, HOWARD
1962   *Mexico: Revolution to Evolution, 1940–60.* New York: Oxford University Press.

DURÁN, MARCO ANTONIO
1967   *El agrarismo mexicano.* Mexico City: Siglo XXI.

EMBRIZ OSORIO, ARNULFO, AND RICARDO LEÓN GARCÍA
1984   *La Liga de Comunidades y Sindicatos Agraristas del Estado de*

Michoacán: Práctica Político-Social, 1919–1929. Mexico City: Fondo de Cultura Económica, Centro de Estudios Históricos del Agrarismo en México.

FOSTER, GEORGE M.

1948   *Empire's Children: The People of Tzintzuntzan.* Washington, D.C.: Smithsonian Institution, Institute of Social Anthropology.

1967   *Tzintzuntzan: Mexican Peasants in a Changing World.* Boston: Little, Brown and Co.

FRIEDRICH, PAUL

1957   *Cacique: The Recent History and Present Structure of Politics in a Tarascan Village.* 2 vols. Ph.D. thesis, Yale University.

1977   *Agrarian Revolt in a Mexican Village.* Chicago: University of Chicago Press (First Printing: Prentice-Hall, 1970). (Translated as *La revuelta agraria en una aldea mexicana*, 1981, Mexico City: Fondo de Cultura Económica, Centro de Estudios Históricos del Agrarismo en México.)

1981   *Agrarian Leadership and Violence in Mexico.* Chicago: University of Chicago Center for Latin American Studies, Occasional Publication no. 2.

GILLY, ADOLFO

1975   *La revolución interrumpida.* Mexico City: El Caballito.

GÓMEZ ROBLEDA, J. (con la colaboración de Alfonso Quiroz, Luis Argoytia, etc.)

1943   *Pescadores y campesinos tarascos.* Mexico: S.E.P.

GONZÁLEZ NAVARRO, MOISÉS

1968   *La confederación nacional campesina (Un grupo de presión en la reforma agraria mexicana).* Mexico City: B. Costa-Amic.

GONZÁLEZ Y GONZÁLEZ, LUIS

1968   *Pueblo en vilo: Microhistoria de San José de Gracia.* Mexico City: Colegio de México.

GRUENING, ERNEST

1929   *Mexico and Its Heritage.* New York: The Century Company.

HANSEN, ROGER D.

1974   *The Politics of Mexican Development.* Baltimore: Johns Hopkins Press.

HART, JOHN M.

1978   *Anarchism and the Mexican Working Class, 1860–1931.* Austin: University of Texas Press.

HUIZER, GERRITT

1970   *La lucha campesina en México.* Mexico City: Centro de Investigaciones Agrarias.

KATZ, FRIEDRICH (ed.)

In   *Riot, Rebellion, and Revolution: Rural Social Conflict in Mexico.*
press   Princeton: Princeton University Press.

LANDSBERGER, HENRY A. (ed.)

1969   *Latin American Peasant Movements.* Ithaca: Cornell University Press.

LEWIS, OSCAR

1951   *Life in a Mexican Village: Tepoztlan Restudied.* Urbana: University of Illinois Press.

1966   *Pedro Martínez.* Mexico City: Editorial Joaquín Mortiz.

LUNA ARROYO, ANTONIO, AND LUIS G. ALCERRECA

1982   *Diccionario de derecho agrario mexicano.* Mexico City: Editorial Porrúa.

MARÍA Y CAMPOS, ARMANDO DE

1939   *Múgica: Crónica biográfica.* Mexico City: Compañía de Ediciones Populares.

MARTÍNEZ MÚGICA, APOLINAR

n.d.   *Primo Tapia: Semblanza de un revolucionario michoacano.* Mexico City.

MENDIETA Y NÚÑEZ, LUCIO

1940   *Los tarascos.* Mexico City: Imprenta Universitaria.

1946   *El problema agrario en México.* Mexico City: Editorial Porrua.

1972   *Las desviaciones de la reforma agraria.* Mexico City: Asociación Nacional de Abogados, Academia de Derecho Agrario.

MEYER, JEAN

1973   *La Révolution mexicaine, 1910–1940.* Paris: Calamann-Levy.

MINTZ, SIDNEY

1974   *Worker in the Cane: A Puerto Rican Life History.* New York: W. W. Norton.

MUMMERT-ZENDEJAS, GAIL

1983   Multiplicité et transformation des formes sociales de mise en value de la terre dans un ejido mexicain, 1924–81. Ph.D. thesis, Ecoles des Hautes Etudes en Sciences Sociales.

NELSON, CYNTHIA

1971   *The Waiting Village: Social Change in Rural Mexico.* Boston: Little, Brown and Company.

NOLASCO ARMAS, MARGARITA

1969   *La reforma agraria en cuatro situaciones culturales distintas de México.* Mexico City: Instituto Nacional de Historia e Antropología.

REDFIELD, ROBERT

1930   *Tepoztlan.* Chicago: University of Chicago Press.

1941   *The Folk Culture of Yucatan.* Chicago: University of Chicago Press.

1950   *A Village That Chose Progress: Chan Kom Revisited.* Chicago: University of Chicago Press.

1961   *The Little Community, and Peasant Society and Progress.* Chicago: University of Chicago Press.

ROMANUCCI-ROSS, LILA
1986   *Conflict, Violence, and Morality in a Mexican Village.* Chicago: University of Chicago Press.

RONFELDT, DAVID
1973   *Atencingo: The Politics of Agrarian Struggle in a Mexican Ejido.* Stanford: Stanford University Press.

SÁENZ, MOISÉS
1936   *Carapan: Bosquejo de una experiencia.* Lima, Peru. Reprinted, 1966, Morelia, Michoacán.

SALAMINI, HEATHER FOWLER
1978   *Agrarian Radicalism in Vera Cruz.* Lincoln: University of Nebraska Press.

SCHRYER, FRANS J.
1980   *The Rancheros of Pisaflores: The History of a Peasant Bourgeoisie in Twentieth-Century Mexico.* Toronto: University of Toronto Press.

SCOTT, ROBERT EDWIN
1959   *Mexican Government in Transition.* Urbana: University of Illinois Press. Rev. ed., 1964.

SILVA HERZOG, JESÚS
1959   *El agrarismo mexicano y la reforma agraria: Exposición y crítica.* Mexico City: Fondo de Cultura Económica.

SIMPSON, EYLOR
1937   *The Ejido: Mexico's Way Out.* Chapel Hill: University of North Carolina Press.

SMITH, PETER H.
1979   *Labyrinths of Power: Political Recruitment in Twentieth-Century Mexico.* Princeton: Princeton University Press.

STAVENHAGEN, RODOLFO
1968   *Neolatifundismo y explotación.* Mexico City: Editorial Porrua.
1971   *Las clases sociales y las clases agrarias.* Mexico City: Siglo XXI.

TANNENBAUM, FRANK
1950   *Mexico: The Struggle for Peace and Bread.* New York: Alfred Knopf.

TAX, SOL
1953   *Penny Capitalism: A Guatemalan Indian Economy.* Chicago: University of Chicago Press.

TAYLOR, WILLIAM B.
1979   *Drinking, Homicide, and Rebellion in Colonial Mexican Villages.* Stanford: Stanford University Press.

TOWNSEND, WILLIAM CAMERON
1952   *Lazaro Cardenas, Mexican Democrat.* Ann Arbor: University of Michigan Press.

UGALDE, ANTONIO
1970   *Power and Conflict in a Mexican Community: A Study of Political Integration.* Albuquerque: University of New Mexico Press.
WARMAN, ARTURO
1976   *. . . y venimos a contradecir: Los campesinos de Morelos y el estado nacional.* Mexico City: La Casa Chata. (Translated as *We Come to Object*, 1980, Baltimore: Johns Hopkins Press.)
WEST, ROBERT C.
1948   *Cultural Geography of the Tarascan Area.* Washington, D.C.: Smithsonian Institution, Institute of Social Anthropology.
WHETTEN, NATHAN
1948   *Rural Mexico.* Chicago: University of Chicago Press.
WOLF, ERIC
1959   *Sons of the Shaking Earth.* Chicago: University of Chicago Press.
1968   *Peasant Wars of the Twentieth Century.* New York: Harper and Row.
WOMACK, JOHN
1970   *Zapata and the Mexican Revolution.* New York: Random House.

Articles

CASO, ALFONSO
1948   "Definición del indio y de lo indio." *América Indígena* 8(4):226–234.
FRIEDRICH, PAUL
1962   "Assumptions underlying Tarascan Political Homicide." *Psychiatry* 25(5):315–327.
1965a   "A Mexican Cacicazgo." *Ethnology* 4(2):190–209.
1965b   "An Agrarian 'Fighter.'" In *Context and Meaning in Cultural Anthropology*, edited by Melford E. Spiro, pp. 117–143. New York: The Free Press.
1966   "Revolutionary Politics and Communal Ritual." In *Political Anthropology*, edited by Marc J. Swartz, Victor W. Turner, and Arthur Tuden, pp. 191–220. Chicago: Aldine Publishing Co.
1968   "The Legitimacy of a Cacique." In *Local-Level Politics*, edited by Marc J. Swartz, pp. 243–269. Chicago: Aldine Publishing Co.
1979   "Dialectal Variation in Tarascan Phonology." In *Language, Context, and the Imagination: Essays by Paul Friedrich*, pp. 299–339. Stanford: Stanford University Press.
1984   "Tarascan: From Meaning to Sound." In *Supplement to the Handbook of Middle American Indians*, general editor Victoria Reifler Bricker, vol. 2, *Linguistics*, edited by Munro S. Edmonson, pp. 56–82. Austin: University of Texas Press.
GALVÁN CAMPOS, FAUSTO
1940   "El problema agrario entre los tarascos." In *Los tarascos*, edited by Lucio Mendieta y Núñez. Mexico City: Imprenta Universitaria.

KATZ, FRIEDRICH
    1974   "Labor Conditions on Haciendas in Porfirian Mexico: Some Trends and Tendencies." *Hispanic American Historical Review* 54(1):1–47.
LEWIS, OSCAR
    1949   "Husbands and Wives in a Mexican Village: A Study of Role Conflict." *American Anthropologist* 51:602–611.
MINTZ, SIDNEY, AND ERIC WOLF
    1950   "An Analysis of Ritual Co-parenthood (Compadrazgo)." *Southwestern Journal of Anthropology* 6(4):341–368.
VAN HORN, LAWRENCE
    1971   "Game Theory and the Strategies of Mexican Cacical Politics and Political Fission." *AAC/AJ* 9(30):6–13.
WATERBURY, RONALD
    1975   "Non-revolutionary Peasants: Oaxaca Compared to Morelos in the Mexican Revolution." *Comparative Studies in History and Society* 17:410–422.
WOLF, ERIC
    1955   "Types of Latin American Peasantry." *American Anthropologist* 57(3):1.

Newspapers (1955–1956, 1966–1967, 1970)

El Excelsior
El Heraldo de Michoacán
El Universal
Jueves de Excelsior
La Voz de Michoacán
Zacapu

Files and Archives

Legal Files and Vital Statistics Files in the Zacapu town hall.
Legal Files in the Morelia archives (exact title lost).
Administrative Files in the Departamento de Asuntos Agrarias in Mexico City.
Letters held by Domitila Tapia.
Records held by Martín Valle.
Diverse records in the Naranja town hall.
Files with the Bank of Ejidal Credit in Zacapu.

Laws

The Criminal Code of Michoacán.
Colección Jurídica: Código Agrario y Ley de Colonización y Disposiciones Relacionadas. 1956. Mexico City: Editorial Olimpo.
Ley de Amparo Reformada. 1956. Mexico City: Editorial Divulgación.

Interviews and Conversations

Some two to three hundred persons were variously interviewed and talked with in what is to a significant degree an oral history. At one extreme were the many peasants of both sexes with whom I conversed, often carrying on an indirect interview; that is, while ostensibly chatting about the crops and the like, I kept coming back to political facts and attitudes. In this "ordinary citizen" category would fall the forty-odd workers in the Celanese factory. Particularly valuable were the many older women (i.e., over sixty) with whom I was on good terms. I discussed Naranja politics with seven priests, including the (arch?)bishop of Morelia and the resident priest in Tiríndaro, Father José Padilla, who was extremely helpful and informative. I would also emphasize that I discussed Naranja (and Tiríndaro) politics with many individuals in other towns, notably Tariácuri, Zacapu, Morelia, and Mexico City. While residing in Tiríndaro for six months with my family I naturally spoke about politics with many persons, including the leader Ignacio Ruíz and his supporters; our wet-nurse, Celina, the widow of a former factional leader there; my host for a while, the orphaned son of a former leader; and Antonio Aparicio, son of the Cristero agrarian leader. While in Naranja I resided for a time in the home of a storekeeper, and so at the node of much gossip, much of it political. Otherwise I interviewed the leaders of both factions and many partisans on both sides, including Martín Valle, Aquiles Caso, Juan Nahua, Camilo Caso, Elías Caso, Pedro González, Daniel Ocampo, Juan Mejía (ejidatario, also a poet), Antonio Serrano, Herculano Ocampo, Héctor Caso, Juan Cruz (of Tarejero), Domitila Tapia, Severo and Félix Espinoza (of Tiríndaro), Raúl Torres (secretary of Zacapu County at the time, a poet), two sons of Joaquín de la Cruz, Luciano Escobar, Ezequiel Peñasco, and many of lesser note or relevance. These interviews ranged from half an hour up, almost all lasted over an hour, and many involved many hours— dozens in some cases. Last and perhaps least were the numerous chance encounters in other towns or while traveling; for example, on a first-class bus I sat down next to two men who turned out to be leaders in the Eleven Pueblos; when they learned that I was studying Naranja they became quite intrigued and now and then provided some helpful tips. I would emphasize, finally, that a sort of head-on interview that is explicitly about politics is often less productive than a general discussion, and that somewhat more remote periods may be more discussable than the immediate present—one reason my data on the thirties are actually much better than what I have on the forties. See also Category 3 in Chapter 7 above.